The Sanctity
of the Synagogue

the case for *mechitzah*—separation between men and
women in the synagogue—based on Jewish law, history
and philosophy, from sources old and new

edited by

BARUCH LITVIN

Third revised and expanded edition

edited by
JEANNE LITVIN

co-editor
RABBI MELVIN TEITELBAUM

KTAV PUBLISHING HOUSE, INC.
UNION OF ORTHODOX JEWISH CONGREGATIONS
5747 : 1987

Library of Congress Cataloging-in-Publication Data

The Sanctity of the synagogue.

  1. Synagogue seating. I. Litvin, Baruch.
II. Litvin, Jeanne. III. Teitelbaum, Melvin.
BM653.2.S26   1986   296.7'4   86-27428
ISBN 0-88125-113-5

Manufactured in the United States of America

BETH TEFILATH MOSES SYNAGOGUE
MOUNT CLEMENS, MICHIGAN

BARUCH LITVIN 1889–1975

dedicated

to the sacred memory of millions of
Jewish martyrs הי"ד to whom the
practices and beliefs embodied in this
volume were the breath of life; and
to the thirteen thousand synagogues
destroyed by the Nazis ימ"ש

contents

Contents

an appreciation of my zeda, Baruch Litvin*

BY JEANNE LITVIN

$\mathbb{A}$T THE Bar Mitzvah dinner of my son, I quoted a verse from the book of the prophet Zechariah that has been a recurring inspiration to me throughout my adult life. This particular verse was first quoted to me by my grandfather Baruch Litvin when I visited him in the winter of 1967 during my vacation from my studies at Stern College for Women in New York. As grandfathers are wont to do, he was offering me advice using this verse to illustrate his point. Ever since, the verse has stuck with me.

"Who art thou, O great mountain, before Zerubavel thou shalt become a plain" (Zechariah 4:7).

I explained to my son, who is named Zechariah, how fortunate he was to have a modern-day Zerubavel, his own great-grandfather Baruch Litvin, as a role model. My message to my son was to look back on his *zeda*'s life and see not only the achievements but the

*Excerpted from an address delivered by the editor at the 1984 National Convention of the Union of Orthodox Jewish Congregations of America at a session entitled, "Twenty-Five Years after Mount Clemens—the *Mechitzah* Controversy in Retrospect."

struggles as well, in order to give him the motivation to conquer whatever difficulties might come his way.

My grandfather was indeed a modern-day Zerubavel! Many people are aware of his accomplishments. Yes, he won the battle for the sanctity of *his* synagogue and published the book by that name documenting that struggle . . . and he published pamphlets for the National Conference of Synagogue Youth (N.C.S.Y.) that are still available for distribution today . . . and yes, he published a second book, entitled *Jewish Identity,* with Ben Gurion's famous query "Who is a Jew?" and the answers to it. But less well known are the personal struggles of Baruch Litvin. I believe there is value in knowing what he had to overcome in order to attain so much so late in his life.

Americans have only recently come around to the realization that there is "life" after 50 . . . 60 . . . and even 70 years of age. Baruch Litvin was a man ahead of his time. He was, perhaps, one of the earliest *baalai teshuvah* of our age, having become one quite late in life, when already in his 50s. Yet, he was to have a tremendous impact in the orthodox world! His actions at the ages of 60, 70, and even 80 strengthened orthodox Judaism in America. He positively altered the lives of his family and all those with whom he came in contact in his travels or through his correspondence. Each and every one of us can learn from his example. We can *all* accomplish our goals—*all* be modern-day Zerubavels in our own right—if we persevere. As demonstrated by Baruch Litvin's example, no one is too old to do so.

My grandfather attended *cheder* in Russia until the age of 14. When he was forced to flee his homeland for political reasons, his formal education ended. He arrived in America with just a few coins in his pocket. Later on

xiv

in life, he always modestly told people that he was "just a *nagar*," a carpenter. This was true because his main means of support through those early years was through carpentry. Later on, he became a chicken farmer and a barber but eventually he returned to the carpentry business, becoming a successful lumber dealer and builder in Mount Clemens, Michigan. The same energy that he applied to "making it" financially in America (he spent over $300,000 to win his court battle and to publish the first two editions of *The Sanctity of the Synagogue*), he also applied to making it in the *Torah* world. He set about acquiring a Jewish education in his own methodical way.

Rabbi Yisroel Wohlgelernter remembers that after World War II, when he was a teenager, Baruch Litvin, then a man in his fifties, came daily to his summer camp to study with him. Rabbi Wohlgelernter further remembers that my grandfather was not satisfied with learning from a translated or secondary source but insisted on learning from original sources (even though he did not *yet* have the proper background to do so).

Rabbi David B. Hollander visited Mount Clemens during the *mechitzah* struggle and wrote the following about his visit to my *zeda*'s home:

> He was certainly not a typical "*baal'e bos*" in a small town in Michigan. But when I came into his home, I was even more taken aback. For such a home would be a discovery even in such centers of orthodox Judaism as New York City. As I entered the huge living room, I found myself in a library containing thousands of *seforim*. But if, at first, I might have thought that he is a sentimental owner of Jewish books, one glance at the huge desk literally covered with half-closed bookmarked *seforim* convinced me that Reb Baruch not only is the *legal*

owner of these books, but he owns them as old, old friends with whom he has been conversant for many years. Later on, as I came to know him better, I learned that he rises before dawn to study and to write.

My grandfather expanded his reach into the areas of Jewish philosophy and Jewish history, learned to read Greek and Latin, and studied texts on such varied subjects as curriculum development and biology . . . all to supplement his understanding of the *Torah* . . . and to help him become a more observant Jew.

But Baruch Litvin did not sit in his study in Mount Clemens and learn just to acquire knowledge. He attempted to encourage others to become more and more involved in *Torah* study. He started with his own family. When Baruch Litvin had become a *baal teshuvah,* his sons had already married and had children of their own. So he went to work on the grandchildren. All ten of his Mount Clemens–born grandchildren attended *yeshivos* due to his perseverence and financial support. But he didn't stop with his family. He travelled from *yeshiva* to *yeshiva.* His first stop at each *yeshiva* would always be the *Bais Hamidrash.* He would walk in unannounced and sit down and start learning with a few of the *bocherim.* He'd manage to find out quite a bit about what they knew . . . and what they didn't know . . . but also what the *yeshiva* might be lacking in the way of *seforim* or equipment. Shortly after his visit, the *yeshiva* would receive the needed equipment or *seforim* from an "anonymous" donor—and the *bocherim* would receive the first of many demanding letters from "Reb Baruch," challenging them to seek answers to his many questions. I have met many of these former *bocherim* who have grown up to be scholars and rabbis. They all fondly remember the re-

xvi

lentless man from Mount Clemens who urged them to dig beneath the surface and search for a complete and valid answer to a question.

I believe the lessons to be learned from my *zeda*'s life are simple ones. There is a lesson for people to do . . . even when they do not think they are capable. All of us, in some way, think that we are "just a *nagar*," or whatever our chosen livelihood is . . . but we can all be more than that—if we apply ourselves conscientiously— as my *zeda* did. There is also the lesson that one can achieve truly *Torah*-committed life even if a *yeshiva* education isn't available from age three and up. Further, one need not be a rabbi to fight a battle for what is *halachically* right. Baruch Litvin was a layman, and yet he fought, and won, the battle for the sanctity of his synagogue . . . without benefit of *semichah*.

My grandfather was nicknamed the "Lone Warrior"—and that he was, a man who gave up the satisfaction of being accepted in his chosen community in order to wage his *milchamah* for what he believed to be right. He did not allow his voice to be stilled although *his* was a minority opinion. The Michigan Supreme Court, in the Mount Clemens case, upheld the cause for which this "lone warrior" struggled.

Baruch Litvin was an *anav,* a humble man, and would not appreciate being talked about today in laudatory terms. However, it would have brought him great satisfaction to know that the story of his struggles has motivated others to alter their lives even slightly toward fighting for *halachic* integrity—wherever those battle lines may be drawn—so that orthodox Jewry will count among its numbers many more Zerubavels in the years to come.

For anyone caught up in a *milchamah,* my hope is

that Baruch Litvin's actions will serve as a guide. Success will then result because his actions were guided by the words of the prophet Zechariah from the verse immediately preceding the one he quoted me so many years ago:

"Not by might nor by power—but by my spirit says *Hashem* . . ."

———

Jeanne Litvin was born and raised in Mount Clemens, Michigan. As a child, she witnessed the battle that took place between her grandfather Baruch Litvin and the rest of the small Jewish community over whether or not Beth Tefilath Moses Synagogue would retain its *mechitzah*. Through her grandfather's intervention, she received her education outside Mount Clemens, attending the Academy in Chicago and then going on to graduate from Stern College for Women of Yeshiva University. Most heart-warming to her grandfather was the year when Jeanne, now a *rebbitzin* (rabbi's wife), returned to Mount Clemens. Her husband, at the time, served as rabbi of the Mount Clemens synagogue.

Like her grandfather, Jeanne has had several careers. For ten years, she was involved in education first as a teacher and day camp owner and director and later as an administrator and guidance counselor for Yeshiva University of Los Angeles High Schools. During the same time period, Jeanne maintained a dairy and vegetarian kosher catering service and administered federal food programs in several *yeshivot*. She has been a kosher food columnist for the *Los Angeles Jewish Bulletin* and the *Jewish Homemaker Magazine*.

Presently, Jeanne is involved in the world of finance working as a mortgage broker, property manager, and real estate agent, except on Passover, when she "moonlights" as a consultant and a *"mashgiach"* for Kosher-for-Passover tours. She was most recently named West Coast Editor of *The Jewish Press*.

acknowledgments to the Third Edition

THE PUBLICATION of this third edition of *The Sanctity of the Synagogue* would not have been possible without the support of the following individuals:

Rabbi Melvin Teitelbaum, my coeditor, who encouraged me every step of the way.

Dr. Lawrence Schiffman, who not only wrote the introduction and conclusion to this edition, but was always available for practical advice on the details of preparing the manuscript for publication.

Rabbi David Rabinowich, Rosh Yeshivah of Ahavath Torah Institute in Jerusalem, who did the initial translations of eleven of Rabbi Moshe Feinstein's *teshuvot* and the article by Rabbi Moshe Sherer.

Rabbi Pinchas Stolper and the U.O.J.C.A. for answering my constant queries and for arranging the session entitled "Twenty-Five Years after Mount Clemens—The Mechitzah Controversy in Retrospect" at the 1984 U.O.J.C.A. Convention in Baltimore, Maryland.

Zachary, Sharone, and Boaz, my three children, who not only tolerated their mother's obsession with their great-grandfather's work but were there to cheer me on with each small victory that brought us closer to our goal of republication of *The Sanctity of the Synagogue*.

Jeanne Litvin

Los Angeles
January, 1987

xxi

introduction to the Third Edition

BY LAWRENCE H. SCHIFFMAN

Professor of Hebrew and Judaic Studies
New York University

I. THE BOOK AND ITS EDITOR

T*HE SANCTITY of the Synagogue,* by Baruch Litvin, of blessed memory, is not just a book; it is part of the history of Orthodoxy in America. This volume chronicles the editor's heroic battle to prevent the conversion of a synagogue in Mount Clemens, Michigan, from an Orthodox synagogue with a *mechitzah,* the traditional separation of men and women in worship and prayer, to one which would have mixed seating. In the course of his struggle, the editor assembled a treasure of essays, responsa *(teshuvot),* and documents regarding this issue and its ramifications, as well as a collection of material relating to its American legal aspects. Accordingly, the book is the best collection of materials arguing for the traditional separation of the sexes, as well as a historical document in its own right.

Baruch Litvin, called the "lone warrior" by Rabbi Emanuel Rackman, was an unlikely person to wage this battle. He was neither a rabbi nor a known leader of the Orthodox community. Yet it was his successful struggle that raised the issue of the *mechitzah* in the American

Orthodox community, at a time when true Orthodoxy was in danger of virtual extinction. The significance of his efforts went way beyond the legal battle regarding the Mount Clemens synagogue. In fact, his real victory was a much more important one. He brought the Orthodox community to understand that the separation of the sexes in worship had become the hallmark of Orthodoxy in America and that its rabbinic leadership had to take a stand on this important issue. He became the conscience of the Orthodox community. His successful championing of this cause created a literature which continues to be a major force in the vibrant development of America's Orthodox community. When Orthodoxy stood at a dangerous crossroads, Baruch Litvin pointed the way. It is no wonder then that this book is now entering its third edition and that this edition contains so much new material pertaining to this very issue and its ramifications.

This was not the only work published by Baruch Litvin. Together with Sidney B. Hoenig, he compiled the volume *Jewish Identity, Modern Responsa and Opinions on the Registration of Children of Mixed Marriages, David Ben Gurion's Query to Leaders of World Jewry* (New York and Jerusalem: Feldheim, 1970). This volume brought together all the important contemporary material on the issue of "Who is a Jew?" and so contributed greatly to the debate on that question.

II. THE HISTORICAL BACKGROUND: ORTHODOXY IN AMERICA

Traditional Judaism established itself with the arrival of Sephardic Jews in North America in the pre-revolutionary period. By the time of Washington's inauguration, six Jewish congregations sent greetings. Among these was the Spanish-Portuguese Synagogue,

Shearith Israel, founded in New York in 1655. These synagogues were traditional in all matters, following the Spanish customs. A traveller in 1748 describes the galleries which "were appropriated to the ladies, while the men sat below." By the close of the Colonial period, a small traditional community, Orthodox in our terms, had been established on this continent.

In the early nineteenth century, Ashkenazic immigrants, mainly German, began to stream to the American shores. The earliest congregations established by these immigrants, whether English or German, were traditional in nature. In 1824, however, the earliest stirrings of a reform movement took place in American Judaism. By 1840 it was clear that numerous American Jews were no longer bound by the Jewish traditions nor connected with the synagogue.

The 1840s saw the continued growth of the Reform movement in America. In 1837 the German Reformist Abraham Geiger had promoted reforms regarding the role of women in Jewish life. Following these views, Isaac Mayer Wise initiated the mixed choir and mixed pews in America. These reforms would have a lasting impact on the American Jewish synagogue.

By 1869 the first major conference of Reform rabbis took place, and in 1873 the Union of American Hebrew Congregations was formed. Although it initially sought to represent all American Jews, it quickly proved to be limited as a Reform organization. By this time, Reform was clearly dominant on the American Jewish scene. But the beginnings of East European immigration would eventually reverse this trend. Already by the 1850s East European Orthodox congregations were being established. Such synagogues spread throughout America, as far west as California. Nevertheless, from early in the nineteenth century there was a tendency, even among some of the traditionalists, toward making reforms. In the 1870s some congregations, essentially forerunners of the organized Conservative movement, had begun to shorten services, institute mixed pews, and make use of the organ. These developments in otherwise traditional synagogues helped to pave the way for the later development of the Conservative movement.

It is probably the year 1885 that marks the date from which the three branches of American Judaism—Reform, Conservative, and Orthodox—can be said to exist in America. In that very year the famous Pittsburgh conference took place at which the position of the Reform movement was clarified. In that year as well the Jewish Theological Seminary of America was founded. In its early days, the Conservatives saw themselves as Orthodox and sought to take the lead in the rapidly developing Orthodox community. In this they were rebuffed by their Eastern European rabbinic counterparts who understood well the important differences in belief and outlook that separated the groups.

Even in this early period, Orthodoxy made great strides. In 1879, the first organization of Orthodox synagogues was founded, in the hope of setting up a chief rabbinate. This attempt failed. In 1896 the Rabbi Isaac Elchanan Theological Seminary, to become Yeshiva University, was founded. In 1898 the Union of Orthodox Jewish Congregations of America was organized.

It was a long way from those early days to the successes of today. Essentially, Orthodoxy had to grow out of the immigrant stage and develop institutions and leaders who would function in the new environment. The first Orthodox rabbinic organization was the Agudas Ha-Rabbonim, formed in 1902. The appointment of Dr.

Bernard Revel as head of the Yeshiva Rabbi Isaac El-chanan was also a major step in developing indigenous American institutions. In addition, other yeshivas, congregational *Talmud Torahs,* day schools, and organizations set up to control *kashruth,* circumcision, and other communal functions gradually appeared.

After World War I, Orthodoxy began to experience the changeover from a European to an American movement. The formal organization of the Young Israel movement took place in 1926, although it had actually begun as early as 1912. In 1935 the American-trained alumni of the Rabbinical Seminary of Yeshiva University founded the Rabbinical Council of America, which became the dominant modern Orthodox rabbinic organization.

The period from 1880 to 1930 had brought vast numbers of Eastern European Orthodox Jews to these shores. In order to enter the mainstream of American life, they found it necessary to assimilate to dominant patterns in many ways. As a result, most discarded their beards and East European dress.

Many of these immigrants, even among the vast majority who were *shul*-goers, had already strayed far from the norms of the *halachah.* Even the truly Orthodox found it difficult to transmit their commitment to their children. In such a situation, it was not unexpected that so many young people, given the worst possible Jewish education, would cease living in the traditional way. In fact, it is a wonder, in light of the poor and often counterproductive education that they received, that they maintained the strong ties to their people that they did. The offspring of most Orthodox immigrants to the United States between 1880 and 1930 soon abandoned Orthodoxy and joined (if they joined at all) Conservative and Reform congregations.

It was among these immigrants that the Conservative movement, now fully organized, gained wide acceptance. The emerging Conservative approach stressed adherence to tradition while allowing certain changes as well. Most prominent among these changes, and accepted by virtually every Conservative congregation in this country (with the exception of the synagogue of the Jewish Theological Seminary itself), was the institution of mixed seating. Interestingly, this innovation was hardly debated. Rather, it was an organic outgrowth of the feeling that only religious compromise would stem the tide of assimilation. The more surprising development is that many modern Orthodox congregations followed suit. Their leaders no doubt thought that it was better to make this one compromise and to retain their members for an "Orthodox" synagogue than to stand on principle. This was a period in which religious compromise was assumed to go hand in hand with Americanization. This tendency was so widespread that if not for the dedication of such people as our editor Baruch Litvin and the soon-to-come immigration in the aftermath of World War II of so many deeply religious Jews dedicated to the *halachah,* this might have become the dominant pattern, even in the Orthodox community.

The period between the World Wars may be seen as an incubation period during which Orthodox institutions were evolving. The day school movement was ever so slowly on the rise. When World War II and the Holocaust brought vast numbers of Jews from Europe to the shores of the United States, the Orthodox community had already evolved sufficiently so that institutions, and patterns of development and growth were already in place. It was left, however, to the new immigrants to develop these shoots into the blossoming community of the second half of the twentieth century.

After World War II, vast numbers of Orthodox Jews came to the U.S. and settled in ethnic Jewish communities, mostly in New York City, and made Orthodoxy an accepted phenomenon in America. It was the children of these immigrants who first populated the new American day schools and yeshivot and pioneered in attaining the best Jewish and secular educations. It was these children who made public demonstrations of Orthodoxy acceptable in America. Even today it is they who constitute a vast market for the innumerable products and services which we in America have come to associate with the Orthodox community.

Most important, this group refused to bow to the dominant forms of Orthodoxy in America, rejecting the tendency toward compromise and the spirit of defeatism that prevailed in the Orthodox community. In this way, it raised the level of education and religious observance in the community, ultimately encouraging the earlier immigrants and their children to achieve a much deeper commitment to Orthodoxy. The children of these post-World War II immigrants have emerged today as leaders in Orthodoxy. It is in their hands that Orthodoxy has re-emerged as the most vibrant and dynamic group within the institutionalized Jewish community in the United States.

It is only in this context that we can understand the reversal of the tendency toward halachic compromise regarding the separation of the sexes in the synagogue which we observed in the earlier Orthodox community. It was the dedication of these new immigrants which showed Americans that life according to the *halachah* was possible; their stance led ultimately to the creation of a truly halachic Orthodox community. More importantly, it became evident in this postwar period that only true adherence to *halachah* would gain for Orthodoxy the respect it deserved as the authentic expression of the Jewish tradition, and that compromise would only detract from this achievement. At the same time, it would become evident, as it is today, that only unstinting dedication to the ideals of Jewish law would attract the allegiance of so many of those whose parents and grandparents had strayed from the traditional path.

III. THE IMPORTANCE OF THIS BOOK AND THE COURT CASE

It is in this setting that we must seek to understand the importance of this volume and of the Mount Clemens court case. By the mid-1950s, it seemed to many segments of modern Orthodoxy that the solution to the issue of the *mechitzah* was to abandon the separation of the sexes in the synagogue. How else could Orthodoxy, the argument went, compete with the other movements for the allegiance of the modern American Jew? In essence, many congregations and their rabbis sought to compromise the standards of the *halachah* in order to insure the future of traditional Jewish practice in the New World. Orthodoxy was then very much on the defensive. It saw itself as unable to compete with the other groups, and the wave of postwar immigrants had not yet had its impact on the American scene. More and more congregations were removing *mechitzahs* or balconies and tending toward mixed seating. At the same time, some elements were campaigning for the conversion of Orthodox congregations into Conservative ones, and departure from the traditional separation of the sexes was certainly part of their program.

In most of these congregations, there was always a dedicated and loyal group of traditionalists who fought, side by side with the rabbi, to stem this tide. Yet usually these people did not succeed. First, they lacked the necessary arguments to deter this seemingly logical action. Second, the times seemed to be against them; how else would traditional Judaism survive?

Our editor Baruch Litvin jumped into this fray. His claim was that to inaugurate mixed seating was a breach of the trust of generations of Orthodox Jews who had lived by the *halachah* and who had built these synagogues in the traditional manner. Such a breach of trust, he claimed, was illegal according to the law of the State of Michigan in which he lived. In this he was supported by the verdict in a similar case in New Orleans in 1954.

But the verdict of the courts was not all that Litvin intended to achieve. Had it been so, his success would have been quite limited. In addition, his intention was to awaken the Orthodox community to the importance of the traditional seating pattern, separation of the sexes with a balcony or a *mechitzah,* and thereby reverse the trend in so many American "Orthodox" synagogues. He sought, in his words, to restore "the sanctity of the synagogue" in this country. He wanted to preserve in North America, in the face of the seemingly insurmountable vicissitudes of modernity and Americanization, the traditional patterns that had kept and preserved the Jewish people for two millenia.

Curiously, this "lone warrior" succeeded. It was not the court victory per se that insured his victory but the publicity that attended it, and the material which he assembled and published in this volume. He raised the issue of *mechitzah* and placed it squarely on the agenda of the Orthodox community. He cried out for the backing of rabbis and laymen and galvanized such support.

By the time Litvin had completed his struggle, the Orthodox community in America knew what the separation of the sexes in the synagogue was for, what its sources were, and why it must be maintained. Even more importantly, they realized that the traditional approach could succeed in America. They understood that the *mechitzah* had to be maintained if Orthodoxy was going to meet the true challenge of modernity, the survival of the halachic way of life in our times.

Indeed, the subsequent history of Orthodoxy in America showed Litvin to have been right. With the help of the many post-World War II immigrants, Orthodoxy began a period of renewal and growth that no one could have imagined. It has emerged today as a vibrant and forward-looking community, dedicated to life under the *halachah*. It was to Litvin's credit that even the most modernized segments of this community maintained the sanctity of the synagogue. One rarely hears about the issue at all, unless a synagogue still without the proper separation installs it. The reverse process has long since ended. The modern Orthodox community went on to thrive while rejecting compromise on the issue of separate seating.

The matter of the use of a *mechitzah* in the synagogue was actually of wider significance than the simple issue itself. Orthodox Judaism is distinguished for its adherence to the *halachah,* the system of Jewish life and law. Litvin and others like him argued that adherence to the system of *halachah* could not be compromised under any circumstances. One might debate about the correct halachic ruling, but the axiomatic subservience of the individual and the community to the laws had to be unquestioned. Indeed, this was one of the most important differences between the Orthodox approach to Judaism and that of the other movements. The issue of separation of the sexes for prayer was, for American Orthodoxy, the test of the entire structure. If Orthodoxy had actually abandoned this principle, it would have succumbed to the centripetal forces of the times and abandoned other aspects of the halachic system as well.

This is not to say that Orthodox Judaism does not adapt to the times. On the contrary, its timelessness is a result of its ability to apply the principles of *halachah*
[Tal]mud and the medieval *Posekim* to all
[app]lication of the law
[pr]inciple, be accom-
[prin]ciples of the *hala-*
[adher]ence to the system
[th]e halachic system is
[as]ide all questions of
[h]ow the Jew was to
[w]hen it was decided
[to] firmly adhere to the
[Late]r, it was also decided
[O]rthodox community,
[the] authority. Orthodoxy
[Ame]rica.

LAW—THE
[TH]E BOOK

[a]s essays and responsa
From all these sources
[o]f argumentation, which
[the] thesis of the work. We

xxxiii

The Sanctuary itself was raised 40 cubits (about 66 feet) and broadened 30 cubits (50 feet).

Court of Women 135 cubits (square) on each side.

The Court of the Israelites was 135 cubits × 11 cubits.

At the end of the Sabbatical year, the King, at Sukkot, read the biblical portion standing on a wooden dias in the center of [court of women] Sot 7:8

shall briefly outline this thesis here so that the reader will be able to see it clearly as it emerges from the volume.

The Mishnah and Babylonian Talmud tells us that a special arrangement was made for the joyous celebration of the *Simchat Bet Ha-Sho'evah* (the Water-Drawing Ceremony) in the Temple in Jerusalem on the second night of the holiday of Sukkot. A balcony was constructed to ensure that the men could not see the women during the celebrations. The purpose of this arrangement was to avoid the social levity which had previously ensued when the sexes had not been separated by a physical structure. From this Talmudic discussion it can be gathered that under normal circumstances the sexes were also separated. It was only that the balcony was necessary for this particular ritual.

There is a Talmudic principle that the synagogue is a sanctuary in miniature (*Mikdash Me'at*). This principle requires that the same level of sanctity observed in the Temple of Jerusalem must be observed in the synagogue. Therefore, it is required that the sexes be separated in the synagogue. Litvin gathered sources, archaeological and historical, to prove that the separation of the sexes by a balcony or by a partition (*mechitzah*) was observed in all synagogues from the Roman period until the advent of the Reform movement. The book argues, therefore, that this is the traditional and historical form of Jewish worship and that it is required by *halachah*.

Among the major authorities in this book some difference of opinion exists about the specific prohibitions involved. All agree that a balcony or partition is required by the law. Rabbi Moshe Feinstein (*ZT'L*) sees both the separation and the structural partition as Torah prescriptions (*de-orayta*—of direct biblical derivation). Rabbi Dr. Joseph B. Soloveitchik sees the separation of the sexes as a Torah law but understands the partition itself as a rabbinic ordinance (*de-rabbanan*—of Talmudic derivation).

We are told at length in this volume that the purpose of the separation is to avoid the distraction of the male worshippers which would result from mixed company. The book stresses that the traditional mode of worship is not intended to indicate any secondary status for women in Judaism. On the contrary, the book argues for the highest regard for women and their place in Jewish tradition and life.

All authorities quoted in this book agree that the requirement of Jewish law is that men and women be separated in the synagogue and that this separation be accomplished by structural means—either a balcony or a partition (*mechitzah*). They all regard it as forbidden to pray in a synagogue in which this separation is not observed. They state clearly that in their view it is better to pray at home than in a synagogue with mixed seating.

V. THE NEWLY EXPANDED EDITION

The first edition of *The Sanctity of the Synagogue,* published in 1959 (Mt. Clemens, Michigan: Baruch and Ida Litvin), was edited from the materials which Mr. Litvin had assembled in the course of his struggle. This edition was quickly sold out, so a new edition appeared in 1962. The third edition, for which this introduction has been written, has been revised and augmented lovingly by the editor's granddaughter, Jeanne Litvin. She has gathered material pertaining to the effects of the editor's struggle and to recent developments regarding the *mechitzah* in the American Orthodox community. In addition, she has undertaken to make any necessary corrections of errors appearing in the previous editions, and to improve the organization of the volume where possible. She has provided an appreciation in which she shares with the reader something of what she and so many others knew of the dedication and heroism of Baruch Litvin. For all this, we, the readers of this new edition, are most grateful.

The significance of this new edition is best gauged from the material which seeks to update the earlier publication. It is here that one sees the true impact of Baruch Litvin's struggle. Here are gathered the stories of the work of others who sought, in the wake of the return to halachic Orthodoxy which we have chronicled above, to restore the traditional separation of men and women to their synagogues. In these stories, we can glimpse the success of Litvin's efforts. In all these accounts, there is no longer any question of the true position of the *halachah*; those struggling for tradition have the force of halachic and communal concensus on their side.

The true contribution of Baruch Litvin to the revival of Orthodoxy in America lies in his having awakened the Orthodox community to the importance of the preservation of the halachic pattern of synagogue worship. His was a major role in insuring the dominance of the halachic system in American Orthodoxy. It remains for the contemporary Orthodox community to continue his work. Mr. Litvin had no choice but to struggle in the courts. Today's Orthodox community, certain of its own stance and secure in its commitment, must carry on this work in a spirit of love for all Jews, so that the entire Jewish community may share in the revival of halachic Judaism in America.

FOREWORD TO THE SECOND EDITION

"Mi yaale behar Hashem umi yokum bimkom kodsho."
"Who shall go up to the mountain of the L-rd, and who shall stand on His Holy place."

In writing these lines on the occasion of the publication of the second edition of the Sanctity of the Synagogue, the above words of the Psalmist come to mind. For the first edition was a mountain-climbing task. Many felt that to publish and sell a book devoted to the theme of, and struggle for, KEDUSHAS BAIS HAKNESSES would be an uphill effort second only to the herculean battle to uphold the laws of Synagogue sanctity — a battle which preceded and gave rise to this magnificent book. The mountain was scaled, the first edition rolled off the press and found its way into thousands of homes, synagogues, universities, colleges and general libraries. But this is not all. Reaching the mountain top is one thing, but establishing a firm, lasting position is something else. As we go to press with the second edition it can be said with quiet pride that this Sefer was no fly-by-night phenomenon. On the contrary, the book has already had such a remarkable effect in communities where the literal and figurative breach of the law was a foregone conclusion, that all the Mesiras Nefesh, that the writing, editing and publication of the Sefer demanded and got from the tireless and dedicated Reb Boruch Litvin stands vindicated.

In the files of Mr. Litvin there are letters of deep and reverent gratitude, showing how plans to overthrow the Mechitza, and with it, the authority of the Torah, would have succeeded but for the dignified and authentic "reinforcements" in the form of this great, heartening Sefer, a sefer which belongs to the category of those books of which it is written Al Ken Yeomar B'Sefer Milchamos HaShem, truly a book that carries on the battle of the L-rd.

Not the least of the accomplishments of this Sefer is, that sacred questions of Torah-law are being more and more decided not by a vote, but by the authority of the law. The old order of Nese Sefer V'nechze, "let us take the book and see what it teaches," will yet be restored.

It may be premature to speak of a "third" edition at the moment, but such an edition may be desperately needed to preserve the sanctity of the synagogue from a new danger and that is the mixed synagogue — the synagogue which satisfies all elements under one roof, the "department-store" synagogue, if you will, where you can have your pick of "Judaism" displayed on various counters. This is not fantasy but sad reality. There are already a few instances where the walls separating the orthodox synagogue from its non-orthodox counterpart are thrown down to make way for a united "Jewish" synagogue.

If the legitimate and necessary Mechitza between the synagogues which are guided by Jewish law and those that ignore it, is breached then the KEDUSHAS BAIS HAKNESSES will meet its sternest challenge.

We of the Metropolitan Board of Orthodox Rabbis are pleased to promote this Sefer and its cause because we have dedicated ourselves to the defence of the Sanctity and uniqueness of Judaism in all its aspects.

May the Alm-ghty to whom we pray these days to be inscribed in the Sefer Hachayim grant us the privilege to uphold the Toras Chayim — the book of life of all Israel.

RABBI DAVID B. HOLLANDER,
President, Metropolitan Board of Orthodox Rabbis

New York City
Erev Rosh Hashonah — 5723

foreword

OD THE EXALTED knows
I greatly feared to write of the matters I wished this work
to contain. . . . But I rely on two precedents: first, in
similar cases our Sages applied the verse, It is time to work
for the Lord: [for] they have made void Thy Torah (Psalms
119:126); secondly, they said, "Let all your deeds be done
for the sake of Heaven" (Aboth 2, 12).

So wrote Judaism's towering luminary, R. Moshe b.
Maimon (Rambam, Maimonides) toward the end of his
introduction to the *Guide for the Perplexed*.[1] I can find no
better opening for this volume, for it was these two precedents which I sought to follow, in my own way, in the long,
often lonely struggle which has given rise to this volume.
In moments of doubt and perplexity they gave direction
and encouragement along a difficult path.

---

1. From the Hebrew translation of R. Judah al-Harizi, Warsaw, 1904.

xxxix

In 1955 I was faced, as a member of my Jewish community, with a dismaying problem. In the synagogue where I had worshipped for many years, a majority of laymen suddenly decided to swerve it from its orthodox ways and to have men and women sitting together at worship. I knew I could not compromise on the religious principle at stake; only one alternative was left me: to fight this proposed desecration with whatever means might be at my disposal.

Would to Heaven all controversy regarding Torah and the faith of the Jew could be resolved in a *beth din,* a Jewish religious court. We are mindful of Maimonides' stringent words: "Whoever submits a suit for adjudication to non-Jewish judges in their courts, even if the judgment they [subsequently] render is in consonance with Jewish law, that person is a wicked man. It is as though he reviled, blasphemed and rebelled against the Torah of our Teacher Moses; for it is stated, *Now these are the ordinances which thou shalt set before them* (Exodus 21:6)—before *them* [the Jewish people] and not before non-Jews, or the unlettered" (*Mishneh Torah, Hilchoth Sanhedrin* 26, 7).

In the present case, as in several others, settlement by a *beth din* was, alas, not to be. The majority of Congregation Beth Tefilas Moses that wished to introduce mixed seating at services, refused to abide by any ruling which a *beth din* might render. A small group, the present writer included, was determined to prevent the sacrilegious change, and safeguard the purpose to which the edifice had been originally dedicated. At the very least, we wished to protect our property rights as members of the congregation, for were the change to take effect, we would have been compelled by religious principle to leave the synagogue permanently and worship elsewhere.

In the source cited above, Maimonides continues: "If

. . . a claimant is unable to recover what is due him through the *beth din,* he must first summon him [the defendant] to appear before Jewish judges; if his opponent refuses to appear, the plaintiff may then obtain permission from the *beth din* to recover his claim through the non-Jewish court."

Again and again I sought to bring the controversy before Halachic authorities. The refusal was absolute. Reluctantly, I received from the following the right to take the case to the civil courts: the Union of Orthodox Rabbis (*Agudath ha-Rabbanim*), Rabbinical Council of America, Rabbinical Alliance of America (*'Iggud ha-Rabbanim*), and the Detroit *Va'ad ha-Rabbanim.*

The struggle has been long, tedious and costly. But in it I have learned a great deal, and perhaps grown a measure. At any rate, when the conflict began, I found it necessary to gather the background material bearing on the subject. For the benefit of the courts it was imperative to assemble authoritative testimony and relevant data from Jewish and secular sources. The material was plentiful; finding it, however, was a most difficult task, and the kindly and generous help of many groups was needed in this great undertaking. I have attempted to repay some small part of my debt of gratitude in the acknowledgments.

Out of the litigation in the courts, out of the array of expert opinion, historical sources, and contemporary Halachic decisions gathered to buttress my case, this volume has grown.

It is my earnest hope that by gathering and presenting this material in one volume, I may contribute significantly to the literature on the subject, and offer essential information to those who seek its knowledge. Even more has it been my wish to provide perspective and encouragement

for those who hold dear the sanctity of the synagogue—
and especially for those who may be called upon some
day to defend ancestral religious practice against innovation and dissension. It may also serve, I earnestly trust,
to give the general reader a depth of understanding in
shaping his attitude to community and synagogue.

But above all else, I have wanted this volume to
make starkly clear how far-reaching are the breaches and
ravages in our religious community life, and in our continuing historical development, when wittingly or unwittingly matters of Halachah are wrested from the hands of
the proper, ordained authorities, and decided by the
ephemeral, evanescent whim of the uninformed and unlettered majority. Such action may well be the gateway
to the disappearance of the Jewish identity.

If this volume will help in some measure to restore
loving respect for the Sages of our Torah, I will feel my
efforts amply rewarded.

As I opened with a quotation, so let me close with one.
Speaking for the eternity of our people's endurance, the
prophet Zephaniah said with simple certainty, *The remnant
of Israel shall not do iniquity, nor speak lies; neither shall
a deceitful tongue be found in their mouths* (Zephaniah
3:13). The Hebrew language knows of one tense, one verb
form, to command and to prophesy. The future tense in
which the Bible commands, also implies the abiding confidence of Zephaniah, that the people of Israel *will* heed
and *will* observe. It is with this confidence that I issue this
book: in the trust that it will reach the abiding core, the
spirit of eternal verities, in America's Jewry, which will
ever listen and respond to God's truth, as our Sages teach it.

Mount Clemens, 1959

BARUCH LITVIN

❧ acknowledgments

It is a most pleasant duty for me to acknowledge my indebtedness to the countless individuals and organizations whose fulsome cooperation, each in his own way, alone made this undertaking possible. To all my thanks.

Regretfully, I can single out but a few for mention here.

My gratitude goes first to Rabbi Joseph Elias, principal of Yeshivath Beth Yehudah, Detroit; he was the architect of the original brochure which was later expanded into this volume.

I was equally blessed with the unstinted assistance of Mr. Saul Bernstein, the editor of *Jewish Life*, and Rabbi Dr. Samson R. Weiss, executive vice-president of the UOJCA. My full thanks also to Rabbi David B. Hollander and to Mr. Samuel L. Brennglass, the "legal brain trust" of the UOJCA; each gave generously of his time and effort.

There is a unique measure of gratitude, which words can barely express, that I owe my dear wife and beloved children: but for their inspiration, abiding cheer, and unfailing encouragement, the task would have been beyond me.

To Rabbi Dr. Howard J. Levine of Stern College for the invaluable assistance rendered by reading the entire manuscript, and contributed to the accuracy of the text, and to Mr. Irving Hunger of their staff, go my thanks for meticulous care and attention to the myriad technical details involved in the printing of such a work. Lastly, I am grateful to Rabbi Elhanan Wengrov for his prodigious labor to prepare the work in final form for publication, including additional research and major counsel regarding both the form and the content of the volume.

May the Almighty reward all as they richly deserve.

B. L.

xliii

✽ The Contributors

I. From the Past

A. SAGES AND RABBINIC AUTHORITIES

R. Isaac Ar'ama (c. 1420-1494): a Sephardic scholar who served as rabbi in various Spanish communities until the expulsion of 1492, when he settled in Naples. The excerpt included here (pp. 187-189) is from his popular work *Akedath Yitzhak,* a philosophical-homiletical commentary on the Pentateuch.

R. Eliyahu Guttmacher (1796-1874): a disciple of R. Akiba Eger who served as rabbi in Plesch (Posen) and, for the most part, in Graetz (Grodzisk, Greiditz), Polish Prussia. A noted Talmudist and kabbalist, he left many writings in print and manuscript. The responsum reprinted in this volume (pp. 198-202) was published in *Zichron Shelomoh* by R. Shelomoh Bigeleisen, Lublin, 1933 (pp. 70-72).

The *Hafetz Hayyim* (R. Israel Me'ir ha-Kohen, 1839-1933): perhaps the most pious and saintly rabbi of his time. His commentary, *Mishnah Berurah,* on *Shulhan Aruch Orah Hayyim* (an excerpt is given on pp. 186-187) is generally regarded as definitive in Jewish law.

R. Hayyim Halberstam (1793-1876): a rabbinical scholar who turned to Hassidism and founded the dynasty of Sanz (Galicia) where he served as rabbi from 1830 on. His essay in this volume (pp. 203-206) is from his collected responsa, *Dibre Hayyim, Orah Hayyim* no. 18.

R. Abraham Isaac Kook (1865-1935): the illustrious chief rabbi of Palestine under the British mandate. His essay on the synagogue in this volume (pp. 96-101) appeared in Jerusalem, 1923.

R. Menahem Mendel Hayyim Landa was an outstanding and key figure in Polish Jewry of a generation ago, a scholar of note who served in various communities. His responsum (pp. 183-186) was printed from manuscript in *ha-Pardes,* vol. 25, no. 10.

R. Hillel Lichtenstein (1815-1891): served as rabbi in various communities of his native Hungary, and from 1867 on, in Kolomea, Galicia. The essay in this volume (pp. 196-197) is from his collected responsa, *Teshuboth Beth Hillel,* Satmar 1908, no. 104.

Maimonides (R. Moses b. Maimon, 1135-1204): philosopher, codifier and medical writer. Considered second only to the first Moses himself, he is best known for his *Mishneh Torah* or *Yad ha-Hazakah,* a Hebrew compendium of the entire Halachah; the philosophical *Guide for the Perplexed;* and his *Commentary on the Mishnah,* an excerpt of which is here included (pp. 182-183).

Maharam (R. Moses) Schick (1807-1879): a disciple of the *Hatham Sofer,* who served as an outstanding rabbi in Hungary, last in Hust (where he was buried); he remained to the end a staunch and valiant battler of Reform Judaism. Included in this volume is one of his collected Responsa, *Orah Hayyim* no. 77 (pp. 193-196).

B. OTHERS

Dr. Joseph H. Hertz (1872-1946): born in Slovakia and educated in New York, he was appointed in 1913 chief rabbi of the British Empire, in which position he spent the remainder of his distinguished life. One of his major works is his Commentary on the Pentateuch, where the essay reprinted here (pp. 266-269) appeared as an Additional Note to Deuteronomy.

Nahida Remy (Ruth Lazarus, 1849-1928): born into a Christian family of Prussian officers, she was attracted to Judaism, and in 1893 wrote *The Jewish Woman,* of which two chapters are here excerpted (pp. 278-287). In 1895 she converted, and married her tutor, Moritz Lazarus.

Solomon Schechter (1850-1915): scholar and founder of the Conservative movement; 1890-1901, lecturer in Talmud at Cambridge; thereafter president of the Jewish Theological Seminary of America. Included in this volume (pp. 269-277) is an abridged essay from his *Studies in Judaism,* volume I, London 1896.

II. From the Present

A. RABBIS

Dr. Samuel Belkin (1911–1976): president (1943–1975) and chancellor (1975–1976) of Yeshiva University. Ordained at the age of 17 in Radin, he held a Ph.D. degree and was an authority on Rabbinic and Hellenistic literature.

R. Israel Brodie (1895–1979): chief rabbi of the United Hebrew Congregations of the British Commonwealth from 1948 until 1965.

His official letter was written in connection with the Mount Clemens controversy.

R. Moshe Feinstein (1895–1986): was rabbi in Luban, Lithuania, before coming to America in 1938. He ultimately became *rosh yeshivah* in Mesivta Tifereth Jerusalem in New York City, which he headed until his death. Considered by many the final authority in Jewish law, he regularly answered legal inquiries from every part of the world. His responsum which appeared first in *Talpioth*, New York, 1949, was part of the first and second editions of this volume. All his remaining responsa on the issue of *mechitzah* appear in a special section in this third edition.

R. Samuel Gerstenfeld (1873–1958): professor emeritus of Talmud at the Rabbi Isaac Elchanan Theological Seminary, a devoted teacher and Talmudic scholar. Born in Austria-Hungary and ordained at the Yeshiva of Klausenberg, he had served as aide to the Chief Rabbi of Britain. His essay reprinted here appeared in *Eidenu*, a memorial volume for Dr. Bernard Revel, New York, 1942.

R. Ezekiel ha-Levi Grubner is the spiritual leader of Congregation Dovid ben Nochim and Director of the Council of Orthodox Rabbis of Greater Detroit in Detroit, Michigan. His essay was written especially for this volume.

R. Isaac Halevy Herzog (1888–1959): from 1936 until his passing, the Ashkenazi chief rabbi in Israel, and as such a noted and impassioned spokesman for orthodox causes and principles, e.g. the *mechitzah*.

R. David B. Hollander: past president of the Rabbinical Council of America, former spiritual leader of the Mount Eden Jewish Center, Bronx, New York, and presently the spiritual leader of the Hebrew Alliance of Brighton Beach in Brooklyn, New York.

R. Dr. Leo Jung (1892–   ): Senior Rabbi of the Jewish Center, New York; author and editor of many books. Born in Moravia and ordained by R. David Hoffmann, he holds degrees from the Universities of London (Hon. B.A., Ph.D.) and Cambridge (M.A.), Yeshiva University (D.D.) and New York University (Hon. Dr. of Humane Letters). His article originally appeared in *Jewish Heritage*, vol. 2, no. 1, Washington, Spring, 1959.

R. Menahem M. Kasher (1895–1985): world-renowned scholar and recognized authority in Rabbinic literature. He devoted over 35 years to his life-work, *Torah Shlemah*, the Hebrew biblical encyclopedia. His essay appeared originally in *ha-Darom*, New York, 1951.

xlvii

R. Aaron Kotler (1892–1962): was dean of the renowned Yeshiva of Kletzk in Lithuania until his arrival here in 1941, when he became dean of the Beth Medrash Gevoha, Lakewood, New Jersey, perhaps the country's leading graduate school in Rabbinics. He was recognized as a principal Torah authority in our generation.

R. Dr. Norman Lamm (1927–   ): former assistant rabbi at New York City's Kehilath Jeshurun and spiritual leader of Congregation Kodimoh in Springfield, Massachusetts, and the Jewish Center in New York City; served on the faculties of Yeshiva University, Brooklyn College, and City University of New York before being appointed president of Yeshiva University in 1976. Dr. Lamm has gained wide recognition for his writings and discourses on interpretations of Jewish philosophy and law in relation to problems involving science, technology, and philosophy in today's society. He was associate editor of *ha-Darom,* a journal of Jewish law and founder and first editor of *Tradition,* where his essay in this volume first appeared.

R. Morris Max was educated at Yeshiva University and was the spiritual leader of the Queens Jewish Center in Forest Hills, New York. His essay was originally published as a pamphlet by the Union of Orthodox Jewish Congregations of America.

R. Dr. David Ochs was the former spiritual leader of the Torath Emeth Congregation, Dean of the M'ril Graubart Yeshiva, and supervisor of the Etz Chaim Schools in Toronto, Canada. His essay was written as a personal communication to Baruch Litvin.

R. David Regensberg (died 1977): was the dean of the Hebrew Theological College, Skokie, Illinois. His letter was written to Baruch Litvin in connection with the controversy in Mount Clemens.

R. Moshe Sherer became executive vice president of Agudath Israel of America in 1951. In 1963, he was elected national president. In 1980, he was elected chairman of Agudath Israel World Organization. Rabbi Sherer's article appeared in Yiddish in the previous editions. It was translated into English for the Third Edition by Rabbi David Rabinowich.

R. Harold P. Smith was the spiritual leader of Congregation Agudath Achim of South Shore (1946–1969) in Chicago, Illinois. His article was originally given as a sermon there, and was subsequently printed in a local publication.

R. Dr. Joseph B. Soloveitchik (1904–   ): the scion of a

xlviii

renowned family of Lithuanian Rabbis, spiritual leader of congregations in Boston and New York, instructor in Talmud and philosophy
at Yeshiva University. He is regarded by many as orthodoxy's
leading thinker and spokesman. Reprinted in this volume are a
message to a convention of the Rabbinical Council of America, an
open letter which appeared in *Conservative Judaism*, Fall 1956, and
an article which appeared in the *Jewish Day–Morning Journal*,
November 22, 1954.

R. Dr. Samson R. Weiss (1910–   ): author and educator,
formerly dean of Yeshivath Beth Yehudah, Detroit, Michigan, and
national director of Young Israel, where he founded the Young Israel
Institute of Jewish Studies. He served as the executive vice-president and is now the executive vice president emeritus of the Union
of Orthodox Jewish Congregations of America. His essay was
written especially for this volume.

B. OTHERS

Dr. Nina H. Alderblum was born in Jerusalem and studied at
Columbia and Paris Universities; she holds the degree of Ph.D. from
the former. A lecturer and member of philosophic organizations, she
has written extensively on Jewish philosophy and ethics. Her essay
appeared originally in *The Jewish Library*, third series, edited by Dr.
Leo Jung. Their permission to reprint it is gratefully acknowledged.

Saul Bernstein was born and educated in England and was the
editor of *Jewish Life* and administrator of the Union of Orthodox
Jewish Congregations of America. Included in this volume are two
chapters from his book *The Renaissance of the Torah Jew*.

Samuel Lawrence Brennglass: appellate counsel, formerly law
secretary to the late Chief Judge Irving Lehman of the New York
Court of Appeals. He was vice president of the Union of Orthodox
Jewish Congregations of America and now holds the position of
honorary chairman of the board. Included in this volume are his
Brief Amici Curiae prepared for the Mount Clemens case and his
analysis of the implications of the final decision in the case.

III. For the Third Edition

A. RABBIS

R. David Algaze is the founder of Havurat Israel, a dynamic
synagogue in Forest Hills, New York, and of a *kollel* and *yeshiva*
currently meeting there. He is also the founder of Eli, a new town in

xlix

northern Israel. Rabbi Algaze's article was written especially for the third edition.

R. David Avigdor is spiritual leader of the Bikur Cholim–Sheveth Achim Synagogue in New Haven, Connecticut. In addition, he is a cantor, certified *mohel, shochet,* and *sofer.* He is also an attorney. Rabbi Avigdor wrote his article especially for the third edition.

R. Simon A. Dolgin served as Rabbi of Beth Jacob Congregation in Beverly Hills, California, for 33 years, during which time he founded Hillel Hebrew Academy. During his residence in Israel, he has served as general and special advisor to the minister of religious affairs, as chairman of the Mizrachi–Hapoel Hamizrachi World Organization and as rabbi of the Ramot Eshkol community. Now Rabbi Dolgin also serves as chairman of the board of directors of Ariel United Institutes in Jerusalem. His article was written especially for the third edition.

R. Oscar Z. Fasman has served as rabbi of Congregation Yehuda Moshe of Lincolnwood, Illinois, since 1964. He is past president of the Rabbinical Council of America. From 1946 to 1964, he was president of the Hebrew Theological College in Skokie, Illinois. In 1982, the high school of the Hebrew Theological College was named the Rabbi Oscar Z. Fasman High School. Rabbi Fasman's article was written especially for the third edition.

R. Dr. Rubin Huttler is rabbi of Congregation Etz Jacob in Los Angeles, California. He is past president of the Rabbinical Council of California and the Southern California Board of Rabbis. Rabbi Huttler has a doctorate in education from the University of Southern California. His article was written especially for the third edition.

R. Milton H. Polin received *semichah* from the Hebrew Theological College and is now spiritual leader of the Kingsway Jewish Center, Brooklyn, New York, and president of the Rabbinical Council of America. Rabbi Polin was chairman of the Rabbinical Council of America Kashruth Committee for five years and served two terms as president of the Va'ad ha-Rabbanim of Flatbush. Rabbi Polin's article in this volume was excerpted from a sermon delivered Succoth, 1979. The sermon, in its entirety, appears in the 1980 volume of the Rabbinical Council of America's *Manual of Sermons.*

Rabbi Shlomo Riskin is the founding Rabbi of Lincoln Square Synagogue and has served there since 1964. He was also a professor

l

of Talmud at Yeshiva University. Rabbi Riskin has a doctorate in Near Eastern Languages and Literature from New York University. He is one of the founders and the Chief Rabbi of Efrat, Israel. Rabbi Riskin founded the Ohr Torah Schools in New York and in Efrat.

R. Pinchas Stolper is executive vice president of the Union of Orthodox Jewish Congregations of America. He founded the National Conference of Synagogue Youth (N.C.S.Y.) and served as its national director for 18 years. He has edited and written more than twenty volumes on Jewish life and thought. Rabbi Stolper's article is adapted from the original which first appeared in *Jewish Action*, winter 1982. His letter was written as a personal communication to Jeanne Litvin.

R. Melvin Teitelbaum was assistant to the rabbi at Congregation Emunath Israel in Manhattan and was spiritual leader of Congregation Ahavath Israel in Hollywood, California, for seven years. He was chairman of the Va'ad ha-Kashruth of the Rabbinical Council of California. He served in the Peace Corps and as a chaplain at state and federal prisons in California. Rabbi Teitelbaum is also an attorney. His article was written especially for the third edition.

B. OTHERS

Paul Cowan, a New York writer, is author of *Tribes in America* and a frequent contributor to the Village Voice. The material for the article on the Pacific Jewish Center–Bay Area Synagogue was adapted from an article by Mr. Cowan entitled "A Renaissance in Venice," which appeared in the special California issue of *Jewish Living Magazine* in April, 1980.

Abraham Dere is one of the two founders of Kol Emes Synagogue in Richmond, Virginia. His article first appeared in the Kol Emes Synagogue Newsletter.

Dr. Lawrence H. Schiffman is professor of Hebrew and Judaic Studies at New York University's Department of Near Eastern Languages and Literatures and serves as associate director of the university's Institute of Hebrew and Judaic Studies. He is a specialist in the Dead Sea Scrolls and in the history of Jewish Law and Talmudic Literature. His publications include *The Halachah at Qumran, Sectarian Law in the Dead Sea Scrolls Courts, Testimony and the Penal Code, Who Was a Jew?* and *Rabbinic Perspectives on the Jewish Christian Schism*. Dr. Schiffman wrote the Introduction and Conclusion especially for the third edition of this volume.

The Fifth Avenue Synagogue, New York, during inaugural services

prologue

note

Wherever reference is made to separation of the sexes, separate seating, separate sections, etc., in the synagogue, it is meant to connote a full separation between men and women, either through the use of a balcony or gallery for the women, or by means of a full physical partition, a *mechitzah*, between the two.

a word
of introduction

FOR YEARS Mr. Baruch Litvin of Mount Clemens, Michigan, has fought courageously for the *mechitzah* in the synagogue. In the course of this battle he and his aides have gathered a great deal of material on this subject, which has been prepared for publication in book form. Since we did not read the bulk of the book, we have to confine our statement to a brief appraisal of Mr. Litvin's efforts for the *mechitzah*.

American Jewry has good cause to be grateful to Mr. Litvin for his energetic and valiant campaign for *mechitzoth*. By virtue of this campaign for the preservation of an essential element in synagogues in accordance with Halachah, Mr. Litvin has strengthened the cause of *kedushath beth ha-kenesseth,* the synagogue's sanctity. He should be encouraged in the publication and distribution of his book on *mechitzoth*.

AGUDATH HA-RABBANIM
(Union of Orthodox Rabbis of the
United States and Canada)

the significance of
a religious victory

BY RABBI EMANUEL RACKMAN
President, Rabbinical Council of America

To HAVE separate seating of men
and women at religious services, with a *mechitzah* separating the men's and women's sections, is one of the
most ancient of Jewish synagogue procedures. There are
well-founded philosophical and psychological, as well as
religious reasons for this practice, which is rooted in Jewish
law. In our day, however, it has been challenged. This
volume is dedicated to its defense. The defender merits
the gratitude of all Jews.

Because of the massive drive to make the synagogues
appear more like churches and because of the general disrespect which those hostile to Halachah—Jewish law—
have sought to foster, especially among women, some synagogues have abandoned this sacred practice during past
years. A number of them have subsequently recognized
the error as a desecration of the sanctity of their synagogues
and have reinstituted the *mechitzah,* and a growing number
of others have newly erected the *mechitzah*. This reversal
of a previous trend is going forward in the face of continuing agitation for abandonment of sacred Jewish seating
practice. It is to the credit of the editor of this volume
that he undertook to combat this agitation in his own community, Mount Clemens, Michigan, and to give, through

this historic publication, potent new force to the defense of our Jewish sanctities.

His effort has even greater significance than that associated with the particular observance to which this book is dedicated. The fundamental issue is whether the Divine sanctity of Jewish law itself shall prevail in the Synagogue and whether Jewish law shall be interpreted by those duly qualified and authorized to do so, or by laymen ignorant of the law and devoid of such qualification and authority. By arrogating to themselves power to make religious changes in their synagogues, such laymen have struck at the very foundations of Judaism.

It would be a fatal distortion of Jewish belief to claim that because the roots of democracy are found in the religious tradition, Judaism therefore equates the will of God with the will of the majority. Majorities can be wrong, and minorities—especially in the spiritual and ethical sphere —can be right. But beyond this point, basic to our faith, is the recognition that the will of God is expressed in the Written and Oral Torah, whose interpretation is the domain of the recognized orthodox Rabbinic authorities. To equate Judaism with the will of the untutored and uncommitted, is to vulgarize and distort it, with disastrous consequences.

The editor of this volume has dedicated his life and his means to the restoration of religious authority in Jewish life to its rightful place—the Rabbinate committed to the Halachah. In this connection it must be underlined that not once on the American scene or elsewhere in the world has any Halachic authority sanctioned mixed seating at religious services. Only those who deny Torah law as the binding force can approve this desecration of synagogual sanctity. This, and more, the present volume makes clear; it is much commended to the attention of the American Jew.

5

this is nought but
the House of God

THE SEPARATION of the sexes in the synagogue, through a physical partition, the *mechitzah*, is universally regarded by the authoritative spokesmen of Torah Judaism as a cardinal principle in the preservation of the sanctity of the House of Prayer. A synagogue without such a *mechitzah* clearly severs its ties with the historic and sacred character of the Jewish House of Worship.

In recent years, the *mechitzah* has been challenged by those who have sought to convert the synagogue to a social hall and meeting place where the habits of the market-place could prevail. As a result, the *mechitzah* has transcended its original, intrinsic importance and has become symbolic of a "sacred wall" which distinguishes the holy from the profane, the religious from the sacrilegious.

It was no doubt an act of Providence that this battle for the preservation of the *mechitzah* should have emerged in Mt. Clemens, Michigan, where the editor of this book almost single-handedly waged the battle for Torah. From this effort there now emerges what promises to be a historic contribution in the documentation of all literature relating to the importance of the *mechitzah* in particular, and the sanctity of the synagogue in general.

One man's selfless dedication of his time, energy, and money has been crowned with success in retaining the sanctity of a synagogue; this is in itself an inspiration. There is, however, an exceedingly more significant lesson

6

to be derived from the Michigan Supreme Court's ruling barring the removal of the *mechitzah*. For, it bears eloquent testimony to our Jewish commitment that in matters of religion the will of an unlearned majority must bow to the authoritative interpreters of the Divine Will.

It is our hope that all serious minded Jews will acquire this volume. It will not alone contribute to an appreciation of a vital ingredient of the synagogue's sanctity, but will help restore authority in Jewish life to the deserving hands of that Rabbinate which is unequivocally committed to the Halachah.

RABBINICAL ALLIANCE OF AMERICA

RABBI SAMUEL A. TURK
President

RABBI BERNARD WEINBERGER
Executive Vice-President

freedom
of choice

BY RABBI EPHRAIM H. STURM
National Director, National Council of Young Israel

THE RIGHT to consciously select a program of religious belief and observance is a fundamental principle of Jewish philosophic thought. To deny *behira,* the freedom of choice, means to uproot the very foundation of reward and punishment, one of Maimonides' thirteen principles of faith. Were every man but an automaton, motivated by drives and instincts beyond his control, he could no longer be held responsible for his deeds; nor might he expect a reward for righteous action. This concept of freedom of conscience is re-enforced in the American tradition, which zealously safeguards freedom of religion, the right to choose to observe, or not.

Conscious choice, in issues affecting the very eternity of the individual, can not be based on temporal and fleeting values, but must be predicated upon knowledge of fundamental principles. One must never equate freedom of choice with guess-work. Before one can consciously select a pattern of observance, a fundamental philosophic standard, one must be certain that he has consulted and understands the underlying principles involved.

This book, edited by Mr. Baruch Litvin, therefore, dramatically addresses itself to these two major areas.

Certainly we cannot deny people the right to consciously choose their mode of synagogue worship. Should they wish to emulate in their prayers certain non-Jewish practices, we may bemoan their choice and may honestly and seriously feel compassion for them because of their distorted ideas. Yet, as American citizens we have no right to deny them the right to make this mistake. However, they on their part owe the same courtesy of religious understanding to their brethren who seek to worship in the synagogue of traditional architectural structure. Therefore, the Mount Clemens decision, cited in this volume, will give strength to those who have built traditional synagogues, through sacrifice and toil, in consonance with their religious beliefs, and who now face new members seeking to foist their non-traditional architectural plans upon the synagogue. The Mount Clemens decision has stemmed the tide which threatened to sweep all orthodox synagogues into the torrents of conservatism, and from there, heaven forfend, into the assimilationist abyss of reform.

Though we may at times feel rancor in the heat of battle against those who would tear the *mechitzah* from the synagogue, in moments of calm and reflection, we come to realize that much of their contemplated plans are a manifestation of freedom of choice based on mis-information or lack of information. In this book Mr. Litvin has therefore gathered all major sources referring to the *mechitzah* from earliest writings until the present. With such a book, both rabbi and layman can exercise *behirah*, free choice, on this issue, with deeper understanding, and thereby retain the traditional mode of worship.

The Young Israel movement is grateful to the author of the book for his comprehensive scholarly undertaking, which undoubtedly will strengthen the hand of all traditional synagogues.

the Sinai Campaign in Mount Clemens

BY RABBI DAVID B. HOLLANDER

WITHIN THE PAGES of this proud volume a great story is told of the redemption of the American orthodox synagogue from shocking neglect by its friends on the one hand, and from massive assault by its "Jewish" adversaries on the other. It is, in a sense, the saga of the decline from royalty to exile, from riches to rags, and a restoration to honor and dignity achieved through a redeemer from an unexpected quarter.

The American orthodox synagogue, which was Jewish royalty itself only three or four decades ago, commanding the loyalty of Jews practically without contest from any source, has in our time suffered an unbelievable decline. It is being challenged not from without, not by anti-religious or even non-religious trends and forces, but by a new "synagogue" based on a new "Judaism." In a matter of a few short years, this challenge has become so serious that there are vast areas, both urban and suburban, where one can no longer find a synagogue that was built and is conducted in accordance with the one and only standard that is acceptable: the Halachah, the laws of Judaism.

This new and latest *hurban bate mikdash me'at* (destruction of the Temples-in-miniature) is all the more disturbing because it coincides strangely enough with an upsurge in the fortunes of Torah in America. Side by side with an impressive increase in Torah education and the consequent appearance of a small but influential American young generation of *bene Torah,* we see nevertheless the orthodox synagogue beset by fear and trembling from within, and by massive assault from without (*mihutz teshakel hereb umehadarim 'emah—Without doth the sword bereave, and in the chambers terror*—Deuteronomy 32:25).

It is this distressing climate of *hurban,* however, which has also (as it has always happened in the annals of the Jews) brought forth *go'alim,* redeemers, champions from unexpected or least expected quarters.

The following pages of this unique volume tell the story of such a *go'el,* a redeemer of the orthodox synagogue. There are at least two odd aspects about the person of the redeemer and the Community which was the battlefield of the now victorious "Mount Clemens Campaign." The person, Mr. Baruch Litvin, is a "mister" and not a rabbi, a builder, a farmer, a merchant, but strictly a layman. The community, Mount Clemens, has now become the model alarm clock for other similarly threatened communities; it is not in Brooklyn's Williamsburgh, or Boro Park, nor even in Metropolitan New York—but in Mid-western Michigan. The two large cities much nearer to it than New York are Detroit and Chicago, two metropolitan centers where the orthodox synagogue has become all but a museum, a relic of the recent past.

It is in this kind of setting that the now successful struggle to stem the tide of the *hurban,* not only in Mount Clemens but in all America, has begun.

We must not underestimate the significance of the role of the layman in this battle. For it reveals that, traditionally, the fight against the alteration of the Torah, the fight against the attempt to replace the Halachah as the one and only standard of the religious conduct of the Jew, cannot and ought not to be carried on exclusively by the rabbis, by the various professional staffs, but must be joined in (not only followed but at times even initiated, as in this case) by the laity.

Indeed, the modern rabbi has become an "indispensable" necessity precisely because the practice and study of Judaism is limited to himself alone. The laity is thus absolved from a daily Torah life by supporting a rabbi.

If a Mr. Litvin (and, indeed we wish there were others half as capable, half as colorful, half as uncrushable as he is) has appeared on the scene to carry on the fight for the sanctity of the Synagogue, it is because he is *not* a member of the new Jewish laity which leaves everything to the professionals claiming that they are the experts and that religion is "their" job. No, he is a layman from a different background, from the age-old Jewish tradition requiring every Jew to be "on his own"—to do his own practicing of Judaism—and not only practicing but *studying* the Torah. The study and the knowledge of the Torah and the inexhaustible tributaries of this vast ocean is not the special domain of the rabbinnate or any other *clerical* group within the House of Israel. To the extent that it *has* become so, to the extent that *yeshiboth* are deemed by some to be *"rabbinical"* schools, as distinguished from schools for *all* Jews, to that extent have we drifted from our moorings. Has not the Torah said, *ve'attem*—you, *all* of you—*tiheyu li mamlecheth kohanim vegoy kadosh* —shall be unto Me a dominion of priests and a holy *nation* (Exodus 19:6). All of us then, not only the rabbis are deemed to be in the "clerical" society.

The story of the Mount Clemens case, therefore, is

not only an account of the struggle to restore the synagogue to the Torah, but also the story of the restoration of the Torah *to the people* where it belongs. But for this role of the Jewish layman, the current fight would either not have begun at all, or it would have bogged down in its early stages due to the shocking attitude of a certain rabbi who literally helped the forces arrayed against the sanctity of the Synagogue.

The natural and expected reaction of a layman to such conduct by a rabbi would have been to drop the whole matter with the glib thought, "I do not have to be more 'religious' than the rabbi." But this was *not* the reaction, because every layman has a "direct wire" to God, and no rabbi can "jam the air-waves"; and most assuredly, if the rabbi takes a stand contrary to the Torah (and contrary, as in this case, to the position of his colleagues) then the layman *must* be more "religious" than the rabbi. (In this connection, it is interesting to note that in many conservative and even reform temples, the rebellion against traditional synagogue procedure led with such arrogance by their "rabbis," has been arrested somewhat by laymen who retained a flavorful memory of what a synagogue should be like, and could not withstand the "modernism" of their spiritual leaders.)

This "by-product" of the Mount Clemens case is, therefore, most significant because it demonstrates that perhaps the most compelling factor in the survival of Torah-Judaism against so many attempts to substitute something else in its stead, has been the fact that Judaism does not have to rely on any clergy to keep it going; that it relies rather on its "grass-roots," on contact with *'amecha,* with the people themselves.

A good illustration of this point is to be found in the

following anecdote. A famous orthodox Rabbinic personality who enjoyed the following and confidence of the orthodox world came to a resort town for a rest cure. Two local Jews noticed with astonishment that this rabbi ate early at dawn before having recited his morning prayers. Actually, the rabbi was justified because the doctors ordered him to eat immediately upon awakening. "Is it not amazing," said one to the other, "that a rabbi should do such a thing?" "It certainly is," answered his friend, "but it only goes to show that even a great rabbi can corrupt his ways." When the rabbi in question was told of this incident he said, "This episode proves the special religious qualities of the *Jewish* laity. Just imagine what the reaction would be if non-Jews saw their spiritual leader eat meat on Friday, for example. Their likely reaction would be, 'If the priest can do it, I certainly can,' whereas in our case it is I the *rabbi* who is tarnished, while the *law* remains sacred and supreme."

It is this typically Jewish trait that the Torah implies when it says, *Let the Lord, I pray thee, go in the midst of us, for it is a stiffnecked people* (Exodus 34:9): God's presence in our midst is implored *because* our people is stiffnecked. Nor is this stiffneckedness an easy task, whether displayed by the rabbi or the layman. In the case of the latter it is even more exacting because the layman is faced, as in the Mount Clemens case, with derision, ridicule and ostracism *by his own class,* the laity. It is always more difficult to be at variance with your own kind than with strangers to your group. The rabbi who resists forces aimed at reducing the authority which he represents has, at least, the comfort of being in a different and perhaps superior class representing the authority of the law. The layman has no such refuge. He meets his adversaries with-

14

out any protective armor. He is instead an attractive target for all their barbs and criticism, and they know the special brand of punishment to be administered to one of their own who turns "traitor to his class."

The writer was in a peculiar position to note this punitive mentality. As the then President of the Rabbinnical Council of America (1954-1956) he was invited by Mr. Litvin to visit Mount Clemens and try to influence the opponents of the orthodox character of the synagogue to drop their fight; for if they would not drop their attack against the sanctity of the law of the synagogue, they would deprive the orthodox from being able to attend it.

It was clear to me soon after my arrival that this lay fighter was disliked intensely and shunned by the leaders of the community. Privately, people told me he was a hypocrite and a fanatic; that the two charges are contradictory—since the first implies inner disbelief, and the second inner sincerity—no one noted. It was clear that prejudice was riding high. The point of view of orthodoxy regarding the specific issue in question, i.e., the proper arrangement for seating for men and women in the synagogue, was not allowed to be presented. The writer appealed both on the basis of Jewish law and on the consideration of fair-play. On the latter point it was stated that whereas the orthodox cannot in good conscience pray in a synagogue which violates Jewish law, the Conservative and Reform Jews are not directed by their conscience to stay away from an orthodox synagogue and that, therefore, an orthodox synagogue actually can serve all religious Jews, and is non-discriminatory. It was pointed out also that the orthodox attended *daily,* whereas they, the advocates of mixed seating, only two or three times a year.

I saw now who were the real fanatics, because however logical the arguments, they made not a dent. It was as though they had all said in unison, "Our mind is made up; don't bother giving us the facts." The prejudice manifested itself also in the anger over bringing in "outsiders" (the writer) to deal with a "local" problem. This claim smacked disturbingly of the "red herring" type of argument employed against lawyers from the North who sought to help Negro prisoners defend themselves against criminal accusations in a prejudice-charged atmosphere.

All these "homespun" pressures were used to persuade the champion of the fight to give it up; but here is again one of those not-too-rare cases in our history when God has strategically placed certain stout-hearted people in areas where they have turned out to be of the utmost importance.

But aside from the unique role of the layman in this struggle, there are several other important facets which are worthy of comment. One strange and bewildering aspect can best be described by referring to one of the best known episodes in the Torah: the case of Jacob who looked like Esau because he wore Esau's tell-tale garments. The situation here was the reverse, for it was a case of Esau hiding in the garb of Jacob. There was a time when secularist Jews fought the Torah openly. That situation was far less dangerous to Torah than the present: for it is supposedly a fight *for* Torah, *for* the Jewish heritage, and actually it is a masked battle for assimilation. In the fight against Torah-authority (which is Esau's strife) some are wearing Jacob's garb—they claim to protect the Torah and the Jewish people even while they are doing all they can to destroy the Torah. In the Mount Clemens case this strategy was repeatedly employed. It is a clever bit of maneuvering, and it works wonders even with sincere (but naive) advocates of the Torah. The strategy is simple: put the blame

16

on the orthodox for disunity, for disinterest in the Jewish people, for consigning to spiritual oblivion all but a handful of "ultra"-orthodox Jews; and finally accuse the orthodox of the crime of all crimes: the so-called *hillul hashem,* the profanation of His sacred Name, of bringing a Jewish, religious controversy to the attention of the courts and the non-Jewish world. This sleight-of-hand trick—here you see it, here you don't—is designed to put the orthodox on the defensive, and picture them as enemies of the Jewish people; consequently, the issue is no longer the authority and sanctity of Jewish law but rather how to cope with the so-called primitive, divisive, parochial orthodox mentality. This strategy was used to the hilt against Mr. Litvin and virtually the whole orthodox Rabbinate which supported him vigorously.

The writer, feeling that whoever will want to read this book will have sufficient objectivity to consider these "charges" dispassionately, will deal with them here briefly.

The charge of disunity has been levelled against prophets and sages. On the surface the charge has some validity, for the true champion of the Torah, now as in previous generations, insists on pointing out the failings of the people and to demand rectification. By so doing he also demands that lines of demarcation be drawn between those who accept the authority of the law and those who go on in their defiance even after due warning. By separating "the wheat from the chaff" one does, of course, establish disunity. But did not Moses cry out, *Whoso is on the Lord's side, let him come unto me* (Exodus 33:26)? and the tribe of Levi alone answered his call. Was he guilty of sowing disunity? Was not the disunity rather a product of a rebellion against an already existing Jewish unity, a unity begun at Sinai when all Jews responded as

17

one, *We will do and we will hear* (*ibid.* 24:7)? ... Those who withdraw and steer a new course are guilty of disunity, a disunity which they can easily cure by returning to the fold. But that is not the unity they want. The "unity" they want is that *all* Jews should join the rebellion against the Torah, and if there are some "die-hards" who do not want to, then they are to be branded as the agents of disunity.

These same gentlemen also appoint themselves as the custodians of religious Jewry, and by the same token they designate as its enemies those who insist that absolutely nothing other than the Torah gives the Jew his identity.

We come now to the next calumny levelled against the orthodox, not only in Mount Clemens but across the board: that we reject Jews who do not accept the authority of the Torah. No, we do not reject any, unless they knowingly, irrevocably and arrogantly reject the Torah. Were we to accept these Jews, too, as full-fledged, not only would we break the hold of the Torah on our people, but we would also dash the possibility of these people *ever coming back to the Torah*. Thus our aloofness and insistence on drawing the line is motivated by our desire not to *lose* these people but to win them back.

Finally, the Mount Clemens case gave new life to the argument which wins almost everyone: that we ought not to take a Jewish dispute to the courts. But what made this a *Jewish* dispute? This was a rebellion against the authority of the Law, not backed up by legal right but by a raising of hands. The power of the vote was simply used against a *religious principle* which is not subject to any vote. The great unfairness of the assault on the established rules of the orthodox synagogue is further emphasized, when we remember this: the people who years ago toiled hard and gave of their meagre earnings to build and maintain an orthodox synagogue, never intended that the synagogue be anything but genuinely *orthodox*. These people are now dead. Is it decent, fair, to knowingly destroy what they built and take over *their* property? *haratzahtah vegam yarashtah*—hast thou killed and also taken possession (1 Kings 21:19)?

These gentlemen are apparently sensitive to *hillul hashem*, profaning His sacred Name. We say "apparently" because when these same people publicly desecrate the Sabbath and dietary laws and often the rules of commercial morality for the non-Jew to see, they are not then concerned with *hillul hashem* as they advertise to the world that the majority of the Jews do not adhere to the laws of Judaism; is the name of God or the Jewish people honored or disgraced in the face of such conduct? But perhaps the real hypocricy of that argument is best proved when we realize that the orthodox went to the *Jewish* tribunals first. Mr. Litvin and his friends waited until all the Jewish tribunals, all the orthodox Rabbinate, had pleaded with the rebels to respect the law; and only after that plea was insultingly and finally rejected and no other avenue was left open to safeguard the rights of the orthodox, did they go to the courts.

The rebels had, in fact, the power to see that no soiled linen was washed in public: by agreeing to the sacred law of the synagogue. This they refused to do, even though they knew that their refusal would take the case into court.

By the mysterious ways of God, out of all this may yet come a *kiddush hashem*, a sanctification of His name; perhaps some of our "modern progressive" Jews will stay their hand from desecrating the sanctity of Jewish law. It may be, even those of our people who, somewhat apologetically, call themselves "modern" orthodox will begin to understand that the Halachah alone is the measure of the rise or decline of Judaism; that all the glib talk about saving the young generation, or attracting more Jews to Judaism by compromise and concession, is calculated nonsense and is used deliberately as a mask for assimilation. The echo of the Michigan decision will reverberate not only in the Jewish world of America but also, hopefully, in Israel. May the Knesset of Israel yet learn from the verdict on the *beth haknesseth*.

A closing story comes to mind. It is related that the famous Kelmer Maggid was once in a very poor Jewish community as a guest preacher. He noticed that the little synagogue had no floor; it stood on the naked earth. He thought and thought of what he could say to them that would make them put in a floor, despite their great poverty. Finally, he told them that when the Messiah would come, the only way poor Jews would be able to get to Israel would be to gather at the synagogue: it would miraculously lift into the air, and, together with its cargo of poor Jews, it would fly to the Holy Land.

"But," continued the Maggid, "unless you put in a floor, the synagogue will fly away, and you will remain here." The application is evident. We are doing many things in Jewish life that are good: building *yeshiboth*, helping the State of Israel, etc.; but all these are products of the influence of the synagogue. It is there that we become inspired and answer appeals for our help. But if we do not plant our feet firmly on the foundation of the synagogue, all will fly away from us, and we will remain stranded amid nowhere. If our children go to *yeshiboth* and grow up to go to a non-orthodox synagogue, and come

20

under the influence of a non-orthodox rabbi, not only will they lose their *yeshibah* training, but whatever is left of that training will be given to the support of a "Judaism" utterly opposed to the Torah.

May the Almighty strengthen the hands of all who support the Torah in its unaltered form, as exemplified in this sacred cause. We view with admiration and reverence the determined *akshanuth,* the stubbornness of a pioneering fighter like Baruch Litvin; taking heart from his shining example, let us not give up the struggle because of the apparent magnitude and power of the enemies of Torah. For he in whose camp the Torah is, is assured of ultimate triumph—a triumph of the House of Israel.

faith and observance

BY DR. SAMSON R. WEISS

The Torah of the Lord is perfect, restoring the soul; the testimony of the Lord is unfailing, making wise the simple.

The precepts of the Lord are righteous, filling the heart with joy; the commandment of the Lord is clear, enlightening the eyes.

The fear of the Lord is pure, enduring forever; the statutes of the Lord are true, they are just, altogether.

(Psalms 19:8-10)

THIS BOOK is concerned with an issue which has aroused much controversy within the American Jewish community. It deals with the separation of the sexes in the Jewish House of Worship. It contains Talmudic and post-Talmudic Halachic sources, complete responsa or pertinent excerpts from the *teshuboth* of Torah authorities past and present, never before collated in similar exhaustiveness on this or any other contemporary issue.

Furthermore, this book contains voluminous material on reported legal cases wherein loyal minorities sought and obtained relief from civil courts in their resistance to the illegal attempts of temporary majorities to introduce mixed seating at worship. The refusal of

22

these majorities to submit the congregational conflict to Rabbinic Tribunals brought the issue of the *mechitzah*—the physical separation between the sexes in the House of Worship—before the courts and thus to the attention of both the Jewish and non-Jewish public. The adjudication of such an issue by the civil courts, notwithstanding the constitutional separation between Church and State, is based on the acceptance by the courts of the obligation to protect the property rights of members whose use of their congregational facilities would be denied to them by the introduction of deviationist innovations which are contrary to their religious convictions. The present volume is, therefore, not only a book of historic Jewish value but also an important American document.

Still, it is difficult to comprehend why so seemingly a minor violation should arouse such strong and persistent resistance. Violations of the Torah regrettably abound in American Jewish life. Protests are being heard, true. Yet, communities have not been split by, nor have the civil courts been called upon to determine, other intramural Jewish issues. Consequently, the exponents of traditional observance have been accused of obstinacy, of quixotic struggles against unavoidable developments, of harming the Jewish prestige and of sacrificing the peace and the harmony of the Jewish community for the sake of maintaining a mere "technicality."

All of these accusations are unjust. They are based either on a deplorable ignorance of Judaism or on demagogic attempts to becloud the true importance of the issue and its variegated ramifications by the use of irrelevant catch phrases. It is only against the background of the fundamentals of the Jewish view that the proper perspective can be gained for an understanding of the Torah-true Jewish position. It is not a random observance which is at stake when the *mechitzah* is being abolished. At stake are the very foundations of Torah Judaism. The eruption of the conflict around mixed seating is never the malady in itself, but rather a symptom and a danger signal that the entire structure of Jewish observance is threatened and that Torah is about to be dethroned, forfend, as the regulative motivation of congregational life.

It is for this reason that it becomes necessary to introduce this volume with a brief outline of those basic considerations which constitute the framework of Jewish faith and observance.

23

THE FAITH OF ISRAEL was established by our father Abraham. Through his contemplation of the universe he recognized the Almighty and His Oneness. In an age of idolatry which had forgotten or discarded the traditions of Noah, Shem and Eber, the great of the preceding generations, Abraham set out to teach mankind the knowledge of God and the truth about the world's origin and purpose, one alone against the prevailing powers and their heathen ideologies. He was chosen by the Almighty to become the father of a people that was to receive His Torah on Sinai and to inherit the Promised Land in which all the precepts of this Torah can be fulfilled.

It is this acknowledgment of the Oneness of the Almighty, of the *ahduth hashem,* which is the cornerstone of our faith. The concept of this Oneness includes the Divine attributes of infinity and eternity, for it bears neither limitation nor division. Time and space in themselves are creations of Him Who is above all confines. Unchangingly the same in His Oneness, He is the source of all existence. His eternity precludes His being preceded by any other thing or being. His infinity extends to all His attributes. Unlimited in His wisdom and power, He is the omniscient and omnipotent creator of all that is, to Whom alone can be ascribed true creativeness.

Creation is the evoking of existence out of the unimaginable void. It is the propulsion into being of *yesh,* substance, *me'ayin,* out of nothingness. Hence, existence *per se* must forever lean on the *metzi'uth hashem,* on the supreme reality of His existence and on His continuous will to maintain His creation. This continuous will is the sole substance of the entire universe. Before pronouncing the *shema',* the acknowledgment of His Oneness, the Jew testifies to the continuity of creation and blesses Him *Who in His goodness renews every day and constantly the works of creation.*[1] Creation is transformed into nature by the constancy of this renewal. Still, even while cloaked in the mantle of nature, the Divine word and command of creation have neither ceased nor changed. Both creation and nature equally evidence His infinite wisdom and power.

Transcending and, so to speak, enveloping His creation, He yet remains unaffected by it in His Oneness. His sovereignty does not depend on His creatures, nor is He in any way conditioned by them. "Were one to imagine that He is not, nothing else could be. And were one to imagine that nothing but He exists, He alone will be forever, unaffected by their voidance; for all existences need Him but He, blessed be He, needs neither all of them nor any one of them" (Rambam, *Hilchoth Yesode Torah* 1, 2-3). While revealed and immanent in His creation, the Eternal and Infinite has not become subject to it or to any of its occurrences. To a people that understands the world as creation, the miracle, the change or the suspension of the laws of nature by His will and intervention, is no more surprising than is the regularity of the universal mechanism.

The revelation of the Almighty through creation is not the final gate to His knowledge. Not even the miracle, so clearly evidencing His mastery over nature, offers to man sufficient insight into the Divine purpose. Creation and the miracle are still mute and do not fill the yearning of the soul for direct colloquy with the One Whom it recognizes from His works. Superior, therefore, to the revelation of creation is prophecy in which the Almighty appears to man in vision and voice and addresses Himself to him.

---

1. [Daily Prayer Book, preceding the *shema'* in the morning prayers.]

Prophecy is the consequence of man's reaching intellectual and moral perfection. Having attained the limit of his spiritual potential, his horizons are further and immeasurably extended by the prophetic view which discloses to him new vistas of the Divine wisdom and which may also make him the recipient of the direct command of God. In prophecy, man achieves his highest affinity with, and knowledge of, his Maker.

It is Abraham the Prophet, not Abraham the philosopher, who is the father of the Jewish people. In prophecy he was told that from his loins would spring forth a nation that was to live, as a blessing to all men, by the precepts of God's law. With Abraham the Prophet the Almighty concluded an everlasting covenant, for himself and his progeny, a covenant enduring through all exiles and sufferings. *And the Almighty spoke to Abraham*[2]—this is the beginning of our history.

On Sinai, the entire people of Israel attained this supreme experience of prophecy, and heard God's voice filling the world with the *anoch'i hashem.*[3] On Sinai, they accepted His Torah upon themselves and all future Jewish generations. Having witnessed in their redemption from Egyptian bondage the Divine intervention, the miracles superseding all laws of nature and returning them for the higher purpose of Israel's salvation to the matrix of creation, they had acknowledged the Creator and followed His prophet Mosheh into the desert. Now, they spoke with Him and perceived in Divine inspiration the purpose of Israel's existence and the purpose of the entire universe.

Torah is the Divine postulate directed to the entire world and in particular to the sons and daughters of Israel,

2. [Genesis 17:15.]
3. [*I am the Lord;* Exodus 20:2.]

26

the seed of Abraham. It is the Divine disclosure of the spiritual substance, and hence of the justification, of all existence. It antedates, as we are told by our Sages, creation itself. From the vantage point of creation, the purpose precedes the instrument, the goal precedes the way, and thus Torah precedes the world. *Bereshith*[4]—"For the sake of the Torah, which is called *reshith* (the first) and for the sake of Israel, that is called *reshith*" He created heaven and earth and all that fills them. The Divine purpose and its human depository were joined in the climactic revelation on Sinai.

Torah, the law emanating from the omnipresent and all-pervading God, addresses itself to every facet, every situation, every contingency and every moment of existence. Therein lies the profound and decisive distinction between Torah and, *lehabdil,* any other religious pattern. Like the Almighty Who envelops in His existence the entire world, so His law too must necessarily envelop us in our totality—without pauses and without reservations.

At no time have the People of the Book submitted to the notion that outer conditions or the flux of circumstances can be permitted to inflict any changes in Torah. The mere admittance of such a possibility would be contrary to its very character and Divine origin. It would make Torah paradoxically submissive to the material world instead of imposing its discipline upon reality. Time would become the master of eternity and space attain dominion over infinity. To make the circumstance supreme and God and His revealed will dependent on it would, in fact, be a reversal of the creative order, a crude, blasphemous debasement of the One Whose omnipresence is verified by all

4. [Literally redenred, *In the beginning;* the first word in the Bible. The quotation which follows is from Rashi *ad loc.*]

existence. It would make man's puny insight supersede Divine wisdom and impose upon the Creator the limitations of human frailty. Surely, a god molded in the image of man is but another idol, whether fashioned in clay or in philosophic abstractions.

The heirs of Israel's unbroken tradition have, therefore, always rejected the attempt to make the Almighty and His word subject to ephemeral adjustments. Following in Abraham's footsteps, they set out to change the world rather than change their faith. They preferred to give their lives rather than deny the unchanging validity of Torah or to relegate its laws to circumscribed spheres of human existence. The recipients of God's postulate, they accepted upon themselves to fulfill His will under any test of circumstance. This is the meaning of *kabbalath ha-torah,* the acceptance of the Law. And this was our response to *mattan torah,* its proffer to us by the Almighty.

Torah, the omnipresent will of the Creator, speaks to man and addresses itself to all his faculties. No fraction of his being is left empty of its norm. Thought and action, soul and body are enveloped by its precepts and commands. Word and deed, inner motivation as well as outer appearance are subject to Torah's statutes. The individual and the group, the family and the nation are equally drawn into the circumference of its regulative character. The acknowledgment of this totality of Torah, as it is based on the omnipresence of the Almighty, is the foundation of true service and observance.

It is strange that in an age given to the over-emphasis of the body and to the satisfaction of all its instincts, lusts and desires, a division between body and soul should be attempted precisely in the realm of faith. While material considerations have replaced in a horrifying measure idealism and spiritual motivations in the lives of men, the approach to the categories of religious belief tends progressively to exclude from its sphere the body and its needs. Faith without action, ideas without deeds are taken as proper religious fulfillment. Discarded—easily and without qualms —are those demands of religion which are directed to physical habits. The claim is heard that religion ought not to concern itself with anything but the soul, and that the outer expressions of man's physical existence are not properly within its orbit. True, whenever this physical existence impinges upon the freedom or the happiness of others, it needs restraint. But for these exceptions, man need best be left to himself if religion wants to exert its ennobling influence upon his soul.

This dichotomy of body and soul is utterly foreign to the Jewish view. Both are created by the Almighty; both are capable of elevation and sanctification; and both are called upon for the Divine task which is the purpose of human existence. They relate to each other in perfect harmony and exercise upon each other reciprocal influences of inescapable force. It is to this unity of body and soul, of matter and spirit, that Torah directs its postulate. The overwhelming majority of its commands, and in the opinion of Maimonides all of them but one, are directed to the body which alone can execute and perform them. By his freedom of choice, which is a faculty of the soul, man is capable of effecting this performance by his body. The conclusions of his intellect become translated into reality only by physical complementation. Any conclusion contradicted by the absence of such realization or negated by contrary conduct, is lacking in value. Conversely, the proper deed, though it may not as yet fully reflect his inner feelings or the desired purity of spiritual intent, will mold the soul and elevate it to ever higher motivation and decision.

To think nobly and to desire goodness—this is not the ultimate attainment. To act nobly and to do good, stands higher. To think *and* to act nobly, to desire *and* to do good, and not to allow any gap to separate the harmonious entity which is man, approximates perfection. Torah teaches us the road, the *Halachah,* to this perfection. Man will become better only by better deeds; only by the nobility of his conduct will he become truly ennobled. Without the *ma'ase ha-mitzvoth,* the actual performance of its commands, Torah and man will remain unfulfilled.

Not only the authority of Torah but its very meaning for man is challenged by the disregard of those of its precepts which pertain to the pattern of human behavior. Aside from being theologically untenable, such disregard bespeaks a grievous lack of psychological insight. Man will never be satisfied unless he can *act* by his convictions. If he is truly inspired by the idea, he yearns to express it not only by word but even more so by deed. A conviction which truly has taken possession of his soul, will in the end only warp him and will bring him misery instead of bliss, unless it also extends to the physical and material manifestations of his life. His yearning for completeness will be denied by such fragmentation of his existence. Ultimately, he will substitute man-made symbolisms and ceremonials to cover his nakedness, and, instead of quenching his thirst with the moving simplicity of Jewish worship and the soul-enriching performance of the *mitzvoth ma'asioth,* fashion for himself his own cults and codes, ever changing them in neurotic search for repose and reaping despair for all his travail.

Even those who see in the Jewish people merely a national and not a spiritual-religious entity, have come to

30

recognize that by this process the bond of Israel's unity, maintained in any adversity, is being shattered and our physical dispersion matched by a spiritual dispersion of even more tragic consequences. *As the number of Thy cities has become the count of Thy gods* (Jeremiah 2:28) —this is the prophetic spectre of the Jewish nation splintered apart by its rejection of the Torah.

There is a profound distinction between transgression and negation, between sin and rejection. The former is the outgrowth of human weakness. It signifies nothing more than a momentary lapse and reversible defeat. The latter is a denial in principle, a *doctrinal* decision justifying the wrong by declaring it to be right. Since man cannot live for any length of time in sin, he has before him two choices. He can repent and endeavor to mend his ways. He can return to his God and beseech Him for forgiveness. Though every night he lay himself down laden with guilt, he will rise rejuvenated in the determination henceforth to master his weakness and to measure up to his task. Or he may seek to escape his burden by adjusting his code to his deeds and by establishing a system of maxims to fit his performance. Within this new code, he will find easy justification. No longer will he need to suffer the heart-wrenching experience of insufficiency. This made-to-measure suit will always fit him. If not, it is easily cut down to his diminishing size.

The theories deviating from Torah are more often than not theologies of convenience. They are not the outgrowth of soul-searching intellectual considerations. Their denial of the obligatory character of Torah is not the cause but rather the consequence of the transgression of its precepts. They are the results of weakness and defeat, twisted into principles of conduct. They substitute man mastered

31

by circumstances for man shaping his world to fit, and to correspond to the Divine will. In the final analysis, these deviations and theories are quickly reduced to the fundamental issue of the acceptance or rejection of prophecy, the communication between God and man by which the Almighty directs His commands to His world, the acceptance or the denial of the literal revelation of Torah on Sinai. Those who accept Prophecy and Revelation will maintain Jewish observance. Those who do not must necessarily experience them as a senseless burden.

Once this decisive doctrinal step is taken, Mount Sinai topples. Revelation is replaced by "the genius of Moses" or "the genius of the Jewish people." Any observance still salvaged from the ruins is placed into a context which fundamentally changes its meaning and its impact. Based on contemporary approval and palatability, it is subject to change by the whim of those who arrogantly set themselves up as judges of religious value. They measure this value by the criteria of public acceptance, congregational attendance, and other subjective responses. Having denied the objective and absolute truth of Torah, their maintenance of some of the observances and some of the traditional forms of worship produces a deceptive outer similarity to Torah-true Judaism. This similarity is unfortunately misleading for the uninitiated. These surface correspondences have no bearing whatsoever on the real issue. Any system, were it even one of complete outer observance, once it is not based on the revelation on Sinai, constitutes a doctrinal deviation to which the term "Judaism" is no longer applicable in either the theological or the historic sense. This term, in spite of its being qualified by the adjective "conservative" or "reform," is still a misnomer when applied to these deviationist theories. A system or a pattern, though

32

adopted and expounded by Jews, does not become Judaism simply because its exponents are members of the Jewish people, just as sin does not become Judaism through its perpetration by a Jew.

This is not a question of mere terminology. Clarification in this area is vitally incumbent upon us, as it has been incumbent upon the Jewish people in every age and against the background of any culture and civilization, because on it depends the very preservation of Torah-true, classic, authentic Judaism which alone may claim the historic and theological right to, and distinction of, the name "Judaism."

Judaism does not read out of its fold any member of the Jewish people, regardless of his observance or non-observance of the Divine precepts. The sharpness of distinction between true Judaism and any theories deviating from it does not imply by any means the negation of the Jewish identity of the expounders and followers of such deviations. On the contrary, Judaism proclaims that its duties and responsibilities are not cancelable by volition and that the substitution of other ideologies is *no escape whatsoever for any Jew from its eternal and divinely imposed obligations.* Beyond that, Judaism proclaims the principle of 'arebuth, of the common responsibility of every Jew for the entirety of his people. This responsibility, too, does not find cessation because of rejection by those who wish to shed the totality or any part of Torah's precepts. That means that the sinner remains the burden and the obligation of the saint, the denier of the believer, and the doctrinal deviationist of the one who has maintained the doctrine of Torah in its undiluted and uncompromising purity. As a consequence of this 'arebuth, our concern is not limited to the observers of Torah. The non-observer is likewise our duty and to regain him for Torah is our sacred task.

Throughout the ages, we have reacted to the sinner with the compassion and forgiveness which we are bidden by the All-Merciful to exercise. To deviation—the sin elevated to a system of thought—we have reacted with the severity commensurate with its danger. Whenever deviation threatened to become a principle of Jewish life, whenever it was to find expression in our public conduct and in the change of our institutions, we have refused to condone it and fought it with all our strength. Transgression symptomizing deviation, change connoting the denial of 'emunath yisra'el, the authority of Torah and its binding character as the literal revelation of God's will, cannot be measured by the yardstick of individual merit or failure. Such deviations and changes must be weighed on scales of an entirely different sensitivity, be they "small" or large. Whether small or large, the sole criterion is that they are fundamental.

On the scales of such measurement, the Jewish people must place its values regardless of any temporary majorities. Religious truth is neither produced nor affected by majority decisions. Often, it has been a minority which has kept alive the Jewish vision and by it the Jewish people. As the prophet must stand alone if need be against the entire people, *whether they will hear or whether they will forbear* (Ezekiel 2:5), so is every Jew bidden to pronounce fearlessly the dictates of Torah and to live by them, though he may stand alone against his entire community. He cannot permit his sacred heritage to be destroyed and its institutions to be perverted by the introduction of any change contrary to the Divine precepts. He cannot, for any transient or social profit, dispense with the strictures of the Halachah and thereby share the guilt of attacking and denying the very foundations of Judaism.

34

The Halachah—the authoritative application of the laws and principles of Torah to the effervescent reality—must remain the supreme motivation and the sole decisive factor in the life of the Jewish community, as it must govern its relation to the outside world. This is the basic norm of Judaism. The fundamental axiom of the Halachah is the reverent acknowledgment that its laws stem from God Who has given them to His people and its Sages to safeguard and to expound. Our duty is not to make a new Torah for every generation, but to apply the Torah in our lives and in the life of the community for all our generations, to mold our existence to Torah's postulate and to discover in it the answer to our vexation. "I have searched and not found it"—this we do not believe, for the shelter of time is eternity and the shelter of man the wisdom and will of the eternal God.

Against the background of these considerations it may be understood why one man, alone in his community, ridiculed and ostracized by his Jewish neighbors, had to stand up to protect the sanctity of his synagogue against the intrusion of a so-called modernization which spells nothing but fundamental, doctrinal deviation. His purpose in the present volume is to collate the sacred sources and the authoritative Halachic statements of the Great of our Torah, of past generations and of our time, concerning the issue of mixed seating.

It is not fortuitous that the onslaught of conservative deviation has centered on the synagogue and its rites. The *beth haknesseth* has served, throughout the millenia of our dispersion, as the anchor of Jewish communal existence. The inroads of assimilation and secularization produced a schism. Those who no longer conceived of the Jewish people as a religious entity necessarily had to establish other centers and gathering places. Nevertheless, the synagogue remained the focal point of religious life. Slowly the trend was reversed. Almost instinctively our people came to recognize that within the local Jewish community Jewish identity can be maintained only by congregational affiliation. Through the synagogue, the family and the individual are tied not only to their faith but also to their people. Without the synagogue, they become quickly dissociated from both and are lost for any Jewish responsibility.

It is the synagogue, then, which forges the character and the physiognomy of any Jewish community or neighborhood. If there exists an orthodox synagogue, though many of its members may regrettably fall short of the full observance of the Divine precepts, the truth of Torah has still a stronghold. The Talmud Torah will reflect the loyalty to the historic teachings of Torah-true Judaism. A Yeshivah can be established and will find the support of the community in which authentic Judaism is represented by its focal institution. The rabbi will be a graduate of an orthodox rabbinic school, maintaining his contact with the great *roshe yeshibah* and gaining from them constant inspiration.

On the American Jewish scene, the rabbi is no longer regarded as a religious functionary. His social standing and his influence are steadily increasing. Guidance and leadership are demanded of him in all matters affecting the Jewish community. This guidance and this leadership are expected to reflect his Torah training. He is asked for his opinion in communal affairs not as a man of administrative experience and sociological insight. He is asked for his opinion as a rabbi, as the *ben torah,* as one steeped in Jewish learning and as the recipient of the Jewish wisdom of the ages.

36

Once the synagogue loses its orthodox character, the entire climate of the community which it serves must, therefore, change. The fortress has fallen and the rallying point of Jewish strength will be occupied by those whose concept of Judaism is theologically and historically a fatal deviation from the Jewish truth and whose preachments, though often under the guise of "traditionalism," are diametrically opposed to Torah and Tradition.

The transgression of mixed seating will thus appear small only to one who evaluates events and trends solely by their surface appearance. The editor of this volume recognized it in its true import. With rare insight, he perceived this issue to be of critical importance for the preservation of authentic Judaism and focused the attention of American Jewry on the fact that the Mount Clemens case is not a local problem but that it must be the deep concern of the entire American Jewish community. By doing so, he has joined the glorious ranks of those who are inscribed in the annals of Jewish history as the courageous defenders of the Jewish principle, as true and loyal sons of Abraham our Father and as true and loyal servants of Torah and the God of Israel.

the religious foundations
of Jewish law

BY SAUL BERNSTEIN

THE PRECEDING PAGES in this volume have set forth the religious principles and ideological premises in whose terms any issue in Jewish life, and certainly one of such basic import as the sanctity of the synagogue, must be judged. It will have been made clear that Jewish law is at all times the sole criterion as to a question of Jewish practice. The present chapter undertakes to explain what is meant by "Jewish law" and to outline briefly its unique character. Thus the reader may understand the frame of legal reference in which a decision as to a Jewish observance may alone be properly reached.

The Jewish religion, as it has come down the ages in unbroken succession finds its origin, mandate and entire content in *Torah,* comprising the Biblical Scriptures and Biblical Tradition. The Bible tells us that to the Patriarchs of the Jewish people (Abraham, Isaac and Jacob) the Almighty vouchsafed Divine communications, entering, with each in turn, into a Covenant applicable not only to them but to their progeny everlastingly. The descendants of the Patriarchs, upon redemption from Egyptian slavery, were the recipients of a Divine Revelation at the foot of Mount Sinai. The content of this Revelation was the Torah, part of which, the Ten Commandments, was pronounced by the Almighty in the hearing of the entire people, the remainder subsequently communicated to them through Moses, in the form of the Five Books of Moses (Pentateuch) and the Oral Tradition. There, at Mount Sinai, Israel in its entirety entered into a further Covenant with the Lord, to worship Him alone, to be a testimony to Him among the families of mankind, to live solely in accordance with His Torah, to observe and to fulfill the *mitzvoth* (commands and precepts) given therein, to hold the Torah to be eternal and unchangeable. This Covenant, in Jewish belief, remains binding upon the Jewish people forever.

In succession to Moses came the Prophets, through whom further Divine communications were transmitted to Israel. With the Pentateuch, the teachings of the Prophets, together with the Sacred Writings which were imparted in the era of Biblical inspiration, complete the Hebrew Scriptures. All of the latter, and the Oral Tradition, are comprehended under the broader usage of the term "Torah."

TORAH

Thus the sole and entire frame of reference for Judaism is that which is comprehended under the term Torah. This word does not lend itself to translation. The word "Law," which is often used as the English equivalent, is inadequate and inaccurate. "Torah" has the significance of Teaching, Doctrine, Creed, Message, Way of Life; above all, in the basic sense in which the term is used, it signifies the Divine Revelation.

When speaking of *the* Torah, the reference is specifically to the Pentateuch. But when reference is made to "Torah" without the definite article, there is signified the entire body of sacred teaching, both Scriptural and Oral, comprising: 1) the Pentateuch (Hebrew, *hamishah humshe Torah,* or *humash*); 2) the Books of the Prophets

39

(Hebrew, *nevi'im*); 3) the Writings (Hebrew, *kethubim;*
the foregoing Hebrew Scriptures are collectively referred
to in Hebrew as *tanach*); 4) the Torah of Oral Tradition
(Hebrew, *Torah she-be'al peh*).

THE ORAL TORAH

The Torah was given as a complete code to live by
under all circumstances and at all times (see e.g., Deuteronomy 29:13-14). Yet the precepts, laws and commandments given in Scripture are frequently synopsized in the
form of general principles and often are not explicit as
to the manner of their application. For example, the commandment to observe the Sabbath, one of the Ten Commandments, whose observance is enjoined in many places
in Scripture and for whose violation Scripture prescribed
the death penalty, is not accompanied anywhere in the
Scriptural text with explanation as to the manner of its
observance or specification as to what constitutes forbidden
labor. Yet from the Scriptural context it is clear that such
explanation and specification was undoubtedly given
through Moses, and similarly in many other cases. This
explanatory and interpretive teaching was the Torah of
Oral Tradition. Without the Oral Torah, orthodox Jews
believe, the Bible cannot be properly comprehended.

Numerous references in Scripture indicate the prov-
enance and function of the Oral Torah, and the fact that
it was communicated to Moses simultaneously with the
Scriptural Torah. For example, Exodus 18:20: *And thou
shalt teach them the statutes and the laws, and shalt show
them the way wherein they must walk, and the work that
they must do;* and Deuteronomy 12:21: . . . *thou shalt
kill of thy herd and thy flock as I have commanded thee—*
since the command herein referred to is not contained any-

40

where in the text of Scripture, it is self-evident that it was previously communicated to Moses orally. This command, whose nature is specified only in the Oral Torah, prescribes the precise form of ritual slaughter of animals—observance of which has been faithfully practiced since Biblical times and whose validity as of Mosaic origin has never been challenged even by the non-orthodox.

While the Scriptural Torah is given in the form of a precise text, every letter of which is specified, the Oral Torah was transmitted through verbal communication. Handed down from generation to generation, the Oral Torah is a body of lore unchanging and unchangeable in its substance, yet fluidly applicable to all circumstances. Transmitted by the process of *midrash* (exegesis) "from Moses to the Elders, from the Elders to the Prophets, from the Prophets to the men of the Great Synagogue (in the era of Ezra and Nehemiah)" (Mishnah, Aboth 1, 1), it was then transmitted to the series of great Sages and Teachers who flourished in the centuries preceding and following the destruction of the Second Temple of Jerusalem. Thus, by elucidation of the Torah of Scripture in the light of the Torah of Oral Tradition, the inspired leaders of Israel expounded through many centuries the teachings of the Jewish religion and derived therefrom definitive prescriptions for all areas of life, alike for the individual and for the community.

HALACHAH

The specific vehicle of Jewish law and religious usage through which the Sages and Rabbis formulated the prescriptions of Judaism is called *Halachah*. This word, signifying "the Path," bespeaks the onward flow of an eternally binding Divine Imperative—the basic law of life, as derived from the explicit commands of Scriptural Torah and the sacred traditions of Oral Torah and applied to all the unendingly diverse exigencies of life by the interpretive wisdom of the great Sages and Rabbis of the people of Israel.

Partaking both of the exactness of Scripture and the fluidity of Tradition, Halachah is ever precise and constant in its definitions and illimitable in its applications. Just as the Written Torah is the Constitution of the Jewish people, and the Oral Torah is the traditional lore which illuminates it, Halachah is the system of constitutional principles, definitions and rulings which constitute the total code of Jewish religious life.

AGGADAH

An instrument auxiliary to Halachah for the transmission of sacred lore is *Aggadah.* This word signifies "the Narration" and applies to the body of essentially homiletic lore, transmitted through the ages, which illuminates the moral and spiritual values of Torah. Aggadah, unlike Halachah, does not bear the character of jurisprudence, and functions only in the area of moral instruction.

THE TALMUD

Under the conditions which prevailed following the destruction of the Second Temple and of the Judean Commonwealth, it was found necessary to compile the accumulated mass of Oral Torah into written form. This compilation, the basic principles, laws and teachings, is known as the *Mishnah,* and was completed in the third century of the Common Era. In the succeeding three centuries, the Oral Torah underwent further authoritative interpretation at the hands of the continuing series of Rabbis and

Sages of the great academies in Palestine and Babylonia, who further clarified, defined and extended by application the laws and teachings contained in the Mishnah. Ultimately, this material was also compiled in written form, and is known as the *Gemara*. Mishnah and Gemara together comprise the *Talmud*. Completing the direct line of Oral Tradition, the Talmud has stood ever after as the fount and authority of Jewish life, in binding interpretation of Divine law and teaching.

The Talmud contains a vast mass of extremely concentrated material, for it represents, so to speak, the Minutes of the discussions of a great number of sages over many centuries. Without an exhaustive knowledge of its endless intricacies, its allusions, cross references, and methodology, and of its total content, character, premises and dialectic, the Talmud cannot be correctly understood. To make the lore of the Talmud more easily accessible in terms of systematic application to daily life, various masters of Talmudic knowledge, through the centuries, organized its data into Codes of Law. (These masters are called *poskim;* singular, *posek.*) The most outstanding such Codes, which have been accepted as authoritative throughout the Jewish world, from the time of their compilation centuries ago to the present day, are the *Mishneh Torah* of Maimonides (Rabbi Moses ben Maimon), the *Tur* of Rabbi Jacob ben Asher and the *Shulhan Aruch* of Rabbi Joseph Caro.

JEWISH LIFE AND JEWISH LAW

It was noted above that the Oral Torah, while unchanging and unchangeable, is fluidly applicable to all circumstances. The same applies, of course, to the Scriptural Torah. However, it must be clearly understood,

43

with respect to the entirety and totality of Torah, that this fluidity operates within a prescribed area and according to its own prescribed rules of interpretation and always in submission to the binding authority of Torah law. *Life in all its aspects and under all circumstances is to be moulded by the commands, requirements and teachings of Torah—and not vice versa.*

This principle has governed Jewish life throughout the ages, and indeed is responsible for the perpetuation of Judaism. *It is inherent in the belief in the Divine origin, immutable character and binding force of Torah, which to orthodox Jews today, as throughout Jewish history, constitutes the very basis of the religion of Israel.* Denial or qualification of this belief is the central point at issue between orthodox Jewry on the one hand and all Liberal, Conservative and other Reformist trends, on the other.

Orthodox Jews maintain that Halachah is subject to continuous *organic* growth—a growth which emanates from the application of the constants of Halachah to the variables of human life. Entailed therein is the continuous exploration within the body of Halachah, *by qualified and recognized authorities,* in seeking the Halachic view and decision in respect to questions and issues of religious observance and practice that arise in the process of unfolding human experience. By its nature, this process can never entail change of Halachah, or invention of new Halachoth to "accommodate" new conditions.

* * *

THE RABBINATE

Following the Talmudic era, the task of expounding and interpreting Torah to the Jewish people, and of interpreting its laws, has continued to be the responsibility and

44

prerogative of the Rabbinate, headed by the recognized religious leaders of each generation. While the Jewish religion requires that every Jew shall be versed in Jewish lore and teachings, and shall study them all the days of his life, it was never conceived that each Jew may determine for himself what Judaism requires of him. It was ever held to be basic that since Jewish law, as prescribed by the Talmud, is binding upon all Jews, every Jew shall submit to the definitions of Jewish law, teaching and practice laid down by the qualified religious authorities. Throughout the ages, this religious authority has been the uncontested province of the Rabbinate.

Great care should be exercised in the understanding of the term "Rabbi." It is properly applicable only to the duly ordained orthodox Rabbi—one who, after rigorous, intensive courses of Torah study through many years under the direction and tutelage of authoritative teachers, has passed exhaustive examinations whereby he demonstrates his mastery of Jewish law, his complete faith in the traditional Jewish religion and his moral fitness to expound it, and who has then received, at the hands of high religious authorities, the Rabbinic ordination knows as *semichath rabbanuth* and *hetter hora'ah*—the authority to pass on matters of Jewish law and religious usage. Only one so trained, so qualified and so ordained may hold the title of Rabbi in orthodox Jewry. And only so long as he continues thereafter to fulfill the full standard of his office may he properly exercise Rabbinic authority. It is obvious that one who questions the Divine origin and binding authority of Jewish law is not qualified to pass upon it.

Within a wide orbit of religious life, each duly ordained Rabbi is considered, in principle, qualified to pass upon the diverse questions of religious law and usage that may be submitted to him. However, questions entailing highly involved or unusual problems of Jewish law, or such as entail the welfare of large numbers of Jews, or derive from unprecedented conditions, are always submitted in turn by the conscientious rabbi in the field to other rabbis of higher authority—to the deans or principal teachers of the great orthodox seminaries, or to other recognized luminaries of the generation.

Thus, as distinguished from the area of everyday law (*din*), religious practice (*dath*), and established custom or usage (*minhag*), which can be adjudged by each duly ordained orthodox Rabbi, adjudications of major questions in the area of Halachah are properly made only by Rabbinic authorities of the highest rank. The opinion of the individual Rabbi is subject to appeal and review by higher authority without reflection upon his Rabbinic status.

The Sanctity of the Synagogue

Yet shall I be for them as a little sanctuary in the lands where they are come (Ezekiel 11:16): Said R. Samuel b. R. Isaac, This refers to the Houses of Prayer and Study in Babylonia [the Exile]. . . . Raba interpreted: What does this verse signify: *Lord, a haven hast Thou been for us in every generation* (Psalms 90:1)? It refers to the Houses of Prayer and Study *(Megillah 29a).*

They shall build Me a Sanctuary, and I will dwell in their midst.
(Exodus 25:8)

R. Yohanan said: He who prays in the synagogue in the present world, it is as if he prayed in the ancient Temple, for it is stated, *Yet shall I be for them as a little sanctuary in the lands* [*where they are come*] (Jerusalem Talmud, *Berachoth 5, 1, version of Yalkut Shim'oni, Psalms 659*).

introduction

IN THE YEAR 1955 the trustees of the Jewish Congregation in Mount Clemens, Michigan, moved to introduce mixed pews in the synagogue. In doing so, they not only challenged a firmly established Jewish religious practice, but the very principle of the authority of Jewish traditional law, the Halachah.

After failing to obtain relief by other means, the defenders of the traditional position filed a civil suit in the Macomb County Court, pleading that they were being deprived of their property rights in the synagogue, since they could no longer worship in it. In support of their case, they made a number of points:

1. The courts have recognized in other cases that traditional Judaism requires the segregation of the sexes in an orthodox synagogue. (Traditional Judaism, as used here and commonly accepted, refers to Judaism as practiced throughout Jewish history, and commonly referred to as "Orthodox Judaism," in contrast to the dissident movements

that arose during the last 150 years, such as Reform and Conservative Judaism.)

2. All recognized spokesmen and authorities on traditional Jewish practice have gone on record that Jewish Law forbids worship in a synagogue with mixed seating of the sexes.

3. This position is fully supported by Rabbinic literature, from ancient times until now.

4. A historical survey of Jewish synagogual practice also proves that the separation of the sexes has always been a fundamental feature of Judaism.

5. Any congregation claiming to follow traditional Judaism is bound to accept the authority of Jewish law, and cannot change it by majority vote.

6. Efforts to change the law and to justify mixed pews are based on the fallacious concept of the "historical evolution of the law" and of the need to do away with supposedly outdated practices such as the segregation of the sexes during prayer. These views, typical of latter-day reforming ideologies, represent a denial of the fundamental Jewish belief in the divine, immutable, and binding nature of Jewish law; and they also fail to appreciate the important and valid psychological and spiritual foundations of the practice required by the law.

7. The fact that some orthodox rabbis have accepted synagogues with mixed pews, in an effort to bring about a return to the correct practice, does not represent approval of mixed pews.

8. For all these reasons, the trustees and majority group of the Mount Clemens Congregation had no right to introduce mixed pews.

These eight points are discussed in the eight chapters of this volume. The sources which follow each chapter give all the background material, documents, authoritative rulings, and articles written on this subject which are referred to in the course of the book.

A special effort has been made to bring in full the outstanding Jewish legal responsa on the subject; the brilliant expositions of the ideas underlying the law of *mechitzah*, written by Rabbis Kasher, Max, and Lamm (chapter VI, sources 2, 9, 10); and the rulings of the civil courts in the Mount Clemens and other cases. It is our hope that the publication of this volume will provide much-needed public enlightenment and aid in the preservation of the traditional sanctity of our synagogues.

I

the issue
as seen by
the civil courts

UDGE HIRT, in the case
of Herman Fisher vs. Congregation B'nai Yitzhok, in the
Superior Court of Pennsylvania, No. 178, in the October
term, 1954, stated that "there is evidence that under the
law of the Torah and other binding authority of the Jewish
Law, men and women may not sit together at services
in the synagogue. In the orthodox synagogue, where the
practice is observed, the women sit apart from the men, in a
gallery, or they are separated from the men by means of a
partition between the two groups" (1).[1]

Judge Hirt confirmed the judgment of the trial judge,
who considered it established *that orthodox Judaism re-*
quires a definite and physical separation of the sexes in
the synagogue, and that an orthodox individual *"could not*

---

1. Numbers in parentheses refer to sources which follow each chapter.

53

conscientiously officiate in a trefah *synagogue, that is,* one that violates Jewish law."

Similarly, in the case of Congregation Chevra Thilim, in New Orleans, La., the court found that "family or mixed seating in Chevra Thilim Synagogue is contrary to and inconsistent with . . . Jewish worship according to the strict ancient and orthodox forms and ceremonies" (2). The court furthermore took the testimony of the Conservative rabbis who appeared in the case to mean that "while they do not agree with the strict orthodox interpretation of the Jewish law . . . they do agree that under [this] interpretation . . . men and women are forbidden to sit together without a separation in an Orthodox Jewish Synagogue." The court therefore upheld the traditional character of the synagogue and prevented the introduction of mixed pews planned by a majority of the congregation.[2]

As an editorial in *Jewish Life* put it (August 1957, pp. 3-7): "It is to be noted that Conservative clergymen testifying in behalf of the proponents of mixed seating contended that Conservatism is a form of orthodox Judaism. Weighing the evidence offered, the judge unqualifiedly rejected this contention, for it was demonstrated beyond all question that Conservatism, by its own definitions, differs profoundly in theology from the orthodox Jewish religion. Thus the premise that practices of Conservatism may be held forth as an acceptable criterion for orthodox Jewish synagogues was exposed as untenable. This was underlined by the admission of the same representatives of Conservatism that Jewish law does in fact require separate seating" (3).

A report on the New Orleans case issued by the Union of Orthodox Jewish Congregations of America, quoted succinctly from the court's ruling: "If men and women are seated together side by side in a synagogue, that synagogue has no separation of any kind, and therefore such a synagogue lacks the necessary sanctity, called *kedushah,* and is not an Orthodox Jewish Synagogue" (4).

Such, ultimately, became also the view of Justice J. Kavanagh of the Michigan Supreme Court in deciding on the appeal in which the present writer was involved: " . . . we are faced under the proofs with these unchallenged facts . . . that under the orthodox Jewish law, orthodox Jews cannot participate in services where there is mixed seating; that if mixed seating was enjoyed in this congregation, orthodox Jews would be prohibited from participating in services there" (chapter VIII, source 7).

---

2. The Supreme Court of Louisiana upheld the authority of the courts to intervene for the purpose of protecting the rights of minority members when the majority radically deviates from the principles upon which the congregation was established.

However, the court found that "the deviation represented by . . . mixed seating does not convince us that the (congregation) is no longer an Orthodox Synagogue . . . as defined and expressed in the Charter . . ."

The evidence before the court showed that:

1) there was dispute within Orthodox Judaism whether or not mixed seating is contrary to "Orthodox . . . Ritual" (in 250 Orthodox synagogues throughout the United States "mixed seating was being practiced");

2) in Jewish custom and practice, a Rabbi has full authority in his synagogue or community (the Rabbi here favored mixed seating and did not see this as contrary to Orthodox Judaism); and

3) the congregation was not "allied" with any ecclesiastical body having authority and ability to impose its doctrinal standards upon the congregation.

The lower court decision was, therefore, reversed. See page 77, *infra,* for citations.

sources for chapter 1

❧ 1 ❧

The Opinion of Judge Hirt

The following judgment was rendered by Judge J. Hirt in the Superior Court of Pennsylvania (No. 177 October Term, 1954), in the case of Herman Fisher vs. Congregation B'nai Yitzhok, appellant. It involved "an appeal from the Judgment of the Court of Common Pleas No. 6 (tried in C.P. No. 5) of Philadelphia County at No. 6279 December Term, 1950." The judgment is marked "177 Pa Super Ct. 359 (1955) 110 A 2nd 881," and was filed January 14, 1955. (See also Michigan Reports vol. 344, March 24, 1956 #3, 1st Protestant Church, p. 624. See North Carolina Supreme Court Decisions, vol. 241 #3, Reid vs. Johnston, Fall Term.)

PLAINTIFF is an ordained rabbi of the Orthodox Hebrew faith. He however does not officiate except on occasion as a professional rabbi-cantor in the liturgical service of a synagogue. The defendant is an incorporated Hebrew congregation with a synagogue in Philadelphia. Plaintiff, in response to defendant's advertisement in a Yiddish newspaper, appeared in Philadelphia for an audition before a committee representing the congregation. As a result, a written contract was entered into on June 26, 1950, under the terms of which plaintiff agreed to officiate as cantor at the synagogue of the defendant congregation "for the High Holiday season of 1950," at six specified services during the month of September 1950. As full compensation for

56

the above services the defendant agreed to pay plaintiff the sum of $1,200.

The purpose upon which the defendant congregation was incorporated is thus stated in its charter: "The worship of Almighty God according to the faith, discipline, forms and rites of the orthodox Jewish religion." And up to the time of the execution of the contract the defendant congregation conducted its religious services in accordance with the practices of the orthodox Hebrew faith. On behalf of the plaintiff there is evidence that under the law of the Torah and other binding authority of the Jewish law, men and women may not sit together at services in the synagogue. In the orthodox synagogue, where the practice is observed, the women sit apart from the men, in a gallery, or they are separated from the men by means of a partition between the two groups. The contract in this case is entirely silent as to the character of the defendant as an orthodox Hebrew congregation and the practices observed by it as to the seating at the services in the synagogue. At a general meeting of the congregation on July 12, 1950, on the eve of moving into a new synagogue, the practice of separate seating by the defendant formerly observed was modified and for the future the first four rows of seats during religious services were set aside exclusively for the men, and the next four rows for the women, and the remainder for mixed seating of both men and women. When plaintiff was informed of the action of the defendant congregation in deviating from the traditional practice as to separate seating, he through his attorney notified the defendant that he, a rabbi of the orthodox faith, would be unable to officiate as cantor because "This would be a violation of his beliefs." Plaintiff persisted in the stand taken that he would not under any circumstances serve as cantor for defendant as long as men and women were not seated separately. And when defendant failed to rescind its action permitting men and women to sit

57

together during services, plaintiff refused to officiate. It then was too late for him to secure other employment as cantor during the 1950 Holiday season except for one service which paid him $100, and he brought suit for the balance of the contract price.

The action was tried before the late Judge Fenerty, without a jury, who died before deciding the issue. By agreement the case was disposed of by the late President Judge Frank Smith "on the notes of testimony taken before Judge Fenerty." At the conclusion of the trial, counsel had stipulated that the judge need not make specific findings of fact in his decision. This waiver applied to the disposition of the case by Judge Smith. Nevertheless Judge Smith did specifically find that the defendant, at the time the contract was entered into, "was conducting its services according to the Orthodox Hebrew Faith." Judge Smith accepted the testimony of three rabbis learned in Hebrew law, who appeared for plaintiff, to the effect: "That Orthodox Judaism required a definite and physical separation of the sexes in the synagogue." And he also considered it established by the testimony that an orthodox rabbi-cantor "could not conscientiously officiate in a 'trefah' synagogue, that is, one that violates Jewish law"; and it was specifically found that the old building which the congregation left, "had separation in accordance with Jewish orthodoxy." The ultimate finding was for the plaintiff in the sum of $1,100. plus interest. And the court entered judgment for the plaintiff on the finding. In this appeal it is contended that the defendant is entitled to judgment as a matter of law.

The finding for the plaintiff in this trial without a jury has the force and effect of a verdict of a jury and in support of the judgment entered by the lower court, the plaintiff is entitled to the benefit of the most favorable inferences from the evidence. Jann v. Linton's Lunch, 150 Pa. Superior Ct. 653, 29 A.2d 219.

58

Findings of fact by a trial judge, sitting without a jury, which are supported by competent substantial evidence are conclusive on appeal. Scott-Smith Cadillac Co. Inc. v. Rajeski, 166 Pa. Superior Ct. 116, 70 A.2d 454.

Although the contract is silent as to the nature of the defendant congregation, there is no ambiguity in the writing on that score and certainly nothing was omitted from its terms by fraud, accident or mistake. The terms of the contract therefore could not be varied under the parol evidence rule. Bardwell v. The Willis Company, 375 Pa. 503, 100 A.2d 102; Mathers v. Roxy Auto Parts Company, 375 Pa. 640, 101 A.2d 680. Another principle controls the interpretation of this contract.

There is sufficient competent evidence in support of the finding that this defendant was an orthodox congregation, which observed the rule of the ancient Hebrew law as to separate seating during the services of the High Holiday Season; and also to the effect that the rule had been observed immemorially and invariably by the defendant in these services, without exception. As bearing on the plaintiff's bona fide belief that such was the fact, at the time he contracted with the defendant, plaintiff was permitted to introduce in evidence the declarations of Rabbi Ebert, the rabbi of the defendant congregation, made to him prior to signing of the contract, in which the rabbi said: "There always was a separation between men and women" and "there is going to be strict separation between men and women," referring to the seating in the new synagogue. Rabbi Lipschitz who was present, testified that Rabbi Ebert, in response to plaintiff's question "Will services be conducted as in the old Congregation?" replied "Sure. There is no question about that" referring to the prior practice of separate seating. The relationship of rabbi to the congregation which he serves does not create the legal relationship of principal and agent. Cf. Reifsnyder et al. v. Dougherty Tr., 301 Pa. 238, 152 A. 98. And Rabbi

Ebert in the absence of special authority to speak for the congregation could not legally bind the defendant by his declarations to the plaintiff prior to the execution of the contract. Davidsville F. Nat. Bk. v. St. John's C., 296 Pa. 467, 472, 146 A. 102. But while the declarations of Rabbi Ebert, above referred to, would have been inadmissible hearsay as proof of the truth of what was said, yet his declarations were properly admissible as bearing upon plaintiff's state of mind and his intent in entering into the contract. 1 Henry Pa. Evid., 4th Ed., 22, 469. "Statements tending to show intent are admissible in evidence although self-serving. Ickes v. Ickes. 237 Pa. 582, 591, 85 A. 885": Smith v. Smith, 364 Pa. 1, 9, 70 A.2d 630.

In determining the right of recovery in this case the question is to be determined under the rules of our civil law, and the ancient provision of the Hebrew law relating to separate seating is read into the contract only because implicit in the writing as to the basis—according to the evidence—upon which the parties dealt. Cf. Canovaro et al. v. Bros. of H. of St. Aug., 326 Pa. 76, 86, 191 A. 140. In our law the provision became a part of the written contract under a principle analogous to the rule applicable to the construction of contracts in the light of custom or immemorial and invariable usage. It has been said that: "When a custom or usage is once established, in the absence of express provision to the contrary it is considered a part of a contract and binding on the parties though not mentioned therein, the presumption being that they knew of and contracted with reference to it": 1 Henry Pa. Evid., 4th Ed., 203. Cf. Restatement, Contracts, 248(2) and 249. In this case there was more than a presumption. From the findings of the trial judge supported by the evidence it is clear that the parties contracted on the common understanding that the defendant was an orthodox synagogue which observed the mandate of the Jewish law as to separate seating. That intention was implicit

60

in this contract though not referred to in the writing, and therefore must be read into it.   It was on this ground that the court entered judgment for plaintiff in this case.

Judgment affirmed.

❧ 2 ❧

Excerpts from a Louisiana Judgment

rendered by Judge F. J. Stich in the case of Harry Katz et al. vs. Gus Singerman et al., July 29, 1957

DEFENDANTS produced as witnesses Rabbi Jacob Agus of Baltimore, Md., and Rabbi David Aronson of Minneapolis, Minn., both being Conservative Jewish Rabbis and very learned scholars and authorities on Judaism.   It is not necessary to analyze in detail the testimony of these two experts, but suffice it to state that it is the Court's appreciation of their testimony that, while they do not agree with the strict orthodox interpretation of the Jewish Law, Scriptures and Text, they do agree that under the strict Jewish orthodox interpretation of Jewish Law, Scriptures and Text, men and women are forbidden to sit together without a separation in an Orthodox Jewish Synagogue.

Defendants attempted to show that Congregation Chevra Thilim has not followed all of the principles of Orthodox Judaism in that, when the synagogue was constructed in 1949, they deviated from some of the principles of Orthodox Judaism in such matters as the lack of a center bimah, an elevated platform in the center of the synagogue.   However, the experts all testified that such fact does not affect the sanctity of the synagogue.

Defendants further contend that there has been no radical departure in the Jewish doctrine by Chevra Thilim Congregation since 1949 by the institution of family or mixed seating in January, 1957, because since 1949, when the new synagogue was constructed and dedicated, there has been a "mingling" of the sexes.

What the Court is called upon to decide in this case is whether or not the action of the Board of Directors, in instituting family or mixed seating, was contrary to and inconsistent with the objects and purposes for which the Congregation was organized and the conditions of the donations made by Benjamin Rosenberg and the Uptown Site & Building Fund of Congregation Chevra Thilim.

The evidence shows that the women are separated from the men by an aisle 4 feet in width and that the pews in which the women sit are located on an elevated platform 6 inches higher than those used by the men and that the ends of the pews, which adjoin and abut the aisle, are 39 inches in height from the platform to the top of the pews, and, further, that these women's pews consist of two sections, each of which is located on the sides of the synagogue abutting the side walls.

The evidence further shows that the practice of separation of the sexes in Chevra Thilim Congregation was in effect since it was founded in 1887 up to the time that the Board of Directors, by its resolution on January 9, 1957, instituted family or mixed seating.

The Court is, therefore, of the opinion that since family or mixed seating in Chevra Thilim Synagogue is contrary to and inconsistent with the "orthodox Polish Jewish Ritual" and with "Jewish worship according to the strict ancient and orthodox forms and ceremonies," and is in violation of the trust imposed by Benjamin Rosenberg and the Uptown Site & Building Fund of Congregation Chevra Thilim, to which said Chevra Thilim Synagogue and Congregation is dedicated, the Board of Directors had no right or authority to institute family or mixed

62

seating on January 9, 1957; and, further, that since the dedication and trust hereinabove mentioned do exist, and so long as it can be carried out, the Congregation is bound thereto and thereby and must abide by same.

For the foregoing reasons, the preliminary writ of injunction will issue upon plaintiff furnishing bond in the sum of $500.00, conditioned as the law directs.

🌿 3 🌿

The Battle of New Orleans

This editorial appeared in Jewish Life, *August, 1957*

A LEGAL DECISION which bears promise of historic import to religious Jewry has recently been issued by a New Orleans court. The case devolved upon the question whether a synagogue may, on the strength of a vote of its members, introduce departures from the orthodox practice to which it is committed and whether the religious and property rights of the congregation in its historic capacity, and of those members opposed to the departure, are thereby infringed.

In this case, suit had been brought by members of Congregation Chevra Thilim, an orthodox synagogue in New Orleans, to enjoin the officers of the congregation from instituting a change from separate to mixed seating of the sexes at religious services. Throughout its 70-year old history, separate seating, in accordance with Jewish practice, had been the rule. The change had been made without reference to recognized authorities in Jewish law and by resort to vote of the congregation's membership.

VIOLATION OF CHARTER AND FAITH

The proponents of the change contended that such procedure was entirely in order, and that the change to mixed seating was conformable with orthodox Judaism. Those demanding retention of the Jewish form of seating charged that its abandonment had constituted a violation of the sanctity and historic character of the synagogue, of the orthodox Jewish religion which it professes, and of its charter, which stipulates that Chevra Thilim shall function in faithful accordance with the tenets and ritual of orthodox Judaism. Accordingly, they maintained, the congregation as such, and those of its members who adhered to its principles, were deprived of the facilities for religious worship prescribed by the charter. The civil rights of donors whose gifts had been made and accepted conditional upon maintenance of strict orthodox observance had been breached. They further held to be invalid the proposition that questions of Jewish law and practice may be determined by vote of the laity.

The court, after hearing exhaustive evidence and testimony from witnesses and experts of both sides, ruled unequivocally in favor of the plaintiffs on all points, the injunction they requested being granted.

It is to be noted that Conservative clergymen testifying in behalf of the proponents of mixed seating contended that Conservatism is a form of orthodox Judaism. Weighing the evidence offered, the judge unqualifiedly rejected this contention, for it was demonstrated beyond all question that Conservatism, by its own definitions, differs profoundly in theology from the orthodox Jewish religion. Thus the premise that practices of Conservatism may be held forth as an acceptable criterion for orthodox Jewish synagogues was exposed as untenable. This was underlined by the admission of the same representatives of Conservatism that Jewish law does in fact require separate seating.

64

Important as is the issue of "mixed seating," the significance of this case lies in the fact that it comes to grips with problems of yet greater consequence, affecting non-Jewish as well as Jewish religious circles.

The problems arise from attempts by dissident elements to impose upon established congregations departures from historic norms integral to their religion. The dissidents, desiring to avoid the onus of schismatism or heterodoxy and the consequent obligation to sever from the group, raise the claim that their doctrines are valid interpretations of those professed by the congregation. They proceed to by-pass the traditionally-recognized sources of ecclesiastical authority, and proclaiming that democracy vests power of decision in the membership at large, seek to attain their ends through a majority vote of the congregation's members. Congregations so affected frequently face an impasse, with the membership divided and—since one party ignores or challenges the jurisdiction of ecclesiastical authorities—with no means of adjudicating the dispute within religious bounds.

Many scores of Jewish congregations have been turned into battlegrounds as a result of such infiltrations. In most cases, *baruch hashem,* the memberships have spurned as gross sophistries the new tenets offered them, but in others the deviationists have succeeded in turning synagogues from the path of true Judaism. In the past, those in the subverted congregations who rose to the defense of their faith have been all too apt heretofore to deem themselves without further recourse in the struggle. The New Orleans case, like a similar development in Mount Clemens, Mich., demonstrates that this assumption no longer prevails.

BASIC PROBLEMS RESOLVED

The New Orleans decision makes history by resolving in definitive legal terms a complex of basic questions. Does the membership of a congregation have the right to effect, by vote

65

of a momentary majority, a change in religious practice not conformable with the origin, historic character and charter of the congregation? The court ruled, in this case, that the membership does not have·such power. Is a congregation subject in its religious practice to the laws and traditions of the religion of which it is begotten and to which it is legally and morally committed? It is, in the light of this decision. Is a congregation simply the membership as of any given time, or is it rather a corporate entity whose franchise is its original religious principles? A congregation is such an entity and is so enfranchised, in the view of this court. And finally, may questions as to the correct interpretation of the laws, tenets, rites, and practices of a religious denomination be determined by vote of lay members of a congregation, or are they subject to the determination of the recognized organs of ecclesiastical authority of the denomination? The latter, and not the former, are competent to pass on such questions, the court held.

NECESSARY RECOURSE

It is unfortunate that religious disputes arising within the Jewish community should be aired in the secular courts. Such a recourse is not only repugnant to Jewish sensibilities—it is contrary to the premise that questions of Jewish law and practice (*halachah*) are to be adjudicated solely by Halachic authorities. Where, however, a party to such a dispute spurns the jurisdiction of Halachic authority, and where a question of public, as well as of Jewish, law is entailed, resort to the legal organs of the general community becomes the sole alternative and it is a necessity to exercise it. However regrettable is the need to resort to this measure, it is infinitely more undesirable to permit, by default of such action, the corruption of synagogues. The Jewish community, and the American religious community at large, are lastingly indebted to the Katz family in New Orleans and to

66

Mr. Baruch Litvin in Mount Clemens, who, with indomitable purpose, have steadfastly pioneered the necessary course in their respective communities. May their example serve to guide and inspire others faced with a like invasion of the sanctity of their synagogues.

It is greatly to the credit of those who formulated the presentation of the case that they addressed themselves to the basic issues, and did so with exacting care. The attorney for the plaintiff, Mr. David Gertler, earned high distinction for the manner in which he prepared and conducted this case. Credit is due also to a committee of the Union of Orthodox Jewish Congregations of America and the Rabbinical Council of America, which, under the chairmanship of Samuel L. Brennglass, gave important aid and guidance. Tribute is likewise due to the group of eminent leaders who presented, to conclusive effect, expert testimony. The group included Rabbi Eliezer Silver, chairman of the presidium of the Union of Orthodox Rabbis of the United States and Canada, Rabbis Solomon J. Sharfman and David B. Hollander, respectively president and past president of the Rabbinical Council of America and Dr. Samson R. Weiss, executive vice-president of the Union of Orthodox Jewish Congregations of America.

In placing the "mixed pews" question in broad legal context, the New Orleans case helps to bring this question into a sound moral and religious perspective also. The attestation given in the case that mixed seating violates Jewish law served to elucidate the point that the violation is at once the product and the instrument of influences foreign to the Jewish religion. Serious as is the violation itself in Halachic terms, the apprehension with which it is regarded derives from the role which "mixed pews" plays as the gateway to the adulteration of Judaism. *Mechitzah* (the separation between the men's and the women's seating sections required by Jewish law) is neither more nor less important than any other mitzvah; *shabbath, kashruth, tzedakah, taharath hamishpachah*—these and every other of the 613 precepts of our faith are equally fundamental. All of them, in the final analysis, are endangered by anti-Torah influences. But the tactic of anti-Torah has focused upon *mechitzah* as a spearhead of insidious attack upon the entire concept of Torah and *mitzvah,* for the logical reason that the psychology of our time lends itself to this tactic.

THE REAL DANGER

The canard that separate seating at religious services marks a position of segregated inferiority for women, clashing with modern standards, was effectively demolished at the New Orleans trial. The concept of "inferiority" of one sex to another is utterly foreign to Judaism, which assigns to men and to women some *mitzvoth* equally applicable to both, as well as others of equal weight, which apply to each sex respectively.

Separate seating is well known to be an institution, characteristic to Judaism, enjoined with the specific purpose of dignifying and honoring womanhood, as well as to foster undistracted concentration upon the Divine at public worship. Mixed seating on its part, far from being a "modern" development, has characterized church practice throughout the centuries of Christian history. The attempt to introduce mixed seating into Jewish worship unquestionably is rooted in the desire, conscious or unconscious, to subordinate Jewish standards to those of the gentile world. Therein, of course, lies its danger to Jewry, and it is in this light that the battle for preservation of Jewish seating is revealed as a key phase of the battle for the total Jewish heritage.

SUPPORT FOR RELIGIOUS FREEDOM

Not the least important aspect of the New Orleans victory is its contribution to the timeless cause of religious freedom. It is grimly ironic that Jews, who among all peoples and faiths have most cause to cherish and uphold religious freedom, should be guilty of attempts to rob their own brethren of this precious right. It is no less ironic that such attempts are usually themselves cloaked in the cry of religious freedom.

American society affords any and every religious element the right and opportunity to establish and maintain its own form of worship. Equal right is afforded to abstain from forms of worship from which one dissents. Those Jews who—however tragically from the traditional Jewish viewpoint—become attached to religious beliefs incompatible with orthodox Judaism, are free to abstain from the orthodox synagogue and to establish, if they wish, their own congregations. It is an unconscionable imposition upon the rights and religious freedom of others for such dissidents to seek rather to impose their beliefs upon orthodox congregations. It is a moral crime against the synagogues themselves, which were instituted and maintained solely for the purposes of orthodox Judaism. It is an outrage against the freedom of conscience of their members, who are told, in effect: you will perforce observe such religious practice as is dictated, not by your conscience and belief, not by the history of your congregations, not by Torah law, but solely by the votes of the majority of members!

An unhappy irony can be seen, too, in the demands laid upon those who resist the violation of their synagogues that they yield in the interest of "unity." The call for unity is a mockery, it is a snare and a delusion, when it is premised upon the abandonment of Torah principle in a Torah synagogue. Even were but a solitary member of the congregation to defend the historical religious character of the synagogue, and the entire remaining membership be ranged against him, there can be no unity at the cost of suppression of conscience.

The opposite case, be it noted, does not hold true. The

tenets of non-orthodox religious groups do not prohibit their adherents from worship in an orthodox synagogue. But the tenets of orthodox Judaism do prohibit worshipping in a non-orthodox house of worship. Thus all Jews of whatever religious belief may in good conscience worship in an orthodox synagogue, just as all Jews, including those who disbelieve in *shemirath kashruth* and *shemirath shabbath,* may eat kosher food and may observe the Sabbath. The issue of unity for an orthodox Jewish congregation can be validly based only upon maintenance of its orthodoxy.

❧ 4 ❧
Report on the New Orleans Case
by the Union of Orthodox Jewish Congregations of America

I. THE CASE

Action by Harry Katz and family with others, aided by the Union of Orthodox Jewish Congregations of America, to prevent Congregation Chevra Thilim of New Orleans from violating its sanctity as an orthodox synagogue, and its charter, by introduction of mixed seating of the sexes at religious services. Defendants were Mr. Gus Singerman and other present officers of the congregation who, upon their election a few months ago, replaced separate seating with mixed seating in this synagogue.

The case came up for hearing before Judge Frank J. Stich of the Civil District Court for the Parish of Orleans, State of Louisiana, running from Thursday, June 27th, to Thursday, July 11th, 1957.

II. THE OBJECTIVE

a. Defense of orthodox Jewish Synagogues against imposition of deviations from Torah Law.

b. Preservation of the historical character of orthodox synagogues.

c. Defense of the moral and civil rights of the founders, members, and donors of orthodox congregations.

III. THE DECISION

On July 29th, the preliminary injunction requested by the plaintiff was granted. A request for suspensive appeal was rejected both by the Civil District Court and the Louisiana Supreme Court. Thus, separate seating had to be restored immediately by the congregation.

IV. SUMMARY

a. For the first time in American Jewish history, legal action has halted the process of converting orthodox Jewish synagogues into Conservative temples.

b. The right of members—even if a minority—to insist that a Synagogue adhere to the traditions and intentions of the original founders, and to the historic character of the Synagogue, has been upheld.

c. A court-approved way has been established to secure the perpetuity of the founders' intentions, which will make certain that any further attempts of conversion of orthodox Synagogues will fail.

d. The Union of Orthodox Jewish Congregations of America stands ready to support before the courts, as in the New Orleans case, congregations threatened in their religious observances.

e. Our Legal Committee offers to our congregations its services in drafting proper charters and/or amendments to existing charters, and in the establishment of trust arrangements for the protection for generations to come, of the orthodox character of their Synagogues.

f. The Union urges all unaffiliated congregations to protect their religious standards by joining the Union forthwith. As the national and authoritative spokesman for orthodox Jewry, the Union works for the advancement of the orthodox Synagogue in all its phases. Affiliation with the Union assures a strong defense against all attempted changes of ritual and observance.

* * *

THE REPORT

The Union of Orthodox Jewish Congregations of America is pleased to report to you a development which may well prove to be an historic turning point for orthodox Jewry in this country.

Congregation Chevra Thilim in New Orleans, La., an orthodox synagogue for over 70 years, decided early this year by majority vote, provoked by persistent propaganda, to introduce mixed seating. A group of members, led by the Katz family, objected. The Union, at its South-Eastern Regional Convention held early this year, unanimously resolved to urge this congregation and its members to abide by the Halachah and to desist from introducing mixed seating. Our call was not heeded and mixed seating was introduced.

The loyal minority, faced with the rejection of Torah authority by the administration, took the case to court, under guidance of the Union. The trial began on Thursday, June 27th and lasted until Thursday, July 11th.

The plaintiffs were seeking an injunction against mixed seating as contrary to the charter of the Synagogue, which prescribes worship according to the "Polish Orthodox rites" and as contrary to a trust, accepted by the Synagogue from an individual donor for building purposes, specifying worship according to "strict and ancient orthodox forms and ceremonies."

72

The Rabbinical Council of America and the Union obtained affidavits from many outstanding orthodox Rabbis to the effect that mixed seating robs a Synagogue of its *kedushah*. Among them were very important pronouncements from Chief Rabbi Isaac Halevi Herzog of Israel and Chief Rabbi Israel Brodie of England, declaring mixed seating as contrary to Jewish Law.

The following experts testified before the court on the Jewish religious Laws governing Synagogue worship:

> Rabbi Eliezer Silver, Chairman of the Presidium of the Union of Rabbis of the United States and Canada;
>
> Rabbi Solomon J. Sharfman, President Rabbinical Council of America;
>
> Rabbi David B. Hollander, Past President Rabbinical Council of America;
>
> Dr. Samson R. Weiss, Executive Vice-President of the Union of Orthodox Jewish Congregations of America.

We cannot cite, within the limitations of this memorandum, the many sources from Jewish Scripture and Halachic literature concerning the *mechitzah* and related laws, quoted by the above experts in direct testimony and during the prolonged cross examinations to which they were exposed. Nor can we enter into the details of the statements made by the opposing experts, Dr. Jacob B. Agus of Baltimore, Md., and Dr. David Aronson of Minneapolis, Minn. It is interesting to note that the defendants had to rely on the two foregoing, who are members of the Conservative Rabbinical Assembly of America, as experts.

1. The Conservative witnesses, presenting arguments long familiar to us, asserted that generally speaking Jewish Law is changeable. They raised the point that some orthodox Rabbis are to be found in the pulpits of "mixed pews" congregations. Our witnesses made it very clear that these Rabbis accepted such calls only under circumstances of urgent necessity to pre-

serve the congregations for orthodox Judaism. Each of these Rabbis affirms that our religious Law does not permit mixed seating and devotes his efforts to restoration of the sanctity of their Synagogues by re-introduction of the separation of the sexes during worship.

2.   In cross examination, the opposing Conservative experts admitted that: 1) they permit travel on the Sabbath to the Synagogue by car or any other conveyance; 2) they do not consider the Laws of *mikvah* and family purity binding, though they admitted that this is contrary even to the Written Law, the simple text of Scripture; 3) they held only a qualified belief, if any, in the Divine Revelation.

Dr. Agus was asked to read and to translate from a prayer book the eighth principle of faith of Maimonides which states: "that the whole Torah now in our possession is the same which was given to Mosheh our Teacher." He admitted that he believes in it not verbatim but only according to his "interpretation," which is not accepted by orthodox authority. Dr. Aronson claimed that, as he himself stated, the thirteen principles of Faith were not the basis of orthodox Judaism.

3.   Our experts testified that: 1) The Torah consists of the Written and the Oral Law, namely the Mishnah and Talmud, the Codes and the Responsa of the Halachic authorities, and of the interpretation and application of this law to any given situation, in every generation and society. 2) This interpretation and application can be given only by recognized Torah authorities. 3) Such authorities must possess a profound knowledge of the Torah Law, must observe this Law in their private lives, and must hold a firm belief in the Divine Revelation and the Divine origin of the Torah, in its all-embracing meaning including the Oral Law as stated above. 4) Anyone lacking either the knowledge or the observance of the faith, is disqualified for any decision in Jewish Law.

74

4. Our experts brought proof that: 1) Conservatism considers itself, by its own statements of policy and ideology too numerous to quote here, as different from, and opposed to, orthodox Judaism; that it is, in fact, a separate alignment with an ideology and theology contrary to authentic Judaism. 2) The differences are basic and fundamental and the elimination of the *mechitzah* by Conservatism is only a deliberate manifestation of a schism which touches the very core of the belief in the Divine origin of the Torah, the Written and the Oral Law. 3) The Rabbinical Council of America would not maintain the membership of a rabbi who considers mixed seating permissible by Jewish Law. 4) It is the avowed purpose of the Union and the Rabbinical Council to educate our congregations and their worshipers to the full acceptance of Jewish Law in their congregational and individual existence.

Resolutions passed by both organizations, upholding the sanctity of our synagogues by maintaining or, wherever missing, by erecting a proper *mechitzah,* were read into the record of the trial.

5. Our experts demonstrated that: 1) There is no foundation in Jewish ideology or practice for the charge that separate seating at religious services marks a position of segregated inferiority for women, clashing with modern standards. They therefore labeled this charge as a canard. 2) The concept of "inferiority" of one sex to another is utterly foreign to Judaism, which assigns to men and to women some *mitzvoth* equally applicable to both as well as others, of equal weight, which apply to each sex respectively. 3) Separate seating is well known to be an institution, characteristic to Judaism, enjoined upon us for the specific purpose of dignifying and honoring womanhood, as well as to foster undistracted concentration upon the Divine at public worship.

In support of the position of honor in which the Jewish

woman is held by the people of the Torah, our experts cited from the Bible, Midrash, Talmud and the Codes numerous passages worthy of special treatment in a separate report.

*   *   *

The court found, as stated above, that orthodox Judaism prohibits worship without separation of the sexes and, therefore, granted the injunction in keeping with the testimony of our experts, inasmuch as mixed seating violates the charter and trust of an Orthodox Synagogue.

"If men and women are seated together side by side in a synagogue, that synagogue has no separation of any kind, and, therefore, such a synagogue lacks the necessary sanctity, called *kedushah* and is not an Orthodox Jewish Synagogue." (From the opinion of the Civil District Court for the Parish of Orleans, State of Louisiana.)

The Civil District Court rejected a suspensive appeal requested by the defendant. The Louisiana Supreme Court also refused, on August 8th, permission for suspensive appeal. Such permission would have stayed the injunction and continued mixed seating until the appeal was determined before the higher courts.[1]

*   *   *

CONCLUSION

The Union of Orthodox Jewish Congregations of America is happy to find in Mr. Harry Katz and his family stalwart fighters for religious rights. They have set an example which will inspire and guide others who face similar problems. The Union records its tribute also to Mr. David Gertler, the able attorney who conducted the case for the Katz family. Appreciation is also expressed to a special committee of the Union and the Rabbinical Council of America which, under the chairmanship of Mr. Samuel L. Brennglass, Vice-President of the Union, un-

76

dertook intensive preparatory work and mapped out the legal strategy, and to the Rabbinic authorities who so effectively testified in behalf of the plaintiffs.

The Union of Orthodox Jewish Congregations of America will be pleased to make available, upon request, copies of the full text of the court decision in the Chevra Thilim case. Send your requests to the office of the Union at 305 Broadway, New York 7, N. Y.

In summary, let it be noted that this historic development underlines the essential importance of working together to uphold our sacred traditions. We repeat our call to all congregations still unaffiliated with the Union to join our ranks. Solidarity among the orthodox synagogues of the country, through the Union of Orthodox Jewish Congregations of America, offers the assurance that our treasured Torah heritage will be steadfastly upheld.

---

1. In rejecting direct appellate jurisdiction from the trial court, the Louisiana Supreme Court in *Katz v. Singerman,* 238 La. 915, 117 So. 2d 56 (1960) transferred the case to the Louisiana Court of Appeal which, at 120 So. 2d 670 (La. Ct. App. 1960), upheld Judge Stich's decision, Subsequently, defendants appealed to the Louisiana Supreme Court which on this occasion, at 241 La. 103, 127 So. 2d 515 (1961) reversed the Court of Appeal. See page 55, *supra.* Plaintiffs then appealed to the U.S. Supreme Court which refused to hear the case. 386 U.S. 15, 82 S. Ct. 136, 7 L. Ed. 2d. 85 (1961). See, also, *Katz v. Goldman,* 33 Ohio App. 150, 168 N.E. 763 (1929).

II

*the position
of the
rabbinate*

HE RULINGS of the civil
courts accurately reflect the position of the competent Jew-
ish authorities. The various orthodox rabbinical associations in the Jewish community, which represent altogether
about 3,100 rabbis [as of 1954], practically the entire
orthodox rabbinate in this country, have gone on record
to stress the illegality of mixed seating in the synagogue.
The open letter of the *Agudath ha-Rabbanim* (Union of
Orthodox Rabbis of the United States and Canada) began
simply, "Jewish law forbids men and women to worship
in the same section of the synagogue, even though they
occupy separate benches" (1). Equally clear were the words
of the Rabbinical Council of America: ". . . a synagogue
which permits the mingling of the sexes during worship
forfeits its sanctity as a sanctuary . . ." (2). And in a letter

to the editor, the *Iggud ha-Rabbanim* (Rabbinical Alliance of America) stated, ". . . a synagogue without a physical separation between the men and the women during services, cannot be designated a Jewish house of worship . . ." (3).

These views were emphatically voiced, too, by local rabbinical groups, as the need arose: e.g., the Council of Orthodox Rabbis of Detroit (4), and the *Beth Din* of Greater St. Louis (5).

The Rabbinical Council of America, not so very long ago, announced the launching of a campaign against the mixed seating of men and women in the synagogue. This effort was undertaken with the endorsement of the outstanding religious authorities of the world, and is devoted to the retention of the synagogue's sanctity and ancient traditions(6). The Union of Orthodox Rabbis of the United States and Canada, the senior orthodox rabbinical body in the country which includes the outstanding rabbinic authorities of this continent, issued a broadside titled, *A Warning Against Reforms,* which reads in part as follows:

MECHITZOTH

1. Jewish law forbids men and women to worship in the same section of the synagogue, even though they occupy separate benches.

2. There must be a proper partition—*mechitzah*—between the men's and women's sections of the synagogue. A proper *mechitzah* is one that meets the requirements of Jewish law. To determine this, competent orthodox rabbis —*rabbanim mubhakim*—should be consulted.

3. *A synagogue which does not have a proper* mechitzah *is not a kosher synagogue, and it is not permitted to pray there.*

79

4. It is not allowed to give any support, moral or financial, to any synagogue which has no proper *mechitzah*.

5. If a person lives in an area where there is only a synagogue without a *mechitzah,* he should endeavor to organize a *minyan* [quorum for prayer] in a private home, and if this is impossible, he should pray without a *minyan* rather than attend services in a non-kosher synagogue.

This call of the Union of Orthodox Rabbis makes reference to a special appeal addressed to American Jewry a generation ago, when the practice of mixed pews in Reform Temples was being adopted by orthodox synagogues because traditional worshippers were ignorant of the position of Jewish law. The appeal was issued by leading rabbis in orthodox Judaism, such as the famed R. Israel Meir ha-Kohen of Radin (the *Hafetz Hayyim*), R. Abraham I. Kook (Chief Rabbi of Jerusalem), R. Dr. M. Hildesheimer (rabbi of Berlin), and others, whose rulings have always been accepted by orthodox Jews everywhere as definitive statements of the Law (7).

Statements issued by the Chief Rabbinates of Great Britain and Israel likewise confirm the legal position. R. Israel Brodie, Chief Rabbi of the United Hebrew Congregations of the British Commonwealth of Nations, wrote on October 11, 1956:

"A properly constituted orthodox community must not introduce an innovation in the service of the Synagogue which is repugnant to Jewish law and practice" (8).

Chief Rabbi Herzog of Israel, on October 19, 1955, warned against plans to abolish the *mechitzah* and permit mixed pews, this being against Jewish law and sacred practice since ages immemorial. In a lengthy discussion of the subject he wrote: "This is to state that the seating together of men and women in the Synagogue is contrary

80

to Jewish law and practice, dating in fact from the times of the Holy Temple in Jerusalem, which had its men's court and its women's court. This law was fully stated and amply explained by my late sainted predecessor, Chief Rabbi Kook, of blessed memory, in the Hebrew pamphlet issued in 1927. . . . The rule so distinctive of Judaism and Jewish places of worship has always been: one synagogue [section] for the men and another for the women. Pray adhere to that rule, sacred and immemorial. . . . If mixing of the sexes has already made inroads in your place of worship, under the influence of Reform, set the matter right immediately in accordance with the directions of a competent orthodox *beth din*. . . . The reasons for this law are vouchsafed by the unimpeachable authority of the Sages, and it is sad in the extreme that whilst praying to the Almighty, the sacred law of Judaism is being violated" (9).

On August 2, 1956, Rabbi Herzog reaffirmed the legal position in the following statement: "The Synagogue has been to us a 'Sanctuary-in-miniature' through the generations. As such, it must follow closely the regulations of the House of God in the Holy City of Jerusalem. The segregation of sexes in the House of Prayer and their separation by a *mechitzah* (partition) are mandatory by Jewish religious law. Mixed pews are strictly forbidden. I plead with my brethren everywhere to help maintain this essential requirement in their Synagogues" (10).

Perhaps the first great authority to address himself directly to this ravaging problem of our times, was the late revered R. Abraham I. Kook, the chief rabbi of the Holy Land. Writing to American Jewry, he poured a heavy heart into his words: "I have heard of the plight of traditional Judaism in your country, and am deeply disturbed by it. . . . Breaches have already been made in our holy structures, affecting entire Jewish communities. . . . What shall we say when this very sanctuary, intended to lift the Jew from his defilement and restore him into the ranks of the just and virtuous, is profaned?" (11).

Like Chief Rabbi Kook and his renowned colleagues, the heads of all the leading orthodox seminaries in the United States have also gone on record in support of the contention that Jewish law does not permit a synagogue to have mixed pews. Thus the late Rabbi E. M. Bloch, Dean of the Rabbinical College of Telshe, Cleveland, Ohio, wrote that "if there is no partition or curtain which should make each section [of the synagogue] a separate and distinct area, it is forbidden to pray there."

Rabbi Dr. Samuel Belkin, President of Yeshiva University, in a paper titled *The Rabbi,* stated: "It is an unquestionable historic fact that . . . mixed pews have always been foreign to the synagogue. [The] real motivation [for instituting mixed pews] was firstly, the desire to imitate the church . . . and secondly, a desire to achieve an actual separation from the traditional rabbinate and the traditional community"(12).

Dr. Joseph B. Soloveitchik, one of the world's most renowned scholars and religious authorities, Professor of Talmudics at Yeshiva University, declared: "I do hereby reiterate . . . that a synagogue with a mixed seating arrangement forfeits its sanctity . . . and is unfit for prayer. . . . With full cognizance of the implications of such a Halachic decision, I would still advise every orthodox Jew to forego group prayer even on the Days of Awe, rather than enter a synagogue with mixed pews" (13). In another instance Dr. Soloveitchik has written how he indeed advised one man in such a case to pray at home on the Days of Awe (14).

R. Moses Feinstein, head of the Rabbinical College

82

Tifereth Jerusalem, New York, has published a detailed essay in which he establishes clearly that the prohibition on mixed pews is by Biblical law (15). A similar responsum has been issued by R. Aaron Kotler, head of the Beth Medrash Govoah of Lakewood, New Jersey, the leading orthodox postgraduate school of rabbinics in America (16).

In conclusion, we may sum up in the words of Dr. Soloveitchik, written in an open letter (17): "I do not know of any orthodox rabbi or Talmudic scholar of high repute who would dare to say that mixed seating is in consonance with our law. . . . The requirement for separation is Halachically so elementary and axiomatic, historically so typical of the Synagogue in contradistinction to the Church since antiquity, and philosophically so expressive of our religious experience that whoever dares to question this institution either is uninformed or consciously distorts religious realities."

sources for chapter II

ᘓ 1 ᘓ

The Stand of the Agudath ha-Rabbanim

(UNION OF ORTHODOX RABBIS
OF THE UNITED STATES AND CANADA)

January 24, 1957

TO WHOM IT MAY CONCERN:

Jewish law forbids men and women to worship in the same section of the synagogue, even though they occupy separate benches.

There must be a proper partition—*mechitzah*—between the men's and women's sections of the synagogue. A proper *mechitzah* is one that meets the requirements of the Jewish law. To determine this, competent Orthodox rabbis—*rabbanim mubhakim*—should be consulted.

A synagogue which does not have a proper *mechitzah* is not a kosher synagogue, and it is not permitted to pray there.

If a person lives in an area where there is only one synagogue, [and that] without a *mechitzah,* he should endeavor to organize a *minyan* [quorum of at least ten Jews for group prayer] in a private home; and if this is impossible, he should pray without a *minyan* rather than attend services in a non-kosher synagogue.

RABBI MEYER COHEN, *Director*

☘ 2 ☘

The Rabbinical Council of America's View

Kislev 2, 5717—November 6, 1956

OFFICIAL STATEMENT:

[The] Rabbinical Council of America, representing 669 orthodox rabbis in all parts of the country, states that Jewish Law is very clear in that a synagogue which permits the mingling of the sexes during worship forfeits its sanctity as a sanctuary, and is unfit for prayer. It is forbidden to worship in such a synagogue.

No rabbi or religious leader has the authority or the moral right to state otherwise.

RABBI SOLOMON J. SHARFMAN, *President*
RABBI ISRAEL KLAVAN, *Executive Secretary*

☘ 3 ☘

A Letter by the Rabbinical Alliance of America

Kislev 23, 5717—November 27, 1956

DEAR MR. LITVIN:

The Rabbinical Alliance of America, comprising some four hundred rabbis serving throughout the United States and Canada, states unequivocally that a synagogue without a physical separation between the men and the women during services, cannot be designated a Jewish house of worship, and has no sanctity as a house of worship from the point of view of Jewish law.

RABBI L. KAHANOW
Chairman, Halachah Committee

WESTERN UNION
TELEGRAM
W. P. MARSHALL, PRESIDENT

DEC 011

PME

DE NA 471 LONG 108 2 EXTRA DL COLLECT=NEW YORK NY 19 331
=DETROIT JEWRY , CARE COUNCIL ORTHODOX RABBIS =
9103 LINWOOD DET=

I AM DEEPLY CONCERNED OVER REPORT THAT A LEADING DETROIT
CONGREGATION WITH ORTHODOX TRADITION OF SEVERAL DECADES
IS ON VERGE OF ABOLISHING MECHITZAH IN ITS SYNAGOGUE .
THIS WOULD INDEED BE A COMMUNAL TRAGEDY AND I CAN
SCARECELY BELIEVE THAT DETROIT JEWRY WILL PERMIT IT .
TIME AND AGAIN AGUDATH HARABONIM PROCLAIMED THAT ABOLITION
OF SYNAGUGUE MECHITZAH CONSITITUES VIOLATION OF JEWISH
LAW AND DESECRATION OF SANCTITY OF SYNAGOGUE , AND
UNDERMINES THE VERY FOUNDATIONS OF JUDAISM .
I CALL UPON DETROIT JEWRY IN GENERAL AND THE MEMBERS OF
RESPECTIVE CONGRATATION IN PARTICULAR TO EXERT THEIR
UTMOST INFLUENCE AGAINST ABOLITION OF MECHITZAH AND THUS
SAVE SAID CONGREGATION FOR TORAH JUDAISM=
RABBI ISRAEL ROSENBERG CHAIRMAN PRESIDIUM
AGUDATH HARABONIM OF U S AND CANADA

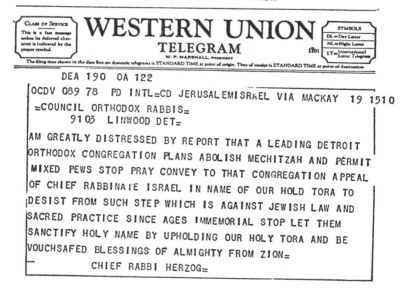

WESTERN UNION
TELEGRAM
W. P. MARSHALL, PRESIDENT

DEA 190 OA 122

OCDV 089 78 PD INTL=CD JERUSALEMISRAEL VIA MACKAY 19 1510
=COUNCIL ORTHODOX RABBIS=
9103 LINWOOD DET=

AM GREATLY DISTRESSED BY REPORT THAT A LEADING DETROIT
ORTHODOX CONGREGATION PLANS ABOLISH MECHITZAH AND PERMIT
MIXED PEWS STOP PRAY CONVEY TO THAT CONGREGATION APPEAL
OF CHIEF RABBINATE ISRAEL IN NAME OF OUR HOLD TORA TO
DESIST FROM SUCH STEP WHICH IS AGAINST JEWISH LAW AND
SACRED PRACTICE SINCE AGES IMMEMORIAL STOP LET THEM
SANCTIFY HOLY NAME BY UPHOLDING OUR HOLY TORA AND BE
VOUCHSAFED BLESSINGS OF ALMIGHTY FROM ZION=
CHIEF RABBI HERZOG=

Further statements, by telegram, *in re* the Mt. Clemens controversy

86

❦ 4 ❦
The Voice of the Orthodox Rabbis of Detroit

Tammuz 15, 5708—July 22, 1948

TO WHOM IT MAY CONCERN:

The undersigned members of the Detroit Council of Orthodox Rabbis wish to state their unequivocal position that men and women must be seated during services in separated sections of the synagogue. The permission of mixed pews, or seating on the same floor without a proper partition between the men's and women's sections, constitutes a violation of religious law, and can not be condoned by orthodox ritual under any circumstances. The women's balcony or section, in our house of prayer, has been a time-hallowed practice throughout Jewish history in all lands, as determined by leading exponents of the code governing public worship in accordance with established Jewish law.

COUNCIL OF ORTHODOX RABBIS
OF DETROIT, Inc.

RABBI LEIZER LEVIN
Congregation Petach Tikvah

RABBI JOSEPH THUMIM
Beth Abraham

RABBI JOSEPH EISENMAN
Beth Tefilo Emanuel

RABBI JOSEPH RABINOWITZ
Beth Shmuel

RABBI ISAAC STOLLMAN
Mishkan Yisroel

RABBI DR. LEOPOLD NEUHAUS
Gemilus Hasodim

RABBI M. J. WOHLGELERNTER
Beth Tefiilo Emanuel

RABBI MOSES SILVER
Anshe Moshe

RABBI MOSES ROTTENBERG
Yeshivath Chachmey Lublin

RABBI SIMCHA WASSERMAN
Yeshivath Beth Yehudah

87

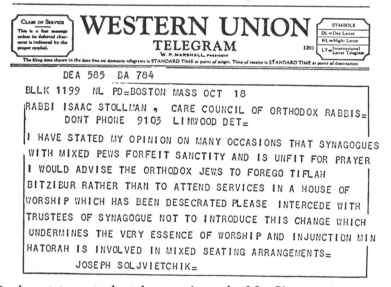

WESTERN UNION
TELEGRAM
W. P. MARSHALL, PRESIDENT

CLASS OF SERVICE
This is a fast message
unless its deferred char-
acter is indicated by the
proper symbol.

SYMBOLS
DL=Day Letter
NL=Night Letter
LT=International
Letter Telegram

1220
(R 11-54)

The filing time shown in the date line on domestic telegrams is STANDARD TIME at point of origin. Time of receipt is STANDARD TIME at point of destination

URFOCO 71 SYB 441

SY FEA 127 NL PD=FE NEW YORK NY OCT 18 1955 =
:JEWISH COMMUNITY OF DETROIT=
    CARE COUNCIL OF ORTHODOX RABBIS 9103 LINWOOD DET=

GREATLY DISTURBED TO LEARN ONE OF OLDEST CONGREGATIONS
IN DETROIT ON THE VERGE OF ABOLISHING TRADITIONAL
MECHITZAH IN SYNAGOGUE • SUCH ACTION THREATENS THE
SANCTITY OF THE SYNAGOGUE AND OF JEWISH LIFE • URGE YOU
TO DIRECT OUR APPEAL TO LEADERS AND MEMBERS TO RECONSIDER
THIS STOP AND TO RESTORE HOLYNESS OF SYNAGOGUE •
TRADITIONAL SEATING, A CARDINAL PRINCIPLE OF OUR FAITH •
    ITS REMOVAL DESTROYS CHARACTER OF SYNGOGUE AS A
SANCTUARY • JEWISH LAW CLEARLY FORBIDS SUCH ACTION • WE
APPEAL TO ALL CONCERNED — SAVE THE SANCTITY OF OUR
FAITH • HOLD FAST TO TRADITIONS OF OUR FATHERS •
THE ALMIGHTY WILL BLESS THOSE WHO SERVE HIM SINCERELY
AND WHO WORKFOR A HOUSE OF WORSHIP THAT IS DEDICATED
TO HIS LAW=
        RABBI DAVID B HOLLANDER, PRESIDENT
        RABBINICAL COUNCIL OF AMERICA=

WESTERN UNION
TELEGRAM
W. P. MARSHALL, PRESIDENT

CLASS OF SERVICE
This is a fast message
unless its deferred char-
acter is indicated by the
proper symbol.

SYMBOLS
DL=Day Letter
NL=Night Letter
LT=International
Letter Telegram

1201

The filing time shown in the date line on domestic telegrams is STANDARD TIME at point of origin. Time of receipt is STANDARD TIME at point of destination

DEA 585 BA 784

BLLK 1199 NL PD=BOSTON MASS OCT 18
RABBI ISAAC STOLLMAN, CARE COUNCIL OF ORTHODOX RABBIS=
    DONT PHONE 9103 LINWOOD DET=
I HAVE STATED MY OPINION ON MANY OCCASIONS THAT SYNAGOGUES
WITH MIXED PEWS FORFEIT SANCTITY AND IS UNFIT FOR PRAYER
I WOULD ADVISE THE ORTHODOX JEWS TO FOREGO TIFLAH
BITZIBUR RATHER THAN TO ATTEND SERVICES IN A HOUSE OF
WORSHIP WHICH HAS BEEN DESECRATED PLEASE INTERCEDE WITH
TRUSTEES OF SYNAGOGUE NOT TO INTRODUCE THIS CHANGE WHICH
UNDERMINES THE VERY ESSENCE OF WORSHIP AND INJUNCTION MIN
HATORAH IS INVOLVED IN MIXED SEATING ARRANGEMENTS=
        JOSEPH SOLJVIETCHIK=

Further statements, by telegram, *in re* the Mt. Clemens controversy

88

⚜ 5 ⚜

A Letter of Encouragement

FROM THE UNITED ORTHODOX COMMUNITY
OF ST. LOUIS

September 3, 1957

DEAR MR. LITVIN:

Your documentation of the Halachic Aspects of Mixed Pews is so thorough and so complete, that it actually leaves nothing to add. It almost seems strange that one should find it necessary to make a case for so basic a concept in Jewish life.

We feel that it is only because of the pressures of our time, and a desire to have Judaism conform to the patterns of other religious faiths, that this question is even raised. And herein lies the danger.

Jewish experience has shown that deviation based on a desire to be like "the others" is unsatiable, and soon grows to monstrous proportions, eating away one basic principle after another. The *mechitzah* therefore becomes ever more significant in our time, in a two-fold manner. It serves as a dividing line between those who desire to retain their Jewishness at all costs, and those who are willing to compromise for some illusory gain. It also serves as a fortress against other encroachment on the sanctity of the Synagogue and all Jewish life. When this fortress falls, the hordes of assimilation swarm over the fallen *mechitzah,* and run rampant. The Synagogue loses its sanctity, and the enemy chalks up another gain.

While we deplore the circumstances that make necessary your fight, we commend you for your documentation and for your staunch heroism in manning the fortress of the *mechitzah*

89

in a time of spiritual crisis for the Jewish people. May it be God's will that your victory will be followed by a closing of the ranks and a strengthening of those forces which are truly dedicated to God and the Torah of Israel.

Most sincerely yours,

BETH DIN (RABBINICAL COUNCIL)
OF GREATER ST. LOUIS

RABBI M. H. EICHENSTEIN
RABBI CHARLES HARTMAN
RABBI GERALD M. JACOBS
RABBI SHOLEM RIVKIN

6

For the Restoration of Sanctity

With the news release which follows, the Rabbinical Council of America initiated a concerted action to turn back the trend to mixed seating in the American synagogue.

RABBINICAL COUNCIL OF AMERICA CALLS FOR RESTORATION OF SANCTITY OF THE SYNAGOGUE

The Rabbinical Council of America, representing the orthodox rabbinate, has announced the launching of a campaign against the spreading custom of mixed seating of men and women in the synagogue.

Rabbi David B. Hollander, of the Mount Eden Jewish Center, Bronx, New York, president of the Rabbinical Council, announced that this effort has been fortified by the endorsement of many of the religious authorities in the world, including the Chief Rabbi of Israel, Dr. Isaac Halevy Herzog; Dr. Samuel Belkin, president of Yeshiva University; and Dr. Joseph B. Soloveitchik, one of the world's most renowned scholars and religious authorities.

In his statement, Dr. Herzog said: The seating of men and women together in the synagogue is contrary to Jewish law; this law dates back to the Holy Temple in Jerusalem, which had separate sections for men and women. . . . Pray adhere to this sacred rule. . . . Think not for a moment that this separation of the sexes in the synagogue implies any inferiority of the women. Nothing was further from the minds of our Teachers and Prophets. . . .

Dr. Samuel Belkin stated: It is a historic fact that as a hallmark of Jewish purity, mixed pews have always been foreign to the synagogue. . . . Those who have attempted to destroy this aspect of the synagogue have been motivated by a desire to imitate non-Jewish practices and to achieve an actual separation from the traditional rabbinate and the traditional community.

Dr. Joseph B. Soloveitchik said: I hereby state that a synagogue with a mixed seating arrangement forfeits its sanctity and is unfit for prayer. With cognizance of the implications involved, I would still advise every orthodox Jew to pray at home, even on the High Holy Days, rather than to worship in a synagogue with mixed seating. . . . No rabbi, however great in scholarship and moral integrity, has the authority to endorse, legalize, or even apologetically explain this basic deviation. Any rabbi or scholar who attempts to sanction the desecrated synagogue casts *ipso facto* a doubt on his own moral right to function as a teacher or spiritual leader in the traditional sense of the word. No pretext, excuse, *ad hoc* formula, missionary complex, or unfounded fear of losing our foothold in the Jewish community, can justify the acceptance of the christianized synagogue as a bona fide Jewish religious institution. . . .

Rabbi Hollander addressed the Rabbinical Council's plea to community leaders everywhere to make an all-out effort to retain the sacred traditions of the synagogue. He noted that the breakaway from tradition, and reforms in the synagogue, have not helped to bring either the youth or the general populace of Jewry closer to the synagogue. The Rabbinical Council, he stated, is determined to wage a strong battle for the retention of the synagogue's sanctity and ancient traditions.

7

A Warning Against Reforms

PROCLAMATION BY
THE UNION OF ORTHODOX RABBIS

THE INTRODUCTION of certain innovations which violate Jewish law and tradition prompts us to issue this Public Statement concerning *mechitzoth,* microphones [on the Sabbath] and the clamps [in circumcision].

MECHITZOTH

1. Jewish law forbids men and women to worship in the same section of the synagogue, even though they occupy separate benches.

2. There must be a proper partition, *mechitzah,* between the men's and women's sections of the synagogue. A proper *mechitzah* is one that meets the requirements of Jewish law. To determine this, competent orthodox rabbis—*rabbanim mubhakim*—should be consulted.

3. A synagogue which does not have a proper *mechitzah* is not a kosher synagogue, and it is not permitted to pray there.

4. It is not allowed to give any support, moral or financial, to any synagogue which has no proper *mechitzah.*

5. If a person lives in an area where there is only a

synagogue without a *mechitzah,* he should endeavor to organize a *minyan* [quorum of ten for group prayer] in a private home; and if this is impossible, he should pray without a *minyan* rather than attend services in a non-kosher synagogue.

             *   *   *

Over twenty-five years ago the greatest and most eminent rabbis of that time addressed a special plea to American Jewry to observe strictly the laws of *mechitzah,* and thereby preserve the sanctity of the synagogue. The following *ge'onim* [great sages] and *tzadikim* [pious men] signed the plea:

The Hafetz Hayyim, RABBI ISRAEL MEIR HA-KOHEN *of Radin*
R. HAYYIM OZER GRODZENSKY *of Vilna*
R. DOB-BER SHAPIRO HA-KOHEN, *Chief Rabbi of Kovno*
R. YEHEZKEL LIFSHITZ, *Chief Rabbi of Kalish*
R. ABRAHAM ISAAC HA-KOHEN KOOK, *Chief Rabbi of Jerusalem*
R. YITZHAK YERUHAM DISKIN *of Jerusalem*
R. ME'IR ARAK, *Chief Rabbi of Tarno*
R. ABRAHAM ISAAC HA-KOHEN BURSTEIN, *Chief Rabbi of Tavrig*
R. DR. ME'IR HILDESHEIMER, *Rabbi of Berlin. . . .*

AGUDATH HA-RABBANIM
(*Union of Orthodox Rabbis of the United States and Canada*)

❊ 8 ❊

A Letter from England

FROM THE BETH DIN, LONDON: COURT OF THE CHIEF RABBI

11th October, 1956—6th Heshvan, 5717

TO WHOM IT MAY CONCERN:

The question of the permissibility of mixed pews has been submitted to my Ecclesiastical Court from various Communities.

93

These Communities have been informed that mixed pews are forbidden, as the sitting together of men and women during Divine Service in Synagogue is contrary to Jewish Religious Law.

A properly constituted orthodox community must not introduce any innovation in the Service of the Synagogue which is repugnant to Jewish Law and practice.

ISRAEL BRODIE
Chief Rabbi of the United Hebrew
Congregations of the British
Commonwealth of Nations

❀ 9 ❀

A Statement from the Holy Land

BY THE LATE CHIEF RABBI,
ISAAC HALEVY HERZOG

THIS IS TO STATE that the seating together of men and women in the synagogue is contrary to Jewish law and practice, dating in fact from the times of the Holy Temple in Jerusalem, which had its men's court and its women's court.

This law is fully declared and amply explained by my late, sainted predecessor, Chief Rabbi Kook of blessed memory [in an essay entitled *As a Little Sanctuary*][1] and in a Hebrew pamphlet entitled תשובה הלכה למעשה בענין סדרי בית הכנסת, Jerusalem, 5683 [1923]—a responsum on the law for arrangements within the synagogue. The rule, so distinctive of Judaism in Jewish places of worship, has always been one synagogue [section] for the men, another for the women. Pray adhere to

---

1. [Reprinted in this volume, pp. 96-100.]

that rule, sacred and immemorial; and if you have no ladies' gallery but must have recourse to a partition (*mechitzah*), do so in strict accordance with directions laid down by a recognized orthodox *beth din* [Jewish religious court].

If, alas, under the influence of Reform, mixing of the sexes has already made inroads in your place of worship, return at once to the ancient paths, and set the matter right immediately, in accordance with the directions of a competent orthodox *beth din.*

Think not for a moment that this separation of sexes in the synagogue implies in the least, inferiority of the women! Nothing was further from the minds of our ancient teachers, the successors of the prophets.

Prophecy is surely the highest degree of human perfection, and our ancient teachers count many women as prophetesses!

The reasons for these laws are vouchsafed by the unimpeachable authority of the Sages. It is sad in the extreme that while [people are] praying to the Almighty, the sacred law of Judaism is being transgressed! Return to the ancient Jewish law and practice in these days of Penitence, and may the Almighty inscribe you all for a happy New Year.

With prayers for *teshu'ah* and the complete redemption. . . .

☙ 10 ❧

And a Public Letter

Menahem-Ab 25th, 5716—August 2nd, 1956

TO WHOM IT MAY CONCERN:

The Synagogue has been to us a "Sanctuary in miniature" through the generations. As such, it must follow closely the regulations of the House of God in the Holy City of Jerusalem.

The segregation of the sexes in the House of Prayer and their separation by a *mechitzah* (partition) are mandatory by Jewish religious law. Mixed pews are strictly forbidden.

I plead with my brethren everywhere to help maintain this essential requirement in their synagogues.

ISAAC HALEVI HERZOG
Chief Rabbi of the Holy Land

11
As a Little Sanctuary

BY RABBI ABRAHAM ISAAC KOOK

TO OUR BELOVED JEWISH COMMUNITIES and individuals in the United States of America and Canada (God preserve them) who are loyal and sincere believers in the Law of Moses, both Written and Oral, and steadfastly uphold the covenant into which God entered with the people of Israel: greetings and blessings from the Holy Mountain in Jerusalem.

Dear Brethren: I have heard of the plight of traditional Judaism in your country, and am deeply disturbed by it. It is reported that there are people who are ready to destroy "God's vineyard" and to forsake the Lord and His true teachings.

We refer to the so-called "reformers," who have succeeded in placing themselves in key positions inside the camp of orthodox Jewry. Many of our people are inadvertently influenced by these *mis*leaders, with the result that they begin to uproot the foundation on which the principles of Judaism are based. Breaches have already been made in our holy structures, affecting entire Jewish communities.

These destructive elements have gone so far as to tamper with the forms of communal life in general, such as the tradi-

tional form of service in the House of Worship, and in many
other spheres relating to hallowed customs and usages handed
down to us by generations gone. Naturally, one evil follows
in the wake of another; one bad step leads to another. For
example, let us take the time-honored custom of having two
separate sections for worshipers in the synagogue: one for men
and one for women. Some time ago these disrupters began
to do away with this hallowed, observant arrangement. What
was the result of this first misstep? We know now that gradually
all the principles of our faith, all that has been dear and sacred
to us from time immemorial, have been forgotten by them
and their children.

Not only that: many of them have forsaken our faith
altogether; they are completely cut off from the fold of Israel
and swallowed up by the environment amid which they live.
And even those who have not severed their ties with the Jewish
people, are like broken-off parts of Israel's national body, continuing their precarious existence devoid of Torah spirit and
the light of true Judaism.

Need we say how depressing this situation is? These
people are to be pitied. Some of them regret their actions
deeply, nay, even resent what their forerunners did. For they
see starkly what calamities the first sinners brought upon them.

And how painful it is today to see traditional Jews, who
otherwise keep aloof from the "reformers," flout our established
custom. They build synagogues to accommodate the male and
female worshippers in one and the same section; they thus emulate the ways and manners of the non-Jews, and hurt the holiness
and purity of our people.

In this connection we might quote a passage from the
Talmud: On the Biblical verse, *As streams are they spread
forth, as gardens by the river's side, as aloe-trees which the
Lord hath planted* (Numbers 24:6), one Sage comments: The

aloe-trees symbolize synagogues, and the Biblical verse is to be understood as comparing synagogues to rivers. As the latter possess the quality of purifying a man from his uncleanness so do the synagogues have the power of purifying a Jew from evil thoughts and lifting him up to the level of a virtuous man (Berachoth 16a).

And now what shall we say when this very sanctuary, intended to lift the Jew from his defilement and restore him into the ranks of the just and virtuous, is profaned; when sanctified customs bequeathed us by our hallowed forefathers from time immemorial, matters of purity, Torah-inspired arrangements, such as the separation of the sexes in two separate sections during services in the Synagogue, are nullified, Heaven forfend, and strange usages of non-Jews are introduced instead!

These extraneous customs verily undermine our holy foundation, and transform our houses of worship and prayer into sinful places. This is nothing else than abusing God's sanctified place, which has given us strength and stamina to withstand the suffering and tribulations heaped upon us in the countries of our sojourn among enemies, during our long *galuth* [exile].

According to the Talmud (Megillah 29a) synagogues are to be looked upon as sacred Temples-in-miniature. It is, therefore, our duty to exalt them to the same level of holiness as our Holy Temple (may it be rebuilt soon in our day). Indeed, our fathers, in establishing two separate divisions for men and women in the House of Prayer thereby continued the system inaugurated in the Temple.

In the same vein Maimonides (the Rambam) wrote: "The women's section [in the Temple] was contained in a balcony in order that the women be placed above and the men below, so that the sexes would not mingle" (*Mishneh Torah, Hilchoth Beth ha-Behirah* 5, 9). And every Talmudical commentator concurs with the Rambam in the observation that in the Temple the women were separated from the men.

Our holy forefathers accepted this custom as a duty to be adhered to in the present day Temples-in-miniature—our Houses of Worship. It is absolutely unthinkable to introduce any changes in the sacred customs our fathers established. And how especially important is it to follow religiously our ancestral customs concerning the principles of the sanctity of our synagogues, the symbols of our Holy Temple.

Now, if it is so urgent a necessity to accommodate male and female worshipers in separate places in the synagogue, how much more important is it to put a stop to the impermissible innovation of having a female chorus in our holy House of Prayer.

This situation is of grave consequences. It is an axiom subscribed to by all Talmudical commentators that female singing in the synagogue is tantamount to lewdness, and should be discontinued under any and all circumstances. It is incumbent upon us to desist from anything likely to excite our imagination during services in the synagogue. The point is that when Jews gather to pray, extra precaution must be taken to have a pure mind, for it is a plain truth that under such circumstances human frailty is rendered less able to withstand the onslaught of passionate inclinations. For this reason the performance of a female chorus in the synagogue during services is a grave transgression; and Jews, constituting as they do a holy people, must have no part of it.

We reiterate as strongly as possible: mixed seating in the synagogue during hours of prayer is a matter proscribed by Mosaic Law. It is a denial of our Torah principles for a Jew to join a congregation guilty of such breaches of Mosaic Law. Nay, it is even forbidden for a Jew to enter a synagogue where such unlawful practices are current.

Some people will fallaciously argue that the mixing of sexes, and women singing in the synagogue, have been declared tabu only by force of custom, and that there is no explicit law in the Torah forbidding such practices. Were we even to grant this false premise for the sake of argument, it would yet not extenuate the gravity of the sin. For all our Talmudical authorities have declared that customs adopted by our forefathers are to be considered as integral parts of our Torah Laws, and, anyone who trifles or tampers with them, is a violator of Torah, pure and simple.

The Jerusalem Talmud (Pesahim 4) records the answer of our Sages to a request for permission to change ancestral custom: "Do not deviate from the customary practices of your fathers whose souls repose in peace." Thus it is implied that to disregard customs instituted by our forefathers to safeguard religious practice from possible infringement, is tantamount to dishonoring our forefathers whose souls rest in peace.

So too Maimonides, in his Code of Jewish Law (*Yad, Hilchoth Mamrim* 1) groups together religious practice based on the force of ancestral custom with religious practice based on pure legal foundation. Jewish Law is constituted of all of these elements, with no distinction drawn between them. "It is written: *According to the Torah which they shall teach thee* (Deuteronomy 17:11); this includes Rabbinic positive enactments, injunctions, and customs instituted to strengthen our Religion. . . . With regard to all three of these categories we are directed by a positive Biblical commandment to heed the words of our Rabbis."

All of this is included in the contents of the Oral Law. There is no ground whatever to treat lightly the customs of our sacred forefathers, and certainly not in matters of public conduct that are founded on the basic sanctity of the Jewish people.

It is therefore my firm belief and hope that our pious

100

brethren, to whom God's word is dear, will hearken to the voice of our eminent spiritual leaders, the members of the Union of Orthodox Rabbis; that they will exercise stringency in adhering to the established customs and rites adopted by our Holy Fathers; and that they will be zealous in maintaining the purity and holiness of our synagogues and houses of worship.

Specifically, let them build these Houses of Prayer in the same style which prevailed formerly: separate sections for men and women. Let them likewise desist from having female choruses in the synagogue, so that our congregation will remain a holy one.

In reward for this noble deed may we all live to see our people reach Zion in happiness and joyous song. And may we also be blessed to speedily see the restoration of our Holy Temple.

☙ 12 ❧

The Rabbi

BY DR. SAMUEL BELKIN

THE JEWISH FAITH is a democratic theocracy that recognizes the potential ability of every human being to commune with God. Man and his Maker require no intermediary. Judaism has, therefore, never known of any distinction between Rabbi and layman with regard to ecclesiastical attributes or religious obligations. The Rabbi is not a super-religious personality, nor does he possess a private door to godliness. Both he and the layman are equally responsible for the fulfillment of the duties placed upon all Jews by the Torah. We might well characterize him in the words of the late George Foot Moore as a "diplomaed Doctor of Law." The Rabbinate, however, without being an

101

association of Jewish ministers, priests or theologians, has, nevertheless, exercised the most profound influence upon the course of Jewish life; so much so, that its very continuity may be said to depend upon the proper functioning of the Rabbinate.

If we understand the real significance and meaning of the Synagogue, we can appreciate, all the better, the character and place of the Rabbi in Israel. The Rabbi is the custodian of the ideals for which the Synagogue stands. He must, first, symbolize the *beth haknesseth*.[1] It is his duty to be the leader of the Jewish community and of all that pertains to community welfare. He is the social worker, better—the social architect. His social activity, however, is motivated and conditioned by a pious outlook and a spiritual purpose which make it in the deepest sense religious. The social or communal function which is given a higher spiritual purpose is no longer a purely social and secular activity, but a genuinely religious one.

Again, the Rabbi must symbolize the *beth ha-tefillah*;[2] he must in his own life personify Jewish piety. Above all, however, the Rabbi must symbolize the *beth hamidrash*,[3] for the reservoir from which he draws his inspiration is the Torah. *A Rabbi, from the historic point of view, is one who is imbued with the conviction of the centrality of Torah learning and Torah practice as the essence of Judaism.* Thus his true function is to be the Jewish scholar, the authority on Jewish Law, teaching the Torah to his Community.

There is more to the Torah than a cursory glance can reveal. Rabbi Judah once said that whoever translates a verse of the Torah in strict literalness is a falsifier, and he who makes additions or changes in it is a blasphemer. It is the Rabbi who must bring to his people the hidden treasures that rest in the

1. ["The House of Assembly."]
2. ["The House of Prayer."]
3. ["The House of Study."]

commentaries and that are contained in the rich repositories of Jewish learning. If one claiming to be a Rabbi does not have the profound knowledge of the Torah expounded in the Oral Law; if lacking *semichah* or true Rabbinic authority he is thus unable to forge a link in the precious chain of scholarship which is the Rabbinate, which traces its way back to the beginnings of our spiritual existence; then he will either ignorantly falsify the essence of the Torah or constantly endeavor to change the Law in order to adjust it to his own outlook—indeed, an act of blasphemy.

One must bear in mind that Judaism does not consist only of theological dogma. The Rabbi is not simply a theologian trained to think of Judaism solely in terms of doctrines, beliefs and articles of faith. Theology, as a separate branch of study, has never been a central element in Judaism. Maimonides, for instance, in his commentary on the Mishnah, enumerates thirteen fundamental doctrines which are, in his opinion, the basic elements of Jewish faith. Although developed through deep study and earnest reflection, accepted by the majority of Jews and incorporated in the prayer book, neither the recitation of these articles of faith nor of those developed by other Jewish scholars in succeeding generations was ever made obligatory. Through the irony of fate, the *yigdal* hymn that contains Maimonides' creed has become part of congregational singing.

This is not to say, as have some modern scholars, that since Judaism requires no confession of faith, it has, then, no dogmas at all. On the contrary, Maimonides' articles of faith are fundamental beliefs of Judaism. Judaism does not, however, recognize abstract beliefs *in themselves* as the fundamentals of its religious life. It is the *duties* and obligations revealed in the Torah that are the fundamentals of Judaism.

Maimonides, for example, includes belief in the Existence and Unity of God as two of the six hundred and thirteen positive and negative commandments. These two commandments surely cannot be fulfilled by simply saying, "I believe in the Existence of God, and in the Unity of God." It is not the theoretical and theological belief in God's existence that is the fundamental element, but the acceptance of *"the yoke* of the Kingship of Heaven." It is through *practical obedience* to the Will of God as manifested in the Torah, that a Jew reveals his knowledge of the Existence of God and the Unity of God. In Judaism, theology per se has no meaning unless interpreted in terms of conduct, in terms of its effect on human activity.

A proselyte who desires initiation into the fold of Judaism is not only instructed in articles of faith or in abstract theological dogmas, but in the duties of the Torah, in the "minor and major" commandments. Rabbi Judah ha-Levi writes: "We do not accept a person who enters our religion through confession alone. We require deeds, including within the meaning of that term self-restraint, purity, study of the Law, circumcision, and the performance of other duties commanded by the Torah." Salvation in Judaism is not obtained by acceptance of theological dogma alone, but through the genuine love of God that *fulfills itself* in action, in the observance of the Law.

Judaism has never endeavored to formulate a definite body of articulated and systematized abstract theology. The existence of God as a father in heaven, who bestows His guidance in particular and universal providence, is not a matter of speculation, but a living reality. The Torah, as the revealed Word of God, is not a matter of academic dispute. It is to the understanding of the law of the Torah as a divine *way of life* that Jews have concentrated their entire energy.

Yeshivoth were, therefore, never "theological seminaries," but schools in which Torah in all its manifestations was studied. For this reason, the "Yeshiva Rabbi" symbolizes, above all, Torah learning and Torah practice. As one who is trained in

104

the Halachah, he knows the true meaning of the Law and as one who has knowledge of the Aggadah he can explain the higher moral and spiritual purpose that one fulfills by the observance of its precepts.

This position is occupied today only by the Orthodox Rabbinate in America. After watching the antics of numerous so-called "Rabbis," the American Jewish community, now reaching maturity, has learned to admire the disciplined attitude of the young American Orthodox Rabbi in his personal and community life. Our "Yeshiva Rabbis" are quickly coming to the fore, as the true leaders of American Jewry.

There are certain problems, however, with which we must seriously concern ourselves. Firstly, the Rabbi alone, cannot be the symbol and embodiment of those things which Judaism requires from each of its members. He cannot be the sole guardian of Jewish ideals nor the community agent for the observance of Torah. Yet how often have we heard tell of communities that are unable to provide a kosher home for the Orthodox Rabbi whom they have requested, if that be his need. The members of the synagogue understand fully that the Rabbi must observe *kashruth,* but see nothing wrong in their own negative attitude towards its observance. The Rabbi thus becomes not only the representative of the Jewish community and the authoritative interpreter of Jewish tradition but the sole personification of things Jewish. This present-day gap between the Rabbi and the laity with regard to religious observance is one of our most challenging problems.

One of the peculiar results of this situation is the assumption by the laity of certain prerogatives not within its purview. The Rabbinate, in carrying out its duty of teaching Torah and Judaism, has always been the accepted authority and guide for Jewish life. No matter how observant or learned a community might have been, all questions pertaining to Synagogue practice and religious observance were always decided by the Rabbi. Even in those communities where layman were as learned as the Rabbi—for the Rabbi has no monopoly on learning—his ruling was always accepted. Was it not for this purpose that he had been chosen by the community as its leader?

Today, however, when our laity openly admits its lack of Jewish learning and its laxity of observance—perhaps, because of these very factors—it has relegated to itself the authority of decision in matters of religious law—an authority which belongs only to the Rabbi, by virtue of his *semichah*—his training and knowledge.

When, for example, a community desires to build a new synagogue or schoolhouse, the Rabbi becomes the prime mover in the campaign, functioning as the leader, the worker and fund raiser. But when fundamental questions arise concerning the structure of the synagogue, the type of instruction to be given in the school and matters of synagogue worship which border along the fundamentals of Jewish law, the members of the congregation assume the authority to take decisions by vote. Synagogue boards disregard the Rabbi, vote to abrogate traditional standards of the synagogue and introduce features which are anti-Jewish in character. Majority rule becomes Jewish Law! But of what value is majority rule if its decisions negate the laws of the Torah, and destroying Jewish tradition, destroy Judaism, as well.

The great Jewish scholar, Nahmanides, was once asked whether, since the rule of the majority is usually the norm in Jewish law, we can accept the view of many general laymen as against the judgment of one outstanding specialist. His answer was, of course, that in a case of that sort the opinion of the specialist must be accepted. Must not this principle, now, be applied to the Rabbi who is the genuine exponent of the traditions of Israel? Since he is the interpreter of Torah Law

106

which is eternally binding upon every Jew, he must be recognized as the indispensable guide for the spiritual and religious needs of his congregation.

True, the Rabbi is not infallible, nor are his teachings or his decisions immune from error. The Rabbi, however, does not merely express his personal opinion. He states the law as found in the *Shulhan Aruch* and that decision is binding upon the community. Unless recognized Jewish authority can prove that the Rabbi has not correctly interpreted the law, his decision must remain binding.

There is another terribly serious matter stemming from this same root with which we must reckon at this time—the matter of separation of men and women in the Synagogue. It is an unquestionable historic fact that as a symbol of Jewish purity, mixed pews have always been foreign to the Synagogue. The past 30 years in America, however, have seen destructive action by irreligious *organized* Temple bodies whose real motivation—let us not be satisfied by rationalizations—was firstly, the desire to imitate the church—*imitation* has been the characteristic feature of the non-traditional Jewish community for the last century—and secondly, a desire to achieve an actual separation from the traditional Rabbinate and the traditional community, much as the early Church, for example, changed the Sabbath to Sunday in order to show a tangible division from Jewish Tradition. Hence, non-Orthodox bodies have not merely tolerated, but actually welcomed and encouraged this breach in Jewish tradition as they have striven for fundamental changes in the Prayer Book, thus abrogating not only Jewish practice but renouncing fundamental beliefs of Judaism.

The problem is presented most challengingly by the synagogues now being erected and by the architectural plans now being prepared for the future. Where some congregations hesitate to make changes in existing structures for sentimental if not religious reasons, they feel hardly any obligation to continue the tradition in a new synagogue. These are facts with which we must reckon and concerning which we must take a united stand.

The Yeshiva will not sanction the abrogation of this essential and characteristic element of the Synagogue. It is the duty of a Rabbi who finds himself in a community which has, through ignorance of Jewish tradition, drifted from an understanding and practice of Jewish observance, to make every effort to restore the true standards of the Synagogue. We dare not, by passive acceptance of a condition not of our own making, permit the Orthodox Synagogue to drift down the already too-well-troden path of immitation and assimilation. Mixed pews can be checked if we make it our responsibility to do so!

Our laity must be shown the destructive results brought about by the breakdown of the traditional Synagogue and their energies must be brought to bear to strengthen and preserve the Orthodox—the *historic*—Synagogue. A few people can no longer be permitted to force the issue at congregational meetings and vote to abrogate basic tradition. All this will require dedication and struggle. The results of acquiescence, however, are obvious. They spell our own destruction.

We require most of all, a strong movement that will lead to an understanding of Orthodox synagogue tradition—a movement that will unite all Orthodox synagogues, still the majority of American synagogues, into one strong and cohesive body. As long as individual synagogues are permitted to drift and thoughtlessly tread their own paths, Jewish Tradition in America will surely be neither the beneficiary nor the spiritual benefactor. Only a forceful and intelligent Traditional Synagogue organization will be able to truly draw the lines of responsibility for the Rabbi and lay leaders of the congregation, so that they will become partners and co-workers in this sacred enterprise. Only

108

if the Traditional Synagogue will base itself upon a single and firm policy toward Jewish observance, will the Synagogue and the Rabbi again become the great unifying and creative forces in Jewish life.

❧ 13 ❧

Message to a Rabbinic Convention

BY RABBI DR. JOSEPH B. SOLOVEITCHIK

I REGRET EXCEEDINGLY my inability to be at this most important conference of our organization. On strict orders of the doctor, I must not engage, for the time being, in public speaking, or even attend public functions. Please accept my heartfelt wishes for very successful and fruitful deliberations and discussions, which should in turn be translated into realities.

I also wish to express to you my deep appreciation of and admiration for your unselfish and untiring efforts in behalf of Torah and traditional Judaism. I know how much you have given to the cause of strengthening the orthodox rabbinate, to solidify its position and to promote its objectives. May the Almighty bestow upon you His infinite blessings and grant you health and fortitude to carry on your good work for many more years. The task is a difficult one; but the harder the mission, the greater is the reward. ‏לפום צערא אגרא‎.

The Rabbinical Council of America stands now at the crossroads; and must decide either to assume boldly and courageously the time-honored, by-ages-sanctified role of the traditional rabbinate which traces its history back to Joshua, Moses and Sinai, and thus be ready to fight for an undiluted Halachah which is often not in the vogue; or to deteriorate into a so-called modern rabbinic group of undefined quality and of a confused ideology, vague in its attitudes and undecided as to its policies.

In particular, I wish to call the attention of the Conference to the *mechitzah* problem. I continually receive reports from laymen from all parts of the country, accusing many rabbis of displaying indecisiveness and even cowardice in this matter. They charge them with laxity and indifference, even in cases when the traditionally minded individuals are willing to organize in defense of the principle of segregation. I have the feeling that a well coordinated, aggressive effort on our part may stop, if not reverse even, the trend of Christianization of the synagogue. However, many of our colleagues choose the *derech ketzarah va'aruchah*, the easy way which leads to doom and disaster.

I do hereby reiterate the statement I have made on numerous occasions, both in writing and orally, that a synagogue with a mixed seating arrangement forfeits its sanctity and its Halachic status of *mikdash me'at* [a Sanctuary-in-miniature], and is unfit for prayer and *abodah she-beleb* [the service of the heart]. With full cognizance of the implications of such a Halachic decision, I would still advise every orthodox Jew to forego *tefillah be-tzibbur* [group prayer] even on Rosh Hashanah and Yom Kippur, rather than enter a synagogue with mixed pews, notwithstanding the fact that the officiating rabbi happens to be a graduate of a great and venerable *yeshibah*. No rabbi, however great in scholarship and moral integrity, has the authority to endorse, legalize, or even apologetically explain this basic deviation. Any rabbi or scholar who attempts to sanction the desecrated synagogue, *ipso facto* casts a doubt on his own moral right to function as a teacher or spiritual leader in the traditional sense of the word. No pretext, excuse, *ad hoc* formula, missionary complex, or unfounded fear of losing our foothold in the Jewish community, can justify the acceptance of the

110

Christianized synagogue as a bona fide Jewish religious institution.

I know beforehand the reaction to my letter on the part of our apostles of religious "modernism" and "utilitarianism." They will certainly say that since a great majority of the recently constructed synagogues have abandoned separated seating, we must not be out of step with the masses. This type of reasoning could well be employed with regard to other religious precepts, such as the observance of the Sabbath, or the dietary laws. However, we must remember that an ethical or Halachic principle decreed by God is not rendered void by the fact that the people refuse to abide by it. Its cogency and veracity are perennial and independent of compliance on the part of the multitudes. If the ethical norm, *Thou shalt not kill* (Exodus 20:13), has not lost its validity during the days of extermination camps and gas chambers, when millions of people were engaged in ruthless murder, but on the contrary, has been impregnated with deeper meaning and significance, then every Halachic maxim assumes greater import in times of widespread disregard and unconcern. The greater the difficulty, the more biting the ridicule and sarcasm, and the more numerous the opponent— then the holier is the principle, and the more sacred is our duty to defend it. In my opinion, the Halachic dictum, *bishe'ath gezerath ha-malchuth 'afillu mitzvah kallah kegon le-shinuye 'arketha de-mesana, yehareg ve'al ya'abor* [at a time of religious persecution through governmental decree, even for a minor custom, such as one involving changing a shoelace, let one suffer death sooner than transgress it] (Sanhedrin 74b), requiring of us a heroic stand in times of adversity, applies not only to political and religious persecution originated by some pagan ruler, but also to situations in which a small number of God-fearing and Torah-loyal people is confronted with a hostile attitude on the part of the majority dominated by a false philosophy.

111

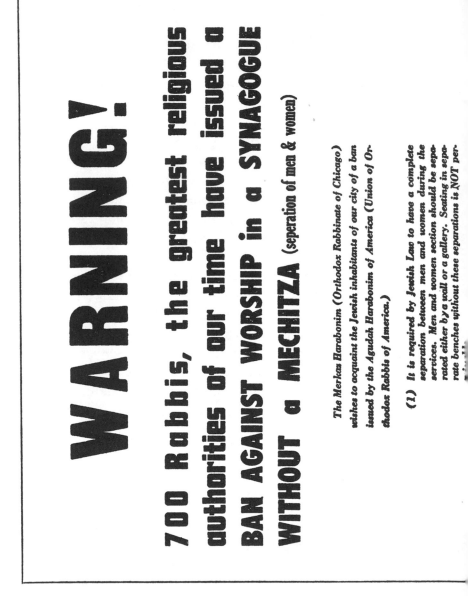

The proclamation of the *Agudath ha-Rabbanim* (source 7, pp. 92-93) was echoed by this broadside, which the orthodox rabbinate of

(3) If no approved synagogue is available in a neighborhood, the people should arrange for a minyon in a private home. If that is not possible, then you should pray in your own home without a minyon. Under any condition do not frequent a synagogue that does not abide to the law regarding mechitzah.

(4) Do not be a member and do not lend your moral or financial support to a synagogue not having a Mechitzah.

(5) Rabbinic authorities should be consulted when in doubt regarding the Kashruth of Mechitzah synagogue.

The greatest Rabbinical authorities of our time sent a special request to American Jewry to uphold the sanctity of the synagogue by adhering strictly to the Mechitzah. The following Rabbis signed this message:

(a) Chofetz Chaim of Radin
(b) Rabbi Chaim Ber Grodzinski of Vilna
(c) Rabbi Abraham Duber Shapiro of Kovno
(d) Rabbi Abraham Isaac Kuk of Jerusalem
(e) Rabbi Isaac Yerucham Diskin of Jerusalem
(f) Rabbi Meir Arak of Tarnow
(g) Rabbi Abraham Isaac Burstein of Tavrig
(h) Rabbi Dr. Meir Hildesheimer of Berlin

The Merkoz Harabonim of Chicago expects all Chicago Jewry to abide by the warnings given by the above named religious authorities and follow the ways set up by our Torah. A Happy and Prosperous New Year to all.

Chicago issued shortly afterward. Paraphrasing and quoting the proclamation, it told Chicago Jewry of the ban.

I call on the convention to make its stand clear on this problem, and to break finally with the policy of evading issues and employing ambiguities and inconsistencies. Matters have gone too far and have reached the state of cynicism, a thing which cannot be tolerated any longer. Let us not try to deceive the American Jewish laity by oral and written protests against deviationist rabbis, while many of our members attempt to emulate them. The American layman is by far more alert and intelligent than we are willing to admit, and we are gradually losing his confidence and trust.

I have perhaps expressed myself in this message a little too forcefully and bluntly. However, since the times of Moses we have known that harsh words are sometimes more expressive of deep sympathy and friendship than soft panegyrics. I realize your problems; I am cognizant of the temptations to which you are exposed; and I also know this should not blind us to our own mistakes. Soul searching, frank admission of errors, and *teshubah* are always in place.

ꕯ 14 ꕯ

On Seating and Sanctification

BY RABBI DR. JOSEPH B. SOLOVEITCHIK

THIS IS THE QUESTION which has been raised: Lately there has been a great increase in the number of synagogues where men and women sit together. Many of them are attended by Jews who designate themselves as orthodox. Shall Orthodox Judaism then consider such synagogues as an inevitable development, and become reconciled to them? Or must it assume a militant stand against them?

114

To make absolutely clear my position on this laden question, I would like to relate this incident:

A young man moved into a suburb of Boston, where the only existent synagogue had men and women sitting together. He asked me what he should do on the High Holy Days, *Rosh Hashanah* and *Yom Kippur;* until then, on account of the mixed seating, he had not entered the synagogue; but on the Days of Awe he was very reluctant to remain at home. I answered him that it were better for him to pray at home both *Rosh Hashanah* and *Yom Kippur,* and not cross the threshold of that synagogue. A few days later he telephoned me again: he had met the man who was to sound the *shofar* in that synagogue, and this man had warned him that if he did not come to the synagogue he simply would not hear the *shofar* at all, for the man would not sound the *shofar* again, privately, for his benefit. The young man practically implored me that I grant him permission to enter the edifice, at least for a half hour, that he might hear the *shofar* blasts. I hesitated not for a moment, but directed him to remain at home. It would be better not to hear the *shofar* than to enter a synagogue whose sanctity has been profaned.

My stringent position regarding the mingling of men and women, arises from several reasons.

First of all, such mingling is forbidden according to the *halachah.* In certain instances Biblical law prohibits praying in a synagogue where men and women are seated together. Such a locale has none of the sanctity of a synagogue; any prayers offered there are worthless in the eyes of the Jewish Law.

Secondly, the separation of the sexes in the synagogue derives historically from the Sanctuary, where there were both a Court of Women and a Court of Israelites. In its martyr's history of a thousand years, the people of Israel have never violated this sacred principle. Moreover, when primitive Chris-

115

tianity arose as a sect in the Holy Land, and began to slowly introduce reforms, one of the innovations which the sect established at once in the externals of synagogue practice, was to have men and women sit together. In many instances mixed seating was the unmistakable sign by which a Jew could recognize that he had found not a place of sanctity for Jews to pray, but rather a prayer-house for a deviating sect; for in those times the Christians had not yet formally differentiated themselves from traditional Jewry. As a secret sect they endeavored to hide their identity, and only through certain definite signs could they be recognized.

It would seem to me that our remembrance of history alone should keep us from imitating today the practice of primitive Christianity almost 1900 years ago.

Thirdly, the entire concept of "family pews" is in contradiction to the Jewish spirit of prayer. Prayer means communion with the Master of the World, and therefore withdrawal from all and everything. During prayer man must feel alone, removed, isolated. He must then regard the Creator as an only Friend, from whom alone he can hope for support and consolation. *Behold, as the eyes of servants look unto the hand of their master, as the eyes of a maiden unto the hand of her mistress; so our eyes look unto the Lord our God, until He be gracious unto us* (Psalms 123:2).

Clearly, the presence of women among men, or of men among women, which often evokes a certain frivolity in the group, either in spirit or in behavior, can contribute little to sanctification or to the deepening of religious feeling; nor can it help instill that mood in which a man must be immersed when he would communicate with the Almighty. *Out of the depths have I called Thee, O Lord* (Psalms 130:1), says the Psalmist. Such a state of being will not be realized amid "family pews."

116

In my opinion, Orthodoxy must mobilize all its forces and wage an indefatigable battle against the "christianization" (I have no other name for it) of the synagogue—a process which is being accomplished by people who possess no sense of *halachah* and no historical-philosophical concept of the nature of prayer; but they do have the arrogance to wreck principles and traditions which have become hallowed through blood and tears.

And I do not believe this battle will be a lost one.

In the mingled seating of women and men I see no progressive idea which should appeal to the person of culture. The American Jew, though he is ignorant in matters of Jewish law, has a great amount of common sense, and a certain intellectual honesty. I am convinced that if the Jewish public were to be truly enlightened on this matter, it would react quite differently to this reprehensible reform. It would understand that the separation of men and women implies not disrespect or contempt for woman, as the representatives of the half-reformed camp would interpret. On the contrary, it is based on the Jewish sense of modesty, a sense identical with the attitude of reverence for Deity, a sense which the Judaism of Abraham and Sarah has shown toward woman as the mother and builder of the people Israel. When *they,* the angels, *said unto him*: *Where is Sarah thy wife*? Abraham simply replied, *Behold, in the tent* (Genesis 18:9).

In practical terms, Orthodoxy has three tasks: (1) to conduct a program of education through the oral and the written word; (2) to morally support those individual laymen and rabbis who often give themselves in self-sacrifice to a battle for the sanctity of the synagogue. Mostly an action for reform will begin with the obstinacy of one despot in the brotherhood or sisterhood. Were the observant Jews well organized, and if they but had a more aggressive attitude, the reform could, in many instances, be averted. (3) Orthodox organizations should undertake to build synagogues in the suburbs and new communities where Jews are settling. If the various synagogue organizations . . . would concentrate on organizing new synagogues and Jewish communities in America, they could accomplish much.

We have not yet lost the battle, for we have not yet begun to fight. We have but abandoned the synagogue, much as the French abandoned Paris before the Germans fired the very first shot. Even today, however, we can yet defend our positions—if we will but have the determination. We must have the will to give battle, for the synagogue is the center of Jewish communal life in this country. No movement or organization is as strong as the synagogue. When we lose a House of Prayer we lose a strategic position. A right battle for principles is always a worthy and honorable endeavor.

Gird thy sword upon thy thigh . . . prosper, ride on, in behalf of truth (Psalms 45:4-5).

❦ 15 ❦

On the Law of Mechitzah

BY RABBI MOSHE FEINSTEIN

THERE ARE LOCALITIES in this our country where people are breaking with the practice of having a *mechitzah* to separate men from women in the synagogue—in the "little Sanctuary" that yet remains to us. Undoubtedly they do not intend wilfully to transgress the law, but rather act from a lack of knowledge of the severity of the prohibition. It is therefore essential to explain the origins of the law, its stringency, and the minimum

118

height of a *mechitzah* [physical separation: partition, screen, etc.] which the law might require.

The basic rule is that even if men are on one side and women on the other, it is still forbidden for them to be without a *mechitzah; and this would seem to be a Biblical injunction.* The proof lies in Sukkah 51a: there the Talmud speaks of the balcony that was erected [in the women's court of the Temple] for the eve of the second day of the Sukkoth Festival, so that the women could be relegated to the upper level and the men to the lower [to watch from there the *simhath beth ha-sho'ebah,* the "festivity of drawing water" for libations].

And the question is raised: But it is written [that David said to Solomon about the Temple plans], *All this is in writing, as the Lord hath made me wise by His hand upon me, even all the works of this pattern* (1 Chronicles 28:19)—[indicating] that it was forbidden to add anything to the structure of the Temple and the courts? Rab replied that they [the Sages] came across a verse in Scripture [Zechariah 12:12, signifying] that it was necessary to have a separation between men and women; see Rashi's amplification *ad loc.*

Quite obviously the import of the reply is that with the verse they found, it is as if the projecting balcony had been explicitly ordained, and there was thus no need to have Gad the Seer and Nathan the Prophet transmit this matter when they gave instruction about the working plans (1 Chronicles 28:29). no 28:29 Now had the balcony been required only by a Rabbinic proscription, it would be impossible to say that a Rabbinic law could override the Biblical dictum that *all this* [all the Temple plans, were given] *in writing* [and hence were not to be modified]— and in Hullin 83 the Talmud makes it quite clear that this is Scripture's ruling.

Therefore, if a balcony was required to separate the men from the women, that too must have been by Biblical law.

119

So it would also seem from a passage in the Jerusalem Talmud, Sukkah 5, 5: Commenting on this addition which amended the Temple structure, it states, "Whence did they learn [that they should build it]? From something in the Bible." Thus, such a separation is referred to as a Biblical matter. And even though its source in the Bible—Zechariah 12:12—is a verse from the prophets (Divrei kabalah), in which case the rule is that it cannot establish any Biblical prohibition, here a Biblical law can well be derived from it: for the verse does not seek to originate any prohibition, but merely requires that mourning be observed in accordance with [apparently pre-existing] Scriptural law—men separate and women separate.[1] We learn similarly of many Biblical laws from the actions of the Prophets, Judges and Kings, out of verses quoted in passages of Oral Tradition.

Our present conclusion finds further confirmation in *Tosafoth* to Zebahim 33, where it is clearly apparent that on account of a Rabbinic proscription alone nothing was to be added to the Temple. . . .

From the Talmud's discussion in Sukkah 51a we learn something more: Even if there is a *mechitzah* (separator), but such as could still permit a state of levity to come about, the same Biblical prohibition remains in force. For originally [in the women's court of the Temple, on this Sukkoth Festival night] women were within and men outside; Rashi explains that actually the former were in the women's court proper while the men occupied the Temple mount and the enclosure within the rampart; there was a great *mechitzah* between them, as the law

---

1. [I.e., the Biblical law is thus implicit in the verse as a pre-existing fact. Zechariah 12:12 reads, *And the land shall mourn, every family apart: the family of the house of David apart, and their wives apart; the family of the house of Nathan apart, and their wives apart.* Verses 13-14 continue similarly.]

120

required, but because people had to stand near the open gate to see the proceedings, it was noticed that levity soon obtained, against which the *mechitzah* availed nothing. It was this situation which Biblical law forbade, and therefore it was decided to build a balcony.

Nor did the Biblical prohibition apply because a man and a woman might seclude themselves (which situation is likewise banned by Scripture), for . . . with so many men and women as were present at this Sukkoth night festivity, there was no reason to fear such seclusion . . . especially as two passageways remained open, and people passed through constantly to leave, through the Temple mount, the rampart enclosure, the women's court, the general courtyard, and thus outside. . . . Hence, necessarily, the problem was only the onset of a frivolous mood.

Now, at first it was thought that perhaps they became frivolous because the men had to look across the women's court [to see the special festivities, since the women were within and the men outside]; although the Sages had known from the beginning that the men would thus have the women in view, this apparently did not in itself warrant their objection, and they permitted this arrangement, not realizing that frivolity would develop. But seeing the spectators reach a state of levity, for, looking at each other they went on chattering idly and illicitly, the Sages decided to reverse the arrangement and have the women outside, behind the men—a better arrangement, as is evident from Sanhedrin 20a (*q.v.* and *Tosafoth* there). Nevertheless levity still came to prevail, for the *mechitzah* did not fully separate them or screen them from one another's view; they could still see right through the open gates. Insofar as a *mechitzah* was required, there was a fully adequate one; but it was of no avail in keeping the men and women separated, since they were still as if commingling, and they yet reached a state of frivolity.

It becomes clear, then, that a balcony was necessary by original Biblical law, so that the women would be above and the men below, and then they would in no sense mingle or communicate. As the Mishnah states: [The wall of the women's court] was smooth at first, and then a balcony traversed its length, so that the women would see [the festivities] from above, and the men from below, and they would not be intermingled (Middoth 2, 5). This proves that originally, though they were separated by an adequate *mechitzah,* they were considered as if commingling; such a situation violated Biblical law, which implicitly demanded, then, a balcony.

The conclusion to be drawn is that in the synagogue as well, where men and women gather to pray, it is best to have a balcony, so that the women will be on the upper level. If for some reason it is too difficult to build a balcony, a physical separation in the full sense of the term must be installed, such as will rule out any possible frivolity. . . . Therefore a *mechitzah* ten handbreadths high [about one yard] is inadequate, for it is worthless as a guard against levity; people can talk and continue to chatter at length without any hindrance, even when seated; this allows for the greatest possible state of levity. Therefore in such a case those present would be regarded as actually commingling, and a Biblical prohibition would obtain—for this is worse than the *mechitzah* which separated the women's court from the rampart enclosure in the Temple: the latter *mechitzah* was far more substantial, yet its open gates rendered it ineffective. A *mechitzah* must be made to such a height as to effectively preclude any possible frivolous mood.

In my humble opinion a *mechitzah* reaching above shoulder-height is sufficient. We have noted that the *mechitzah* need not prevent the people's glimpsing one another, for originally an arrangement was sanctioned in the Temple with the knowledge that it would permit such glimpsing, but by itself this was no cause for concern. Even after the great amendment [of building the balcony for the women] only the balcony is mentioned, built of boards laid on a platform of beams extending out [from the wall], and "balcony" does not imply any screen or curtain [to hide its occupants from view]. . . . If, then, the balcony was uncurtained, the women on it were visible, at least to those in the middle of the court if not to those underneath the balcony. Yet this did not trouble the Sages. . . . Only when such visibility can lead to frivolity should a prohibition be in effect. And so, if women are on an upper level, even without a screen or curtain, or if they are below but behind a veritable, high *mechitzah,* so that there need be no fear of levity, it is of no consequence if the women are visible. . . .

Hence, if a *mechitzah* is of above shoulder height, it seems reasonably certain that no state of frivolity can develop, and the *mechitzah* should be sanctioned. This requires a height of three *'amoth* or eighteen handbreadths [about five and one half feet], as would appear from Shabbath 92. . . . Although the heads are visible in such a case when people stand, we need not be concerned, for it is highly unlikely that such circumstances can lead to frivolity. If people are more stringent, and make the *mechitzah* tall enough so that the heads too are not visible, may they indeed be blessed, especially as many women are lax about keeping their heads covered. However, if the *mechitzah* is but eighteen handbreadths high, it may be legally sanctioned, although many women will appear with uncovered heads: for the sage author of *Aroch ha-Shulhan* has already ruled that since in our time our sins have merited that there are many such women, one may pray in their presence. And so there is no reason to object. But if the *mechitzah* is less than eighteen handbreadths in height, it is condemned by law, and should be fought against with all possible strength. For were it but forbidden by Rabbinic law, one should fight to replace it; how much more when it is a matter of Biblical law that is at stake, as I have humbly endeavored to show.

It might be argued, however, that only in the Temple was such separation required by Bible law, because of the injunction in the verse, *My sanctuary ye shall reverence* (Leviticus 19:30, 26:2), for if one is frivolous he is certainly not reverent; hence, it may be argued, in the synagogue this law may obtain only because the Sages extended the ban against levity to the synagogue. . . . And yet, during prayer the Name of Heaven and matters of Torah and holiness are mentioned; it is therefore reasonable to assume that the injunction here is Biblical too. Indeed, R. Nissim in his Novellae to Megillah, folio 26, writes that *kedushah,* the doxology of sanctification, was instituted in synagogue prayer, because in essence the synagogue was designed to recite therein matters of holiness. Now, if these "matters of holiness" are themselves not recited under conditions of sanctity, why institute the prayer of *kedushah* especially for the synagogue? It would therefore seem quite certain that during prayer the Biblical laws about holiness apply to the synagogue. Frivolity during prayer would then be proscribed by Scripture.

Necessarily, the Scriptural law must further apply to any occasion where people gather. For it is derived [from the verse, *And the land shall mourn, every family apart: the family of the house of David apart, and their wives apart* (Zechariah 12:12), which indicates that men and women should be separate]. Nowhere do we find that this instance of future mourning is to be in the Sanctuary. . . . It therefore indicates that wherever men and women must gather they are forbidden to be without a dividing *mechitzah* between them, so that they cannot reach a state of levity. . . . And so in our synagogues too, where people gather to pray, there must be a *mechitzah,* and it must be such that a mood of frivolity will be quite out of the question. This means either a balcony for the women, with the men below,

124

or a *mechitzah*—a partition—of not less than eighteen hand-breadths in height.

* * *

In a personal communication, the author of this responsum, one of the recognized poskim, *final authorities in Jewish law, of our generation, wrote further concerning his legal opinion:*

June 17, 1957

Dear Mr. Litvin,

In reference to what is written in my name, that "the prohibition of mixed pews is Biblical law," it would be better to change the words to read: "the prohibition against praying in a synagogue without a *mechitzah* of at least eighteen *tefahim* (handbreadths) or sixty-five inches high, is a Biblical law." Stronger emphasis should be put on the point that it is prohibited to pray in a synagogue without a proper *mechitzah*, even though there is separate seating.

Sincerely yours,

Rabbi Moshe Feinstein

🌼 16 🌼

A Responsum on Mixed Seating

BY RABBI AARON KOTLER

I HAVE BEEN ASKED to clarify, according to the laws of our sacred Torah, whether it would be permissible for an ortho-dox congregation to change its traditional seating arrangement so as to have men and women sit together in the synagogue. I am amazed to find that anyone could have any possible doubts on this matter, when in fact it has been obvious to Talmudic Sages through all generations right up to our day, that for men and women to sit in a synagogue without a proper partition between them is expressly forbidden by the laws of our Holy Torah. Not one Sage has ever found grounds for permitting it.

This prohibition was accepted, and followed by all Jews throughout history and in all communities the world over, until destructive elements emerged who cast off the yoke of the Torah and its commandments, and violated the sanctity of Israel.

I shall now cite, with the help of the Almighty, some of the sources drawn from Talmudic writings to establish this prohibition.

1. The Mishnah in Sukkah (51b) relates that "they made an important innovation"[1] in the Holy Temple. The Gemara (*ibid.*) explains that the innovation was the building of a balcony in the Court of Women so that the women could sit above in the balcony, and the men below. Even before this innovation, men and women did not mingle during celebrations in the Holy Temple, as it is expressly stated in the Gemara (*ibid.*): "The women stood outside the courtyard, and the men stood inside"; but because of the fear that even with such an arrangement there would still be improper levity, the balcony was built. The Gemara proves from Scripture that there should be a strict separation of men and women, by quoting Zechariah (12:12), *All in the land shall eulogize*[2] . . . *the family of the House of David separately and their wives separately.* The Gemara then states: "Does it not follow *a fortiori*? If even in the days to

---

1. The Mishnah deals with the celebration of the drawing of the water during *Sukkoth* (*simchath beth hasho'ebah*) when the men came to the Court of Women in the Temple to celebrate. In order to make provision for the women who were in the Temple to watch the celebration, but could not enter their court because the men were there, the balcony was built. (The Gemara is the later Talmudic commentary on and interpretation of the Mishnah. The two together constitute the Talmud.)

2. This refers to the eulogy for the Messiah *ben Yosef* (of the tribe of Joseph) who according to tradition, will be killed in the Great War that will precede the coming of the second Messiah, a descendant of David.

come [the days of the Messiah] when the people will be occupied with eulogies, and evil desires will not be present in them (see Rashi *ad loc.* that these are two separate reasons why it would not be likely for improper levity between men and women to take place: firstly, because people occupied with mourning are not frivolous, and secondly, because the Lord had said that in the days to come *I shall remove their heart of stone* [Ezekiel 36:26], which means that the Lord will remove the evil desires in people), nevertheless the Torah said men should be separate and women separate, and this in the Temple—now that people are joyous and evil desires are present, how much more certainly must there be separation between men and women." Thus the Gemara.

Now, how much greater still is the conclusion that we must draw: if in the Temple with its great sanctity, where ten miracles took place constantly before all Israel, as related in the Mishnah (Aboth 5, 5), where all fulfilled the commandment *Thou shalt fear My Sanctuary* (Leviticus 26:2), the Sages nevertheless felt it necessary to build a balcony to separate men and women, and thus guard against improper levity, though previously they had not mingled (as mentioned above)—in our generation that is so inferior to them in all matters dealing with sanctity and the fear of God, as is obvious to any sensible person, it is surely a far greater necessity to separate men and women to preserve the sanctity of the synagogue.

That our generation is inferior may be inferred from the Gemara (Shabbath 112b), which states: "If the previous generation were as angels then we are as people, and if the previous generation were as people then we are as donkeys." This was said by one generation of Tannaim [Sages of the Mishnah] about the generation immediately preceding it. The great Tanna, R. Judah ha-Nasi, who was called simply *rabbenu ha-kadosh,* "our holy Teacher," said, "As great a difference as there is between the holiest of the holy and the most profane, so is there a difference between my generation and that of R. Jose"—i.e., a Sage who had preceded him by one generation. What can we now say, removed as we are, so many generations from the Golden Age of the Talmud?

The very fact that there is a desire to bring about the mingling of the sexes in the synagogue, shows how far our generation has strayed from the path of holiness.

2. The Gemara (Megilla 29a) states: "It is written, *Yet am I to them as a little sanctuary* (Ezekiel 11:16); this denotes the synagogues and Houses of Study in Babylonia [i.e., in Exile]." In many other places in the Talmud the idea is expressed that the synagogues in the Diaspora have a sanctity comparable to that of the Holy Temple, though a lesser one. Thus, the prayers were instituted in place of the daily sacrifices brought in the Temple (see Berachoth 26b); and in the Sanctuary we find a special court for women only. It is asked in the Talmud (Kiddushin 52b), "How is it that a woman would be in the courtyard of the Temple?" From this question we see that women were not found at all in the courtyard. Although the Talmud was only discussing the theoretical question of whether a man could betroth a woman in the courtyard with the meat of a sacrifice, nevertheless the whole question is dismissed because there was no possibility at all for a woman to be found in the courtyard. Despite the fact that the Gemara says (Taanith 26a), "Whenever a person brought a sacrifice, he was required to stand beside it in the courtyard of the Temple," and women as well as men were obligated to bring sacrifices, nevertheless women did not enter the courtyard so they would not mingle with the men; how much more certainly should women not be allowed to mingle with men in the synagogue.

That we derive laws governing the synagogue from the laws governing the Holy Temple, is shown explicitly in *Orah*

Hayyim (152, 1) where we read, "It is forbidden to destroy anything in a synagogue because it is as if one would destroy a stone from the walls of the Sanctuary, which is forbidden." This can also be derived from the Gemara (Megillah 28a), which states, "A synagogue that is destroyed still retains its sanctity, as it is written (Leviticus 26:31), *I shall destroy your sanctuaries*—which implies that although they are destroyed their sanctity remains." While the verse has reference to the Temple, the Talmud nevertheless infers from it a law concerning synagogues, and calls them sanctuaries. See also the *Bi'ur ha-Gra* (*Orah Hayyim* 151, 24) by the great Talmudic scholar R. Eliyahu of Vilna, famous as the Vilna Gaon. Commenting on R. Joseph Caro's uncertainty whether it would be permissible to use the second floor of a synagogue for secular purposes, the Gaon explains that the problem is whether the second story of a synagogue can be compared to the roof and top stories of the Temple courtyard, which were not sanctified, and so could be used for secular purposes; or whether it might be compared to the second story of the Temple proper, which was sanctified and could not be used for secular purposes. In any event, we see that the synagogue is regarded as comparable to the Holy Temple.

3. The *Rama* (R. Moses Issereles) states in *Yoreh De'ah* (265, 11) that according to an ancient custom, when a circumcision takes place in the synagogue a woman may help in the ceremony by bringing the child to the synagogue door, whereupon her husband would take it from her. The *Rama* is careful to emphasize that the woman brought the child *to the synagogue* and not into the synagogue. Thus we see that though the woman was taking part in the fulfillment of the commandment of circumcision, and her husband was the *sandek* [who would hold the child on his knees during circumcision] nevertheless she did not enter the synagogue.

129

4.   It is expressly stated in Talmud, Berachoth (24a) and in all Rabbinical codes, that the uncovered hair of a married woman is considered indecent, and it is forbidden to pray or read the Shema in the presence of such hair even if it belongs to one's own wife or mother, let alone if it belongs to someone else's wife or other forbidden relatives (sister-in-law, aunt, etc.). According to many Rabbinical authorities, this prohibition is included in the Biblical injunction, *that He see no unseemly thing among you* (Deuteronomy 23:15).   It is stated in *Orah Hayyim* (75, 2) that the basic reason for this prohibition is that uncovered hair can induce indecent thoughts.   It is also stated (*ibid.*) that one who has transgressed this prohibition and has prayed or read the Shema before uncovered hair has not fulfilled his obligation of prayer or reciting the Shema.

If while praying or reciting the Shema, a person should even gaze on a woman and thereby come to have evil thoughts, it would also be included in this rule.   And when you have men and women not separated by a proper partition, it is impossible to guard against this.

5.   It is expressly stated in Talmud, Abodah Zarah (20b) that a man is forbidden to gaze upon the fancy clothes of a woman whom he knows, even if she is not wearing them at the time.   It is surely proscribed if the woman is wearing the clothes.   The reason, as explained by Maimonides (*Yad ha-Hazakah, Hilchoth 'Issure Bi'ah* 21, 2) and in *Shulhan Aruch Eben ha-Ezer* (21:1) is that such gazing would bring one to have indecent thoughts.   Therefore it is expressly forbidden during prayers, and is included under the commandment, *that He see no unseemly thing among you.*   It is impossible to avoid gazing on women's clothes during prayer when there are many people present and the sexes are not properly separated.

In his Commentary on the Mishnah, Succah 5, 2, Maimonides states that the balcony was built in the Temple so that the men "would not gaze" upon the women (see also the *Tosafoth Yom Tob ad loc.*). And the *Mordechai* (Sanhedrin, Chap. 2) questions the custom that had the women lead funeral processions. "How were the women permitted to march before the men? The men would come to gaze upon them? . . ." He further quotes the *Riba* (*ibid.*) who explains that women walked *behind* the men in a funeral procession *to* the cemetery, but were first to leave the cemetery on the way back, so that the men should not have to pass the women on the way back.

6. It is expressly stated in the Commentaries *Bayith Hadash Beth Shmu'el* on *Shulhan Aruch Eben ha-Ezer* 62, that the formula, "We will bless our God in whose abode is joy," is not to be recited at the Grace after a wedding feast [as it usually would be], if men and women are found together in one room—because there is no joy in God's dwelling when the *yetzer hara'* (Evil Impulse) is present.

In Berachoth (45a) the Mishnah states that women are not counted with men to make up the necessary quorum of three or ten to say Grace after meals as a group, although according to some authorities (e.g., R. Asher, R. Nissim *ad loc.*) women are obligated to say the special Grace among themselves as a group, when there is the necessary quorum made up solely of women.

7. It is generally known that the most important part of prayer is sincerity and purity of thought, as it is expressed in Sifre and the Gemara (Taanith 2a): on the verse, *to serve Him with all your heart* (Deuteronomy 11:13) they comment that this means prayer; and according to Maimonides it is a positive commandment of the Torah. Now, *with all your heart* denotes that all one's powers and desires should be subordinated to the prayer; the Sages interpret *with all your heart* to mean "with both your wills"—both the will to do good and the will to do evil should be subordinated to the service of the Lord.

This is expressly stated in numerous places in the writings of our early Sages.

Nothing is as disturbing to prayer as indecent thoughts, which render the prayers impure and unacceptable before the Lord. And how much more unacceptable is prayer when the people incite their evil desires by deliberately seating men and women together, in contradiction to the Laws and traditions of our Nation. This is pure wilfullness, which must bring about improper sights and improper thoughts. Beside the fact that this is in itself a serious transgression, it is even more contemptible when it takes place in the Palace of the King of Kings, the holy synagogue. According to the Law such people are not fulfilling their obligations in praying or in the reading of the Shema; all is voided and unacceptable before the Lord. In addition, whenever the name of God is uttered at such services, it is uttered in vain.

The *Yalkut Shim'oni* (1, 934)[3] cites the *Seder Eliyahu:* "A man should not pray among women" because as the commentary there explains, he may be distracted by them. It has been stated by the foremost rabbinical authorities that a person should pray alone at home even on Rosh Hashanah and Yom Kippur rather than pray in a synagogue where men and women are not separated by a proper partition. Even if he must miss hearing the shofar, or the reading of the *megillah* on Purim, he should still pray at home rather than attend a synagogue that is not conducted according to law.

8. Since our ancestors instituted the custom of separating men and women in order to prevent improper thoughts and levity, and have maintained it through all generations, then even if the basic law required no such separation, we are yet

---

3. This passage was shown me by the eminent *rosh yeshibah,* Rabbi Ruderman of Baltimore.

obligated to follow in their footsteps, for it is written, *Forsake not the teaching of thy mother* (Proverbs 1:8), and the Gemara (Pesahim 50b) interprets it that we must maintain the prohibitions which our ancestors instituted as a defense against committing other transgressions. No *beth din* (court of Jewish law) may remove such prohibitions.

This is expressly shown in the Gemara (*ibid.*) in the case of the family of Baishan whose forefathers had instituted the custom in the family not to travel to market on Friday, so as not to interfere with the preparation for the Sabbath. The children of Baishan came before R. Yohanan and asked to be absolved of this prohibition, and be allowed to travel to market on Friday. He told them, "I cannot absolve you, because your forefathers instituted this custom, and you are duty-bound to follow it—as the Torah commands, *Forsake not the teaching of thy mother.*" Such prohibitions, accepted as custom, are binding on all generations.

In our case, not only is it forbidden per se, according to the Law, to mingle the sexes, but it is also prohibited by the age-old custom, not of one family alone, or even one city alone, but of all Jews the world over, in order to guard against committing other sins (improper thoughts, etc.). Surely the Biblical injunction of *Forsake not,* etc., applies here, and no absolution in the world can avail.

9.   Beside the prayers, the sanctity of the synagogue itself is profaned by the mingling of the sexes, for this sanctuary is turned into a place expressly designed to induce a number of serious transgressions such as improper thoughts, etc. There is no need to dwell at length on the fact that it is impossible to guard against such transgressions where many men are brought together with women for a long period of time. To so profane a holy place is the greatest ignominy.

10.   There is, further, a question of usurpation of property

rights. Most, if not all, of the original contributors to the construction of the synagogue proffered their money to build an Orthodox synagogue in accordance with the Laws of the Torah and the decisions of the Talmudic Sages. Their express intention in contributing was to perform a meritorious deed by helping in the building of a holy place that would glorify and sanctify the name of God. Under no condition did they intend to have the synagogue changed into a place where it would be forbidden to pray—a place that would not only bring them no merit, but would make them, Heaven forbid, partners to the incitement of base desires and the resultant transgressions mentioned above. Particularly when many great Sages, especially those of Hungary, foremost of whom was the great *Hatham Sofer,* of blessed memory, placed a ban on synagogues that are not maintained in accordance with the Law, and forbade even entering such a synagogue. Surely the founders would not have contributed a penny to the building of such a synagogue. There can be no doubt that the proposed change is completely contrary to their intentions; it would therefore be, according to the Laws of our holy Torah, a usurpation of the property rights of both the living and the dead. Even a *minority* of the contributors, or even *one* contributor can prevent such a change, as we shall see later, when I discuss the laws of partnership in detail (section 12).

11. There are surely members of the congregation who inherited their rights and places in the synagogue from their fathers; and it was certainly the will of their fathers, as their actions demonstrated, that the synagogue be maintained only in accordance with the Law. Therefore on the heirs devolves the Talmudic injunction (Gittin 14b), "It is an obligation to fulfill the wishes of the deceased"; they should not alter the makeup of the synagogue in any way. Further, any such change would mean a breach of the Biblical commandment, *Honor*

134

thy father, etc. (Exodus 20:12), which means to honor him in his lifetime and also after his passing (Kiddushin 31b).

12. Another consideration arises in regard to property rights, if even a minority òf the members objects to any change. Although in matters pertaining to a partnership the majority decides, majority rule *does not apply where changes are proposed to the basic agreement whereby the partnership was set up.* Then certainly according to the Law, a minority can prevent any change. Consider, for instance, if most members of the congregation would decide to convert the synagogue into a theatre; are we to follow the majority, when the partnership was originally set up for a synagogue? In such a matter basic to the partnership, the partners are dependent on each other for consent. So it is in our case. The original intent of the partnership was to maintain an orthodox synagogue, and any one who wishes to change this is at a legal disadvantage.

We see this in the Mishnah, Pe'ah 4, 1: The Mishnah states that the corner of a field of grain should be left unharvested, the grain standing in the ground, and the poor should come and cut the grain themselves. However, the owner of the field and all the poor have the right to agree to have the owner cut the grain and distribute it to the poor. But the Mishnah goes on to say: "Even if 99 poor men say the grain should be distributed by the owner and only one says the poor should cut it themselves, they are all obligated to listen to this one, for he has spoken in accordance with the law." Hence, if the majority would make any changes, even with the power of the constitution of the congregation, it would be a gross usurpation of the property rights of the minority, who cannot now enter the synagogue and pray.

13. It is well-known that one transgression leads to another (see Mishnah Aboth 4, 2). Any change toward mingling the sexes brings many other violations of the laws pertaining

to the synagogue, because the general administration of such a synagogue is far from the spirit of Torah. No observant rabbi, no Jew who has the fear of God in his heart, would want to have anything to do with such a synagogue. Lacking proper leadership, the synagogue would therefore stray further and further from the path of Torah; and who would venture to predict what this could lead to. Any well-informed person remembers the Mendelsohn period in Berlin, which began with only "minor" changes in the synagogue similar to those proposed now, and in a relatively short time half the Jewish community of Berlin had converted to Christianity and assimilated.

14. It is explicitly stated in many places in the Bible and the writings of our Rabbis that prayer is the outpouring of one's soul before the Lord, and communion with Him, to such an extent that all earthly considerations are forgotten. We find this in Berachoth (30b) about the *hasidim ha-rishonim* (the early pious men) and R. Akiba (*ibid.* 31a), of whom it is said that "one left him at the beginning of his prayer in one corner of his house, and found him at the end of his prayer in another corner," because of the ecstasy of his communion with the Divine. The prayers themselves are of very ancient origin, having been instituted by the Patriarchs Abraham, Isaac and Jacob (Berachoth 26b). Prayer is what is meant by *abodah*, service to the Lord—one of the three pillars (the other two are Torah and Charity) on which the world rests (see Mishnah Aboth 1, 2). One who prays properly is called a "servant of the Lord," as we find in the statement of Rabban Yohanan b. Zakkai about R. Hanina b. Dosa (Berachoth 34b):[4] "I am like a minister before a king and he is like a servant before a king."

---

4. The Talmud relates that once the son of Rabban Yohanan b. Zakkai was very ill. He sent to R. Hanina that the latter should pray for the boy to become well. Rabban Yohanan's wife asked him, "Is it possible that his prayer should help more than yours? You are greater than he in the knowledge of Torah." Rabban Yohanan then gave the answer quoted.

The Gaon R. Elijah of Vilna explains that one is like a *minister* before a king when he has attained the highest level in the study of Torah, but like a *servant* before a king when he has attained the highest level in *abodah,* prayer. Although Rabban Yohanan b. Zakkai was greater than R. Hanina b. Dosa in the study of Torah, and therefore attained the higher rank of "minister before a king," nevertheless R. Hanina b. Dosa was a "servant of God": because of his great piety and greatness in prayer, he was closer to Him; his prayers were more readily answered by God, for he was like a servant who serves his master personally, and may therefore come before him at any time with a request.

It is quite impossible to set down here even a small fraction of what has been written by our great Sages on the importance and sanctity of prayer. And though we are far from the heights of sincerity and sanctity that our ancestors attained, nevertheless it is incumbent upon us to maintain at least the outward forms of prayer as they were instituted by previous generations. In this way we may at times have some moments of sanctity and feeling similar to those of our ancestors. Those who wish to change the outward form of prayer by instituting the mingling of the sexes, show that they wish to vulgarize the prayers and to change completely the whole traditional concept of what a synagogue and place of worship should be. By their actions they demonstrate that they wish to create a conception of prayer as being just another activity aimed at providing them with ordinary pleasures. I hesitate to dwell at length on this point out of respect for the honor of the Jewish people.

15. It is expressly proven according to the Laws of the Torah, in the collected responsa of the *Hatham Sofer* (1767-1839) and in the responsa of many great Sages of his generation, that it is forbidden to make any changes in the laws governing a synagogue. All the great Sages of that generation also placed

a ban on any synagogue that instituted any of the changes proposed then, or any that would be proposed in subsequent generations.

Surprisingly enough, although the Reform Jews of that period were so radical that they removed any mention of the Messiah from the prayerbook, and brought an organ into the synagogue, it never occurred to them to have men and women together, for even they understood that such an arrangement would be highly improper. Throughout our long history and in all our wanderings there is no evidence that the question of "mixed seating" was ever raised in any Jewish community.

16. In answer to those who wish to abolish the separation of men and women in the synagogue because they claim that this separation is an indignity to the women, we need but cite the words of our Sages on the verse in Psalms (45:14), *All glorious is the daughter of the king within,* that modesty is a woman's true dignity.

I have set down only a small portion of the reasons and citations from the writings of our Sages that establish the fact that any changes in the synagogue are forbidden. I have been forced to be brief because the request for my opinion reached me very late (I was in the Yeshiva in Lakewood at the time). Because of my many duties and the fact that an immediate answer was required, I have not had the time to organize my answer properly. Nevertheless it is obvious from even a part of what I have cited that the proposed change is forbidden.

I turn to all the members of the congregation and to all those who have any influence in this matter to preserve the glory of God and His Torah; to defend the honor of our ancestors; and to not permit this change, that is a desecration of our Torah, to be put into effect. They should also have compassion for their own souls and those of their children, for if they will, Heaven forbid, institute this change, all their prayers in this

138

synagogue will be considered unworthy and unacceptable before God; and they will cause subsequent generations to become completely alienated, Heaven forbid, from God. I fervently hope that the people of Israel will not commit a grievous wrong.

Even those who do not understand the reasons I have set forth to prohibit this change, are obligated to accept the decision of the Sages of Israel of all generations. Even if there are those who are far from the Torah and its spirit, and are therefore in doubt about the matter, let them consider carefully the possible dangers involved in such a change as I have set them forth here, and they will certainly not wish to risk such serious peril.

May all those who aid in defending the integrity of the Law of the Torah be graced with the Biblical benediction, *Blessed be he who shall uphold the words of this Torah* (implicit in Deuteronomy 27:26). The merit of the whole community shall be their portion.

Presented and signed for the sake of the glory of the Torah and the sanctity of the synagogue.

❦ 17 ❦

An Open Letter

BY RABBI DR. JOSEPH B. SOLOVEITCHIK

FIRST, LET ME REITERATE in precise and unequivocal terms my position with regard to the seating arrangement in a house of worship. The separation of the sexes in the synagogue is a basic tenet in our faith. It dates back to the very dawn of our religious Halachic community, and constitutes a Pentateuchic injunction (*'issur de'oraitha*) which can never be abandoned by any legislative act on the part of a rabbinic or lay body regardless of its numeric strength or social prominence. What

139

was decreed by God can never be undone by human hand. In my opinion, mingling of the sexes is by far a more flagrant violation of a great principle than installing an organ or praying with bare heads. Unfortunately, while every traditionally minded Jew understands that the latter practices tend to strip our synagogue of its Judaic quality, and are tantamount to an attempt to christianize our ritual, many well meaning and sincere Jews are being misled with respect to the mixed seating arrangement.

I wish to state that I do not know of any orthodox rabbi or Talmudic scholar of high repute who would dare to say that mixed seating is in consonance with our Law. Neither the orthodox rabbinate of America, consisting of three major organizations, nor the chief rabbinate of Great Britain and its Dominions, nor the rabbinate of the Holy Land would ever even vaguely suggest that such a practice is permissible. The requirement for separation is Halachically so elementary and axiomatic, historically so typical of the Synagogue in contradistinction to the Church since antiquity, and philosophically so expressive of our religious experience, that whoever dares to question this institution either is uninformed or consciously distorts religious realities.

As to whether or not the Halachah also requires segregation, I wish to say that there is certainly a requirement for the erection of a partition, and the synagogue which fails to erect one is guilty of violating a very sacred tradition. However, there is a basic difference between this wrong and that of the complete mingling of the sexes, for, as I indicated above, separation has its origin in the Bible itself, whereas the requirement of a *mechitzah* must be attributed to a Rabbinic ordinance. The Biblical passage from which the Talmud derives the interdiction against mixed pews [Zechariah 12:12 in Sukkah 51b], and also the Pentateuchic injunction, *Let Him see no unseemly thing in thee* (Deuteronomy 23:15), deal with separation only.

140

There is no mention, however, of segregation. The latter has been introduced in accordance with the old maxim, *va'assu seyag latorah,* "Make a fence around the Law" (Aboth 1, 1), as a safety measure in order to prevent the mingling of the sexes. The Biblical law itself, however, only requires separation. Although complete segregation is important, since we have no authority to amend even a Rabbinic institution, yet it should not be treated on a par with the principle of separation. While the latter determines the very essence and sanctity of the synagogue, the former, if violated, does not place the congregation in the class of a reform temple.

In conclusion, let me say that it is completely irrelevant to our problem whether fifty or five percent of the membership of the Rabbinical Council of America occupy pulpits in synagogues with improper seating arrangements. The violation of a religious or ethical principle does not affect its validity and cogency, even though a large segment of the community is engaged in doing so. A transcendental tenet is binding regardless of its unpopularity with the multitudes. Was the commandment against murder declared null and void while the Nazi hordes were practicing genocide?

III

sources
in
Jewish law

N VIEW of the unanimity
among orthodox authorities as to the legal position, to quote
the classical sources on which these authorities have based
their decisions, may only serve to buttress an already impregnable stand.   However, a brief reference to the origins
of these strong opinions, will add a necessary dimension of
historical perspective.

1.   Both Temples had a special women's section (1).
The changes in the structure of the women's section referred to in the Talmud do not disprove, but rather confirm,
that the Women's Court existed prior to the repairs.   See,
for example, the responsum of R. Moshe Feinstein (chap.
II, source 15).   And the late beloved R. Samuel Gerstenfeld has clearly shown from the Talmud's question about
the changes (Sukkah 51b) that its Sages were certain be-

yond doubt that the second Temple was a precise replica of the first (except for specific minor changes)—including a Women's Court which might not ordinarily be altered (2). This matter is also treated in R. Menahem M. Kasher's fine essay (chap. VI, source 2). Except for specific ritual functions, for which a woman was admitted to the inner Temple court, men and women were always separated; see Josephus, *Wars of the Jews,* V, 5, 2 (1C). Even when women were admitted on such occasions, the Sages indicated special provisions to prevent the slightest possibility of levity (chapter VI, source 2).

As the Mishnah, Middoth 2, 5, interprets Ezekiel 46:21 (1B§1), there will be exactly the same Women's Court in the Sanctuary of the Messianic future (so also Rashi to Ezekiel 44:19). This fundamental symbol of the principle of separation will thus never be forgotten or relegated to the past. Rooted in Talmud and Scripture, it remains part of our program for the spiritual renaissance of future time.

2. Interpreting Ezekiel 11:16, the Talmud calls the synagogues of the Exile "little Sanctuaries" (3§1). To a lesser degree, our synagogues have been our Sanctuaries, ever since the Temple itself was destroyed. This concept is affirmed in Talmud and Midrash (3); many passages see prayer as the successor to Temple offerings; and for one Geonic responsum the synagogue is, in effect, our Holy of Holies (3§5). Nor is this mere poetic or homiletic fancy; the Talmud derives the times for daily prayers from the times for the daily burnt-offerings in the Temple (3§3); a late Talmudic work applies a Bible law on the Temple directly to the synagogue (3§4); an Early Code (*Eshkol* 5) cites two Talmud passages on the relation of prayer to sacrifices, as a legal principle; *Tur Orah Hayyim* 150 discusses

details of synagogue ararngement required because it must parallel the Sanctuary; and two Early Authorities cite this principle as the basis for Talmudic laws governing reverence for the synagogue (3§6-7). When the *Shulhan Aruch Orah Hayyim* includes these laws (151), the late sainted *Hafetz Hayyim* simply notes in his definitive commentary *Mishnah Berurah* that it is because the synagogue is a Sanctuary-in-miniature; hence frivolity is strictly forbidden there. Now, because of the prohibition against levity, the separation of men and women was so strictly carried out in the Temple, and it therefore follows logically that synagogues were from the beginning required to have the same separation of sexes as the Temple.

3. The principle that men and women remain apart at times of great spiritual experience, is quite perceptible in Scripture itself: after the rescue at the Red Sea, Moses and the men sing praise separately, Miriam and the women separately (Exodus 15:1, 20-21); before the Revelation at Mount Sinai, Moses commands the Israelites, *Come not near a woman* (*ibid.* 19:15). In the Oral Torah this principle began yet in Noah's Ark and continued throughout Jewish history (4), down to Talmud times, when rabbis insured that men and women remained apart when all came to hear their lectures (4§7).

At Mount Sinai, Moses first informed the women of the forthcoming Revelation, and then the men—separately; they were to stay apart until the great moment; and witnessing the Divine manifestation, they remained separate: so we read in the Midrash *Pirke de-R. Eliezer* 41 (4§3). Commenting in the Biblical encyclopedia *Torah Shelemah* (XV, 94, §183), R. Menahem M. Kasher writes: Here is a most reliable source for the prohibition against men and women being mingled in the synagogue: If in the wilderness, at Mount Sinai, at a time as holy as the Revelation, our Sages say that men and women were separate—and there is some evidence for this in the verse, *Come not near a woman*—how much more necessary is such separation in the synagogue the year round.

That men and women require separation at every festive or sacred occasion, continues to be clearly stated in the writings of the Geonim and Early Authorities (5).

In one Midrashic passage, the verse, *the Lord thy God is a devouring fire* (Deuteronomy 4:24, 9:3) implies that men should not pray in the midst of women (4§6). This was elaborated splendidly by R. David Ochs (Toronto) in a personal communication to the editor (6).

4. The Codes do not specifically discuss the special women's gallery in synagogues. This omission is probably for the same reason that the Mishnah fails to give particulars about the laws of *tzitzith* (fringes) and *tefillin* (phylacteries)—because *the observance was so widespread as to be common knowledge*; thus Maimonides in his commentary on Mishnah, Menahoth 4, 1 (7). Moreover, this observance was not in fulfillment of a specific law referring to the synagogue, but merely the application of a general, clearly stated law to synagogue conditions: "The law of the Torah for the separation of the sexes to prevent frivolity applies to all places where crowds gather, not just to places of worship"; so wrote R. Moshe Feinstein, referring to Talmud Sanhedrin 20a and *Mordechai ad loc.* There is no law requiring a synagogue to have a women's section; however, if women come to worship, then, for the protection of the sanctity of the Synagogue and the undisturbed devotion of the worshippers, a women's section is specifically required. In other words, the women's gallery is the obvious formal expression, in the synagogue, of an existing

law, rather than some entirely novel institution—as R. Menahem Hayyim Landa, a prominent Torah authority of Poland, asserted (8). Our definitive latter-day authority, R. Israel Meir ha-Kohen (the *Hafetz Hayyim*) notes in another connection (*Mishnah Berurah* 151, 1b): ". . . iniquity becomes so much more heinous in a sacred place. . . . There is no comparison between sinning in private and sinning in the royal palace, in the king's very presence"; these words recall what another authority wrote, in a similar vein, several centuries earlier: in his Bible commentary *Akedath Yitzhak,* R. Isaac Ar'ama also stressed that a public sin by a group is so much more serious a crime as to be of a different degree or quality from the private sin of the individual (9). These points apply with peculiar cogency and force to the question of *mechitzah.*

5. The separation of the sexes in a regular place of worship is, moreover, a necessary consequence of the legal rule (Talmud, Berachoth 3, quoted in *Shulhan Aruch Orah Hayyim* 75) that under many conditions prayers may not be read in the immediate proximity of women; see in this connection Abodah Zarah 20 and *Shulhan Aruch 'Eben Ha'ezer* 62 (10). This prohibition applies even to private prayer; but where larger numbers of worshippers are present, more formal arrangements are required. The women's gallery was the answer to this problem.

6. The many incidental references to women's sections that occur in the Rabbinic literature throughout all ages prove that the existence of these women's sections could be taken for granted. The Jerusalem Talmud refers to the women in the Great Synagogue of Alexandria as being above (11§1). Authorities of the 12-14th centuries mention the women's section in passing, while writing of other matters (11§2-7). For instance, one authority requests that at

146

the time the *shofar* is sounded, to avoid disturbance, the little ones be sent to the *women's section* of the synagogue (11§4).

A later decision which implies the existence of a women's gallery as a legal requirement, is given by R. Moses Isserles in *Shulhan Aruch Yoreh De'ah* 265; he also cites the references of two Early Authorities to women's synagogues (*ibid. Hoshen Mishpat* 35; 11§3, 7). And *Ture Zahab* to *Shulhan Aruch Orah Hayyim* 315, 1 cites a medieval authority about erecting a temporary partition when men and women require separation (5§6). Note that no early authority suggests that women be permitted to sit in the men's section and the erection of a partition foregone.

7. In the 19th century, when for the first time reform tendencies raised questions about the need for a women's gallery, this need was unequivocally affirmed in *all* responsa, among them those of the great Rabbinic authority, R. Moses Sofer (*Hatham Sofer, Responsa, Hoshen Mishpat* 190 and *Orah Hayyim* 28), and of *Maharam Schick* (*Orah Hayyim* 77), both of whom pointed out that the mixing of the sexes is forbidden no matter what the consequences may be in regard to synagogue attendance and religious practices (12). In the responsa *Teshuboth Beth Hillel* 50, it is clearly stated that where there is no proper *mechitzah*, "it is forbidden to enter the synagogue even if no women are present, because the violation has desecrated the Synagogue and has left it devoid of the sanctity of a miniature sanctuary" (13). In this vein, another typical responsum, condemning strongly even the use of an inadequate partition, was sent by the noted R. Eliyahu Guttmacher (14). One could go on, page after page, enumerating all the similar responsa, without a single dissenting orthodox legal opinion, which appeared over the last 150 years.

147

8. These responsa also pointed out that the change to mixed pews, like most innovations introduced at that time into the Synagogue, was imitative of non-Jewish practice, and therefore in direct violation of the Torah's law prohibiting the imitation of non-Jewish religious forms and practices in our worship (12). This was stressed particularly in the responsa *Dibre Hayyim, Orah Hayyim* 18 by the renowned Hasidic Rabbi of Sanz (15).

9. R. Aaron Kotler, one of the leading Rabbinic authorities of our time, points out that in our days there is an additional legal rule against the abolition of women's sections (chapter II, source 16). Since this practice has been adhered to by our forefathers in all generations and in all countries, it would have the force of law—by virtue of the Biblical rule, *Forsake not the teaching of thy Mother* (Proverbs 1:8, 6:20)—even if there were no law requiring this practice as such. This was also stressed by Chief Rabbi Kook in a responsum issued in 1927 (chapter II, source 11). It has been further clarified by R. David Regensberg, dean of the Hebrew Theological College, in a communication to the editor (16).

10. Jewish law also stresses that where a community has traditionally established certain practices no changes should be made that would redound to the disadvantage of any of the members of this community (17). A change, therefore, which would make it impossible for members of the congregation to worship there, would be a violation of Jewish laws relating to property rights.

Many of the sources mentioned above, in Talmud and Early Authorities, et al., have been ably reviewed by R. Ezekiel Grubner, showing the inevitable conclusions to which they lead (18).

We may then summarize the position in the words of

Dr. Soloveitchick (chapter II, source 17): "The separation of the sexes in the Synagogue is a basic tenet of our faith. It dates back to the very dawn of our religious community . . . [and] can never be abandoned by any legislative act on the part of a rabbinical or lay body."

sources for chapter III

❦ 1 ❦

The Women's Court in the Two Temples

SOURCES FROM TALMUD, EARLY COMMENTARIES, ETC.

A. IN THE FIRST TEMPLE

1. *And the spirit of God clothed Zechariah the son of Jehoiada the priest; and he stood above the people, and said unto them: "Thus saith God: Why transgress ye the commandments of the Lord, that ye cannot prosper? because ye have forsaken the Lord, He hath also forsaken you." And they conspired against him, and stoned him with stones at the commandment of the king in the court of the house of the Lord* (2 Chronicles 24:20-21).

R. Judan asked of R. Aha: Where did they kill Zechariah—in the Women's Court or in the Court of the Israelites? He answered him: Neither in the Court of the Israelites nor in that of the Women, but rather in the Court of the *kohanim* (priests) . . . (Jerusalem Talmud, Taanith 4, 5—69a).[1]

2. *And he built the inner court with three rows of hewn stone, and a row of cedar beams* (1 Kings 6:36).

The inner court: this was the court of the *kohanim* (priests) and the court of the Israelites; it was located before the porch.

---

1. Since the murder occurred under Joash, the eighth king of Judah, who reigned from 836 to 798 BCE (see 2 Chronicles 24), the passage concerns the first Temple. The passage is also found, with minor variants, in *Pesikta de-R. Kahana', 'Echah* (121a); *'Echah Rabbathi,* Proems 5 and 23; *Koheleth Rabbah* 10, 5.

Scripture calls it "inner" because it was farther within than the women's court (Rashi *ad loc.*).[2]

B. IN THE SECOND TEMPLE

1. The Court of the Women was 135 [cubits] in length by 135 in width; there were four chambers at its four corners, each of forty by forty cubits, and they were not roofed over; and so are they destined to be [in the Temple of the future], for it is stated, *Then he brought me forth into the outer court, and caused me to pass by the four corners of the court. . . . In the four corners of the court there were courts inclosed . . .* (Ezekiel 46:21-22). . . . It [the Women's Court] was bare at first, and then they surrounded it with a balcony, so that the women could look on from above and the men from below, in order that they should not be mingled. Fifteen steps rose from it to the Court of the Israelites, corresponding to the fifteen [Songs of] Ascents in the Book of Psalms (120-134), and upon them the Levites [stood and] chanted hymns. . . . There were chambers underneath the Court of the Israelites which opened into the Women's Court, where the Levites would store stringed instruments,[3] cymbals, and all kinds of musical instruments. . . . Corresponding to these [four southern gates],

---

2. In Mishnah Middoth 2, 5 (cited below in B §1.) Ezekiel 46:21-22, *Then he brought me forth into the outer court*, etc., is quoted to prove how the Women's Court will be in the Temple of the Messianic future; hence "the outer court" is taken to denote the Women's, and so R. David Kimhi interprets in his commentary to Prophets *ad loc.* So also Rashi to Ezekiel 44:19. The phrase, "the inner court," used here in regard to the first Temple, suggests that there was also an "outer court," i.e., a Women's Court. Hence its existence in the first Temple is directly implied by the present verse. See also the commentaries of R. Samson of Sens and R. Asher b. Jehiel to Mishnah Kelim 1, 8, and *Tosafoth* to Pesahim 92a, s.v. *tebul yom*, which tally a passage in the Mishnah with another in the Gemara, indicating that the first Temple had a Women's Court in Jehoshaphat's time.

3. Hebrew, *kinnoroth u-nebalim,* variously translated as harps, lyres, lutes or psalteries.

on the north side, starting from the west corner,[4] were the Gate of Jeconiah, the Gate of Offering, the Women's Gate, and the Gate of Song . . . (Mishnah Middoth 2, 5-6).

The Court of the Women was 135 [*cubits*]: from east to west. *by 135 in width:* from north to south. . . . *It,* i.e., the Women's Court, *was bare at first:* for there were no joists whatever over it. *and they surrounded it with a balcony:* they set brackets in the wall all around, and built an upper level on them (R. Asher b. Jehiel, Commentary *ad loc.*).

It [the Court] was *bare* in that it was quite open, and no wall enclosed it. It has already been explained toward the end of Tractate Sukkah (52b) that there the people gathered for the rejoicing in the days of the [*Sukkoth*] Festival; out of fear lest the women mingle with the men, they surrounded it with filled arches to which some kind of stairway led, so that the women should watch from there when the people Israel gathered there for the Festivity of Drawing Water . . . (Maimonides, *Commentary to Mishnah, ad loc.*).

It was bare at first: that is to say, [the balcony][5] was quite open, with no wall surrounding it on its four sides; it merely stood on columns. *and they surrounded it with an exostra:*[6] that is, a screen of lattice-work; for the women would gather there to see the Festivity of Drawing Water, while the men stayed in the Court; and in order that the women should not commingle with the men[7] they surrounded it with these screens (Me'iri *ad loc.*).

---

4. Literally, close to the west.

5. This addition is clearly required by what follows. This interpretation by Me'iri differs widely from the others; the first comment seems to follow Maimonides (above), but is applied differently; what follows, concerning a screen, suggests the comments of the first R. Isaiah di Trani, given below, end of §2.

6. This is the Latin version of the Mishnah's *ketzoth-terah,* and means balcony or gallery. Me'iri, however, interprets quite otherwise.

7. I.e., communicate through speech or looks.

152

Fifteen steps rose out of it [the Rampart] which descended from the Court of the Israelites to that of the women; the height of each was half a cubit, and its depth was half a cubit (Yoma 16a).

2. They said: He who has not seen the Festivity of Drawing Water [for Libations] has never seen rejoicing in his life. At the conclusion of the first Festival day [of *Sukkoth*] they would descend to the Women's Court and make a great improvement there. . . . And Levites without number with harps, lyres,[8] cymbals, trumpets and other musical instruments were on the fifteen steps which descended from the Court of the Israelites to that of the Women, corresponding to the fifteen Songs of Ascents in the Book of Psalms (120-134); on these the Levites stood with their instruments and chanted hymns. Two *kohanim* (priests) stood in the upper gate, which led from the Court of the Israelites down to that of the Women, with two trumpets in their hands . . . (Mishnah Sukkah 5, 1-2 and 4).

They would descend: *kohanim* and Levites would go down from the Court of Israelites, which was higher than the Women's Court, for the latter was below it along the incline of the mountain (Rashi *ad loc.*).

A great improvement: that is to say, of great benefit; for the people would prepare one place for men and another for women, the place for the men being above the one for the women, so that the former would not gaze at the latter (Maimonides, *Commentary to Mishnah, ad loc.*).

What was the great improvement? Said R. Eleazar, It was as we learned: it [the Women's Court] was bare at first,[9]

---

8. See note 3.
9. One MS reads, "At first it was divided between the men and the women"—which might mean that the area was divided into two, the Women's Court for the women, and the Rampart for the men (Rabinowitz, *Dikduke Soferim, ad loc.*).

and they surrounded it with a balcony and instituted that women should sit above and men below (Mishnah Middoth 2, 5). Our rabbis taught: Originally the women were within and the men outside, and they would reach a state of frivolity; it was then ordained that the women sit without and the men within, but they would still reach a state of frivolity; it was [finally] ordained that women were to sit above and men below. But how could they do so? It is written [of the Temple plans], *All is in writing, as the Lord hath made me wise by His hand upon me* (1 Chronicles 28:19)?[10] Said Rab, They came across a verse, which they interpreted: *And the land shall mourn, every family apart: the family of the house of David apart, and their wives apart* (Zechariah 12:12); they reflected: In this instance, surely we can reason from the lesser to the greater: If in the [Messianic] future when they will be occupied in mourning, and the Evil Impulse will have no power over them, the Torah ordains that men be apart and women apart, now, when they are engaged in rejoicing, and they are subject to the Evil Impulse, how much more certainly must they be separated (Sukkah 51b-52a).

It, the Women's Court, *was bare at first*: and no brackets projected from the walls. *and they surrounded it with a balcony*: they set brackets in the walls to extend from them all around, and every year they would arrange balconies there [on the brackets] out of boards . . . so that women could stand there during the Festivity of Water-Drawing, and look on; this was the "great improvement" of which we learn in the Mishnah, that was constructed every year. *within*: in the Women's Court proper. *without*: along the expanse of the Temple Mount and the Rampart. *But how could they do so?* how could they add or alter anything in the construction of Solomon?

---

10. Since the Temple plans were of Divine origin, how might anything be altered?

154

It is written: of King David, when he instructed Solomon about the measurements for the Temple and its construction [that he said], *All is in writing, as the Lord hath made me wise by His hand upon me—even all the works of this pattern*—which the Holy One (blessed be He) transmitted to him through Gad the Seer and Nathan the Prophet. *They came across a verse*: that it was necessary to separate men from women, and erect a "fence" in Israel, so that they should not come to grief. *And the land shall mourn*: in Zechariah's prophecy he foretells how in time to come the Messiah of the tribe of Joseph will be eulogized, for he will be slain in the battle of Gog and Magog; and it is written, *the family of the house of David apart, and their wives apart*—[indicating] that even in time of sorrow men and women must be separated. *when they will be occupied in mourning*: at that time, and one who grieves will not be frivolous; and furthermore, *the Evil Impulse will have no power over them*: as the Writ states, *I will remove the stony heart* (Ezekiel 11:19, 36:26); and below [the Talmud] declares that the Holy One (blessed be He) will slay it. . . . *now, when they are engaged in rejoicing*: and close to becoming frivolous, and furthermore, now *they are subject to the Evil Impulse*— how much more surely must they be apart (Rashi *ad loc.*).

They would reach a state of frivolity: for they [the men] would enter among the women. And so they made a balcony round about the Court, projecting from the wall, with an arched roof over it . . . (R. Nathan b. Jehiel, *Aruch,* s.v. *gezuztera'*).

. . . *It was as we learned* . . . Originally the Women's Court was bare, and no brackets extended from the wall; and afterward *they surrounded it with a balcony*: they had brackets extending out, on the inside of the walls of the Court, round about—either by building them on or by means of holes that they made there [in the walls]; beams were set upon them, and boards atop those, so that the women could stand on them

155

and observe the festivity from above, while the men would stand below, in the Court. The men could not gaze at the women, for it [the balcony] had screens round about, made like a kind of latticed windows, so that the women within could see out, while those without could not see in. As it was taught: *Originally the men were within and the women outside,*[11] *and they would reach a state of frivolity: for the men would come and go among the women. it was then ordained that the men stay outside and the women within, and they would still reach a state of frivolity: for the men would enter and leave among the women. it was then ordained that the men be without and the women within, and yet they would come to be frivolous:*[12] for they would regard one another and communicate with their eyes. It was [ultimately] enacted that the women were to watch from above and the men from below. *How could they do so? It is written, All is in writing, as the Lord hath made me wise by His hand upon me—even all the works of the pattern—* and we have not permission to alter the construction, to add or lessen anything (The first R. Isaiah di Trani, *Rulings to Sukkah, Sam Hayyim,* Leghorn 1801, 25a).

3. What improvement would they make there? They would set the men off by themselves, and the women by themselves, as we learned elsewhere (Middoth 2, 5): It [the Women's Court] was bare at first, and they surrounded it with a balcony, so that the women could watch from above and the men from below, in order that they should not be intermingled. Whence did they learn [to do so]? From something in the Torah: *The land shall mourn, every family apart* [etc.] (Zechariah 12:12). Two *amora'im*[13] [differed on this]: one said, it refers to the

---

11. This and the texts which follow differ markedly from our version.

12. From the comment which follows, the arrangement now seems to have been such that one could not actually go from one group to another.

13. Sages of the Gemara (the later part of the Talmud) who discussed, interpreted and elaborated on the Mishnah.

156

mourning for the [slain] Messiah; and the other said, It signifies the mourning in regard to the Evil Impulse. The one who holds that it refers to the mourning for the Messiah [would explain the reasoning thus]: if at a time that people mourn you see that the men are to be by themselves and the women by themselves, how much more certainly must it be so when people are rejoicing. The one who holds that it signifies mourning concerning the Evil Impulse [would explain the reasoning thus]: if at a time that the Evil Impulse no longer exists, you see that the men are to be by themselves and the women by themselves—when the Evil Impulse is alive, how much more certainly must they be separated (Jerusalem Talmud, Sukkah 5, 2).

4. Originally, when they watched the Festivity of Water-Drawing, the men would look on from within and the women from the outside. Once the *beth din* (high court) saw that they reached a state of frivolity, they built three balconies in the Court, facing three directions, where the women would [sit and][14] observe; and so when they watched the Festivity of Water-Drawing they were not [any longer] intermingled (Tosefta ed. Zuckermandel 4, 1).

5. *Speak unto the sons of Israel. . . . And he shall lay his hand* [*upon the head of the burnt-offering*] (Leviticus 1:2, 4)—the *sons* of Israel rest [their hands on the heads of animal sacrifices] but not the daughters of Israel. R. Jose and R. Simeon say: Women have the option to do so. Said R. Jose: Abba Eleazar told me, Once we had a calf for a peace-offering, and we brought it into the Women's Court, where the women laid their hands upon it—not because this is incumbent on women, but to give them satisfaction of spirit (Hagigah 16b).

---

14. So in one MS. The Women's Court in the second Temple is also mentioned in Talmud, Sotah 40b-41b, *q.v.*

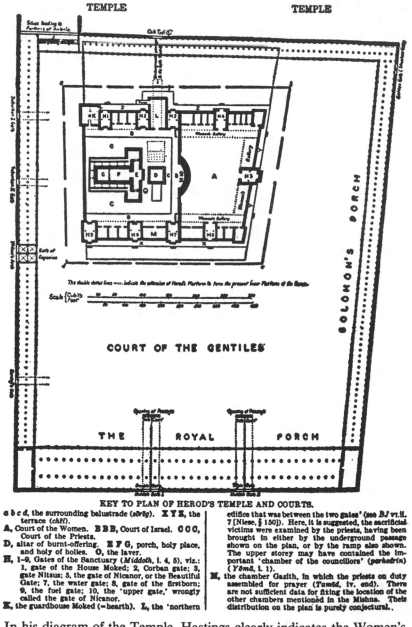

COURT OF THE GENTILES

SOLOMON'S PORCH

THE   ROYAL   PORCH

KEY TO PLAN OF HEROD'S TEMPLE AND COURTS.

a b c d, the surrounding balustrade (*sôrêg*). X Y Z, the
    terrace (*chêl*).
A, Court of the Women. B B B, Court of Israel. C C C,
    Court of the Priests.
D, altar of burnt-offering. E F G, porch, holy place,
    and holy of holies. O, the laver.
H, 1–9, Gates of the Sanctuary (*Middoth*, i. 4, 5), viz.:
    1, gate of the House Moked; 2, Corban gate; 3,
    gate Nitsus; 5, the gate of Nicanor, or the Beautiful
    Gate; 7, the water gate; 8, gate of the firstborn;
    9, the fuel gate; 10, the 'upper gate,' wrongly
    called the gate of Nicanor.
K, the guardhouse Moked (=hearth). L, the 'northern

edifice that was between the two gates' (see *BJ* vi. ii.
    7 [Niese, § 150]). Here, it is suggested, the sacrificial
    victims were examined by the priests, having been
    brought in either by the underground passage
    shown on the plan, or by the ramp also shown.
    The upper storey may have contained the im-
    portant 'chamber of the councillors' (*parhedrín*)
    (*Yômâ*, i. 1).
M, the chamber Gazith, in which the priests on duty
    assembled for prayer (*Tamîd*, iv. end). There
    are not sufficient data for fixing the location of the
    other chambers mentioned in the Mishna. Their
    distribution on the plan is purely conjectural.

In his diagram of the Temple, Hastings clearly indicates the Women's
Court (A), with the women's gallery on three sides.

C. OTHER SOURCES

1. Since there was a partition built for the women on that side, as the proper place where they were to worship, there was a necessity for a second gate for them; this gate was cut out of its wall, over against the first gate. There were also on the other sides one southern and one northern gate, through which was a passage into the court of the women; for the women were not allowed to pass through the other gates; nor, when they went through their own gate, could they go beyond their own wall (Josephus, *Wars of the Jews,* V, 5, 2).

2. Entering by the "Beautiful Gate," (H5), one found oneself in the colonnaded *court of the women*—so called because accessible to women as well as men. This was the regular place of assembly for public worship. . . . The women were accommodated in a gallery which ran round the court (Mishnah Middoth 2, 5), probably above the colonnades as suggested in the plan. . . . The west side of this court was bounded by a wall, which divided the Sanctuary into two parts, an eastern and a western. As the level of the latter was considerably higher than that of the eastern court, a magnificent semicircular flight of fifteen steps led up from one to the other (Hastings, *Dictionary of the Bible,* p. 902a).

❧ 2 ❧

The Ezrath Nashim in the Synagogue

BY RABBI SAMUEL GERSTENFELD

THIS QUESTION is "a matter of controversy in our gates."[1] Congregations are formed or dissolved in consequence of it. What usually happens is this: Members who have prospered

---

1. [See Deuteronomy 17:8.]

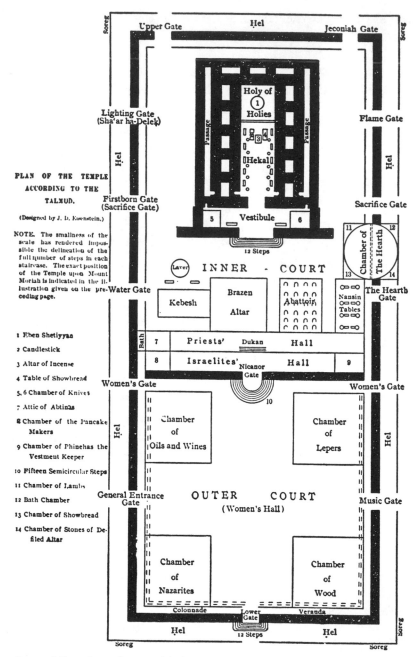

Dotted lines have been added to show where the balcony was built.

and attained wealth and position, become possessed of a spirit of innovation and imitation. They begin to be critical and find fault with the Synagogue in its traditional form. They clamor for an organ, a mixed choir and commingling of the sexes. And to our sorrow, as in the time of the Judges, we are without the restraining hand of a central authority, "everyone doing what is upright in his own eyes."[2]

The consequences are: Either the innovators get the upper hand and then the synagogue becomes reformed and the remnant of Israel, "of the seven thousand that have not knelt to the *Baal* of innovation,"[3] have to withdraw and build another synagogue conducted along traditional lines; or the innovators are outvoted and then is realized the plaint of the Prophet, *Israel has forgotten its Maker and built temples* (Hosea 8:14). The position of the rabbi in a modern synagogue is unenviable and unstable. He is frequently put to the test. Shall he court poverty and lose his position by not yielding, or shall he enjoy well-being and sit firmly in his position by being pliant, thus abjuring the tenets inculcated at his alma mater?

To enter into a controversy with confirmed reformers would be labor wasted and in vain. What is purposed in these lines is to strengthen the hands of those that doubt and waver, "that halt between two opinions," and that have not yet crossed the line dividing orthodoxy from reform.

The crux of this question is whether the separation of the sexes in the synagogue is a *recent addition* to Judaism and is therefore no integral part of the Jewish ceremonial law or whether it is a law of ancient standing that provided for an *ezrath nashim* to keep the sexes apart, and is therefore part and parcel of Jewish law.

Research and investigation prove that at all periods of the

---

2. [See Judges 17:6, 21:25.]

3. [See 1 Kings 19:18.]

Temple as well as of the Tabernacle, the sexes were not to mix during prayer.

The main authority for this custom is the Halachah. The Halachah alone is our most authentic history. No one can profitably read our *halichoth olam,* our history, who neglects the study of our *halachoth.* By the searchlight of our laws alone we are enabled to trace the antiquity of the custom of segregation of the sexes during public worship.

Now according to the following data (Maimonides, *Yad,* Laws of the Temple, 7, 5; R. Aaron ha-Levi, *Hinuch,* 362), the Temple of Jerusalem with its environs was subdivided, with regard to degrees of sanctity, *as its prototype the Tabernacle of Moses,* into three parts. Within the walls of Jerusalem up to the Temple Mount (corresponding to the square formed about the Tabernacle in the wilderness within the hosts of Israel) was the Israelite camp, *mahaneh Israel.* From the Temple Mount to the Gates of Nikanor, the portals of the Temple (corresponding to the square formed by the hosts of Levites surrounding the Tabernacle) was the Levite camp, *mahaneh leviah.*

The place within the Gates of Nikanor (corresponding to the court of the Tabernacle) was called the "divine camp," *mahaneh shechinah.* According to the same sources, within the "camp of the Levites" in its western part, close to the Gates of Nikanor, was the women's section, *ezrath nashim;* while within the "divine camp," *mahaneh shechinah,* in its eastern part, was the men's division, *ezrath Israel.* Farther west, nearer the altar, was the priests' section, called *ezrath kehunah.* For sacrificial purposes these distinct sections, *azaroth,* were nonexistent. Except for the case of a *sotah* (see Maimonides, Laws of Sotah, 3, 16.) all might traverse to the altar in connection with an offering. But for the sake of prayer or other religious gatherings, the distinction of *azaroth* was rigidly observed and

162

enforced. When once R. Meir's disciples discussed the contingency of a priest's wedding a woman with his portion from the sacrifices which must be consumed only within the *mahaneh shechinah,* i.e., *ezrath kehunah* and *ezrath Israel,* and must not be carried beyond to the *ezrath nashim,* which is located in the *mahaneh leviah,* R. Judah, displeased at being troubled with any hypothetical questions, exclaimed, וכי אשה בעזרה מנין? Is the event of a woman's presence in the *mahaneh shechinah* possible? (Kiddushin 52b).

Who knows with certainty? And yet we may declare with the highest degree of probability that the institution of *ezrath nashim* originated with the Tabernacle of Moses. The phrase repeated in the Writ, of "the women that congregated at the door of the Tabernacle,"[4] which, according to Onkelos and Ibn Ezra, alludes to prayer meetings *at the door of the Tabernacle,* at *mahaneh leviah,* points to the later *ezrath nashim* situated in *mahaneh leviah,* at the eastern side of the Gates of Nikanor.

And as there was an *ezrath nashim* in the second Temple, so there was one also in Solomon's Temple. For, the second Temple was like the first. Its plan was merely a copy of the first drawn up by King David according to the instructions of Samuel with the assistance of Gad the Seer, and Nathan the Prophet. When King David fled and narrowly escaped the emissaries of Saul, he hid himself at Ramah, where he met Samuel for the second and last time and where the plan of the future Temples was worked out (see 1 Samuel 19:18; Zebahim 54b). Except for the double curtain of the second Temple, which replaced the *ammah teraksin,* the cubit-wide double partition of cedar, and other minor changes, both Sanctuaries were alike (Yoma 51b; Maimonides *Mishneh Torah, Hilchoth Beth ha-Behirah,* 2).

The statement by Dr. Mosessohn in "The Jewish Tribune"

---

4. [Exodus 38:8; 1 Samuel 2:22.]

(June 8, 1923), that "the Temple built by Solomon had no provision for a women's apartment," thus contradicts the facts. Is he disinclined to grant the same amount of credence to our annals as he would grant to a tale by Strabo, Herodotus or Xenophon? We may exclaim with the Talmud, "Shall not the priest's wife be accorded an authority at least equal with that of the saloon keeper?" Shall not our Torah, which is perfect, be at least as the idle gossiping of theirs? The fact is that Solomon's Temple did have an *ezrath nashim* for the use of women for the purpose of prayer. And according to the *Tana D'be Eliyahu* [ed. Friedmann, chapter 9] as quoted in *Yalkut Shimoni* [I, 934] the Biblical injunction, *Let thy camp be holy,* etc. (Deuteronomy 23:15), is a direct order that men and women shall not sit together in the synagogue.

An important historic reference bearing on our subject, is the narrative of Sukkah 51b (see Maimonides, *Mishneh Torah, Hilchoth Lulab,* 8):

It is told in that Baraitha that "at the end of the first Festival day of *Sukkoth,* the priests would go down to the women's apartment, *ezrath nashim,* and make extensive repairs therein." Asks the Talmud, "What was the nature of the repairs?" Says R. Eliezer, "It was as is explained elsewhere: It was originally smooth and they surrounded it with projecting beams." (Rashi: The walls of the *ezrath nashim* were originally smooth, there having been no projecting beams; then came the priests and fixed them permanently, and annually they came and covered them with boards, thereby enabling the women to view the rejoicing.) Then the Talmud proceeds to quote a Baraitha: The Rabbis have taught: Originally the women were inside and the men outside (the women in the *ezrath nashim* and the men in the broad square of the Temple mount and by the wall). This arrangement led to levity; so they provided that the men be inside and the women outside. Yet misconduct was not

164

prevented. Therefore it was finally arranged that the women be seated on the upper part (on the balcony of the *ezrath nashim* —Rashi) and the men below.

The Talmud proceeds to question the legality of the addition to the building. "How did they do so when it is written, *All this the Eternal made me understand in writing with His hand upon me?* (How did they add and change anything in Solomon's plan? Is it not written by King David when leaving word before his death to Solomon about the dimensions of the Temple and its structure, all the work according to the pattern communicated through Gad the Seer and Nathan the Prophet?) Says Rab: קרא אשכחו ודרשו — they found a verse and expounded it (they found a verse that it is necessary to separate men from women and to make a "fence" in Israel to prevent misconduct —Rashi).

The following thus becomes evident: that the *ezrath nashim* existed prior to these innovations or extensive repairs; that previous to these repairs either the men were inside and the women outside, or vice versa, but never together; that the Talmudic criticism was directed *not* against the introduction of separation, but against adding permanently fixed beams to a structure whose plan was drawn up by a king through a seer and a prophet, according to Divine instruction. And since the fixed beams objected to were in the *ezrath nashim,* we have the strongest possible evidence that in the second Temple the *ezrath nashim* itself was not a departure from, but in conformity with the plan of the first Temple.

Rab's answer conveys the lesson that in all gatherings, whether festive or mourning, separation is to be insisted upon, and is of such vital importance, that it outweighs the illegality of making structural changes [in the Sanctuary].

Maimonides in quoting this Talmudic passage says: "Though it is a duty to rejoice on all holidays, on *Sukkoth* the rejoicing was greater than on all other holidays; as it is said,

You shall rejoice before the Lord your God seven days (Leviticus 23:40). How did they do it? On the eve of (in the Mishnah, the evening after) the first Festival day they prepared seating for the women in the Temple on the upper part, and for the men beneath, so that they would not mix one with another."

Dr. Mosessohn, however, discounts the decision of Maimonides because Maimonides does not set it down as a law but as an historical narration, and says: "Its very contents prove that Maimonides has not made it as a law . . . this is history of the past and not a law for the future." He thinks that Maimonides does not give this the dignity of law, because Rab, when replying to the criticism of innovation, uses the phrase of קרא אשכחו ודרשו. And the use of this phrase, accordingly, (*Lehem Mishneh,* on Maimonides, Talmud Torah 4, 1; see also *Shach, Yoreh De'ah* 246, 8) minimizes the legal value of anything so derived. He must have supposed that this innocent phrase is a magic spell, that overthrows *halachoth.* He fails to notice an apparently slight distinction which makes big differences. When the Talmud apologizes for R. Meir, for his having studied from Aher, it states: קרא אשכח ודרש. This does not necessarily imply the rejected opinion of an individual.

This singular form probably conveys the meaning that Rabbi Meir stands alone in this view (see Tosefta Hullin 11b, Kiddushin 3, 1 and elsewhere). But in our case, concerning the alterations in the Temple made for the separation of sexes, the plural form is evidence of general concurrence (see Gittin 20a and 77a, and *Tosafoth, ibid.*). Surely Maimonides in quoting this historic fact, meant to convey to us the custom which has the sanctity of law, that sexes are not to mingle in the synagogue as they did not in the Temple. The narrative form does not prove that it is merely intended "as a history of the past and not as a law for the future." Even the narrative part of our literature is written with a purpose, viz., to deduce laws for life's conduct. The Zohar (quoted by *Baal Akedah* 7) echoes this doctrine in the following words: Said R. Simeon b. Yohai, "Woe to that man who says this Torah came to present mere history and secular things. Were it so, even today they could manufacture a Torah, and perhaps a more attractive one, etc." Were the Mishnah and Maimonides bent merely on telling a story and not on setting up an example for imitation, why have they left out such thrilling stories, so graphically narrated by Josephus and others, of what befell the Jewish people at that time? Perforce must it be admitted that their records of the past are *ipso facto* examples for the future.

So far it is proven that the *ezrath nashim* is an ancient institution existing in both Temples and, according to *Yalkut*, is part of a Biblical commandment. Now what about the Synagogue? Ezekiel says (11:16), *Therefore say: Thus saith the Lord Eternal, Although I have cast them off among the heathens, and although I have scattered them among the countries, yet I will be to them a little sanctuary in the countries whither they shall come.* The *mikdash me'at*, or Temple-in-miniature, is, according to the Rabbis (Megillah 29a), an allusion to the Synagogue, which is the Temple of the diaspora.

The Codes, indeed, do not yet directly mention an *ezrath nashim*. Yet it is mentioned incidentally and as a matter of course. It is stated that for the two-fold purpose of chanting praises and preventing a fire, some are accustomed to have vigil on the night of *Yom Kippur*. However, when slumber overtakes them, they may lay themselves down either at the entrance, on the western side, or in the *ezrath nashim*, when no women are present (see *Hagahoth Maimunioth* to end of Maimonides' Code, *Hilchoth Shebithath 'Asor*).

The silence of the Codes on this point is rather due to the fact that the custom of separate worship was so well known and the practice of setting apart an *ezrath nashim* was so clearly in vogue, that the Codes could afford to be silent about it. Just as the Mishnah omits particulars about the laws of *tzitzith* and *tefillin* (see Maimonides, Commentary on Menahoth, 4) because their observance was so general and widespread, so was this considered too obvious a custom for further inquiry.

The old synagogue bears witness to the continuity of the law concerning *ezrath nashim,* and its acceptance by Israel. We may well exclaim with R. Eliezer (Baba Metzia 59b): כותלי בית המדרש יוכיחו: — "the walls of the synagogue shall corroborate my statement." Every synagogue still extant with a history of centuries behind it, has an *ezrath nashim.* And when, after the commencement of the Mendelsohn era, synagogues were erected in western Europe without an *ezrath nashim,* a mighty shout of protest rang out and was echoed from one end of the Diaspora to the other. All contemporary great Rabbis denounced it as a violation of a sacred custom.

It is thus demonstrated that the *mikdash me'at,* the Temple-in-miniature, the synagogue, conformed to the law of an *ezrath nashim* as it did conform to all laws that are motivated by decorum, decency and good conduct.

To prove his contention "that there was no segregation of the sexes during public prayers," Dr. Mosessohn quoted Megillah 23, where it is stated, "All may be called up (on Sabbath) to fill up the number of seven, even a minor, even a woman; but the Sages said, a woman should not read from the Torah because of the honor of the community." He reasons that "it is obvious that if a woman may be called to the Torah which is read in the synagogue, she was not separated from them, but sat with them and prayed with them." He seems to think that then, as today, a reader would recite in behalf of the person called, and that everyone was therefore eligible, and that if a woman was called up, it is conclusive evidence that she was one of the congregants. Else why not call up one of the *minyan?*

168

The fact, however, is that till the time of R. Asher b. Jehiel, the *Rosh* (see Megillah 3, 1), to be eligible as one of the seven, one had to be able to read from the scroll. Not everyone was therefore able to read the Torah. When there were no seven scholarly men present, they may have had to forego or discontinue reading the week's portion. Under such conditions, the question would arise whether to invite a scholarly woman to read.

Now, since Torah reading and studying—and when Hebrew was the vernacular, reading the Torah in public was not a dry mechanical *mitzvah*, but a real study—are conducive to pure and moral thoughts (see Sotah 21a), the Sages would permit a woman to read before the *minyan;* but because of the shame of ignorance that would accrue to the congregation, they forbade such reading. So we see that for prayer or any religious gatherings in the synagogue, an *ezrath nashim* is as ancient as our Torah.

A synagogue without an *ezrath nashim* is a violation of the Law and ought altogether to be shunned. Rather than bring about that *He will turn away from thee* (Deuteronomy 23:15), a consequence resulting (according to the *Yalkut*) from non-separation in the synagogue, it is better to pray alone and be with Him that hears all prayers and who promised, *In every place where I shall* permit *my name to be mentioned I shall come to thee and bless thee* (Exodus 20:21).

❁ 3 ❁

The Synagogue as a Sanctuary

SOURCES IN TALMUD, MIDRASH, GE'ONIC AND EARLY AUTHORITIES

1. YET SHALL I BE FOR THEM *as a little sanctuary in the lands where they are come* (Ezekiel 11:16): Said R.

Samuel b. R. Isaac,[1] This refers to the Houses of Prayer and Study in Babylonia [the Exile]. . . . Raba interpreted: What does this verse signify: *Lord, a haven hast Thou been for us in every generation* (Psalms 90:1)? It refers to the Houses of Prayer and Study (Megillah 29a).

2. R. Yohanan said: He who prays in the synagogue in the present world, it is as if he were praying in the ancient Temple, for it is stated, *Yet shall I be as a little sanctuary for them in the lands* [*where they are come*] (Jerusalem Talmud, Berachoth 5, 1, version of *Yalkut Shim'oni*, Psalms 659).

3. R. Joshua b. Levi said: [The Men of the Great Assembly] instituted the prayers to correspond to the daily burnt-offerings. . . . We have learnt a *baraitha* supporting R. Joshua b. Levi: Why did they say, the time for the morning prayer is till noon? Because the daily offering of the morning could be sacrificed at any time until noon. . . . Why did they say, afternoon prayers may be recited until the evening? Because the daily offering of the afternoon might be brought until evening. . . . Now why did they say that evening prayers have no time limit? Because the limbs [of burnt-offerings] and suet [of other sacrifices whose blood was sprinkled before sunset] which were not consumed [by the altar fire] by evening, might continue to be consigned to the flames that entire night. Why did they declare that the additional prayers may be recited at any time

---

1. Where variations from printed editions occur, please consult the Hebrew texts and notes. For the translations the likeliest readings have generally been adopted, with no attempt to note the variants.

In addition to the excerpts cited here, many passages in Talmud and Midrash regard prayer as a substitute or equivalent for the Temple sacrifices, e.g., §3 below. See Jerusalem Talmud Berachoth 5, 1 (8d); *Mishnath R. Eliezer*, p. 234; *Sifre*, Deuteronomy 41, end; *Shemoth Rabbah* 38, 4; *Bamidbar Rabbah* 18, 17; *Shir ha-Shirim Rabbah* 4, 11 and 5, 2; *Pesikta' de-R. Kahana', Shubah*, end; *Sifra, Behukothai* 6 (cited in 6 below); R. Israel Al-Nakawa, *Menorath ha-Ma'or*, II, 5-6 and 171; see also *Tosafoth* to Baba Bathra 8a, s.v. *yathib*, and R. Samson b. Zadok, *Tashbetz* 202.

during the day? Because the additional offerings [for any special day] might be sacrificed at any time on that day (Berachoth 26b).

4. *Nor shall she come into the sanctuary* (Leviticus 12:4): [a woman ritually unclean from childbirth] has no permission to enter Houses of Prayer or Study (*Baraitha de-Massecheth Niddah*, 30-33).

5. . . . And should you say, the land is defiled—Israel is a holy people, and does not take defilement; the Torah is hallowed; and the Houses of Prayer and Study stand in place of the Holy of Holies for us today . . . (from a Geonic responsum in *Otzar ha-Geonim, Kethuboth*, p. 182).

6. *Thou shalt fear thy God* (Leviticus 19:14, *passim*): He has commanded that when a man enters the Sanctuary, a synagogue, or a House of Study, he is to behave toward them with reverence and respect, for it is written, *Ye shall keep My sabbaths, and reverence My sanctuary* (*ibid.* 26:2). It was taught in a *baraitha* in Yebamoth (6b): *and reverence My sanctuary*—do not fear the Sanctuary, but rather the One who adjured you about the Sanctuary—meaning the Holy One (blessed be He). Now we find the House of Prayer or Study called a Sanctuary, as we read in *Torath Kohanim* (*Behukothai* 6): *I will bring your sanctuaries* (mikdeshechem) *unto desolation* (Leviticus 26:31): [it contains three words:] *mikdash* (sanctuary), *mikdashi* (My sanctuary), *mikdeshechem* (your sanctuaries)—and thus includes Houses of Prayer and Study. And in Megillah (29a): *Yet shall I be,* etc.[2] Thus we learn that when Scripture says, *Ye shall reverence My sanctuary,* Houses of Prayer and Study are included. Scripture does not explain in what such reverence consists, but the Sages have defined it by their views, each in accordance with his concepts of sanctity. About reverence for the Sanctuary we learn in the

---

2. See above, §1, for the passage which follows.

Mishnah, Berachoth (54a): A man should not act in disparagement before the eastern gate [of the Temple], for it is opposite the Holy of Holies. And Rab commented: This applies only from *tzofim* toward [the Sanctuary, an area from which it was visible] and if he actually can see it. Similarly, R. Yohanan added: If no fence intervenes, and when the Shechinah (Divine Presence) rests there. . . . We learned further (*ibid.*): A man should not ascend the Temple Mount with his walking stick, shoes, or bag; nor with the dust [of his journey] on his feet; nor should he make it a general thoroughfare.[3] . . . Thus we learn what constitutes irreverence toward the Temple Mount. As for the synagogue and the House of Study, we learn in Mishnah Megillah (28a): In a synagogue which has become a ruin, one is not to hold mourning eulogies, spread nets, set out fruit on its roof,[4] or fasten bundles; nor is it to be made a thoroughfare; for it is stated, *I will bring your sanctuaries into desolation* (Leviticus 26:31): they remain sanctified though they are desolate. . . . In a *baraitha* in Megillah (*ibid.*) we read: Synagogues and Houses of Study are not to be treated with heedless disparagement; one should not eat there or drink there, use the premises for pleasure, or stroll there; nor should one enter on hot summer days to escape the sun, or in rainy weather to escape the downpour; they should be swept and washed. . . . We have thus clarified disparagement and reverence in each case; *give to a wise man, and he will be yet wiser* (Proverbs 9:9): let one guard against any irreverent act similar to the examples of which our Sages have taught, and certainly against anything more serious (R. Eliezer of Metz, *Sefer Yere'im* 324).

7. . . . The synagogue is considered a little Sanctuary, as we learn further in the chapter (Megillah 29a). It is there-

---

3. To use it to reach other destinations, or for similar ulterior motives.
4. The latter two, to dry.

fore proscribed to demolish anything of the synagogue; for we read in *Sifre* (Deuteronomy 61): How do we learn that if one demolishes even one stone of the Temple, altar or court, he transgresses a negative precept? From the verses which state, *Ye shall break down their altars . . . . Ye shall not do so to the Lord your God* (Deuteronomy 12:3-4; *Mordechai,* Megillah 826).

❦ 4 ❦

The Principle of Separation

SOURCES IN TALMUD, MIDRASH AND COMMENTARIES

1.   R. LEVITAS OF YABNEH said: All that came to the Ark had the males separated from the females, for it is stated, *Noah went in and his sons, and his wife and his sons' wives* (Genesis 7:7)—the males were then to one side, and the females on another. When they went out, males and females were re-united, for it is stated, *Go forth from the ark, thou and thy wife, and thy sons and thy sons' wives, with thee* (*ibid.* 8:16)—man and wife together (*Pirke de-R. Eliezer* 23).

2.   *Then sang Moses and the sons of Israel*[1] *this song. . . . I will sing unto the Lord, for He is highly exalted. . . . And Miriam the prophetess . . . took a timbrel in her hand, and all the women went out after her. . . . And Miriam sang unto them: Sing ye to the Lord, for He is highly exalted* (Exodus 15:1, 20-21).

Miriam sang unto them: Scripture tells us that just as Moses sang praise for the men, so did Miriam chant for the women: *Sing ye to the Lord,* etc. (*Mechilta, Shirah,* end).

At the paean for [deliverance from] Egypt, the men pre-

---

1.   Literal translation.

ceded the women; at the paean of Deborah (Judges 5) the women preceded the men: for here deliverance came through men, as it is stated, *Moses and Aaron did all these wonders* (Exodus 11:10); there, however, it was women who brought deliverance—Deborah (Judges 4:6-10, 14) and the wife of Heber the Kenite (*ibid.* 17-22; *Lekah Tob,* Exodus 15:20).

3.   R. Pinhas said: The day before Sabbath, the Israelites stood at Mount Sinai arranged with the men apart and the women apart. [On the Monday before,] the Holy One (blessed be He) bade Moses, "Go, ask the daughters of Israel if they wish to accept the Torah": for usually men follow the opinion of women; as it is stated, *Thus shalt thou say to the house of Jacob* (Exodus 19:3), i.e., the women; *and tell the sons of Israel* (*ibid.*), i.e., the men . . . (*Pirke de-R. Eliezer* 41).

The day before Sabbath: At the beginning of chapter 46, this Midrash states that the Revelation, when the Torah was given, occurred on the day before Sabbath; it continues on the verse, *Thus shalt thou say,* etc., which occurred before the Revelation, on Monday, as we read in *Mechilta'* and Shabbath (86b); however, the statement that they stood arranged with the men and women separate, seems to refer definitely to the day of Revelation, for earlier there was no need for them to separate and stand apart. But because it wishes to interpret the verse that Moses was to speak to the women first, it begins by relating that on the sixth day the women also stood, arranged by themselves: hence Moses was bidden to speak to them apart, for they were also to attend the Revelation (R. David Luria, Commentary *ad loc.*).

Here is a most reliable source for the prohibition against men and women being mingled in the synagogue: If in the wilderness, at Mount Sinai, at an event as holy as the Revelation, our Sages say the men and women were separate, how much more necessary is such separation in our synagogues the

174

year round (R. Menahem M. Kasher, *Torah Shelemah*, XV, 94, Commentary §183).

4. R. Helbo said: On the day that Moses our Master (peace upon him) died, he wrote thirteen Torah scrolls, one scroll for every tribe, and noon had not yet come [when he was done]. He then called every tribe and bequeathed it the Torah and its precepts. That [thirteenth] Torah scroll [which remained], he put beside the Ark [in the Tabernacle]. He adjured and admonished every single [tribe] separately, the men apart and the women apart, saying to them: Be careful of the honor of the Torah and its precepts (*Midrash on the Passing of our Master Moses*).[2]

5. *Now there was a certain man of Ramathaim*, etc. (1 Samuel 1:1). Elkanah would go up [on pilgrimages to Jerusalem] four times a year: three by the Torah's precept (Deuteronomy 16:16), and one which he had taken on himself; as it is stated, *This man went up out of his city from year to year*, etc. (*ibid.* 3). Elkanah himself went up, and with him his wife, sons, daughters, brothers, sisters, relations in general, as well as all the members of his household. . . . Why did he take them all with him? When they went up on the way, they would camp for the night in a city square, and the men [of the city] would gather separately, and the women apart: for a man would talk with a man, and a woman with a woman, an adult with an adult, and a child with a child. The entire countryside would take notice of them, and would ask, "Whither do you go?" And they replied, "To the house of God that is

---

2. Reprinted in J. D. Eisenstein, *Otzar Midrashim*. A slightly different version is given in *Da'ath Zekenim* to Deuteronomy 31:26. For other passages indicating the separation of women see *Pesikta' Rabbathi* MS cited in *Sefer 'Aggadah* 373a; Tosefta 'Arachin 2, 1; Kiddushin 52b: "How would a woman come to be in the Men's Court?" as interpreted by Rashi, Me'iri and *Tosafoth R. Isaiah di Trani;* Sanhedrin 20a, Rashi and *Tosafoth* s.v. *nashim, ad loc.;* *Mordechai,* Sanhedrin 684; Jerusalem Talmud Sanhedrin 4, 4 (20b).

in Shiloh, from which Torah and precepts emanate; why do you not come with us, and we will go together?" At once their eyes would well with tears; they would ask, "Shall we go up with you?" And the reply would be, "Yes!" (*Seder Eliyahu Rabbah,* ed. Friedmann, 9).

6. A man should not stand among women and pray, because he will mind the women.[3] Let a man consecrate his camp four cubits to the north, four to the south, four to the east, and four to the west.[4] If he is within a house,[5] let him consecrate it entirely, even if it be 100 cubits; for it is stated, *The Lord thy God is a devouring fire*[6] (Deuteronomy 4:24, 9:3; *Seder Eliyahu Rabbah,* ed. Friedmann, 9).

7. Abbaye[7] set a row of jugs; Raba[8] arranged grass reeds (Kiddushin 81a).

Jugs: Where men and women would gather, either for the rabbi's lecture or for a wedding, he would arrange many earthenware pitchers between them, so that if they should approach each other, these would be struck, and would give off a sound. ... *arranged grass reeds* ... so that if anyone passed over them, their sound would be heard (Rashi *ad loc.*).

---

3. So *Zeth Ra'anan* on *Yalkut Shim'oni* 1, 934; literally, because of the mind of the women.

4. *Yalkut Shim'oni* reads: Let him rather consecrate his camp five cubits in each direction. But Berachoth 22b tends to confirm our reading.

5. *Yalkut Shim'oni* has: within his camp. Our reading suggests Berachoth 25b: an entire house is like the four cubits about one.

6. *Yalkut Shim'oni* cites: *the Lord thy God walketh in the midst of thy camp* (Deuteronomy 23:15).

7. Religious leader in Pumbaditha, 322-337.

8. Religious leader in Mehoza, 337-351.

❦ 5 ❦

Further on the Principle of Separation

SOURCES FROM GE'ONIC AND EARLY
(MEDIEVAL) COMMENTARIES

1. WHAT IS THE LAW about having men and women intermingled at a celebration? It is forbidden to do so; rather
must the men be apart and the women apart: for if at a time
of mourning, when there is lamentation and weeping, it is writ,
the land shall mourn, every family apart (Zechariah 12:12),
at a time of festivity and feasting, when there is happiness and
the Evil Impulse is rampant, how much more certainly must
each group be by itself, so that their inclination shall not contemplate sinning, at the joy of the feast (*Ma'asim li-Bene Eretz
Yisra'el,* ge'onic work, MS fragment in *Tarbitz,* I, 1, p. 97).

2. It is forbidden for women to mingle among the men,
either at a ritual meal or at any other occasion; rather must
women be apart and men apart, for we reason from the lesser
to the greater: if for a time of mourning it is written that the
House of Israel shall lament every family apart, *the House of
David apart and their wives apart,* how much more is separation
necessary at feasting and rejoicing, for then the Evil Impulse
is provocative (*Sefer ha-Pardes,* 19b).

3. Do not mingle sons amid daughters, lest they sin.
[We read:] *Then shall the virgin rejoice in the dance*—alone;
but *the young men and the old together* (Jeremiah 31:13). So
also, *boys and girls playing in its broad places* (Zechariah 8:5)—
boys apart and girls apart. And again toward the end of Psalms
(148:12), *Young men and also maidens;*[1] it does not read,
"Young men with maidens," like [the continuation], *old men*

---

1. Literal translation.

with children (*ibid.*). [The extra word] *also* signifies that, in addition, women should also be separate (*Sefer Hasidim,* ed. *Mekitze Nirdamim,* 60).

4.   Whoever would recite [before the Grace to a wedding meal] the benediction ["Let us bless our God] in whose dwelling is joy," must ascertain if Scripture's dictum, *rejoice with trembling* (Psalms 2:11), has been observed: if there is "trembling" [awe] in the place of rejoicing. But if he [the bridegroom] is marrying an unsuitable woman . . . or if women are sitting among the men, where there would be illicit thoughts, it is not fitting to say, "in whose dwelling is joy." Concerning people such as these is it said, *I sat not in the assembly of them that make merry, nor rejoiced* (Jeremiah 15:17); and again, *For all tables are filled with filthy disgorgement, and no place is clean* (Isaiah 28:8) . . . (*Sefer Hasidim,* ed. *Mekitze Nirdamim,* 1176).

5.   Our master R. Jacob the Levite said: Hence it was written as normative in *Sefer Rabiah* that it was the custom to permit spreading prayer robes[2] to separate men from women, on the Sabbath at the time of the rabbi's lecture, for the sake of chasteness (R. Jacob b. Moses Moelln, *Sefer Maharil,* Cremona 1565, 38a).

6.   It is forbidden to set up any screen whatever on the Sabbath, unless it is for chasteness in general . . . but a screen made for general chasteness is permitted: for example, the divider that is put up for the rabbi's lecture, between the men and the women, may be set up on the Sabbath (*Mordechai,* Shabbath, 311).

---

2.   Or perhaps, cloths or robes in general.

178

🎋 6 🎋

A Letter

BY RABBI DAVID OCHS

(*Translated by Rabbi Shapiro of Milwaukee*)

TO THE DISTINGUISHED MAN OF LETTERS who wages the battles of the Lord, Mr. Baruch Litvin: peace and blessing.

To my great regret I cannot undertake to be present at the time of the court suit, to have the honor of standing by you, as I am not in the best of health. May the Blessed One grant that His cause which you bear, the defense of the sanctities of our people, will meet with success.

In regard to your question, whether among the arguments of the opponents there are specious ones, let me say this: It is certainly impossible to arrive at any true decision in Halachah unless one believes in the sacred character of the Torah and its Halachah, and in its revelation at Sinai. Their attempts to interpret questions of immorality and indecency in Jewish law, and the Writ involved, differently from the way in which our Sages have interpreted, are naught but windblown distortion; they put a construction on Torah that is at variance with our sacred ancestral Halachah.

The sources of the prohibition against praying in a synagogue without a *mechitzah* (physical separation) or a women's gallery, are all known. In the Talmud, Sukkah 51b, it is clearly indicated that even before the "great amendment" was made[1] there was a partition which separated the men from the women, for originally one group was without and another within. The amendment was instituted to prevent any possibility of levity at any time.

---

1. [For the passage in full see above, source 1, §2.]

In a passage cited from *Seder Eliyahu Rabbah* 9 in *Yalkut Shim'oni* I, 934 we read: One should not stand among women and pray because he will mind the women; he should rather sanctify his site five cubits on each side; and if he is within his own camp let him sanctify it in its entirety, for it is stated, *The Lord thy God walketh in the midst of thy camp* (Deuteronomy 23:15). . . .

It is clear from this passage that on public grounds, which can be but a transient setting for prayer, if no alternative is possible, it is sufficient to set off a distance of five cubits all around; but as for a synagogue, it must be sanctified in entirety, so that one cannot come to entertain illicit thoughts.

In his responsum[2] R. Moshe Feinstein has written that in every synagogue where a state of levity can be reached, the Scriptural precept *My sanctuary shall ye reverence* (Leviticus 19:30, 26:2) is being violated, for the synagogue is a sanctuary-in-miniature. All this applies even when the women are dressed properly, in accordance with Jewish law. However, if they are not so dressed, then even in one's own house is it forbidden to recite the *shema'*, and all the more certainly in the synagogue, a dwelling place for holiness; for according to a prior passage cited in *Yalkut Shim'oni* (*loc. cit.*) such unholiness would deprive the synagogue of its sacred character: it reads, *That He see no unseemly thing in thee, and turn away from thee* (Deuteronomy 23:15)—this teaches us that indecency repels the Divine Presence (*Sifre, Debarim* 258).

The view of *Mordechai* to Megillah 28a is that the Torah itself equates the sanctity of the synagogue with that of the Temple. Perhaps this is also the thought of Maimonides when he writes in his enumeration of the precepts, at the beginning of his Code, negative precept 65: [We are obligated] not to destroy

---

2. [Reprinted in this volume as source 15 to chapter II.]

the Sanctuary, synagogues, or Houses of Study . . . for it is stated, *Ye shall surely destroy all the places wherein the nations . . . served their gods. . . . Ye shall not do so unto the Lord your God* (Deuteronomy 12:2, 4).

Even R. Nissim, who in his Novellae to Megillah 26 holds that a synagogue is holy only by Rabbinic ordinance, has himself ruled in a responsum that during prayer the synagogue is sacred by Biblical law.

Moreover, the desire to remove the *mechitzah* touches on the violation of the many injunctions of the Torah that *neither shall ye walk in their* [the nations'] *statutes* (Leviticus 18:3), as Maimonides enumerates them in his Code, *Hilchoth 'Abodah Zarah* 11. There is also a ban against demolishing any part of the Temple, etc. This has all been dealt with at length in the Responsa of *Maharam Schick, Orah Hayyim* 71, which see in its entirety, as well as 77,[3] where he is most emphatic about such innovations. See also the Responsa titled *Dibre Hayyim,* I, 3, that even if the synagogue is holy by Rabbinic law alone, nevertheless the demolition of a synagogue or any part of it is Biblically forbidden.

In any case, *Maharam Schick* has already written that the matter does not depend on the severity of the transgression, for we have been adjured to observe a "minor" precept as carefully as an "important" one.

As for the argument that even in orthodox synagogues study groups are held for men and women together, and this is also considered "Divine service" or "worship"—it is true that study is also a form of Divine service, as Maimonides has written in his *Sefer ha-Mitzvoth,* positive precept 5: ". . . *to serve him* (Deuteronomy 11:13) denotes prayer, and it denotes study. . . . Serve Him through His Torah, serve Him in His Sanctuary."

---

3. [Reprinted below as source 12.]

Nevertheless there are distinctions; for there are three types of service: (1) sacrificial offerings at the Temple; (2) study of the Torah; (3) prayer, which is called the service of the heart—and each one has special laws. Proof is that only for group prayer is a *minyan,* a quorum of at least ten, needed, but not for group study of Torah.

In support of this the opinion of the *Bayith Hadash* may be cited. He states in *Eben ha-Ezer* 62 (quoted in *Beth Shmu'el* 11) that one should not recite the formula, *she-ha-simhah bi-m'ono* [in whose dwelling is the rejoicing—usually said in the Grace after a wedding meal] if there is no separation between men and women, for there is no Divine joy where the Evil Inclination has dominion; however, the *sheba' berachoth,* the seven wedding benedictions, are to be pronounced, as his words plainly indicate. It is clear then that the prohibition here under discussion applies only to prayer in the synagogue with women present, because of the necessary sanctity of the "camp" and reverence of the Sanctuary-in-miniature.

I am in prayer that the Almighty awaken the hearts of His people to return to Him in truth; and may He vouchsafe you His Divine aid.

I close with greetings to you and yours.

ꙮ 7 ꙮ

On Laws which are Common Knowledge

BY RABBI MOSES BEN MAIMON (MAIMONIDES)

THE LAWS of *tzitzith* [fringes; Numbers 15:38], *tefillin* [phylacteries; Deuteronomy 6:8, 11:18] and *mezuzah* [the scroll on the door-post; *ibid.* 6:9, 11:20], the manner of making them, the blessings that must be recited over them, and all other matters of law connected with them, as well as what has been said about them in responsa—all these are not, properly speaking, subjects for discussion here, according to the adopted purpose of this work; for it is but a commentary, and the Mishnah does not speak of these precepts in particular, to include their especial laws, so that it should require explanatory commentary. The reason for this [silence of the Mishnah], it seems to me, is that these matters were common knowledge at the time the Mishnah was composed; they were known and practiced by the entire people, in general and in particular, and not one detail was beyond anyone's ken; therefore he [the redactor of the Mishnah] saw no need to speak of them, just as he did not set down the order of the prayers, or what the reader of the congregation should do, for this was all common knowledge; hence no order of prayers was composed, but rather the Gemara [as a commentary on the Mishnah] and its explanation (Maimonides, *Commentary to Mishnah*, Menahoth 4, 1).

8

Responsum to an American Rabbi

BY RABBI MENAHEM MENDEL HAYYIM LANDA

TO MY ESTEEMED FRIEND AND PUPIL, R. Raphael Abigdor Landa, Manchester, New Hampshire: Your letter has reached me, in which you write of those who brazenly do away entirely with the women's section in the synagogue, pray with men and women seated intermingled, and yet call themselves orthodox, claiming that they nullify no law of our Codes, because in our compilations of laws it is not mentioned at all that there must be a women's section, especially for women.

Know that these are *a brood of sinful men* (Numbers

32:14), who wish to break through the "fences" of our fathers, in order to be like the non-Jews; they would uproot the guards for chasteness which have ever distinguished our ancestors.

The matter is explicitly indicated in the Mishnah, Middoth 2, 5 which deals with the Court of the Women in the Sanctuary: "It was bare originally, and then they surrounded it with a balcony, so that the women could look on from above and the men from below, and then they would not be mingled." It is clarified in Sukkah 51b: "What was the great amendment? Said R. Eleazar: As we learned . . . Originally, the women were within and the men without, and they came to be frivolous; it was then ordained that the men sit outside and the women within, but they yet reached a state of frivolity; then it was ordained that the women sit above and the men below. [Then it was asked,] How could this be done? etc. [We derive from a verse that the original Temple plans might not be altered.] Said Rab, They [the Sages] found a verse which they interpreted, etc.[1] If in the [Messianic] future when people will be engaged in mourning, and the Evil Inclination will have no power over them, the Torah declares that men and women should be separate, now that they were involved in festivity, how much more necessary was such separation."

Now, in the *Shulhan Aruch* (Code of laws) there is no mention that a women's section is to be provided in the synagogue, because the *Shulhan Aruch* notes only matters which *must* be observed. But there is no absolute obligation to have a women's section in the synagogue, since women are legally exempt from group prayer.[2] However, this custom was automatically adopted everywhere: to have a separate section for

1. [For the continuation see above, source 1, B §2.]
2. [Hence a synagogue may well remain without a women's section if no women attend. This has been the practice to this day in many Houses of Prayer of the Hasidim.]

the women who would come to pray although not required to do so—just as women have stringently accepted the precepts of *shofar* and *lulab*. This section is generally made as it was in the Sanctuary: to have the women on an upper level and the men on a lower, so that they will not mingle.

This is obviously most stringent a matter if the Sages permitted erecting a balcony [in the Sanctuary] although it was generally forbidden to add anything to the Temple structure as it had been made by the builders in prophetic times. No matter what—once women also came to that court, for the Festivity of Water-Drawing for Libation, the Sages permitted an addition to the structure so that there could be no mingling of men and women—as the Talmud in Sukkah clearly states.

Actually, it appears that in the Sanctuary, originally, the women's court was not at all reserved particularly for women; the outer court was merely called that of the women because the latter were permitted to come there. Farther within, beyond the wall, however, women did not go: according to Rashi (Kiddushin 52b, s.v. *vechi 'ishah*) because they were forbidden there; according to *Tosafoth* (*loc. cit.*) because they were not in the habit of going there. And so the outer court was called the Women's Court, because their custom was to go there if they happened to come; but it was not a fixed place for women alone, as it was not their habit to come regularly to the court. And under Bible law, it did not have the sanctity of a regular court; if we find in the Mishnah, Kelim 1, that the Women's Court was hallowed, it was by Rabbinic enactment, as is indicated in Yebamoth 7b. . . .

Now originally no amendment was needed there, since women came only infrequently, by happenstance. It was only in the later generations that women betook themselves to the court with greater regularity, and especially after the Sages instituted the Festivity of Water-Drawing for Libation to remove the belief of the Sadducees, who held heretical views about the libation of water. Then many women would come to see this religious rejoicing. And it was seen that although they did not actually mingle, for the women sat within and the men in the outer part, they nevertheless reached a state of levity. Then was it ordained to erect a balcony and have the women above, etc. Now the balcony was made in the women's court itself, and the men too sat in that court, below; it was not at all designated especially for women. Further, entry to the court of the men was only by way of the women's court; there was no other way to get to that court. Thus it was not in the least peculiarly a *women's* court; it was so called only because the end of this court was as far as women went when they came to the Temple.

And so in the synagogue there is no obligation to have a women's section; it is only that since generations before our time women have grown accustomed to come to pray in the synagogue. Therefore the practice was instituted to have a section for women on an upper level, or even at the side, but separated by a complete physical partition.

The proper way is to endeavor with soft words to correct these people's erroneous views, and to show them that what they do runs counter to an enactment of our Sages yet from the time of the Temple.

May peace dwell amid the people Israel.

☙ 9 ❧

On Public Iniquity

1. IDLE CONVERSATION, which means even any secular talk for the sake of one's livelihood, which is permissible elsewhere, is forbidden in the synagogue; and especially so con-

versation that is altogether idle, from which it is always fitting
to refrain. The holy Zohar on pericope *vayyakhel* enlarges on
the great seriousness of this sin.[1] And in the synagogue or House
of Study one should certainly beware of the sin of forbidden
talk, such as malicious gossip, talebearing, quarreling or discord:
for not only are these great sins in their own right, but the
wrongdoing is so much greater in the hallowed place, since the
honor of the Shechinah (Divine Presence) is thus deprecated.
There is no comparison between sinning alone, by oneself, and
transgressing in the royal palace, in the presence of the king.
And the evil is here so much greater, since many are brought
to grief by crimes such as these . . . (*Mishnah Berurah* 151, 2).

2. In the Midrash (*Bereshith Rabbah* 50, 7) we read:
This one came to sojourn and he would play the judge (Genesis
19:9)—the law which the early inhabitants enacted, you come
to undo. Said R. Menahem in R. Bibi's name: Thus had the
people of Sodom agreed among themselves: they said, Whatever
traveller stops off here, we will use him immorally and arrogate
his money.[2] . . . They were entirely bent, then, on abolishing
hospitality from their midst and having no one come there from
anywhere at all. . . . Now this clarifies Ezekiel's meaning when
he says, *Behold, this was the iniquity of thy sister Sodom, etc;
neither did she strengthen the hand of the poor and needy*
(Ezekiel 16:49); he means that they made this their law and
norm. . . . That night they followed their usual practice, and
their measure of sin overflowed, for it was filled from before

---

1. The passage reads: Once the holy congregation has gone up into
the synagogue [on the Sabbath] it is forbidden to be occupied with anything,
even the needs of the synagogue, except matters of doxology, prayer and
Torah, as it is fitting. If a person takes up other matters, worldly matters,
this is a man who is desecrating the Sabbath; he has no portion amid the people
Israel. Two angels are assigned to him on the Sabbath day; and they rest
their hands on his head and say, Woe to so-and-so, who has no share with
the Holy One, blessed be He (Zohar II, 205b).

2. Or, more likely, his wealth, goods, possessions, etc.

with every kind of casual and wilful iniquity, and thus they incurred annihilation. From here we derive a satisfactory explanation about the men of Gibeah (Judges 19-20): for if they followed the practice of the Sodomites in these two respects, namely, to put an end to anyone's passing through, and to permit this bestiality, such practice was not made part of their statutes, and was not sanctioned by their laws, perish the thought; they were rather like a people with good laws who do not, however, observe them. Therefore we need not puzzle why brimstone and fire did not rain down on them from the Lord in His heaven; yet by their own laws this [action of theirs] was a criminal offence, and the judges of the city or the tribe were obligated to extirpate them from this world; since these judges looked on and did not seek to stay their hand, or they closed their eyes to what was done so openly, the guilt lay on the entire tribe,[3] and it was the blessed Lord's will to visit retribution upon all, once those who sought justice were satisfied. And this is the rule for any transgression which individuals in any group may commit, violating some one of the Torah's prohibitions, such as drinking non-kosher wine, eating non-kosher cheese, wearing clothes of wool and linen (Leviticus 19:9, Deuteronomy 22:11), etc. If the blind eye which the judges and leaders turn on this practice gives the transgressors tacit permission, as though they were allowed by law, then the sins of the individual have been converted into the group sins of all. . . . Indeed, if but public opinion accords with it, and it becomes the rule of the courts to raise no objections, then the smallest sin becomes a statutory crime and wickedness, and is the iniquity of the entire group; it can find atonement only through retribution upon the group, as it happened with the Benjaminites for their participation in

---

3. The original has "tribes"—perhaps in the sense that the other tribes were required to redress the great wrong by waging a war of annihilation against the tribe of Benjamin.

the sin. . . . It were therefore far better that those who sin with their very souls be decimated, burnt or stoned, rather than let one letter of the Torah be uprooted with public consent. . . . He who does not accept this has no share of understanding and no portion in the Godly Torah (R. Isaac Ar'amah, *Akedath Yitzhak,* I, 20).

10

On Chasteness, Immodesty and Indecency

SOURCES FROM TALMUD AND CODES

1. SAID R. ISAAC: A handbreadth of a woman's body [if exposed] constitutes an indecency. In regard to what? If we say in regard to gazing at her, R. Shesheth has already stated: Why did the Writ list outer jewelry together with intimate jewelry [in Numbers 31:50]? To inform you that whoever gazes at [even] the little finger of a woman, it is as if he stared licentiously. Rather does this apply to one's own wife, in regard to reciting the *shema'*. R. Hisda said: The leg of a woman [if exposed] constitutes an indecency, for it is written, *uncover the leg, pass through the rivers* (Isaiah 47:2), and Scripture continues, *Thy nakedness shall be uncovered, yea, thy shame shall be seen* (*ibid.* 3). Samuel said: A woman's voice [singing][1] is sensually arousing, for it is stated, *sweet is thy voice,*[2] *and thy countenance is comely* (Song of Songs 2:14).[3] R. Shesheth said: A woman's hair is sensually arousing [if visible], for it is

1. So *Me'iri* and *Shittah Mekubetzeth ad loc.*

2. Since the verse praises her for this, it is apparent that this makes her desirable (Rashi).

3. In the version of the Jerusalem Talmud, Hallah 1, 4, the proof-text is Jeremiah 3:9, *from the voice of harlotry the land was polluted.*

stated, *thy hair is as a flock of goats*[4] (*ibid.* 4:1; Berachoth 24a).

2. If a handbreadth of a woman's body [is revealed] in a part which is usually covered, even if she is one's own wife, it is forbidden to recite the *shema'* in her presence. If the hair of a woman's head which is usually covered [is visible], it is forbidden to recite the *shema'* in her presence (even if she is one's own wife).[5] . . . One should beware of hearing a woman singing while he recites the *shema'* (R. Joseph Caro, *Shulhan 'Aruch 'Orah Hayyim* 75, 1-3).

3. . . . *thou shalt keep thee from every evil thing* (Deuteronomy 23:11)—[this indicates] that a man should gaze neither at a beautiful woman, even if she be unmarried, nor at a married woman, even if she be ugly, nor yet at the colorful clothes of a woman [for he will remember the woman as she looks in them, how they beautify her, and his thoughts will dwell on her].[6] . . . R. Judah quoted Samuel: Even if they are hung on the wall ('Abodah Zarah 20a).

4. It is the practice in Cracow that at the meal [in honor of the groom and bride] given on the second night [after the wedding] one recites the blessing, *who hast created joy and gladness* [following the Grace after the meal] but not [*Blessed be our God*] *in whose dwelling is gladness*, [before the Grace]. This is puzzling, and I have found no explanation for it, unless it is because this is a small meal and the men and women are seated together in one room, and it is written in the Customs that the blessing, *in whose dwelling is gladness*, is not recited where thoughts of transgression are suspected (R. Joel Sirkes, *Bayith Hadash* to *Tur 'Eben ha-'Ezer* 62, s.v. *ve-yesh 'omrim*, end).

---

4. See note 2.
5. Gloss of R. Moses Isserles.
6. Rashi *ad loc.*

5. The [author of] *Bayith Hadash* has written that when men and women are in one chamber, the blessing *in whose dwelling is gladness* is not to be said, for there is no gladness where the Evil Impulse is rampant (*Beth Shmu'el* to *Shulhan Aruch 'Eben ha-'Ezer* 62, 11).

⚜ 11 ⚜

The Women's Section in the Synagogue

AS MENTIONED IN TALMUD AND EARLY (MEDIEVAL) AUTHORITIES

1. SAID R. JUDAH: Whoever did not see the Diplaston [basilica synagogue] of Alexandria has never in his days seen the glory of Israel. It was like a great basilica,[1] having a colonnade within a colonnade; at times it held twice as many as had left Egypt. . . . Who laid it waste? The wicked Trajan . . . [his] legions surrounded it and slew them [the men within]. Said he to their wives, Yield yourselves to my legions, and I will not slay you. They retorted, What you did on the ground do on the upper level.[2] He thereupon merged their [the women's] blood with theirs [the men's], and the sea ran red until Cyprus (Jerusalem Talmud, Sukkah 5, 1).

2. It is the custom of some men to sleep in the synagogue [the night of *Yom Kippur*] for during most of the night they recite psalms, hymns and prayers of praise; some do so for the sake of guarding the candles [they sleep there to guard that none

---

1. I.e., it had two areas separated by ranges of columns, with a raised platform at one end. According to S. Krauss (*Synagogale Alteruemer*) the Jews adopted this Greek style of architecture for synagogue construction, and eventually the early Christians copied it from the Jews.

2. It is thus clear from this tragic account that the men were generally below, and the women on a gallery. This tallies with archaeological findings of the synagogues of second century Galilee; see chapter IV.

191

of the many candles sets fire to the synagogue] . . . and such was the practice of our master R. Me'ir [b. Baruch Rothenberg], although he would sleep at the western end [of the synagogue], far from the place of prayer, or in the women's synagogue when there were no women there (*Hagahoth Maimunioth* to *Mishneh Torah, Hilchoth Shebithath 'Asor*, end, s.v. *kol nidre*).

3. Three are believed on [the identity of] a firstborn [among twins, etc.], viz., the midwife, his father and his mother: the midwife, immediately [after birth] . . . (Kiddushin 74a): I have heard the ruling, derived from this, that a person is believed about whatever he is occupied with, and no other, as in the case of the midwife. This applies practically to . . . matters occurring in the women's synagogue, about which we would rely on women's testimony (R. Alexander Zuslin ha-Kohen, *Sefer ha-'Agudah* 106a-b).

4. Our master R. Jacob the Levite [Moelln] said that it was strange, past his understanding, whence came this bad custom of people to bring the little children to the synagogue, so that they should hear the sound of the *shofar*. This is well and good for the reading of the Scroll of Esther, when it is done for the sake of merriment; but why here? only when small children reach the age for education is it obligatory to train them. And so, if a woman cannot leave her child at home, it is better if she keeps him in the women's synagogue (R. Jacob b. Moses Moelln, *Maharil*, Cremona 1569, 50b).

5. Our master R. Jacob the Levite preached that it is a custom for the people to spend the night of *kol nidre* [*Yom Kippur*] in the synagogue, to recite a great many hymns of praise . . . and if one would go to sleep let him go off to the western end, away from the place of prayer, or to the women's synagogue when there are no women there (*ibid.* 59b).

6. . . . In your city, however, where the women's synagogue is in the [wine] cellar of the sexton, [lighting candles there]

192

would be considered for the sake of the meal,[3] in order to [be able to] draw wine at night; this is the more certainly so if [Sabbath candles] are lit in a women's synagogue near the wine . . . (*idem,* Responsa of *Maharil* 53).

7. Leah and Rachel[4] are disputing over seats in the women's synagogue: Leah has brought two women [to attest] that the seats are hers, while Rachel has proffered a man who testifies that the seats are hers. Which testimony is the weightier, that of the two women or the man's?

Response: The law would seem to depend on the present possession of the seats . . . if Leah now holds these seats, and Rachel is trying to wrest them from her, Leah need not even take an oath to refute Rachel's witness . . . for since Leah has two women attesting to her claim, she is free of any obligation. Now, although generally a woman's testimony is legally invalid, in this case, where they would be wont to observe more accurately than men, they are well believed. . . . It would seem that regarding seats in the women's synagogue as well [as in similar cases] men are not likely to know which seat belongs to which woman . . . (R. Israel Isserlein, *Terumath ha-Deshen*, I, 353).

❊ 12 ❊

A Responsum on a Changed Mechitzah

BY MAHARAM (RABBI MOSES) SCHICK

Hust, Hungary, 1878

NOW [AS I UNDERSTAND IT] this is your inquiry: Brazen members of a certain congregation have hitherto had their

---

3. And therefore permissible and in order, since Sabbath candles must ordinarily be lit for the Sabbath meal.

4. Random names to designate two women, like "Jane Doe." For an earlier reference to women's remaining apart during prayer, see *Tosafoth* to Rosh Hashanah 27b, s.v. *veshama'*.

shops closed on the sacred Sabbath; now certain wicked men have dared to set hand to the partition which divides the women's section from the men's [in the synagogue], so that there will no longer be a complete separation by boards but only by slats, permitting people to see and be seen. Many say that, with the blessed Lord's help, I can battle them with a strong hand, but the wicked ones threaten to secede from the community and begin at once to have their shops open on the Sabbath too—which may easily lead others as well to violate the sacred Sabbath. Hence you know not what plan to devise, how to act in accord with the Law: to battle them and let them go to the devil—give the wicked rope and let him hang himself[1]—or perhaps, since others will emulate them and be ensnared by their influence, it were better to keep silent.

It were sacrilege for you righteous men to keep silent on this insolent breach by the brazen ones! for it is by law that we are required to separate the men's section from the women's, as it was in the Sanctuary, each section apart. In those days, when they had the Festivity of Water for Libation, a "great amendment" was instituted [i.e., a balcony for the women] as we read in the Talmud, Sukkah 51b; it is there derived from a Scriptural verse that an amendment was needed so that the men should not see the women, since they could thus be led to a state of levity and further transgressions.

These brazen violators also transgress the Bible's admonition, *Ye shall not do so unto the Lord your God*[2] (Deuteronomy 12:4), since the synagogue is a sanctuary—a "sanctuary-in-miniature."

There is a duty to protest such action, and to chastise the transgressors. Those righteous men who have it in their

---

1. [Literally, Give the wicked one his fill to swallow, and let him die.]
2. [This follows the command to destroy the temples and idols of the conquered heathen nations.]

power to object strenuously [and do not] are disobeying the positive command, *Thou shalt surely rebuke thy neighbor* (Leviticus 19:17); indeed this applies to anyone in whose power it lies to protest. Further, we have it as law in *Shulhan Aruch Yoreh De'ah* 157 that when such people fail to protest it is as if they committed the crime themselves, and they are caught up in the guilt.

Granting even that these wicked men speak truth, that for the sake of the change in the partition they will not open their places of business on the Sabbath, it is nevertheless an established rule that we may not say to a man, "Sin so that your fellow will win merit," where it means wilful transgression; this is clarified in *Magen Abraham* 306, 28-9. How much more does this apply in our case, where it might be said, "Since the rabbis were silent we may conclude that it was acceptable to them"; this would be a desecration of His Name, especially in our generation, when the insolent transgressors are determined about this violation. This might well be likened to the Jewish custom about a shoelace, for which one is obligated to sacrifice his life if need be (Sanhedrin 74b).

Yet more than this: it is an established decision, since most authorities agree with R. Moses Isserles in *Shulhan Aruch Yoreh De'ah* 334, 1, that if one has incurred excommunication he is to be excommunicated, even if there is reason to fear that as a result he may leave the faith. Had we the authority to excommunicate these insolent transgressors, we would be obligated to do so, as is clear from the source cited (*ibid.* 43): one of the twenty-four crimes which warrant excommunication is contemning even the words of the Sages. But we most certainly have no right to accede to their demands, since silence is tantamount to consent; and if they secede, why, let them secede.

I have written thus far according to the view of the esteemed questioner. But in truth we well know that this would be but the beginning of their breach of the Torah's word; one sin draws another in its wake (Aboth 4, 2). As our Sages (of blessed memory) said, "This is the *metier* of the Evil Tempter: today he tells one, Do this; tomorrow he bids him, Do that— until he says to him, Go and worship idols" (Shabbath 105b) or, Desecrate the Sabbath, which is equivalent to idolatory. [Of them] is it written, *Whose mouths speaketh falsehood, and their right hand is a right hand of lying* (Psalms 144:11). If they separate from the congregation, it will be a fine departure for them and for all. And should the income of the community stand to be diminished as a result, nothing impedes the Lord from helping, through many or a few. The Lord will give blessing to those who uphold His Torah, as is His desire. . . .

☙ 13 ❧

Concerning a Thin Partition

BY RABBI HILLEL LICHTENSTEIN

Friday, New Moon Day, Adar 1873, Kolomea, Austria; to my dear, beloved friend, the reverent scholar R. Wolf Leb . . . peace:

YOU ASK with your very soul, if it is permitted to enter a synagogue where the partition (*mechitzah*) dividing the women's section from the men's is so gossamer thin that the men can see the women—i.e., if one is not of the defiant transgressors, but wishes to submit to the verdict of the *beth din* (religious court).

I do not know what there is to question here. It has already been clearly stated that it is forbidden to make the partition in such a way that the men can regard the women, and if the

196

partition has already been so made, one should not enter there. This applies all the more strongly in your instance, for originally the division there was thick and well made, and people changed it with the intention of [thus] joining the violators and innovators. . . . Moreover, even if there is not a single woman in the synagogue, it is forbidden to enter and pray there: for on account of this wilful violation it has become desecrated and is no longer a "sanctuary in miniature."

Since I find your words so appealing, I will answer insofar as my poor hand is able. Now you are stirred by the question, Why were curtains not put up at the Festivity of the Water for Libation, in the Temple, so that the men could not gaze at the women? The answer seems to me to lie in Maimonides' comment to the Mishnah, Sukkah 5, 2: "A great amendment— i.e., of great value, because the people used to prepare a location for men and another for women; and the place for the women was above the one for the men, in order that the men should not gaze at the women." If we note his language carefully, we see that he could have said simply, "the place for the women was above, in order that the men" etc.; why state, "the place for the women was above *the one for the men*"? It therefore seems to me that Maimonides means just this: it was arranged for the men to sit precisely underneath the balconies, but not beyond them, for if the latter the men could still have stared upward. He therefore is intentionally specific [to intimate that the] location for the men was only the space underneath the balconies. . . . Hence there was no need for a partition. . . .

Do not take it to heart or take it ill that you will pray alone; for the Writ says, *Better is a dinner of herbs where love is, than a stalled ox and hatred therewith* (Proverbs 15:17). God grant us the merit to see Him fulfill His word for all: that *the Lord thy God will circumcise thy heart . . . to love the Lord thy God with all thy heart* (Deuteronomy 30:6).

On the Grave Importance of Mechitzah

BY RABBI ELIYAHU GUTTMACHER

I WAS FURTHER ASKED: In the synagogue there, a *mechitzah* was erected to partition the men's section from the women's; however, it was to be but eighteen cubits high [about five and one half feet] so that from the shoulders up the women would be easily visible from the men's section. Now you are in some doubt on this, insofar as opinion [on related matters] is divided in *Shulhan Aruch Orah Hayyim* 75.

Now, first let me convey that by the views you hold this can in no way be permissible, since the exposed women's hair would legally constitute an indecency. If R. Moses Isserles expresses a lenient view in this regard because women's hair is wont to extend beyond the bounds of the head-covering, this offers but scant permission: for such is not the way of reverent, wholly observant women, but rather of the brazen. Perhaps, though, in his locality such permission became widespread.

Yet, granting for the moment that his view can be stretched to somehow sanction our case, what can we say when women go about with bared backs? And as regards the wife of one's fellow, even if less than a handbreadth is improperly exposed, it legally constitutes indecency. *Magen Abraham* (*Shulhan Aruch, loc. cit.*) writes that even under thick covering, if part of a women's body is visible, a ban exists. In paragraph 6 there the *Shulhan Aruch* states that with closed eyes it is permissible to pray under such circumstances; but *Ture Zahab, Magen Abraham* and *Eliyahu Rabbah* (*loc. cit.*), by whose words we live, differ decisively with this view; *Peri Hadash* (*ibid.*) adduces proofs aplenty that shutting the eyes does not bring permission [to recite the *shema'* and pray]. . . .

So much can be said, then, in behalf of a lenient view, based on *Shulhan Aruch Orah Hayyim* 75. But alack and alas if permission is thus extracted from this source. Were the *Shulhan Aruch* to grant full, unequivocal permission, it would yet not cover our case: for that Code treats only of an instance where *it happens by chance* that a man must recite the *shema'* [under such circumstances; then the question is] shall he recite it or not. But to establish such a situation in the synagogue to begin with, as a fixed state of affairs—·to invite the Evil Inclination into a sacred place—this is certainly forbidden. There are parallel instances in the laws of *kashruth* involving meat and milk, where if something has happened, the food may yet be eaten, but to deliberately make this happen remains forbidden.

Our case is even more severe, for the Talmud states explicitly: R. Isaac said, A handbreadth of a woman's body constitutes an indecency [if exposed; and it is asked,] To what does he refer? Shall we say, staring at a woman? but R. Shesheth has already declared . . . Scripture tells you that whoever stares even at a woman's little finger, it is as if he stares licentiously. Rather, then, he refers to one's own wife when one must recite the *shema'* (Berachoth 24a). If such a sight sullies the eyes, can there be a greater desecration than to regard women in a gathering for the sake of Heaven? *O, the Heavens be confounded at this* (Jeremiah 2:12). See what the Talmud says: *Thou shalt keep thee from every evil thing* (Deuteronomy 23:10)—[this means] that a man should not regard a beautiful woman though she be single, nor a married woman though she be ugly, nor yet the colored raiments of a woman; said R. Judah in Samuel's name: even if these last are hung on the wall, if he but recognizes their owner (Abodah Zarah 20a). Maimonides (*Hilchoth 'Issure Bi'ah* 21) and the

199

Shulhan Aruch (*'Eben ha-'Ezer* 21) cite these rules as normative law. What argument can yet be advanced when in such
a case women will be in view bedecked with hats and jewelry—
in the synagogue, in the House of the Lord?

Can it be right for a man to go up and take a Torah
scroll from the Ark, and then turn around, and standing elevated before the sacred Ark, have women in his vision and
come to entertain alien thoughts—all the while holding the
Torah which writes of capital punishments by Heaven and
beth din (Jewish religious court) for immorality? Shall *kohanim*
(priests) go up to give the priestly blessing and have their
vision encounter defiling immodesty? And if they are supposed
to close their eyes and not dare to look up, lest they see the
women, the enormity of the snare is only too plain: for this very
action will arouse within them impure thoughts at a time when
extra holiness is needed, when they should fulfill the written injunction, *Sanctify yourselves and be ye holy* (Leviticus 11:44,
20:7); as the Sages interpreted it: If a man sanctifies himself
slightly, he becomes greatly hallowed; if he sanctifies himself
here, below, he is hallowed from above; if he sanctifies himself
in the present world he will be hallowed in the future world[1]
(Yoma 39). If eyes must be shut against the sight of women and
their raiments all about the *kohanim,* there will rather be fulfilled
Scripture's admonition, *Neither shall ye make yourselves unclean
with them, that ye should be defiled thereby* (Leviticus 11:43),
[which is interpreted:] If a man defiles himself somewhat, he will
become very unclean; if he defiles himself here, below, he will
become impure from above; if he defiles himself in the present
world, he will be defiled in the future world.

What more need we than to ponder this Talmudic passage:

---

1. [Since the verse is apparently redundant in its repetition, these
interpretations give it the sense, If you sanctify yourselves, you will be hallowed. Similarly the verse and interpretations which follow.]

200

They [the Sages] came across a verse and interpreted it: *And the land shall mourn, every family apart: the family of the house of David apart, and their wives apart* (Zechariah 12:12). Said they: Can we not reason from the lesser to the greater? If in the [Messianic] future when they will be occupied with mourning, and the Evil Inclination will have no sway over them, the Torah says that men and women shall be separate, now that people are engaged in festivity, and they are subject to the Evil Inclination, how much more certainly must they be separate (Sukkah 52a). If our Sages spoke thus when the women did not go with heads or backs bared, what is there for us to say? Is it not the purpose of present-day women to thus attract men's glances? The synagogue would then become a place of which the Lord might well say, *Who hath required this of your hand, to trample My courts? Your new moons and your appointed seasons My soul hateth. . . . And when ye spread forth your hands*—[to give the priestly benediction]—*I will hide Mine eyes from you* (Isaiah 1:12, 14, 15). As the *kohanim* shut their eyes on such sights, so will the Lord shut His eyes [so to speak] to their blessing.

Many years ago I was asked by a Godfearing man to write to his rabbi (of blessed memory) because of this very question: a short partition—but a huge breach of the Law—was to be installed in the synagogue, to separate the women's section. I gladly complied with the request; but the rabbi consulted his wife, and she frightened him against opposing the innovation. In the end the Lord visited upon him the iniquities of all the congregation; as our Sages say, "the righteous man is seized for the sin of the generation"; *those close about Him are judged most critically, to a hair* (Psalms 50:3):[2] for he would not wage

---

2. [The word *nis'arah* is here connected with *sa'ar*, hair, to yield this meaning. Jewish Publication Society renders: *round about Him it stormeth mightily*.]

the battle of the Lord. The very season in which the new synagogue building was completed, standing before the Ark on the Sabbath of Repentance to preach, a sudden and strange death seized him (may we be spared), and he was taken lifeless from the pulpit. His great righteousness merited this much, that he should not preach in such a synagogue.

Therefore, O my brethren, do not commit evil; betray not the Lord. Let your ears hear what you utter, as the Law requires of you, when you say, *And thou shalt love the Lord thy God with all thy heart and with all thy soul* (Deuteronomy 6:5). Do you then fear that the women can decrease your earnings or your esteem? Cry out to them that they should take care, and not go at all to such a synagogue. The women will heed if you but appeal to them out of heartfelt distress, as though they were going to deprive you of a livelihood; and you will find that the Lord is with you.

It is incumbent on me to inform you, and all your congregation equally—men, women and children—that I am of greater authority for your community than other rabbis. The matter cannot remain as it is; let poles be set up at the ends, and a beam be put on them; a lattice is to go in the middle, and let curtains hang over all.

If for our many iniquities one breach has been made in our sacred tradition, and the center has been abolished from many synagogues—something most strictly prohibited, for which the guilty congregations will have no answer at judgment—nevertheless, whatever can be repaired to return the synagogue to its original state of grace, we are required to repair.

202

ꙮ 15 ꙮ

A Responsum from Sanz, 1864

BY RABBI HAYYIM HALBERSTAM

the renowned Hasidic leader of Sanz

TO THE WORTHY, distinguished and reverent seekers of the Torah's truth, the esteemed heads of the Jewish community of Miskolcz: Your letter has reached me, in which you ask of me whether it is permissible to establish a house of prayer literally similar to a non-Jewish place of worship, and to have as reader before the Ark a cantor and choir who will sing non-Jewish melodies, and will bow and genuflect in ways alien to us.

Know, my dear friends, that the very fundamentals of the religion of our hallowed Torah, are founded up on the Oral Torah which our Sages and guides have taught us, having themselves received their teaching through an unbroken line of tradition; this tradition has been transmitted from person to person, and goes back to our Teacher Moses, who received the hallowed Torah at Sinai. For without the Oral Torah we should not know what any precept is: e.g., what exactly are the *frontlets between thine eyes* (Deuteronomy 6:8)? or the *fruit of goodly trees* (Leviticus 23:40)? by what ceremony does *a man take a wife* (Deuteronomy 24:1)? and what precisely is *a bill of divorcement* (*ibid.*)? and so on. Most of the Torah's precepts are principally known only through the tradition of our Sages; so also were most of the punishments and admonitions established through their knowledge. And Scripture itself warns us: *According to the law which they shall teach thee, and according to the judgment which they shall tell thee, thou shalt do; thou shalt not turn aside from the sentence which they shall declare unto thee* (*ibid.* 17:11). Many times has the Writ adjured us on this; it is a fundamentum of our faith.

Out of the blessed Lord's lovingkindness toward His people, He has shown this wonder: a very long time has passed, and we have been dispersed through many lands, and yet we remain one people, with one Law for us all; if differences of opinion arose among the Sages, the majority view has become law, but nothing has been changed from country to country, far or near. Our faith stems from one source, and there is no basic deviation in it (Heaven forfend). There are differences in customs: for where the law is permissive (as all would agree) some Sages have chosen to impose stringency on themselves, and hence on their followers and local adherents—much as one may take a vow of abstinence about something generally permitted. Of course, in such cases, many of our people would not wish to accept the added stringency, and thus there are different customs: in one country a stringency may have been accepted, but not in another. But in such a case the lenient ones cannot be called transgressors, for all agree that the Torah permits leniency, and it is only the people in one country who desire the extra severity, much as any individual might take a vow of abstinence or become a Nazir.

The laws of the Torah, however, the entire people Israel observe uniformly, in all countries, even to the end of the world. And even as regards local customs, our Sages have enjoined us that an individual is forbidden to deviate from the practice of the general community in which he lives.

It is therefore certainly forbidden to vary and build a synagogue in a fashion other than the custom which we have ever followed in this country; and especially to emulate a house of worship other than our own, and to have a reader for the congregation sing melodies that are not ours, and alter the traditional bowing and genuflection—this is totally forbidden.

204

The Talmudic dictum is known that even the least of Jewish cutoms, involving perhaps a shoelace, we must observe at the cost of our lives, if need be, for it is a Jewish practice.

Nor let us feel shamed by those who would calumniate us and deride our faith and our laws. It is quite known that in every other faith there are practices and statutes which seem unacceptable to those who are not of that faith, and outsiders may indeed regard some such statutes with scorn; yet those who uphold that faith will disregard those who deride their belief, and will not give up their practices because of the scoffers. How much more must we, who believe in the religion of our hallowed Torah, never give up right laws on account of the calumniators; here Jeremiah's words apply: *Send unto Kedar, and consider diligently, and see. . . . Hath a nation changed its gods, which yet are no gods? But My people hath changed its glory for that which doth not profit* (Jeremiah 2:10-11).

Then may Heaven forfend that our people build a synagogue or conduct prayers in ways that are not ours; Heaven forfend that we ever alter any detail of our fathers' ways, and thus wreck our entire faith. For go out and see what has happened with the new "sect" which has contemned the rules of the Sages: they are almost alienated from the people of Israel, and commit many transgressions wilfully. Principally: whoever does not have faith in the teaching of the rabbis who have received the Oral Torah, has no care for the customs of our fathers, sees the Sages' words as contemptible, and chooses for himself whatever seems fit in his own view—he has left the ranks of our faith. For the mainstay and basis of our faith are the words of the Sages; whoever does not believe this, is not committed to our sacred religion. Nor does he practice any other religion, for other faiths seem equally contemptible in his view; he chooses for himself whatever his whim finds fit. Such a man is not religious at all, for he acts with no purpose of observing any faith, but only as seems pleasing to him. He thus cannot at all be included among those who have a faith.

And so beware to enter any house of prayer built in such new fashion, or to pray therein. It is forbidden to listen to the melodies of those who chant[1] without religious devotion or reverence for the Lord.

I have written only generally, and have not indicated any source for my statements—some printed work or authoritative legal decision; this for two reasons: (1) this matter is very obvious, as is well known, to anyone with the least knowledge of our sacred literature, unless he has gone off into apostasy, and his eyes have gained nothing from the sight of the truth; with the slightest investigation one can find clear statements in Scripture, Talmud and later authorities; why shall I then carry on at length? and (2) it is known that the new "sect" derides the words of our Sages of blessed memory; how shall I then quote from them to prove my statements? All their words will only sound ludicrous in the ears of those fools. . . . Hence I have cited no proof whatever for my words, but merely stated the truth in itself.

It was indeed *as a heavy burden, too heavy for me* (Psalms 38:5) to reply on such a matter, *but who can withhold himself from speaking* (Job 4:2)? We are commanded to inform those who seek the truth, but briefly; he who will, will hear. . . .

Therefore, my friends, obey the Torah and do not follow the views of those who detest the faith of our sacred Torah; keep far from their opinions, and all will be well with you.

---

1. [The Hebrew has *mesorerim*, "who rebel or go astray," rather than *meshorerim*, who chant. Either it is a typographical error, or a double meaning is intended.]

☙ 16 ❧

The Mechitzah as a Minhag

BY RABBI DAVID REGENSBERG

DEAR MR. LITVIN:

It is a well established rule in Jewish religious law that a custom (technically called *minhag*) is Law, whether there is or is not any legal basis for the observance of the custom. The very acceptance of a custom by the community of Israel bestows upon that custom the status of law.

A law thus established is not subject to any process of change. It is stated in the Talmud, Yebamoth 102, that even if the prophet Elijah were to return to earth he would be without authority to change a custom. The great rabbinic authority R. Abraham b. David (RABaD) in his glosses to the Code of Maimonides (*Hilchoth Mamrim* 2, 2) cites this as definitive: that even Elijah would lack the authority to change an accepted custom. Maimonides (*ibid.* 3) states that if a rabbinic court decreed the enactment of a rule which became established and observed by the people, and if such a rule is a *seyag* (a "hedge" or preventive measure, designed to prohibit acts which might lead further to violations of Jewish law) it might not be abolished by even a more authoritative court (i.e., greater in scholarship and number). The *mechitzah* undoubtedly falls into the category of *seyag*.

☙ 17 ❧

On the Inviolability of Traditional Rights

IF ONE does not allow the poor to glean [gather what is dropped or forgotten during reaping, or what grows in a corner left for the needy],[1] or allows one [poor person to glean] but not another, or helps one of them, he is in effect robbing the poor. Concerning this is it said [in Scripture], *Do not move the boundary of those who have risen* (Proverbs 22:28; Mishnah Pe'ah 5, 6).

R. Jeremiah and R. Joseph [both interpreted *those who have risen*]: One said, They are the people who went up out of Egypt. The other said, They are those who have gone down in their fortunes, [so called in the sense that] a blind man is called "light-filled" (Jerusalem Talmud *loc. cit.*, 19a).

One said . . . out of Egypt: in other words, Do not move the boundary . . . set for those who left Egypt, meaning the precepts of the Torah (R. Isaac b. Melchizedek Simponti, *Commentary ad loc.*).

As for [the Mishnah's] reading *'olim* (those who have risen) while the Writ has *'olam* (of old), do not regard this as a difficulty, for this is by way of interpretation . . . *'olim* denotes those who went up from Egypt, and the verse refers to the precepts and statutes which the Almighty commanded them (Maimonides, *Commentary to Mishnah, ad loc.*).

The other said . . . "light-filled": that is, *'olim* is interpreted in the sense of "risen," and is applied to the poor as a euphemism of respect, just as the blind are called by this other euphemism of respect (R. Samson of Sens, *Commentary ad loc.*).

❀ 18 ❀

A Review of the Sources

BY RABBI EZEKIEL HA-LEVI GRUBNER

TO MY ESTEEMED AND VERY DEAR FRIEND, who with pure heart stands in the breach to wage the Lord's battle, a

---

1. Leviticus 19:10-11, 23:22; Deuteronomy 24:19-21.

man now hailed in the circles which revere the Lord, Mr. Baruch
Litvin:

At your suggestion I hereby set forth my views about
this evil matter, in which people have acted to destroy the
sanctity of the synagogue, saying [as it were] "Let us now see
how the others serve God, and we too will act thus."[1] Their
intention is but to emulate the non-Jews and the wilful transgressors of our people: they would commit the deed of Zimri
(Numbers 25:14) and seek the reward of Phinehas (*ibid.*
11-13). They bring "strange fire" into the sacred service,[2] to
"play the harlot" in the House of Jacob, and say they come
to adorn and elevate the House of our Lord with a beautiful
choir and lovely services. Woe to us, how astoundingly the
principles of Torah have fallen: men of frivolous minds who
sin against their very souls, have come forth and diverted their
neighbors into their evil ways, to separate from the pathways
of our fathers and go seeking after strange creations which are
forbidden us.

To its furthermost reaches the people Israel has had
from time immemorial, a uniform, traditional format for its
synagogues, patterned after the Sanctuary, as I will explain;
hence no concern was felt to specify plans, insofar as the
matter was so obvious and well known. In general, women
are free of the obligation to pray in a group, and so there is
no mention [of a women's section in the synagogue] in the
Talmud or in Maimonides' *Mishneh Torah, Hilchoth Tefillah*
11, where he deals in detail with the order and arrangements
of a synagogue. It is only that a long time afterward women
of themselves acquired the practice of attending the synagogue
to pray; then women's sections were set up for them. Therefore

---

1. [See Deuteronomy 12:30.]
2. [See Leviticus 10:1.]

is it not mentioned in our Codes of law. This is all obvious and well known to the lettered, beyond any question. I have thus not come now to render a decision or to demonstrate anything new: for this evil matter in question has already been declared utterly forbidden by early and later Sages, the saintly who have passed into eternal life. I will merely seek to gather and set in order the sources from Mishnah and Gemara [which together form the Talmud] and from the writings of our Earlier and Later Masters.

Firstly we have the Mishnah in Sukkah 51a: The evening following the first day of the Festival [of *Sukkoth*] they would go down to the women's court [in the Temple] and establish there a great amendment. On the following page the Gemara asks: What was the great amendment? Said R. Eleazar, As we have learned: It [the women's court] was bare originally, and then they surrounded it with a balcony, and instituted that women were to sit above and men below. [The Gemara continues:] Originally the women were within and the men outside, and they would reach a state of levity; it was ordained that the women occupy the outer part and the men the inner, but they yet reached a state of levity. It was then enacted that women were to sit above and men below. [Then it is asked:] How could they do this? It is written, *All this [do I give thee] in writing, as the Lord hath made me wise* (1 Chron. 28:19).[3] Rab replied, They came upon a verse which they interpreted (that it was essential to separate men from women and establish a guard in Israel to keep the people from coming to grief —Rashi): *And the land shall mourn, every family apart: the family of the house of David apart, and their wives apart* (Zechariah 12:12); said they: We can surely reason from the

---

3. [Indicating that the plans for the Temple which David bequeathed to Solomon were of Divine origin, and hence not subject to any change.]

lesser to the greater; if in the [Messianic] future, when they will be engaged in mourning, and the Evil Inclination will not hold sway over them, the Torah asserts that men and women are to be apart—now that people are in the midst of festivity, and the Evil Inclination has dominion over them, how much more certainly must they be separated.

Tosefta, Sukkah 4, 1 adds: so that the women would sit there and watch the Festivity of the Water for Libation, and they would not mingle. This is also found in the Jerusalem Talmud, Sukkah 5, 2; there it is clearly indicated that the prohibition involved was Biblical; for in speaking of the addition of the balcony, it states: What amendment would they make there? they would set the men off by themselves and the women by themselves . . . whence did they learn [to do so]? from a matter in the Bible.

The original passage about this [balcony] is in the Mishnah, Middoth 2, 5: The court of the women . . . was originally bare, and they surrounded it with a balcony, so that the women could look on from above and the men from below, in order that they should not mingle. Now the words of the Mishnah, that originally the court was bare or smooth, are explained in several ways: Rashi comments: No beams extended out from the walls; while Maimonides writes: It was open to the winds, and no wall enclosed it. The *Aruch,* s.v. *gezuztera,* explains: It was as smooth as a hill, and they came to be frivolous because they [the men] would enter among the women. About the balcony Rashi comments: Beams extended out from the wall all around, and every year boards would be arranged on them so that they [the women] could stand there during the Festivity of Water for Libation, and watch; this was the great amendment which, as we learned in the Mishnah, they would set up every year. Maimonides writes: They surrounded them with filled arches, and set some kind of steps

211

to them, so that the women could look on from there. The *Aruch* explains: They built a balcony about the court, coming out of the wall, with an arched roof over it; the women would stand above, on the balcony, and the men below, in the court . . . they established three balconies, facing three directions. . . . And *Me'iri* writes: They surrounded it with a balcony which had a lattice-like partition, for the women would gather there to observe the Festivity of Water for Libation, while the men would be in the court; it was in order that men and women should not mix together that they surrounded it with these screens.

In his Commentary to the Mishnah, Sukkah, Maimonides writes: A great amendment, meaning that it was of great value; because the people prepared a place for men and a place for women, the area for the women being above the one for the men, so that the men would not gaze at the women. In his Code, *Mishneh Torah, Hilchoth Lulab* 8, 12, he writes: They would prepare places in the Temple, for the women above and for the men below, so that one group would not mingle with the other. And he writes similarly in the same work, *Hilchoth Beth ha-Behirah* 5, 9: The women's court was surrounded by a balcony, so that the women could observe from above and the men from below, in order that they should not become merged. In *Sefer Mitzvoth Gadol*, positive precept 163, R. Moses of Coucy words it thus: They surrounded it with a balcony so that the women would look on from above and the men from below, at the Festivity of Water for Libation, as the Talmud states in Sukkah, so that they would not be mingled.

What emerges clearly, then, from all the statements of the Early Commentators, is that it is necessary to separate the men from the women. On the Mishnah, Sukkah 5, 2 *Tosafoth Yom Tob* comments: Men's gazing upon women indeed

212

leads to a state of frivolity, for it is written, *He shall rule over thee (Genesis* 3:16).[4]

Now these are Josephus' words in his *Wars of the Jews,* V, 5, 2: . . . of necessity [there were] two [gates] on the east; for since there was a partition built for the women on that side, as the proper place where they were to worship, there was a necessity for a second gate for them. He writes further: There were also on the other sides one south and one north gate, through which was a passage into the court of the women: for the women were not allowed to pass through the other gates, nor when they went through their own gate could they pass beyond their own wall or partition.

In the first Temple there was also an area designated as a women's court: Rashi to 1 Kings 6:36 writes, Scripture calls it inner because it was farther within than the women's court.

We thus see that in the Sanctuary care was taken that even when there was no prayer there should be no mingling of the sexes; and synagogues have always taken the Sanctuary as their model, as appears from Tosefta, Megillah 3, cited in *Tur Orah Hayyim* 150: The doors of synagogues are to open on none but the eastern side, for so we find in the Temple, that its door was toward the east, as it is stated, *Those that were to pitch before the Tabernacle eastward, before the Tent of Meeting toward the sunrising, were Moses and Aaron and his sons, keeping the charge of the Sanctuary* (Numbers 3:38). See also *Bayith Hadash, Orah Hayyim* 90, based on the Jerusalem Talmud, Berachoth 5, 1, that a synagogue is to have a forecourt, similar to the porch of the Sanctuary, so that a person entering will pass through two doorways. In a similar vein Maimonides writes in *Mishneh Torah, Hilchoth Tefillah* 11, 2—and it is quoted as law in *Tur Orah Hayyim* 150, 2: A

---

4. [The tendency for male dominion over the female is thus implicit in the natures of both, and in their interrelations.]

synagogue should be built in none but the high part of the city, for it is stated, *She* [wisdom] *calleth at the head* [the top] *of the noisy streets* (Proverbs 1:21). And so is it also derived from the Temple that a synagogue must be taller than the other houses of the city. See also Talmud, Shabbath 11a; and *Hilchoth Beth ha-Kenesseth,* that there is a view that it is forbidden to tear down any part of a synagogue, for it is called a sanctuary-in-miniature, and if one pulls down a stone of the Temple he violates a negative command: *Ye shall break down their altars. . . . Ye shall not do so unto the Lord your God* (Deuteronomy 12:3-4); (thus *Sifre ad loc.* interpretes these verses). So also R. Moses Isserles in *Shulhan Aruch Orah Hayyim* 152, quoting *Mordechai,* Megillah 4, 826; and similarly in many instances the Talmud likens a synagogue to the Temple as regards building or tearing down.

To quote *Mordechai* again (beginning of Tractate Shabbath), Our sanctuary-in-miniature is to be regarded as having a sacredness essentially similar to that of the Temple. Thus too the comment of the Talmud, Megillah 29a on the verse, *Yet shall I be to them as a little sanctuary* (Ezekiel 11:16): Said R. Isaac, This denotes the synagogues and Houses of Study in Babylonia; and what does this verse signify: *Lord, Thou hast been our dwelling-place in all generations* (Psalms 90:1)? It applies to the synagogues and Houses of Study. See also *Sefer Yere'im* 324, that reverence for the synagogue and the House of Study is incumbent by Biblical precept, out of the verse, *My sanctuary ye shall reverence* (Leviticus 19:30, 26:2), which covers as well the synagogue and the House of Study. *Tosafoth* to Baba Bathra 8, s.v. *yahib,* states that whatever is contributed to a synagogue counts as a sacrificial offering, and hence such contributions may be accepted from non-Jews.

For this reason, throughout the dispersed communities of the people Israel, wherever they settled, be they Sephardic

214

[from Spain and Portugal] or Ashkenazic [from France, Germany or Eastern Europe] the basic plan of the synagogues is uniform; one does not vary significantly from another, for by our ancestral heritage, all are in emulation of the Sanctuary. In our time synagogues were still extant which had been built about a thousand years ago; to our misfortune many of them have been torn down and destroyed by the Nazis (be their names extirpated); all of them followed one plan as regards the women's section, for we follow but one sacred teaching.

To quote again from the *Shulhan Aruch,* which derives this from the Responsa *Terumoth ha-Deshen* 353 and *Sefer Agudah, Asarah Yuhasin:* It is an enactment of the Early Authorities that in a location where men are not wont to be, such as the women's synagogue . . . women are relied upon [as witnesses] (*Hoshen Mishpat* 35). It is thus explicitly indicated that men could not see what was happening in the women's section.

Even in a private dwelling, not in a synagogue, and not during prayer, our Sages are stringent about the mingling of the sexes: Do not mix sons among the daughters, lest they cause sin; [the Writ states] *Then shall the virgin rejoice in the dance* (Jeremiah 31:13)—alone—but *the young men and the old together* (*ibid.*). So also should young boys and girls play in their respective streets, the boys apart and the girls apart; thus, toward the end of Psalms (148:12) we read, *young men and also maidens,*[5] but not "young men *with* maidens," in the way that the verse continues, *old men with*[5] *children;* the word *gam*[6] (too) is to add that women too should be apart. So wrote R. Judah he-Hasid in the 13th century in *Sefer Hasidim* (edition of *Mekitze Nirdamim,* Berlin 1891, Frankfort a. M. 1924, 60).

---

5. [Literal translation.]

6. [It is a principle of Rabbinic interpretation that the participle *gam* (also) extends the meaning or application of a verse.]

Thus too we read in the Talmud, Sanhedrin 20a: Where it is the custom for women to follow the bier [in a funeral procession] they are to do so; where it is their custom to precede the bier they are to do so; and Tosafoth comments (s.v. *nashim*): There is also the practice of having them follow after the bier, and the men before it, since it disgraces daughters in Israel to have men regarding them.

Again, Tosafoth to Kiddushin 81a (s.v. *sakba*) writes: The meaning is that these Festival days are the worst of the days of the year as regards seclusion of couples and sin, for there is a gathering of men and women to hear the rabbi's exposition, and one casts an eye upon another; some say that this is why it has become the practice to fast after *Pesah* (Passover) and after *Sukkoth*. In *Mishneh Torah, Hilchoth Yom Tob* 6, 21 Maimonides writes: The *beth din* (Jewish court) is obligated to appoint guards for the Festivals to make the rounds and look through the gardens, orchards and river banks, in order that men and women should not gather there to eat and drink, and thus be enticed into sin. See also *Shulhan Aruch Orah Hayyim,* end of 529.

Ture Zahab to *Shulhan Aruch Orah Hayyim* 315 cites *Mordechai*, Shabbath 3, 311 that "a *mechitzah* (partition) for the sake of mere propriety is permitted [to be set up on the Sabbath]—for instance, a *mechitzah* installed between men and women for the duration of the rabbi's exposition, may be set up on the Sabbath, as is indicated in 'Erubin chap. 9." . . . Again, Rashi to Kiddushin 81a, s.v. *gulfi,* comments: In a place where men and women would gather for the rabbi's exposition, Abaye used to make partitions of earthenware jars, and Raba, of reeds.[7] In a similar vein we find this passage in *Seder Eliyahu*

---

7. [So that no man could approach a woman, or vice versa, without causing disturbance.]

216

Rabbah 9, in regard to Elkanah and his men: When they would go up journeying on the way [to make the pilgrimage to Jerusalem for a Festival] they would sleep in a city square; whereupon the men [of the city] would gather separately, and the women separately, for a man [of Elkanah's party] would talk with a man, and a woman with a woman [to convince them to join the pilgrimage]. . . .

Now all these authorities deal only with a time of festivity and rejoicing, when no one is praying or reciting the *shema'*. When men had to be in the women's court [in the Temple] the Talmud speaks of a "great amendment" that had to be made on that account. How much more certainly must there be a high, solid partition separating the women from the men in our synagogues, where people come to recite the *shema'*, prayers and everything holy.

To cite the Talmud once more: Said Raba . . . If an indecency [is visible] in a mirror, it is forbidden to recite the *shema'* before it; *that He see no unseemly thing in thee* (Deuteronomy 23:15) said the Compassionate One, and here such can be seen. In similar vein Maimonides in *Mishneh Torah, Hilchoth Keri'ath Shema'* 3, 15: Every part of a women's body constitues an indecency [if exposed]; therefore one should not regard a woman's body while reciting the *shema'*, even if she is his own wife; if a handbreadth is exposed, he should not recite this portion in her presence. And so *Shulhan Aruch Orah Hayyim* 75, 4: It is forbidden to recite it before any indecency. On this the *Mishnah Berurah* comments: Since it is writ, *The Lord thy God walketh in the midst of thy camp . . . therefore shall thy camp be holy, that He see no unseemly thing in thee,* etc.; from this verse the Sages learned that wherever the Lord our God "walks with us"—i.e., when we are engaged in reciting the *shema'* or prayer or the study of Torah—nothing immoral is to be seen about us, which means that nothing of

217

indecency should face him who recites [the *shema'*] or prays, as far as he can see.

Such an unchaste sight may be exposed hair or a revealed handbreadth of the body; see *loc. cit.* 2. There, note 10, the *Mishnah Berurah* continues: "This involves a Biblical ban, since it is written, *The priest shall . . . let the hair of the woman's head go loose*" (Numbers 5:18). In *Sifre ad loc.* it is derived from this verse that "daughters of Israel are to cover their hair"; and so Rashi comments on the verse. The Talmud, Kethuboth, puts it thus: It is an admonition to the daughters of Israel that they ought not to go out with loose [uncovered] hair. Such is also the law in the *Shulhan Aruch ibid.* 90, 26 in regard to prayer; see *Mishnah Berurah* there note 82; such is also the law regarding the study of Torah or any holy matter.

There is, further, the passage in *Seder Eliyahu Rabbah* 9, quoted in *Yalkut Shim'oni* I, 934, on Deuteronomy 23:15 (given above): One should not stand among the women and pray, because [he will have his] mind on the women; let him rather sanctify his camp five cubits on each side, and if he is amidst his own camp let him sanctify its entirety, for it is stated, *The Lord thy God walketh in the midst of thy camp.* And again, *Yalkut Shim'oni* I, 601 has: Why was the portion of [Scripture beginning with] holiness (Leviticus 19 *et seq.*) set near the portion on immorality *(ibid.* 18)? To teach you that wherever you find a "fence" against immorality you find holiness; whoever "fences" himself off from immorality, is called holy. We thus see that the term "holy" is the opposite of the immoral; how can we then have men and women seated together in the synagogue, a hallowed place, when it is considered an indecency for a man to pray in the presence of women? . . .

Teshubah me-'Ahabah 229 states succinctly: To have a woman in the House of the Lord, the men's synagogue, is like having an idol there. Maimonides writes in *Mishneh Torah, Hilchoth 'Abodah Zarah* 2, 3: So did our Sages state: *that ye go not about after your own heart* (Numbers 15:39), refers to heresy; *and after your own eyes* (*ibid.*), to immorality. . . . Talmud, Sotah 8a has: Said Raba, It was learned that the Evil Inclination has power only in regard to what one's eyes see.

In the Jerusalem Talmud, Berachoth 1, 5 we read: It is writ, *Thou shalt not commit adultery* (Exodus 20:13), and again, *That ye go not about after your own heart and your own eyes:* said Resh Lakish, the eye and the heart are the two agents for sin; spoke the Holy One (blessed be He), If you give Me your heart and eyes, then I know you are Mine. *Midrash Rabbah* and *Midrash Tanhuma* comment on this verse (Numbers 15:39): The heart and eyes are agents for the body, for they nourish the body; therefore is it stated, *that ye may remember and do all My commandments* (*ibid.* 40).

It was Job who said, *I made a covenant with mine eyes; how then should I look upon a maid* (Job 31:1)? . . .

And so we can draw our conclusion, how very great is the obligation to remove any possibility of sinful thoughts; as the *Hatham Sofer* wrote in his Responsa (Addenda, *Hoshen Mishpat* 190), such thoughts are like flame in dry straw. And in our instance it is a question of men and women sitting together in actual closeness. . . . A Midrash to *sidrah beshallah* states: Whoever touches a woman who is not his [wife] brings death upon himself; and this passage is ancient. How is it then possible to consider breaching our traditional guard and permitting prayer under such reprehensible conditions during the Holy Days of Awe?

Come and see the revealing words of the hallowed Targum of Jonathan ben Uzziel to Genesis 6:2: The sons of the great [chieftains or justices] *saw the daughters of men that they were fair,* that they painted their eyes, rouged their faces, and went about exposing themselves; and they lusted to cohabit, *and took themselves wives, whomever they desired.*[8]

To sum up, if men and women are intermingled in a synagogue during prayer, it is forbidden to join in the services there, for four reasons: (1) the sanctity of the traditional arrangement of the synagogue has been altered; (2) women are improperly in view; (3) when anything morally improper is in sight it is expressly forbidden to recite the *shema'* or pray; (4) physical contact with another's wife touches on the ban against adultery.

Therefore, my dear good friend, in my opinion it is incumbent on you to resist with all your strength this attempt to destroy the House of the Lord. Do not grow afraid of the militant, strident voices that will be raised against you, verbally and in writing. Let not your heart quake before any attempts to frighten you, for the Lord battles for you. . . . The *Maharam Shick* stressed the duty to fight such actions and to admonish the transgressors, for otherwise the righteous share in the guilt (Responsa, *Orah Hayyim* 77).

I have written at such great length because the arrogance here involved makes one's hair bristle if a spark of Judaism still glows in one's heart. . . . I do hope they will retract and leave matters as they have been traditionally, in glory and beauty, rather than defile the holy. May the Lord turn back the hearts of the Children of Israel to their Father in heaven; and may they uphold the ways of their forefathers.

---

8. [According to *Midrash Bereshith Rabbah* 26, they took wives indiscriminately, even women already married, and thus helped bring on the Flood.]

IV

the historical background

E HAVE MADE repeated reference to the fact that the separation of sexes in the synagogue was such a universal practice throughout all ages as not to require any special emphasis in the Codes of Law; and we have clearly shown this to be a fundamental principle of Jewish worship. It is, therefore, appropriate to trace the existence of separate women's sections through Jewish history.

Phillip Johnson, Director of the Department of Architecture of the Museum of Modern Art in New York, writes in the foreword to Rachel Wischnitzer's *Synagogue Architecture in the United States* (Jewish Publication Society, 1955): "Jews have historically built in the styles and disciplines of the times without being bound by traditional architectural styles" (p. vii). It is all the more significant that the separation of women remained a basic feature of synagogue construction.

George Loukomski, writing on the European synagogues, says: "Synagogues . . . in the course of centuries underwent considerable evolution in form . . . for their form often depended upon local forms and influences. . . . Yet, in spite of this factor, logical and inevitable as it was, the Jews succeeded in holding fast to traditions in creating their own specific forms" (George K. Loukomski, *Jewish Art in European Synagogues*, London, 1947, p. 27).

In a last work on the synagogue, the erudite authority S. Krauss put it thus: "To sum up what the expert Alfred Groette wrote (*Juedisches Lexikon*, V, 809), there is no especial national style of the Jews in the Diaspora. Pinkerfeld justly states: 'The discontinuity of all organic links between one period and another, one land and another, has fragmented the history of Jewish architecture into many islands, isolated in time and space.' What we can point to alone, is the basic Jewish groundplan, which is truly original, in accordance with the laws and requirements of the ritual" (Samuel Krauss, *Koroth Bate ha-Tefillah be-Yisra'el*, New York, 1955, p. 231).

In the 1906 edition of the Jewish Encyclopedia, Professor Deutsch of the Hebrew Union College (Reform) wrote: "The separation of the sexes in synagogues is most likely coeval with synagogue services" (1). There naturally have been changes in the actual manner of carrying out this separation. The very founder of Conservatism in America, Solomon Schechter, wrote: "I am rather inclined to think that the synagogue took for its model the arrangements in the Temple, and thus confined women to a place of their own" (chapter VI, source 5).

Again: "A characteristic feature of the modern

222

orthodox Synagogue is the women's gallery. This, however, is certainly not primitive, even though there is evidence of its existence in the IInd century synagogue at Capernaum, and perhaps in that of Beth Alpha. The segregation of sexes, indeed, was obligatory. . . . But this was possible without a pillared gallery. There are instances of latticed enclosures for the women below the men's Synagogue (Comtat Venaissin), or level with it (Ferrara, etc.); and, when more elaborate architectural arrangements were introduced and the women were placed on a higher physical plane (for example, at "El Transito," in Toledo, Spain, or in most of the extant ancient *scuole* of North Italy), the lattices are flush with the walls, and do not project over the interior of the building. The pillared "women's gallery" . . . seems to be a Northern European innovation, popularized perhaps by the Spanish and Portuguese Synagogue of Amsterdam." Thus writes Cecil Roth, the well-known Jewish historian, in his introduction to Loukomski's book (page 21). While we may be able to show that the pillared gallery was somewhat more popular in medieval times than he thinks, he certainly is correct in pointing out that separation of the sexes was a uniform practice, and that it took a variety of forms in the course of Jewish history.

In some of the earliest synagogues whose ruins have been excavated, we find that the usual style was the Basilica, and that they had a balcony, mostly on three sides, for women, following the pattern of the Temple. These were synagogues in second century Galilee. Thus, Ernest W. Gurney Masterman describes the archaeological findings in the Tell Hum (Capernaum) synagogue which show that a gallery ran along three sides, and concludes, "This gallery, judging from modern analogy, may have been for the women" (*Studies in Galilee,* Chicago, 1909,

223

pp. 112-114). S. Krauss is by no means so tentative: in his definitive *Synagogale Altertuemer* (Berlin, 1922) he gives the evidence for such galleries in several other Galilean synagogues as well, found on later expeditions (pp. 338-339); on pp. 355-357 he sums up these findings, and states: "We may consider these galleries the place for the women, who were thus separated from the men's section by a balustrade. . . . Rather than by literary means—we refer especially to the silence of the Talmud—instances of women's sections in the synagogue can thus be shown. . . . What we know of the Temple in Jerusalem, we can designate as the model for the arrangement in the synagogues of Galilee. On the Temple mount, in the Women's Court, it was found necessary . . . to construct a balcony for the women. . . . It was set along *three* sides of the Court (Tosefta Sukkah, 4, 1), and we find exactly the same thing in the synagogues of Galilee."

Nor was the idea of separation as a religious principle limited to the Talmud and to that part of the Jewish people which followed its traditions. Philo describes an analogous practice among the Therapeutae, a communal group of pietists similar or related to the Essenes and/or the Qumran community: "The common sanctuary in which they meet every seventh day is a double enclosure, one portion set apart for the use of the men, and the other for the women. . . . This arrangement serves two purposes: the modesty becoming to the female sex is preserved, while the women sitting within ear-shot can easily follow what is said. . . . The order of reclining [for the meal] is so apportioned that the men sit by themselves on the right and the women by themselves on the left" (*The Contemplative Life,* Loeb Classical Library, IX, 131-133, 155).

Particularly illuminating is the Talmud on the destruction of the Diplaston Synagogue in Egypt (dating from Temple times) in 166 CE: it clearly indicates that women used a separate balcony (chapter III, source 11, §1).

While it is generally agreed by scholars that the sexes were separated at worship, some have raised the question whether this was not merely a matter of separate benches or other temporary barriers, rather than fully separated sections; they point, for instance, to a passage in Kiddushin 81a (chapter III, source 4, §7) as proof. However, the present-day Israeli scholar Eliezer Levi points to the fact that in this Talmudic passage the barriers were placed for public gatherings, and not during prayer (2). There are instances of synagogues not having a permanent gallery or separation, particularly in Babylonia. Undoubtedly, these synagogues were for the use of men only (we find such with great frequency in the Middle Ages); or possibly it was not customary in those places for women to attend synagogue services, and makeshift measures were taken for the special occasion when they would be present. Thus Krauss writes in his posthumous Hebrew work: "In Germany a partition would sometimes be made between men and women by hanging up cloths (or robes; *Sefer Maharil,* Cremona 40a). I have myself seen such things done in villages, where only with the greatest difficulty could space be set apart for the women. And this year [1946] I have seen this occur even in London, in small, itinerant congregations" (S. Krauss, *Koroth Bate ha-Tefillah be-Yisra'el,* p. 239). On the following page he writes: "The traveller Ibn Sapir (volume 2, p. 7) relates that in all Arabia the women do not pray in the synagogues—for example, in Aden, etc. Hence there is no need for a women's section, and they are not concerned with it."

225

For the Middle Ages, the evidence is, of course, voluminous and quite unambiguous. "Women are segregated in synagogues almost everywhere and are placed behind bars [railings] in galleries (even when placed high up in the building, they are, in addition, enclosed by bars [railings]: at Leghorn, Cordova, etc.). There are, however, many special synagogues for women" (Loukomski, *op. cit.*, p. 29).

Thus, in Prague there were separate synagogues for men (built between 1034 and 1350) and for women (built in the twelfth century). In Worms there are also two synagogues joined by an arch (built in the tweltfth century); and in Frankfurt there were two connected by apertures. Two rooms, connected by small wall openings, characterized the house of worship at Ratisbon (built in the thirteenth century and destroyed in 1519). This synagogue served as a model for a large number of other European houses of worship. The synagogues in Toledo (12th century) and Aleppo also had the women's sections hidden. However, it is interesting that as early as 1550 we find the synagogue at Nikolsburg, Bohemia, with a projecting women's gallery, and likewise the "Istanbul Synagogue" in Jerusalem; similar structures for prayer appeared at the same time in Italy (Venice, Leghorn, etc.), in 1624 in Lemberg, Poland; 1675 in Amsterdam; and 1701, in London.

Here we might quote Alfred Groette: "That the construction of a women's synagogue was regarded as a special event, is best shown by a manuscript of the Jewish community of Worms [France], dating from 1559; it contains copies of earlier inscriptions on stone tablets in the Worms Synagogue. One such inscription reads: This House did R. Me'ir b. Joel the *kohen* build for the glory of God in the year 4973 (1213). May he be remembered before God for good; and may everyone who learns of this answer Amen. That this edifice has been built as a prayer-house for women who trust in the Lord and His kindness, is here thus engraved with an iron stylus, for all time" (*Deutsche, boemische und polnische Synagogentypen,* Berlin, 1915, p. 21).

It should be pointed out that this pattern—which also obtained in the Karaite synagogues—disproves the assertion that separate women's sections were a result of prevalent social attitudes about the place of women. The women's section was a feature of synagogues in all countries, at all times, irrespective of social mores. This is easy to understand if it is remembered that it did not imply a negative view of women's importance, but rather expressed the concept of sanctity to be attained by the separation of the sexes.

When we turn to the American continent, we find that the ancient traditions were continued. The oldest house of worship, the Mill Street Synagogue of Congregation Shearith Israel in New York (1730), had a women's gallery on three sides; and it is interesting to note that non-Jews, though used to separate seating in some churches. considered this complete separation unusual.

The synagogues that followed, however different in architecture, had the same seating arrangement: among them the famous edifice of prayer in Willemstad, Curacao (1732) and the Touro Synagogue (1763) in Newport, Rhode Island. In 1827 the Elm Street Synagogue was built in New York. During the spread of the Reform movement congregations laying claim to orthodoxy determinedly retained the women's gallery.

The year 1824 may be accepted as the date at which

the Reform movement made a beginning in the United States; it is subsequent to this date, and parallel with the unfolding of Reform, that changes in synagogue seating occurred. In 1847 the Worcester Street Synagogue was built in New York; it featured a choir and orchestra, and the seating was mixed. Another synagogue identified with mixed seating and the Reform movement was Temple Emanuel.

The reasons for the changes may have been the desire for the imitation of Christian forms (a factor of major importance in Europe), the prominence accorded the sermon, and the different concepts of worship associated with "reform-minded Synagogues" (Wischnitzer, *Synagogue Architecture in the United States,* p. 61).

To counter the spread of reform the traditional elements of the community strongly reasserted their stand, and identified orthodoxy with women's galleries. In the 1840's a German group in Cincinnati decided that the "ritual was to be orthodox and the women were to be seated in the gallery." In 1842 Congregation Rodeph Sholem (Philadelphia) inserted a condition in its lease that a gallery had to be provided. In March 1858 S. Oettinger wrote an article in "The Occident" attacking the reform practice on the basis of traditional law. It is no wonder, then, that while the reform movement spread, congregations laying claim to orthodoxy retained and emphasized the women's galleries. Thus, H. Wilson in the New York Almanac of 1850 describes the New Anshe Chesed Congregation in New York: "There are galleries . . . which are devoted exclusively to the female portion of the congregation, who in all Jewish congregations are separated from the males."

In December, 1906, the *Architectural Record* (New

228

York, XX, 6) published an article titled *The Story of the Synagogue,* by Abram S. Isaacs (pp. 464-480). He wrote: "The inner history of the synagogue is intensely human. . . . Here the bridegroom worshipped on the Sabbath after his marriage . . . wearing the praying-scarf [*tallith*] which his bride, who sat so proudly in the latticed gallery, had embroidered and given him as her wedding gift" (p. 468). "In the old synagogues there was either a latticed gallery or a special room for women worshippers . . . while in reformed American congregations family pews have been introduced. . . ." (p. 480).

It is clear, then, that in the public mind and, specifically, in the thought of the Jewish community, until the most recent times, all synagogues other than Reform required women's sections as a matter of principle, and the existence of women's sections veritably became a touchstone of orthodoxy. Not only orthodox, but other spokesmen as well, recognized that "orthodox Jewish law clearly and unequivocally requires the two sexes to be separated either by a curtain or by an elevation high enough to consider the women's section a balcony" (Dr. Solomon Faber, quoted in *Conservative Judaism,* Fall 1956).

We can in truth say, then, that until the nineteenth century no synagogue is known to have had mixed seating; that in the nineteenth and twentieth centuries mixed seating appeared as an integral part of the reform movements in Judaism; that orthodox or traditional and historical Judaism has been, and is, characterized by the *mechitzah*; and that synagogues which change to mixed seating, even though otherwise adhering to orthodoxy, commit a serious violation of both Jewish law and Jewish religious practice.

sources for chapter IV

❦ 1 ❦

The Jewish Encyclopedia on the Women's Section

FRAUENSHUL OR WEIBERSHUL: That part of the synagogue which is reserved for women, whether an annex, as it
is in the Altshul of Prague and in the synagogue of Worms,
or a gallery. It is generally in the rear of the building, on
the west side, sometimes on the east side, but at other times
on the north side. Some of the modern synagogues have two
galleries, one above the other. The separation of the sexes in
the synagogue is most likely coeval with Synagogual Services,
although it is not mentioned in the old sources, and the ruins
of ancient synagogues found in Palestine are not in such a
state of preservation that conclusions can be reached in regard
to their interior arrangements.

    According to Talmudic reports, which most likely rep-
resent genuine tradition, there was in the Temple at Jerusalem
a women's gallery, so built that its occupants could witness
the ceremonies, while a grating hid them from the view of
the men. *Sukkah 51b; Middoth 2, 5; Maimonides, Mishneh
Torah, Beth ha-Behirah 9.*

230

❧ 2 ❧

The Talmud's View on Separation

BY ELIEZER LEVI

ABBAYE set a row of jugs; Raba arranged grass reeds (Kiddushin 81a).

Jugs: Where men and women would gather, either for the rabbi's lecture or for a wedding, he would arrange many earthenware pitchers between them, so that if they should approach each other, these would be struck, and would give off a sound. . . . *arranged grass reeds* . . . so that if anyone passed over them, their sound would be heard (Rashi *ad loc.*).

THE TALMUD is not speaking here at all about a synagogue, as certain scholars suggest;[1] we cannot, therefore, conclude that men and women sat together in the synagogue, one group beside the other, with only earthenware jugs separating them. On the contrary, we can derive that even at gatherings outside the synagogue women sat separately (*Yesodoth ha-Tefillah,* Tel Aviv 1947, p. 109).

---

1. Leopold Loew, *Der Synagogale Ritus,* p. 64; Ismar Elbogen, *Der Juedische Gottesdienst,* p. 467.

V

religious
authority
in Judaism

HE SIGNIFICANCE of the unanimous stand of orthodox religious authorities and the uniformity of its practice, has been questioned for a number of reasons.   Above all, we hear arguments that "there is no provision in Jewish life for hierarchical authority. It is therefore left to every rabbi and congregation to determine the particular forms which their religious practice are to take."

It is true that there is no Jewish hierarchy which could issue or cancel religious laws.   But that does not mean that rabbis or congregations have the authority to determine *religious principles*.   Judaism provides for a "nomocracy," rule of the Law. The belief in the Torah as God's law has always been a cornerstone of Judaism; and until the rise of Reform movements all Jews subscribed to the immutability of the Torah. It was clearly understood that the rules laid down by the Torah were devised to fit the most diverse conditions and times without themselves standing in need of change.

The duty of the ordained rabbi, therefore, was not forming or reforming the law, but applying it to religious questions, according to the established legal rules. "These are not subject to change and are to be interpreted only by those who have the proper authority and knowledge, and whose study of the Law is guided by the desire to learn what the Law has to say" (statement of the Rabbinical Council of America, September 1955).

In the application of the law, of course, doubts can arise occasionally about one detail or another. Therefore recourse is had to outstanding authorities. But these, again, do not make the law: they are listened to because they have proven their mastery of the law and their ability to apply it correctly. *If any of them issued a decision in conflict with the established principles and practices of Jewish law, he would no longer be an authority for orthodox Jewry; and this applies equally to individual rabbis of congregations that would take such liberties.* They may exercise leadership in seceding or reforming congregations— but they are no longer orthodox rabbis.

Confusion about the governing role of the law in Judaism is evident in the Ohio case of Katz et al. versus Goldman, et al. (33 O.A. 150) which has often been quoted. In this case the court refused to interfere and protect traditional practices because it felt that it had "no jurisdiction, in the presence of a final church tribunal, to assume the monitorship of the religious faith of the members. . . . There is a deadline which is an impregnable barrier to a judicial tribunal, and that is the right of a congregation to the conduct of its worship in such form and manner, and with such ceremony, as agrees with the constituted authorities of the church." These, the court felt, were represented in the case of a Jewish congregation by the Board of Trustees, for "there is nothing in the record which forbids the conclusion that the church in question is congregational and independent in its character and administered exclusively by and within itself in accordance with the rule of the majority of its membership."

It should be noted that the court recognized, however, that there were some limits to the independence of a congregation and to the actions of a majority group in a congregation. It explained that its decision was governed by the fact that, in its view, "there is such a variety of opinions in regard to orthodoxy and traditional doctrine that it would be impossible to grant any relief. . . . There must be, in order to grant the relief prayed for, such a perversion and diversion of the original principles and purposes upon which the church was founded as would either partially or totally destroy the institution as a Jewish identity." In such a case majority rule would not apply.

If the court, in this case, had followed this line of thought to its logical conclusion, it would have realized that any rejection of the binding character of Jewish law as such, or of any particular unequivocally recognized rule of Jewish law (such as separation of the sexes at worship) does indeed pervert the original and fundamental purposes of orthodox Judaism. As Maimonides ruled, on the basis of Talmudic law, anybody who rejects even one detail of the Law excludes himself from the Jewish community. For this is what he wrote in his monumental Code of Law: "There are three [sorts of people] who heretically reject the Torah: one who states that the Torah did not originate

234

with the Lord; then even if he says of one verse, or yet one word [of the Torah], 'Moses expressed this of his own accord,' he in effect rejects the Torah heretically. And so also one who denies [the authoritative character of] its interpretation, which is the Oral Tradition . . ." (*Mishneh Torah, Hilchoth Teshubah,* 3, 8).

VI

is the Law subject to change?

HE AUTHORITY of the Torah law has been challenged on the grounds that it is itself subject to historical changes: "The unchangeability of the Law is a myth; it changes with the times."

The orthodox Jew categorically refuses to admit this. In *The Difference Between Orthodoxy and Conservatism,* Rabbi Harold P. Smith shows very clearly that the so-called "socio-historical evolution of Jewish law" is exactly the point over which the modern reform movements have broken with traditional Judaism. "Traditional Jewish belief maintains that the times are the rock and our religious observances are the chisels that shape the rock, and not, as the non-traditionalists by necessity have to say, that the Jewish religion is the rock and the times constitute the chisel which shapes the rock. Orthodoxy says that our religion is a Divine instrument to shape the ages, rather than clay which the ages are to shape" (1).

It is true, of course, that Judaism knows many controversies over details of the Law, and that there is no one book which contains *the* entire, undisputed resume of Jewish Law. But while no one book can claim such authority, the Law as a whole can, and while there are differences over legal details, these differences are all within the Law. In other words, we find differences of rabbinical opinion on details, even on such a subject as the exact manner in which the sexes are to be separated in the synagogue, or on the exact quantity of matzoth to be eaten on the first night of Passover—but: (1) these differences do not touch fundamentals (such as the duty to separate the sexes, or to eat matzoth); (2) they are not the result of adaptation to contemporary socio-cultural conditions; they rather arise from legalistic differences in the application of the fundamentals; (3) thus they are not a challenge to the principle of the rule of the Law; and the Law, indeed, provides its own self-regulating techniques for solving such differences of opinion, namely, appeal to outstanding authorities for their correct application, or majority decisions of competent rabbis, or mediating principles laid down by the Law itself, as defined by the rabbis, etc. Jewish history indicates that the Law has indeed enjoyed absolute continuity of observance. It has itself arbitrated between controversies over its application; it has turned its back only on those who dispute the entire principle and system of the Law, and see it as a mere by-product of historical evolution.

In defense of the latter view, great play has been made of so-called shifts in the orthodox position toward reform tendencies; obviously, it has been said, orthodox legal principles cannot be immutable if ninety years ago the absence

237

of a *bimah* in the synagogue, or sermons in the vernacular, were causes for "excommunication," while today they are readily accepted by orthodoxy. In reality, these arguments merely reveal ignorance of the legal principles involved.

Sermons in the vernacular and (according to some legitimate legal rulings) the absence of a *bimah* were not wrong per se: they were banned at one time because they were then examples of imitation of non-Jewish practice and, as such, they became both legally objectionable and dangerous. When these considerations were no longer of significance, the prohibitions naturally lapsed. On the other hand, such a rule as the separation of the sexes at worship is prescribed by the Law irrespective of circumstances.

Efforts have been made to establish the time-bound character of laws such as the separation of the sexes, by calling them the result of social-historical conditions and an outgrowth of antiquated ideas about the inferiority of women. There is absolutely no justification for this view. As Chief Rabbi Herzog put it, "Think not for a moment that this law implies the least inferiority of women. Nothing was further from the minds of our ancient teachers, the successors of the prophets. Prophecy is surely the highest degree of human perfection, and our ancient teachers count many women as prophetesses" (chapter II, source 9). The Bible thus describes Miriam (Exodus 15:20), Deborah (Judges 4:4), and Huldah (2 Kings 22:14). The Talmud lists them, together with Sarah, Hannah, Abigail and Esther. And from Genesis 21:12 the Midrash derives that Sarah was indeed Abraham's superior in prophetic power (*Shemoth Rabbah* 1, 1; *Tanhuma' Shemoth* 1).

The existence of a women's section in the synagogue is in no way a symbol of degradation, but actually a natural consequence of the fact that the Torah exempts women from the obligation of regular public prayer: not because they are inferior, but because they have other duties in the home, which in the eyes of the Jewish religion must take precedence. Beyond that, of course, there is the injunction of the Torah against levity or frivolity at public gatherings, and, in particular, at public services (see chapter II, above). Its purpose is to assure maximum decorum, to put the individual into a prayerful mood, and to lead him toward the transcending ideal of holiness. This has been cogently elucidated by Rabbi Menahem M. Kasher in his eloquent essay on the hallowed nature of the synagogue (2).

THE JUDAIC CONCEPT OF WOMAN

On woman's place in Judaism there are passages galore scattered throughout Talmud and Midrash, which tell their own clear tale. A representative selection, given after this chapter, shows a rare insight into, and appreciation of, woman's proper role in Jewish family life, as well as her qualities of compassion and intuitive understanding; and Jewish law treats her with tender regard for her nature (3). Citing such sources and others, the late Dr. Joseph H. Hertz has written an impassioned short essay to refute thoroughly the "hostile misrepresentation that exists in regard to the woman's position" in Judaism (4). His teacher, Solomon Schechter, depicts in an earlier essay the role of "woman in Temple and synagogue"; he shows how, from earliest times to the present, women have participated in love and reverence in Temple and synagogue worship— although segregated (5). In this connection we might quote an inscription found by the late E. L. Sukenik (Israel's foremost archaeologist) in the remains of a synagogue in Na'aran, near Jericho, dating from about 300 CE. In a mosaic pavement at the entrance hall are the words:

239

May Halifo the daughter of R. Safrah be remembered for good, because she supported this sacred place; Amen (E. L. Sukenik, "Ancient Synagogues in Palestine," *Rimmon*, V, Berlin, 1923, p. 20). And from the 17th and 18th centuries we have tombstone inscriptions of women (recorded in such works as Marcus Horovitz, '*Abne Zikkaron*, Frankfurt, 1901) which bear lasting witness to their scrupulous, pious regular prayers, and their faithful attendance at synagogue. Apparently attending regularly in the women's section was not regarded as a mark of inferiority but as a matter for praise.

But perhaps only women can speak with final authority for their own kind. Nahida Remy, a 19th century Christian woman, studied with growing fascination the life of the Jewess, past and present, especially as compared with woman's lot in other cultures and other lands (she ultimately became a proselyte). Out of her study she wrote a book, *The Jewish Woman*, from which we have appended sections of two chapters (6). What can be more eloquent than this: "The special care for woman and the reverential regard for her [in Bible and Talmud] are remarkable, and fall nothing short of homage." Even more eloquent, in its own way, is an essay by the present-day Nina Alderblum, an "insider," who was reared in a family steeped in Jewish tradition. To choose a random sentence from *The Elan Vital of the Jewish Woman*: "The Jewish soil is fertile for nurturing the creative ideals of womanhood" (7). Neither author sees any hint of inferiority in the traditional life of the Jewish woman. Another woman writer points out in a recent book that the Jewish woman's religious status cannot very well be considered inferior if it is given to her to usher the Sabbath's holiness into her home by lighting the Sabbath candles (Evelyn Garfiel, *The Service of the*

240

Heart, New York, 1958, pp. 126-127). Earlier in the book she notes that R. Elijah Levita (*R. Eliyahu Bahur*) translated the daily Prayer Book, in the 16th century, into early Yiddish, expressly for the benefit of the women, that they might understand the prayers—a sign of a great degree of literacy among the women, and a mark of the care felt for women's religious welfare (*ibid.* p. 38).

A modern exponent of our ancestral tradition has recently written in moving fashion on what marriage has been, and can be, in the lives of observant Jews. In his essay, *Married Love in Jewish Law,* Dr. Leo Jung shows how the age-old laws, rituals and symbols surrounding Jewish marriage make for happy, rewarding life, even in our age of upheaval (8).

But we have digressed; let us resume the main thread —the question of *mechitzah* per se.

Elucidating the question from the point of view of our current modes of living, Rabbi Morris Max writes: "Although we are living in an age when the intermingling of the sexes in schools and public gatherings is commonplace, there is no doubt that when absolute concentration is necessary, as in prayer, and when the mind is apt to wander as the individual strives to conceive and feel the ideas of Godliness, the presence of the opposite sex that may lead to socializing may become a distracting factor" (9).

To say that this outlook reflects an outdated strictness of social behavior, and should therefore be discarded, means overlooking the very serious moral, social, and psychological problems that have been created by our contemporary lack of strict standards. A brilliant exposition of the psychological factors involved was recently published

241

by Rabbi Norman Lamm (10). The Torah's insistence on the sanctity of the relation between the sexes has undoubtedly been one of the means for protecting the Jewish people from most of these problems during its long pilgrimage through history. Here, again, the traditional Jew sees an indication of divine wisdom, revealed by the Torah, which is superior to contemporary social modes, and cannot be changed by, or for, the times.

sources for chapter VI

❀ 1 ❀

The Difference Between Orthodoxy and Conservatism

BY RABBI HAROLD P. SMITH

THIS IS A QUESTION concerning which there prevails much confusion and misinformation, and therefore one concerning which there is great and urgent need for clarification.

People will say to me almost every day in the week, "The difference between Orthodoxy and Reform I can see and understand. But I cannot see the difference between Orthodoxy and Conservatism. I pray in this and this Conservative Synagogue and then I pray in this and this Orthodox, or Traditional, Synagogue, and I cannot see the difference. What *is* the difference?"

This is a legitimate question which deserves a legitimate, forthright answer.

In terms of fairness, let it be said at the outset, that if you are starting with the impression that the present writer is an Orthodox rabbi and has emotional, theological, and philosophical predilections in favor of Orthodoxy, your impression is correct. What I will attempt to give here is an Orthodox rabbi's answer to the question: "What, according to *you*, is the difference between Orthodoxy and Conservatism?"—an answer which he cannot always give to each one individually because it calls for some development and for a "settled listener" situation.

243

One of the problems involved in the answering of this question is that Conservatism came on the American scene in a framework of socio-religious confusion—wherein many American Jews mistook sociological factors for religious philosophy.

Let me explain very simply.

There are many who can remember, probably as children, being in Orthodox Congregations where despite the devoutness of some of the worshippers, the decorum was very poor, with people getting up and walking about, even chatting and exchanging greetings, during the prayers and the reading of the Torah; where sermons were delivered only in Yiddish, despite the fact that you may not have understood Yiddish; and where not a single English prayer was ever read.

There was an element on the American Jewish scene of religious observance to whom all this disorder was objectionable and offensive to their sense of religious refinement. What is more, they wanted English prayers and English sermons. So they went elsewhere and brought all this about, with the thought that they had discovered a new religious product. What they did not know or realize was that all this disorder in the synagogue was not Orthodox but a picture of the gravest *violation* of Orthodoxy. The *Shulhan Aruch,* Orthodoxy's authority for procedure, states specifically that it is forbidden even to utter one word during religious services or during the reading of the Torah, except what is required for conduct of the service. These disorderly people who moved around and chatted—these walkie-talkies, as it were—were, then, unwittingly bringing forbidden practices into the service—reforms, you might call them. It was not realized that these nervous people with the unfortunate, unstable conduct were immigrants who had recently undergone a revolutionary upheaval in their own lives, and were therefore guilty of unstable conduct for which they could not altogether be blamed, but which nevertheless was not Orthodoxy.

244

There were those who thought that the English sermon, rather than the Yiddish, was un-Orthodox, and therefore, Conservatism —when, in fact, there was no religious objection whatsoever to the English sermon, any more than there was to the Yiddish sermon, except that the older Rabbis, transplanted from another continent, were hardly in a position to start learning a new language. It was not realized that there were no objections to English prayers, for the *Shulhan Aruch* specifically states that *korin shema' bechol lashon*—that it is perfectly acceptable to *add* prayers in *any* language in the synagogue.

And now I can tell you a little secret.

It is because so many of our people had many false impressions of what Orthodoxy really stood for, that the classification Traditional Synagogues was introduced. We wanted to avoid some of the terribly wrong impressions some of our people held about Orthodoxy, so we called ourselves Traditional and they came and saw what Orthodoxy *really* stands for—decorum, dignity, meaningful worship and meaningful instruction.

There was some talk that the Conservative elements had come upon the scene to restore equal rights to the woman. This was—and still is—the most powerful *misimpression* ever foisted upon the minds of our co-religionists.

Assuming that there is such a thing as total equality in all areas of living—and I'm not sure, because I have never yet heard of a case where two people got married and tossed a coin to see whether to take his name or her name—but assuming there *is* such a thing, the fact is that in the history of the world there has never been a people and a religion which, in its family life, had placed its women on so high and revered a pedestal as the Torah Jewry of the centuries. There are dozens and dozens of examples and citations from our religious literature and history to prove this. There *still* is not a woman president of the United States in modern America, which would be the equivalent to the position held by Deborah in the period of the Judges some *3,000 years ago.*

To interpret separated seating, as some have interpreted it, to mean inequality of women, is either deliberate mental fraud or pathetic misinformation. If anything, it is inequality of the man, for its purpose is not to separate the women from the men but to separate the men from the women. Men, because their nature is not as basically gentle and kindly as that of women, are *required* by Judaism to pray, to help mold and guide their character and religious personality. That is why they are required to make up the *minyan*. Women, blessed with the tenderness that comes with the Divine gift of motherhood, and considered by our Sages to have a better and more delicate control of their habits and conduct, were deemed to be not in such dire need of the softening influence of worship as the men who are in the harsh give-and-take of a relentless business world. Therefore they, the women, as far as a *minyan* is concerned, were *invited* by Torah law to pray, but *not required* to pray.

Now, when Jewish Tradition separated the sexes in worship, this had no relationship to rights or equality, but simply constituted a realistic realization that man, weaker in moral strength than woman, might not remain totally pure and completely wrapped in elevated and elevating thoughts of Divine Communion, if some very charming woman were sitting next to him. You can agree or disagree with the reasoning, but the fact is that some modern Christian Churches have instituted separate seating, possibly on the advice of psychologists on their board. But one way or another, it has no relationship to the *equality* of the sexes.

However, this is not yet the basis for a distinction between Orthodox and Conservative Synagogues. There are Orthodox synagogues which have gradations of mixed seating, and there are Conservative synagogues with *separated* seating; in fact, the synagogue of the Jewish Theological Seminary, the one and only Conservative Seminary in the world, has *separated* seating. All we must grant is that a synagogue with separated seating and which is Orthodox in other respects is more Orthodox and certainly *more* true to the sacred traditions of our people than one which has mixed seating.

What, then, is the *real* difference between Orthodoxy and Conservatism? The answer lies in a *religious philosophy*. Those who align themselves with an Orthodox, or Traditional, synagogue, are affiliating themselves with *one* religious philosophy, and those who join a Conservative Synagogue are affiliating themselves with another—and totally different—philosophy, even if there be little difference in the *personal* observances of these two individuals, or even the two Congregations.

Let us understand one fact clearly. The word "Orthodox" is a word in the English language, given to the traditionalists by their non-Traditionalist co-religionists, and, surprisingly enough, is a combination of two Greek words, "ortho doxo," meaning "correct opinion."

Obviously, there is no such word as "Orthodox" in basic primary Jewish sources such as the Talmud or *Shulhan Aruch*. If, then, a synagogue *says* it is Orthodox, this means, in my opinion, that it commits itself to a philosophy generally associated with Orthodoxy, and if a synagogue *says* it is Conservative, then regardless of the degree of its observance, it automatically commits itself to *another* philosophy—and the individual who joins either, commits *himself* or *herself* to the philosophy it represents.

What *are* these two very clear and distinct philosophies? They are, in simple words, the philosophies which answer the simple question: "Is our religion God-given or man-given?" Is our religion of Divine source or is it of human origin? Have the Torah and the Talmud and our religious observances come down to us as mere folklore?

Here is the basic difference. Orthodoxy says that our religious observances come from God and that all our religious observances and beliefs are the transmission of a Divine message to our children and our future generations—*Torah min ha-shamayim.*

On the other hand, Conservatism does not accept the doctrine of *torah min hashamayim,* i.e., that our religious beliefs and practices are of Divine origin, but simply something that started with man and developed through the ages. In Conservative circles, you hear much about adjusting your religion to the times.

Orthodoxy feels terrified at the thought that you will take a time like the present, when far more money is spent for either liquor or horse racing than for education, when divorces take no longer to acquire than it takes to get a dog license, when the heroes of our youth are the Hollywood stars who marry five, six and seven times, when Kinsey reports tell us that promiscuity of relationships is the rule rather than the exception—you take such a time and say you want to adjust your religion to the times. Think of it, rather, as the sculptor chiseling the rock. Orthodoxy says that the times are the rock and our religious observances are the chisels that shape the rock, and not as the non-Traditionalists will by necessity have to say, that the Jewish religion is the rock, and the times constitute the chisel which shapes the rock. Orthodoxy says that our religion is a Divine *instrument* to shape the ages, rather than the *clay* which the *ages* are to *shape.*

Orthodoxy believes that every non-Orthodox approach—whether Conservative or Reform—has in itself the seed of self-destruction. The moment you extend to each generation the invitation to mold our religion to suit its particular whims,

248

then it is a definite certainty that, after you have rejected what does not suit you, and then preached how vital is what you have kept, for the preservation of the Jewish religion *your* grandchildren will come along and eliminate these as unsuitable to them—and *why not?*—and where are you then? When you admit that what is Judaism in one land is not Judaism in another land—then the Judaism of the ages, universally applicable to all times and all places, must of necessity become a thing of the past.

In the records of the proceedings of the Conventions of the Conservative Rabbinate, we already find, in our own lifetime, that what their authorities said 20 years ago should be forbidden, the current authorities have already changed to permissibility. What better proof do we need of the validity of our thesis?

Orthodoxy says that when Rabbi Akiba and many other great Rabbis of his time, and hundreds of thousands of Jews throughout the centuries, knowingly gave their lives for their religion because it contained their God-given message it was a great *kiddush hashem* for Jewry, "sanctification of the name of God." On the other hand, if they gave their lives for something which is mere folklore, then they did a very foolish thing. I would not recommend to any Jew to offer his life for the preservation of the Jewish custom of eating gefilte fish. Folklore or not, it simply isn't worth it.

Now!—the man or woman who joins a Conservative Congregation is subscribing to a *philosophy*—the philosophy of the movement—that our religious beliefs and practices have no direct Divine implications. Even if that Congregation may be thoroughly observant (and there are some observant Conservative Congregations), one who joins has automatically subscribed to the philosophy of the United Synagogues movement with which this Congregation is affiliated.

On the other hand, take a man who is himself not observant —perhaps one who eats in all restaurants, does not observe the Sabbath, and so on—yet joins an Orthodox Congregation. What about him? People will say he is a hypocrite. But what this man or woman is, in essence, saying is this: "I join this movement because I believe there is something God-given about our religion, and if I do not observe our religious practices, it is because of some reason or another of my own, perhaps even some inadequate rationalization, perhaps some weakness on my part; but I do not believe that our people as a whole ought to repudiate these religious practices and abandon them." In short, it is a question of whether he wants Jewry as a whole, including his Rabbi, to abandon these practices or whether he thinks Judaism in the totality would be better off if they did not consider *his* non-observance as the norm, or as an advisable maximum for all Jewry.

This, my friends, is the basic difference—a very mighty difference, in fact, which affects ultimate survival—between Orthodoxy on the one hand and all non-Orthodox movements, be they Reform or Conservative, on the other hand.

Contrary to what some think, Orthodoxy can well afford to invite thought and examination of its doctrine; for, it alone has, through the ages, stood the tests both of time and thought.

❦ 2 ❦
The Hallowed House of Worship
BY RABBI MENAHEM M. KASHER

ONE OF OUR SAGES was once asked if any one word could define the aim and purpose of most of the Torah's precepts. He replied tersely, "Holiness"; [as Scripture puts it,] *Ye shall be*

250

holy, for I the Lord your God am holy (Leviticus 19:2). This is the focal point toward which all the Torah's precepts lead.[1] Every precept invests with greater holiness him who observes and maintains it.[2] And this is what we stress when we say in every benediction over the performance of a precept, *who hast hallowed us by Thy commandments.*

Now, the Creator of the world, who gave us the Torah, is Himself called holy in Scriptures (Leviticus *ibid.* and 20:26, Isaiah 6:3); in the words of *Midrash Tanhuma* (*Kedoshim* 3), He is sanctified with every kind of holiness.[3] The Torah too is called sacred;[4] and so is Israel designated as hallowed: *ye shall be unto Me a kingdom of priests and a holy nation* (Exodus 19:6); *Israel is hallowed unto the Lord* (Jeremiah 2:3).[5] Jerusalem in turn is named the holy city (Isaiah 52:1), and the Land of Israel is called the holy land (Zechariah 2:16). About the Tabernacle the Torah states, *Let them build Me a sanctuary*[6]

---

1. *Midrash Tanhuma, Tazria' 5*, reads: Said R. Akiba, The Holy One (blessed be He) gave the precepts to Israel only to prove them therewith. See also Makkoth 24a: Along came Habakkuk and established them [the principles of Judaism] as one: *The righteous shall live by his faith* (Habakkuk 2:4).

2. Thus, in *Mechilta, Mishpatim, Kaspa* 20: Issi b. Judah said, When the Almighty gives Israel a new precept He invests them with greater holiness. See also Nahmanides (*Ramban*), Commentary to Exodus 22:30.

3. R. Bahya writes in *Kad ha-Kemah* (s.v. *kedushah*): Each holy person may derive his sanctity from another of [greater] holiness . . . until [we come to] the Supreme Cause: He (be He blessed) is the power and well-spring of all sanctity; He is thus called holy because He is the source of all blessings.

4. *Mishnath R. Eliezer*, p. 243, reads: The Torah is called sacred, for it is stated, *The fear of the Lord is the beginning of wisdom, and the knowledge of the holy ones is understanding* (Proverbs 9:10); so great is its holiness that Moses had to sanctify himself by abstaining forty days from even bread and water, before he could receive the Torah. [The second part of the verse signifies the Torah, and connotes its holiness; it is missing in *Mishnath R. Eliezer*, but included in R. Israel Ibn Al-Nakawa, *Menorath ha-Maor*, III (New York, 1931) 375f. who cites this passage.]

5. *Mechilta* (*loc. cit.* in note 2) interprets emphatically: *Ye shall be unto Me holy men* (Exodus 22:30)—when you are holy, then are you Mine.

6. Hebrew, *mikdash,* same root as the word for holy.

251

(Exodus 25:8); and the synagogue is subsequently called *a little sanctuary* (Ezekiel 11:16 as interpreted in Megillah 29a). The Israelite community is commanded, *Therefore shall thy camp be holy* (Deuteronomy 23:15). In the prayer-book the Sabbath is called *a day of rest and holiness;* while the Writ refers to the Festivals as *holy convocations* (Leviticus 23:4); in our Festival prayers we bless the Lord, *who hallowest Israel and the Festive Seasons.*

The sanctity of the Torah spreads abroad and illumines space, time, and the very limbs of a person which fulfill the precepts.[7] And what indeed is the ultimate purpose of the people Israel in this world? To hallow the Divine Name on this earth, as we declare and proclaim in our prayers: *We will sanctify Thy name in the world.*

When an Israelite prays every day enwrapped in *tallith* (prayer robe) and *tefillin* (phylacteries), he accepts the yoke of the kingship of Heaven; his is "the service of the heart." And he thereby invokes for himself, every morning anew, a refreshing climate of sanctity and purity; as our Sages of blessed memory put it, people may enter the synagogue and *beth midrash* (House of Study) full of sins, and leave full of merit (*Yalkut Shim'oni* 1,771). When ten Jews [a *minyan*] recite together the *kedushah* ("sanctification") they give strong, exalted expressions to the Torah's command, *Let Me be hallowed among the children of Israel* (Leviticus 22:32).

Our Sages of blessed memory have clarified at great length the principles of holiness and prayer. To cite a few examples: He who prays must direct his heart toward Heaven (Berachoth 31a). He who prays has to regard himself as if the Shechinah (Divine Presence) is before him, for it is stated, *I have set the Lord always before me* (Psalms 16:8; Sanhedrin 22a). A man

---

7. Through observing the precepts a man attains holy concepts, sanctified speech, purity of vision, cleanliness of hands, etc. (see *Sefer Haredim*).

252

must purify his heart before prayer (*Shemoth Rabbah* 22, 4). The Writ cautions the Israelites: When you are praying before the Almighty, you are not to have two hearts [as it were], one for the Holy One and one for other matters (*Midrash Tanhuma, Ki Thabo* 1). At the time you stand in prayer, direct your eyes and heart to Heaven (*Midrash Tehillim* 142). When a man stands in prayer let him be happy that he serves a God who has no equal in the world, and let him not act frivolously before Him, but rather in reverence (*Yalkut Shim'oni, Psalms* 623). One is not to stand on public grounds and pray, because he will mind the people [passing by]; nor is one to stand among women and pray, because he will mind the women; let him rather sanctify his site five *amoth* in each direction (*Yalkut Shim'oni,* I, 934).

The *Shulhan Aruch* (our standard Code of Law) states clearly, One is to put aside all thoughts which trouble him, until his mind and attention remain pure for his prayer. . . . One is required to meditate on humbling thoughts, and not on matters involving frivolity (*Shulhan Aruch Orah Hayyim* 98, 1). And again: One is not to pray where there is anything which will distract him (*ibid.* 2).

Our Sages of blessed memory have asserted: Whoever brings himself to licentious thoughts will not be admitted into the inner sphere of the Holy One, blessed be He (Niddah 13b). This principle, that licentious thoughts must be avoided, also extends to any environment or circumstances which will necessarily induce such thoughts in a person: whoever does not keep well away from such environment or conditions, especially at the time of prayer, will certainly be unable to enter the inner domain of the Holy One.

Anyone reading these passages can see clearly that the fundamental condition for the purity and sanctity of prayer is to direct and concentrate the heart's reflection toward the service of the blessed Lord. In a sacred place the hallowed atmosphere can infuse one with holiness, and fire his spirit to commune in devotion with his Creator—everyone according to the level of his understanding and his degree, be it greater or lesser. Even for those who are far removed from what has been written here, who would be in the category of people who "go to the *beth midrash* but do nothing, who have merit only for going there" (Aboth 5, 14), the refining experience of reciting the *shema'* with devotion in a hallowed setting has yet the power to purify and sanctify a man for the entire day.

To permit us to call any quarters a "holy place," whose atmosphere is fit for the Shechinah to dwell there, the first condition was set by our Sages of blessed memory, in the Midrash: Said R. Judah b. Pazzi, For what reason was the section [of Scripture] on immorality[8] placed near the portion on holiness? This is but to teach you that wherever you find a restraint against immorality [in Scripture] there you find [mention of] holiness. This is in line with what R. Judah b. Pazzi said [elsewhere]: Whoever "fences himself off" from immorality is called holy (Vayyikra Rabbah 24, 6).[9] On this, *Yefeh Tho'ar,* citing *'Akedath Yitzhak,* comments: Since the passage speaks of a "fence" against immorality rather than a "prohibition," it evidently means more than mere abstinence from immoral behavior; it implies adding a barrier, an obstacle against licentiousness, so that one will not succumb through frivolity, gay abandon, or fantasies arising from improper thoughts or sights, all of which can bring one to grief.

From our Sages' words we learn that keeping distant from ideas of sinning, through guards and barriers, is the gateway to holiness. If they gave this as a general rule in daily living,

---

8. More correctly, incest and adultery; so throughout. The two sections here referred to are respectively Leviticus 18 and 19.
9. So also in the Jerusalem Talmud, Yebamoth 2:4; see as well *ibid.* Sanhedrin 10, 2.

254

how much more does it apply to quarters which we designate for sanctity and prayer. A synagogue without an atmosphere of holiness is but as a lifeless body.

Knowing as they did the nature of man in all its hidden aspects, the conflicts and contortions in man's thinking, our Sages realized that a people chosen and designated to become a "holy nation" would have to have "fences and barriers." This was indeed the first task of the Men of the Great Assembly, who stated as a key principle, "Make a fence around the Torah" (Aboth 1, 1)—based on the verse, *Ye shall guard my charge* (Leviticus 19:30), which the Sages interpreted to mean, Set a guard about My charge (Mo'ed Katan 5a). Along the same lines they said, There is no resemblance between a vineyard enclosed by a fence and one that is not thus enclosed (Aboth de-R. Nathan B, 1). In this vein we find the Sanhedrin (great court) called a "hedge" (1 Chronicles 4:23), for they "fenced in" the lawlessness of Israel (Baba Bathra 91b). In Chronicles Moses is called *abigdor,* "the father of fences" (1 Chronicles 4:18), according to the Midrash, which comments: Many "fence-makers" arose for Israel, but he [Moses] was father to them all[10] (*Vayyikra Rabbah* 1, 3). The very first paragraph of our Mishnah, which our saintly Teacher R. Judah ha-Nasi chose to begin this great work, sets down this norm: Why [says the Mishnah] did the Sages say [that at night the *shema'* may be recited only] until midnight? To keep a man distant from transgression[11] (Berachoth 1, 1). Along the same lines they said, A *beth din* (court) may impose lashes and [other] punishments . . . in order to erect a fence around the Torah (Yebamoth 90b).

---

10. I.e., predecessor or prototype.
11. Under original law, the nighttime *shema'* may be recited at any time of night, until dawn. But the Sages, fearing one might delay it unduly until its time would be passed, limited the period until midnight only; i.e., they established a "fence."

It should be noted that the need for "fences" or "defenses" against transgression first arose through a woman, out of a tragic experience of hers. Scripture relates, *And Tamar put ashes on her head, and rent her garment of many colors that was on her, and she laid her hand on her head, and went her way, crying aloud as she went* (2 Samuel 13:19) [because Absalom had seduced her and then rejected her]. Our Sages add: It was taught in the name of R. Joshua b. Karhah, She gave rise to a great fence, for it was then people said: If this can happen to princesses, how much more to commoners; if this can happen to the chaste, how much more to the wanton. Said R. Judah in Rab's name: There and then a ban was established against seclusion with an unmarried woman (Sanhedrin 21a). Elsewhere they declared: In that generation [of the wilderness] the women would fence off whatever the menfolk transgressed (Bamidbar Rabbah 21, 11). And again: It is a common saying that one fences in only that which is contained (*Yalkut Shim'oni Psalms* 731). A barrier can be erected only for one who is self-possessed; for the lawless it is doubtful if a fence will avail anything.

As to the claim which some make that the physical separation in the synagogue relegates the women to an inferior position, and connotes a slight to her esteem—this is piffle. The orientation of our Sages is expressed in the Jerusalem Talmud (Kiddushin 1, 7): *For thou art a holy people* (Deuteronomy 7:6; 14:2, 21)—the men and the women alike. And again: I call heaven and earth to witness—whether a non-Jew or a Jew, man or woman, the holy spirit will rest upon a person only in accordance with his deeds (*Seder Eliyahu Rabbah* 9). In *Seder Olam* (chapter 21) we read: Forty-eight prophets and seven prophetesses uttered revelation to Israel.[12] Women, then, reached the very summit of holiness: for example, Sarah the

---

12. So also in Megillah 14a.

mother of prophecy; Rebekah, Rachel and Leah, the mothers of prayer; Miriam the mother of deliverance; the womenfolk in the wilderness, mothers of faith; Ruth of Moab, mother of royalty; Queen Esther, mother of Israel's rescue; the daughter of Mattathias, and Hannah of the seven sons, mothers to sanctification of the Divine Name. And in every age there have been righteous women by whose merit we are destined to be redeemed. In Niddah 45b the Talmud concludes that "the Holy One, blessed be He, endowed women with greater understanding than men."[13]

As regards the mingling of men and women, the Sages had insight into the uttermost depths of the human mind; said they: A man's nature desires and longs for the gains of theft and immorality (Makkoth 23b); most become involved in theft, and a minority in immorality (Baba Bathra 165b).

Consider well what has been written thus far, and you will grant this as true: When a man finds himself amid unrelated women, even if his wife be with him, is not the atmosphere then most unhallowed, farthest from the special environment a man must have when he would pray and commune with his Lord and Maker? Does not the atmosphere of levity root out every trace of holiness, the very soul of prayer?

How then can observant Jews not quiver or quake to breach the traditional fences which have held for our people since time immemorial—fences whose entire being is to safeguard the purity of man's thought in time of prayer? And how can spiritual leaders dare to nullify the basic requirement for a synagogue's holiness, to rob the pious Jew of his chance to attain the emotions of holiness when he stands in prayer? Let it be noted that in essence the practice of men and women mingling is the fruit

---

13. This conclusion has its effect in Jewish law: The vows of a girl require investigation [if they are binding] after she is twelve, but those of a boy only after he is thirteen.

of an exile in which our people *mingled themselves with the nations and learned their actions* (Psalms 106:35). It is in imitation of the usage of non-Jews, against the Torah's command, *Ye shall not walk in the customs of the nations* (Leviticus 20:23).

These men sin against the generations to come; they have destroyed the basic character of the House of God, and have substituted for it a "people's house."[14] They have robbed their

---

14. Perhaps this is what our Sages (of blessed memory) had in mind when they declared: For a sin of two words the ignorant die . . . they call the synagogue a "people's house." Rashi comments: [It was] a derogatory name [denoting a place] where everyone gathers. (See also Jeremiah 39 and Rashi *ad loc.*) *Maharsha* comments: A "people's house," as though it were designated for the people, for their needs, and there were no Divine element in it. In other words, they were punished for perceiving no distinction between a "people's house" and a synagogue—that the latter is a House of God, a sacred place, while a "people's house" designates a secular place, where men and women gather for all occasions, but not for prayer. These ignorant men made a "people's house" out of the synagogue.

And apparently for this reason the laws of the synagogue in our Codes do not specify that there must be a physical separation or partition between men and women—since the name "synagogue" denotes a sacred place, and this requirement is implicit; quarters where men and women mingle would be called a "people's house." This distinction was apparently so generally well known that no need was felt to give it the emphasis of the written word. But see *Shulhan Aruch Orah Hayyim* 315, 1, about setting up a partition on the Sabbath, that one put up merely for modesty is permissible; *Mishnah Berurah ad loc.* citing *Mordechai* to Shabbath, comments: "For instance, to separate men from women when they are listening to the rabbi's address." Clearly, then, even where they did not regularly assemble, but both men and women merely came to hear the rabbi expound, a partition was required for the sake of modesty. See *Shulhan Aruch ibid.* 88 on whether a woman may enter a synagogue to pray during the days of her uncleanness.

Some believe that in early times it was the custom that women in general did not attend the synagogue but prayed at home (there is the well-known letter of R. Elijah, the Vilna Gaon, to his household; see also the present writer's *Torah Shelemah*, XV, chapter 5, on prayer in the synagogue); they went only to hear the rabbi's exposition (as would appear from Kiddushin 81a, *q.v.*, as well as Rashi and *Tosafoth ad loc.*) and that infrequently. With the passing of the generations they began going to the synagogue for prayer, and women's sections were established for them. However, a women's section

children of the vision of a hallowed synagogue, the "little sanctuary" to which Jewry has turned in every generation, in a spirit of reverence for God. They have converted it into a general public hall, devoid of the true, exalted spirit of holiness which was preserved and transmitted to us by generation after generation through tradition-bound synagogues, conducted by the laws of the Torah.

At the very time the Torah was to be given, the Israelites were commanded, *Approach not near a woman* (Exodus 19:15). In *Pirke de-R. Eliezer* (chapter 41) we read: "R. Pinhas said, The Israelites stood at Sinai arranged, the women apart and the men apart." If it was so at Mount Sinai, where both time and place were imbued with holiness, how much more necessary is this arrangement in the synagogue the year round?

In that historic situation we find our Sages considering the women more highly esteemed than the men: The Holy One, blessed be He, bade Moses, *Thus shalt thou say to the House of Jacob, and tell the children of Israel* (Exodus 19:3),

---

did not have the status of a synagogue in Jewish law, as is apparent from the ruling in *Hachmath 'Adam* 86, 15: A synagogue wall may not be torn down to allow for windows for the women's section; insofar as a women's section has no synagogual sanctity whatever; hence, even if [the tearing down] is not done as destruction, it is forbidden by Rabbinic law. Similarly in the Responsa of *Maharam* of Lublin, 59: The site where the men's synagogue section stood is to remain intact, for there is the main sanctity.

On the other hand, from the Talmud Tractate Soferim it would appear that it was the custom for women to come to the synagogue: By law [it reads] every portion [of the Pentateuch] and the Prophets [read in the synagogue] is to be translated [into Aramaic] for the people, the women, and the children (Soferim 18, 6, *q.v.*). This is also suggested by the account in Sotah 22a: A certain widow . . . came to pray in the academy of R. Johanan. Similarly, *Yalkut Shim'oni* 1, 871: It happened that a woman . . . came before R. Jose b. Halafta. . . . Said she to him . . . I rise early for synagogue every day. Elsewhere (*Torah Shelemah*, XVII, Supplement, p. 316) I have cited *Shibbale ha-Leket* that the essential function of rendering the Scriptural portions in the synagogue into the vernacular, is to explain the Torah to the women. Note, however, Mo'ed Katan 18a: A woman in the *beth midrash* is unusual.

and our Sages interpreted: *the House of Jacob* refers to the women (Shabbath 87a). The women were thus approached first, before the men, about accepting the Torah and respon· sibility for the sanctity of the House of Israel.

Again, at the hymning by the Red Sea it is written, *Then sang Moses* (Exodus 15:1), *And Miriam took,* etc. (*ibid.* 20), *And Miriam sang,* etc. (*ibid.* 21). *Mechilta* comments: The Writ shows that just as Moses sang praise for the men, so did Miriam sing praise for the women: *Sing ye to the Lord,* etc. (*ibid.*; *Mechilta, Shirah,* end). So also Philo in his *De Vita Mosis*: Moses stood at the head of the men, and his sister Miriam with the women (*Torah Shelemah* XV, 239). Quite simply, singing their great hymn of deliverance, the men stood apart, and the women apart.

If you really wish to know how earnest our Sages were about guards for the sanctity of the synagogue, go and learn it from *Targum Jonathan* to Exodus 38:8[15]—"*And he made the laver of brass* . . . out of the mirrors of [polished] brass of the modest women; and when they would come to pray forgiveness at the Tabernacle door they would then stand [there] while their sacrifice was being offered up, and they would give praise and worship." This is clarified in a Commentary to Chronicles by a disciple of R. Saadiah Gaon, and *Recanate* to Leviticus, pericope *Vayyikra*: The officiating *kohen* (priest) had to offer up the woman's sacrifice in her name [and he would therefore need to know who she was], and yet he was forbidden to look at her visage. Hence the laver [fount or basin] was made of highly reflecting material: the woman would stand near, regarding it, while the *kohen* would look at the laver, recognize her, and offer up the sacrifice on her behalf.

These words illustrate impressively how stringent our Sages

---

15. See the present writer's lengthy discussion of this passage in *Horeb,* Spring, 1937.

were about protecting modesty and guarding the sanctity of the Israelite community. In their view, the Torah ordained a special kind of vessel in the Tabernacle so that the *kohanim* should not transgress the ban against regarding women,[16] even where a precept of sacrifices might require it. If mere looking is treated so stringently, how much more the mingling of men and women? Such a practice in holy quarters would be unthinkable to our Sages!

It is well known that the Temple contained a women's section or court, as the Talmud makes clear in Middoth 2 and Sukkah 51b: "They [the Sages] ordained that women were to sit in the upper part and men below. . . . They came across a verse, which they interpreted [that it was necessary to keep men and women separate, and to erect a "fence" in Jewry, so that people would not come to grief —Rashi]: *And the land shall mourn, every family apart: the family of the house of David apart, and their wives apart,* etc. (Zechariah 12:12).[17] The

---

16. *Sefer Yere'im*, precept 12 (392) regards the verse, *Let thy camp be holy, that He see no unseemly thing in thee* (Deuteronomy 23:15) as a negative precept; a derivative is the dictum that "a hand-breadth of a woman's body constitutes an indecency [if exposed], as regards reciting the *shema'* and praying"—stated in Berachoth 25b, *q.v.* So also *Sefer Mitzvoth Katan* 83; see as well *Shulhan Aruch Orah Hayyim* 75: The verse, *Thou shalt keep thee from every evil thing* (*ibid.* 10) is interpreted in Abodah Zarah 20b to signify that a man is not to regard a woman . . . or let his mind dwell by day, etc. *Sifre* 254 reads, *Thou shalt keep thee*—beware not to let your thoughts dwell on licentiousness. Similarly in Berachoth 12b: *And ye shall not go about after your own heart and your own eyes* (Numbers 15:39)— this refers to licentious thoughts.

17. In *Piske Massecheth Sukkah* 45 (printed in *Sam Hayyim*) the earlier R. Isaiah writes: What was the great innovation? Said R. Eliezer, It was as we learned: It [the courtyard] was at first level [ground], and they erected a balcony so that the women could see from above, and the men from below. Thus we learned in the Mishnah, Middoth. . . . They set up beams, and boards atop them, so that the women could stand on them and see the festivities [during Sukkoth] from above, while the men would stand below in the courtyard; and the men could not gaze at the women because it [the balcony] had screens all around made of plaited material [to leave many

Jerusalem Talmud (Sukkah *ad loc. q.v.*) reads: "What amendment did they institute there [in the Temple]? They placed the men by themselves and the women by themselves, etc." Thus it was derived that at every gathering men and women are required to be separate.[18]

From that day to this, the Jewish people have undertaken, in every region where they have settled, that any synagogue they would build was to have a special women's section, separated by a partition. The assimilationists alone breached this "fence" in order to ape the ways of other peoples. R. Asher b. Jehiel in his Work on Pesahim, 3, cites the Jerusalem Talmud (Pesahim 4, 1): "Do not alter the usage of your fathers. . . . Your fathers built a fence," etc. Hence such a practice [i.e., which our fathers kept] is considered a "fence." In another connection *Mahzor Vitry* (p. 375) has: Whatever was instituted at the time of the Temple, and its ban has spread throughout Jewry, that matter becomes as though it had been ordained at Mount Sinai. In the same vein we read in a responsum of R. Saadiah Gaon: Since the Prophets bade the people Israel act thus . . . and

---

small] openings, so that the women within could see out, while those without could not see within—as we learned in a *baraitha*: Originally the men were within and the women outside, and they would reach a state of levity—that is, the men would enter and leave with the women; it was then ordained that the men be outside and the women within [this is not the version of our printed editions], and still they would become frivolous—that is, they would gaze and then wink at one another; it was ultimately ordained that the women should watch from above and the men from below.

R. Isaiah's view is clearly that the screen was such that the men without could not see within. This tallies with Maimonides' words in his Commentary to Mishnah, Sukkah *ad loc.*: "so that the men would not regard the women." See also *Me'iri* and *Yad David ad loc.*

18. And so Rashi in *Sefer ha-Pardes*, 19b: It is forbidden for women to mix among the men, whether at a ritual meal or any other occasion; rather must the men be separate and the women separate. It is derived *a fortiori*: if at a time of mourning it is written that the House of Israel lamented *each family apart, the family of the house of David apart, and their wives apart,* etc.

262

Daniel so did . . . and Jewry has followed this practice on the Prophets' word, it has become a precept [binding] on all Jewry in exile to observe, like any precept ordained by the Divine word (Geonic Responsa, Lyck, 1). These statements apply, then, even to customs and innovations.

The Holy One, blessed be He, had a precious gift in His treasure-house, and "holiness" was its name. At the time the Torah was given, He transmitted it to the Jewish people, and called us *a kingdom of priests and a holy nation* (Exodus 19:6). Through long exile the Jewish people has kept guard over the sanctity of the Torah, and the Torah has safeguarded the holiness of the Jew, from birth to burial: There were ever the holy covenant of ritual circumcision, the education of children in sacred studies, the celebration of the Bar Mitzvah, when the yoke of Heaven's kingship was assumed, marriage into a family life of purity and modesty, and a hallowed meal-table; and above all, the scrupulous observance of Sabbath and Festivals. Tragically, for part of Jewry this world of the spirit has been destroyed; all these sanctities have been profaned; while some observe the precepts in a secular form and manner, having utterly dispelled the sacred character inherent in the precepts.

What is yet left us? Only the synagogue, the domain of the sacred, the House of God. To our despair, even this saving remnant is being desolated before our eyes: it is being changed into a "people's house." The Shechinah has been driven from the synagogue proper, forced to take refuge on the lower level, in the *beth midrash,* where people yet pray on weekdays— groups composed for the most part of the middle-aged and elderly, and those who recite *kaddish.* These are the meager quarters assigned the Shechinah, there to cling to the sanctity of Jewry.

Shall we drive the Shechinah from this its last corner as well? We dwell in prayer that He who dwells on high will send

263

forth a spirit of purity from above to open the eyes of the blind who walk in darkness, that they may see the glory and the splendor hidden in our people's Torah and in the spiritual leadership of generations past; that they may yet sense the incandescent luminosity of Jewish sanctity, and transmit this rare essence to their desecndants until the end of the generations.

Guardian of a holy nation, guard Thou the remnant of a holy people, and let not a holy nation perish.

❦ 3 ❦

Woman in Talmud and Midrash

A SELECTION OF SOURCES

SAID R. ELEAZAR: Whoever has no wife, is [thereby] not truly a man (Yebamoth 63a). It was taught: Whoever has no wife remains without beneficence, without a helpmate, without joy, blessing or atonement. . . . R. Simon quoted R. Joshua b. Levi: He remains also without peace. . . . R. Hiyya b. Gamdi added: Nor is he a whole man (*Bereshith Rabbah* 17, 2).

Our rabbis taught: Who is wealthy? . . . R. Akiba said, Whoever has a wife of beautiful deeds (Shabbath 25b). The heart's joy—is a woman (*ibid.* 152a). Said Raba: Come and see how beneficent is a good wife . . . since it is written, *Whoso findeth a wife findeth a great good* (Proverbs 18:22; Yebamoth 63b).

Our rabbis taught: If one loves his wife as himself, and honors her more than himself . . . Scripture says of him, *Thou shalt know that thy tent is in peace* (Job 5:24; Yebamoth 62b). Said Rab: A man should ever be careful not to mortify his wife, for since a woman cries easily, she is easily hurt.[1] . . . If your

---

1. Or, her hurt readily brings reprisal (Rashi).

wife is short, bend down and listen to her. . . . Said R. Helbo:
A man should ever take great care to respect his wife, for blessing will frequent a man's house only for the sake of his wife
(Baba' Metzia' 59a). R. Pinhas ha-Kohen b. Hama' said:
When a woman remains chastely retired in her home, just as
the Temple altar atones, even so does she bring atonement to
her household (*Midrash Tanhuma', Vayyishlah* 6).

Said R. Eliezer: Whoever divorces his first wife, even the
Temple altar sheds tears for him (Gittin 90b). And R. Yohanan
said: Whoever loses his first wife, it is as if the Temple were
destroyed in his time. . . . Said R. Alexandri: For any man
whose wife dies in his lifetime, the world grows dark. . . . R.
Samuel b. Nahman said: For everything there is a substitute,
except for the wife of one's youth. . . . R. Judah taught his son
R. Isaac: A man finds satisfaction of spirit only with his first
wife (Sanhedrin 22a).

The school of R. Shila' said: Women are compassionate
(Sukkah 14b). We learn that the Holy One (blessed be He)
gave woman extra understanding, more than man (Niddah
45b).

Where the tithe for the poor is distributed, a [poor] woman
is to be given [her share] first. Why? because of the shame;
[it would shame her to wait]. Said Raba: At first, if a man and
a woman came before me to sue [their respective defendants]
I would resolve the man's conflict first. . . . Once I heard this
ruling, I settled the woman's case first [thereafter] (Yebamoth
100a). Our rabbis taught: If a male and a female orphan
come to receive sustenance [from the community charity][2] the
girl is provided for first, and then the male orphan: for it is
proper for a male to go about and ask alms at doorsteps, but
it is not proper for a girl. If a male and a female orphan both
come [for charity to be able] to marry, the girl is to be married

---

2. Rashi *ad loc.*

off first, and then the boy; for a woman suffers greater shame than a man (Kethuboth 67a-b).[3]

4

The Position of Woman in Judaism

BY DR. JOSEPH HERMAN HERTZ
late Chief Rabbi of England

IT IS ASTONISHING to note the amount of hostile misrepresentation that exists in regard to the woman's position in Bible times. "The relation of the wife to the husband was, to all intents and purposes, that of a slave to her master," are the words of a writer in the *Encyclopedia of Religion and Ethics.* That this judgment is radically false may be proved from hundreds of instances throughout Scripture. God created man and woman in His image (Genesis 1:27)—both man and woman are in their spiritual nature akin to God; and both are invested with the same authority to subdue the earth and have dominion over it (*ibid.* 28). The wives of the Patriarchs are almost the equal of their husbands; later generations regard them as quite alike. Miriam, alongside her brothers, is reckoned as one of the three emancipators from Egypt (Micah 6:4); Deborah is "judge" in Israel, and leader of the war of independence; and to Hannah her husband speaks: *Why weepest thou? . . . am I not better to thee than ten sons?* (1 Samuel 1:8). In later centuries we find a woman among the Prophets (Huldah —2

3. This principle is incorporated in our Code of law, *Shulhan Aruch Yoreh De'ah,* 251, 8: "If a man and a woman come to ask for food, the woman is given precedence over the man; the same is the law if they come seeking clothing. So also, if a male and a female orphan come to be married off, she is given in marriage first." And in 252, 8: "A woman is to be ransomed from capture before a man." (On clothing and ransom see Horayoth 13a.)

Kings 22:14, 2 Chronicles 34:22); and in the days of the second Temple, on the throne (Queen Salome Alexandra). Nothing can well be nobler praise of woman than Proverbs 31; and as regards the reverence due to her from her children, the mother was always placed on a par with the father (Exodus 20:12, Leviticus 19:3). A Jewish child would not have spoken to his grief-stricken mother as did Telemachus, the hero's son in the Odyssey: "Go to the Chamber, and mind thy own house-wiferies. Speech shall be for man: for all, but for me in chief; for mine is the lordship of the house."

The property rights of women became clearly defined in the Talmudic period. Her legal status under Jewish law "compares to its advantage with that of contemporary civilizations" (G. F. Moore). In respect of possessing independent estate, the Jewish wife was in a position far superior to that of English wives before the enactment of recent legislation (Abrahams). An infinitely important proof of her dominating place in Jewish life is the undeniable fact that the hallowing of the Jewish home was her work; and that the laws of chastity were observed in that home, both by men and women, with a scrupulousness that has hardly ever been equaled. The Jewish Sages duly recognized her wonderful spiritual influence, and nothing could surpass the delicacy with which respect for her is inculcated: "Love your wife as yourself, and honor her more than yourself. Be careful not to cause a woman to weep, for God counts her tears. Israel was redeemed from Egypt on account of the virtue of its women. He who weds a good woman is as if he had fulfilled all the precepts of the Torah" (Talmud).[1]

The respect and reverence which womanhood enjoyed in Judaism are not limited to noble and beautiful *sayings*. That respect and reverence were translated into life. True, neither

---

1. [See respectively Yebamoth 62b, Baba' Metzia' 59a, Sotah 11b, Yebamoth 63b.]

minnesingers nor troubadours sang for Jewish women; and the immemorial chastity of the Jewess could not well go with courts of love and chivalric tournaments.

And yet one test alone is sufficient to show the abyss, in actual life, between Jewish and non-Jewish chivalry, down to modern times.

That test is wife-beating.

On the one hand both Rabbenu Tam, the renowned grandson of Rashi, and R. Meir of Rothenberg, the illustrious jurist, poet, martyr, and leader of thirteenth century Judaism, could declare: "This is a thing not done in Israel"; and the *Shulhan Aruch* prescribes it as the *beth din's* duty to punish a wifebeater, to excommunicate him, and—if this be of no avail— to compel him to divorce his wife with full *kethubah* [payment as per the marriage contract] (*Eben ha-Ezer* 154, 3).

Among non-Jews, on the other hand, no less an authority on the Middle Ages than G. G. Coulton writes: "To chastise one's wife was not only customary, not only expressly permitted by the statutes of some towns, but even formally granted by the Canon Law." Even in our own country (England), as late as the fifteenth century, "wife-beating was a recognized right of man, and was practiced without shame by high as well as low" (G. M. Trevelyan). In the reign of Charles II this recognized right of man began to be doubted; "yet the lower ranks of the people who were always fond of the Common Law still claim and exact their ancient privilege" (Blackstone). Even more strange was the public sale of wives that was not unknown among the very poor. Thomas Hardy wrote his powerful novel, *The Mayor of Casterbridge,* on such a sale. Some years ago, the [London] *Times* (January 4, 8, 11 and 17, 1924) traced a number of these sales throughout the nineteenth century; and Professor A. R. Wright has shown that folk-custom to have survived in various parts of England into the twentieth century.

268

In modern times, friend and foe of the Jew alike speak with admiration of his home, and echo the praise of the heathen seer: *How beautiful are thy tents, O Jacob, thy dwelling places, O Israel* (Numbers 24:5). The following description may well be quoted here of the Sabbath eve of a humble toiler in the London ghetto a half century ago: "The roaring Sambatyon[2] of life was at rest in the Ghetto; on thousands of squalid homes the light of Sinai shone. The Ghetto welcomed the Sabbath Bride with proud song and humble feast, and sped her parting with optimistic symbolisms of fire and wine, of spice and light and shadow. All around, their neighbors sought distraction in the blazing public houses, and their tipsy bellowings resounded through the streets and mingled with the Hebrew hymns. Here and there the voice of a beaten woman rose on the air. But no son of the Covenant was among the revelers or the wife-beaters; the Jews remained a chosen race, a peculiar people, faulty enough, but redeemed at least from the grosser vices—a little human islet won from the waters of animalism by the genius of ancient engineers" (I. Zangwill).

✿ 5 ✿

Woman in Temple and Synagogue

BY SOLOMON SCHECHTER

(an abridgement)

THE LEARNED WOMAN has always been a favorite subject with Jewish students; and her intellectual capabilities have been fully vindicated in many an essay and even fair-sized book. Less attention, however, has been paid to woman's claims as

---

2. [A legendary river which ran turbulently all week and rested on the Sabbath.]

a devotional being whom the Temple, and afterwards the Synagogue, more or less recognized. At least it is not known to me that any attempt was made to give, even in outline, the history of woman's relation to public worship. It is needless to say that the present sketch, which is meant to supply this want in some measure, lays no claim to completeness.

The earliest allusion to women's participation in *public* worship is that in Exodus 38:8, to the women who assembled at the door of the "tent of meeting," of whose mirrors the lavers of brass were made (cf. 1 Samuel 2:22). Philo, who is not exactly enamored of the emancipation of women, and seeks to confine them to the "small state," is here full of their praise. "For," he says, "though no one enjoined them to do so, they of their own spontaneous zeal and earnestness contributed the mirrors with which they had been accustomed to deck and set off their beauty, as the most becoming first-fruits of their modesty, and of the purity of their married life, and, as one may say, of the beauty of their souls." In another passage Philo describes the Jewish women as "competing with the men themselves in piety, having determined to enter upon a glorious contest, and to the utmost extent of their power to exert themselves so as not to fall short of their holiness."

The Septuagint speaks "of the women who fasted by the doors of the Tabernacle." But most of the old Jewish expositors, as well as Onkeles, conceive that the women went to the Tent of Meeting to pray. Ibn Ezra offers the interesting remark, "And behold, there were women in Israel serving the Lord, who left the vanities of this world, and not being desirous of beautifying themselves any longer, made of their mirrors a free offering, and came to the tabernacle every day to pray and to listen there to the words of the commandments."[1] When we

---

1. [It might be interesting to add a passage from *Midrash ha-Gadol* to Exodus 38:8 (recently published): R. Eliezer said, Come and see what the

find that in 1 Samuel 1:12, *Hannah continued to pray before the Lord,* she was only doing there what many of her sisters did before and after her. We may also judge that it was from the number of these noble women, who made religion the aim of their lives, that the "twenty-two" heroines and prophetesses sprang who form part of the glory of Jewish history. Sometimes it even happened that their husbands derived their religious inspiration from them. Thus the husband of the prophetess Deborah is said to have been an unlettered man. But his wife made him carry to the Sanctuary the candles which she herself had prepared, this being the way in which she encouraged him to seek communion with the righteous.[2]

The language in which the husband of the "Great Woman" of Shunem addresses his wife, *Wherefore wilt thou go to him* [the prophet] *today? it is neither New Moon nor Sabbath* (2 Kings 4:23), proves that on Festivals and Sabbaths the women used to attend some kind of worship, performed by the prophet, though we cannot say in what this worship consisted. The New Moon was especially a women's holiday, and was so observed even in the Middle Ages, for the women refrained from doing work on that day. The explanation given by the Rabbis is that when the men broke off their golden earrings to supply material for the golden calf, the women refused to contribute their trinkets, for which good behavior a special day of repose was granted to them. Rather interesting as well as complimentary to women is the remark which the Rabbis make with regard to the "Great Woman." As will be remembered, it is *she* who says, *I perceive that this* [*Elisha*] *is a holy man of God* (*ibid.* 9). Referring to this verse the Talmud says, "From this fact we

righteous women of that generation did; [this verse] teaches us that each and every one brought one copper mirror, to make a separate contribution, memorializing themselves alone.]

2. [*Seder Eliyahu Rabbah,* ed. Friedmann, beginning of chapter 10.]

may infer that woman is quicker in recognizing the worth of a stranger than man" [Berachoth 10b].

The great woman, or women, continued to pray and to join in the public worship also after the destruction of the first Temple. Thus Esther is reported by tradition to have addressed God in a long extempore prayer before she presented herself before the throne of Ahasuerus to plead her people's cause; and women were always enjoined to attend the reading of the Book of Esther. When Ezra read the Law for the first time, he did so in the presence of the men and the women (Nehemiah 8:3). In the Book of the Maccabees we read of "the women girt with sackcloth . . . and the maidens that ran to the gates. . . . And all holding their hands towards heaven made supplication." In the Judith story, mention is also made of "every man and woman . . . who fell before the Temple, and spread out their sackcloth before the face of the Lord . . . and cried before the God of Israel." In the second Temple, the women, as is well known, possessed a court reserved for their exclusive use. There the great illuminations and rejoicings on the evening of the Feast of Tabernacles used to be held. On this occasion, however, the women were confined to galleries specially erected for them. It was also in this Women's Hall that the great public reading of certain portions of the Law by the king, once in seven years, used to take place, and women had also to attend at the function.

The three hundred maidens who were employed for the weaving of the curtains in the Temple cannot be looked upon as having stood in closer connection with the Temple, or as having formed an order of women-priests or girl-devotees (as one might wrongly be induced to think by certain passages in Apocryphal writings of the New Testament). But, on the other hand, it is not improbable that their frequent contact with the Sanctuary of the nation produced in them that religious enthusiasm and zeal which may account for the heroic death which—according to tradition—they sought and found after the destruction of the Temple. It is to be remarked that, according to the law, women were even exempted from putting their hands on the head of the victim, which formed an important item in the sacrificial worship. It is, however, stated by an eye-witness that the authorities permitted them to perform this ceremony if they desired to do so, and that their reason for this concession was "to give calmness of the spirit, or satisfaction, to women" [Hagigah 16a].

Still greater, perhaps, was "the calmness of spirit" given to women in the synagogue. We find in ancient epitaphs that such titles of honor were conferred upon them as "Mistress of the Synagogue," and "Mother of the Synagogue," and, though they held no actual office in the synagogue, it is not improbable that they acquired these titles by meritorious work connected with a religious institution, viz., charity. There was, indeed, a tendency to exclude women from the synagogue at certain seasons, but almost all the authorities protest against it, many of them declaring such a notion to be quite un-Jewish.

I am rather inclined to think that the synagogue took for its model the arrangements in the Temple, and thus confined women to a place of their own. But . . . there can be no doubt that the Jewish women were great synagogue-goers. To give only one instance: One Rabbi asks another, If the members of the synagogue are all descendants of Aaron, to whom would they impart their blessing [to answer Amen]? The answer is, To the women [and children —Jer. Talmud, Berachoth 5, 5;9d].

Of the sermon some were even more fond than their husbands. Thus one woman was so much interested in the lectures of R. Meir, which he was in the habit of giving every Friday evening, that she used to remain there so long that the

273

candles in her hourse burnt themselves out. Her lazy husband, who stopped at home, so strongly resented having to wait in the dark, that he would not permit her to cross the threshold until she gave some offence to the preacher, which would make him sure that she would not venture to attend his sermons again.[3]

The prayers they said were the Eighteen Benedictions which were prescribed by the law. But it would seem that occasionally they offered short prayers composed by themselves as suggested by their personal feelings and needs. Thus, to give one instance, R. Yohanan relates that one day he observed a young girl fall on her face and pray: "Lord of the world, Thou hast created Paradise, Thou hast created hell, Thou hast created the wicked, Thou hast created the righteous; may it be Thy will that I may not serve as a stumbling-block to them."[4] The fine Hebrew in which the prayer is expressed, and the notion of the responsibility of Providence for our actions, manifest a high degree of intelligence and reflection. It was said of Jewish women, "The daughters of Israel were stringent and laid certain restrictions on themselves." They were also allowed to form a quorum by themselves for the purpose of saying the Grace, but they could not be counted along with males for this end [Berachoth 45b].

One privilege was left to women—that of weeping. In Judges 11:40, we read of the daughters of Israel that went yearly to lament the daughter of Jephthah; while in 2 Chronicles 35:25, we are told how *all the singing men and the singing women spoke of Josiah in their lamentations*. Even in later times they held a public office as mourning women at funerals. In the Talmud fragments of compositions by women for such occasions are to be found. Indeed, woman became in these

---

3. [Jerusalem Talmud, Sotah 1, 4; *Bamidbar Rabbah* 9; *Debarim Rabbah* 5.]

4. [Sotah 22a.]

274

times the type of grief and sorrow. She cannot reason, but she feels much more deeply than man. Here is one instance from an old tradition: Jeremiah said, "When I went up to Jerusalem [after the destruction of the Temple] I lifted my eyes and saw there a lonely woman sitting on the top of the mountain, her dress black, her hair dishevelled, crying, 'Who will comfort me?' I approached her and spoke to her, 'If thou art a woman, speak to me. If thou art a ghost, begone.' She answered, 'Dost thou not know me? . . . I am the Mother, Zion.' "[5]

In general, however, the principle applied to women was: *The king's daughter within the palace is all glorious* (Psalms 45:14), but *not* outside of it. In the face of the "Femina in ecclesia taceat," which was the ruling maxim with other religions, Jewish women could only feel flattered by this polite treatment by the Rabbis, though it meant the same thing. We must not think, however, that this prevented them from attending the service of the synagogue. According to the Tractate Soferim, even "the little daughters of Israel were accustomed to go to synagogue" (18, 8). In the same tractate (18, 6) it is laid down as "a duty to translate for them the portion [of the Law] of the week, and the lesson from the prophets" into the language they understand. And thus being ignorant of the Hebrew language women prayed in the vernacular. Many famous Rabbis of the twelfth and thirteenth centuries express their wonder that the "custom of women praying in other [non-Hebrew] languages extended over the whole world." Some even recommended it, as, for example, the author of *The Book of the Pious,* who gives advice to women to learn the prayers in the language familiar to them. Nor was it unknown for a pious Jew to compose a special hymn for his wife's use in honor of the Sabbath.

How long this custom of women praying in the vernacular

---

5. [Pesikta' Rabbathi 26.]

lasted, we have no means of ascertaining. Probably it was already extinct about the end of the fifteenth century. For R. Solomon Portaleone, who lived in the sixteenth century, already regrets the abolition of "this beautiful and worthy custom." "When they prayed in the vernacular," he says, "they understood what they were saying, whilst now they only gabble off their prayers." As a sort of compromise we may regard the various *tehinoth,* "Supplications"; they form a kind of additional prayers supplementary to the ordinary liturgy, and are written in German. Chiefly composed by women, they specially answer the needs of the sex on various occasions. These prayers deserve a full description by themselves, into which I cannot now enter.

It is also worth noticing that the manuals on the "Three Women's Commandments" (mostly composed in German, sometimes also in rhymes) contained much more than their titles would suggest. They rather served as headings to groups of laws, arranged under each commandment. Thus the first (about certain laws in Leviticus 12 and 15) becomes the motto for purity in body and soul; the second (the consecration of the first cake of the dough) includes all matters relating to charity, in which women were even reminded to encourage their newly married husbands not to withhold from the poor the tithes of the bridal dowry, as well as of their future yearly income; whilst the third (the lighting of the Sabbath lamp) becomes the symbol for spiritual light and sweetness in every relation of human life.

As another compromise may also be considered the institution of *forzugerin* (woman-reader) or the *voilkennivdicke* (the well-knowing one) who reads the prayers and translates them into the vernacular for the benefit of her less learned sisters. In Poland and in Russia, even at the present time,[6] such a woman-reader is to be found in every synagogue, and from

6. [Two or three generations ago, and so below.]

what I have heard the institution is by no means unknown in London. The various prayer-books containing the Hebrew text as well as the Jewish-German translation, which appear in such frequent editions in Russia, are mostly intended for the use of these praying women. Not uninteresting is the title-page of R. Aaron ben Samuel's Jewish-German translations and collections of prayers which appeared in the beginning of the eighteenth century. He addressed the Jewish public in the following terms: "My dear brethren, buy this lovely prayer-book or wholesome tonic for body and soul, which has never appeared in such German print since the world began; and make your wives and children read it often. Thus they will refresh their bodies and souls, for this light will shine forth into your very hearts. As soon as the children read it they will understand their prayers, by which they will enjoy both this world and the world to come."

An earlier translator of the prayer-book addresses himself directly to the "pious women" whom he invites to buy his book, "in which they will see very beautiful things." Recent centuries seem, on the whole, to have been distinguished for the number of praying-women they produced. The virtues which constituted the claim of women to religious distinction were modesty, charity, and daily attendance at the synagogue morning and evening. In the memorial books of the time hundreds of such women are noted. Some used also to spin the *tzitzith* (fringes) which they presented to their friends; others fasted frequently, whilst "Old Mrs. Hechele" not only attended the synagogue every day, and did charity to poor and rich, but also understood the art of midwifery, which she practised in the community without accepting payment for her services. According to R. Ch. J. Bachrach women used also to say the prayer of *kaddish* in the synagogue when their parents left no male posterity.

✾ 6 ✾

The Jewish Woman

BY NAHIDA REMY

MODERN RESEARCH, which continually discloses the re-
motest mementoes of all civilized peoples, has, proportionally,
brought to light only a few of the treasures of Jewish lore, which,
however, have influenced, though unnoticed, the rise and development of civilization.

The investigator will be astonished to find how much old
Jewish thought and custom have contributed to the amelioration
of family life, and the social standing of woman.

It is the Bible which, from the very beginning, shows that
man and woman were alike created in the image of God. Even
the formation of the term in Hebrew, איש man, and אשה woman,
are alike, except for the necessary feminine ending, *ah*.

Among nearly all the ancient nations woman was considered a dependent, enslaved creature, or an object of luxury
and amusement. Let us turn to the Bible and the Talmud to
find how woman was treated among the Jews. Both these books
are replete with the most important laws and statutes which,
developed by a thousand years of experience, are still valid in
modern legislation.

The regulations and rules for the position and treatment
of woman are found to be the most original ones. Before entering into a detailed examination, one is induced to ask: Have
the ancient Jews been so much ahead of their time, or did
modern legislators retrograde so far behind the ancient Jews?

The special care for woman and the reverential regard for
her are remarkable, and fall nothing short of homage. A striking difference prevails in the very way in which the birth of a

child was greeted among the Jews, in comparison with other nations. The newborn human being, whether a girl or a boy, was received with all the love and tender care which its touching helplessness required.

There are no rules to be found in old Jewish legislation concerning how the children should be brought up, how they should be cared for and treated—for it seemed self-evident to them that it should be done. This question is discussed the first time in the Mishnah, and the Jewish scholars agreed that children of either sex, had the very same right to parental care.

The grown-up girl is given in marriage by the parents, or put into a home where the master, or the son of the master, wishes to marry her later. Even where there is a question of a "sale," the father, it is true, receives a compensation, and the girl "serves" in the house of the "master," but when the master, or the son, has not married her within six years, she is *free*, and no one, not even her own father, can prevent her from going, for she is protected by the law.

What a vast difference between this independence gained in a few years, and the condition of slavery to which girls and women of other nations were subjected during entire lives.

Her master, who was not permitted to send her to any other place during the six years, was bound, if the marriage did not take place, to indemnify her for the work she had done in his house. Under all circumstances, there was not only care taken of her physical wants, but also of her moral development. Many a proverb and Talmudical saying illustrate this seemingly dependent, but really self-directed, relation of the girl in the house of the master who would probably become her husband.

Strange and hazardous seems the custom that the father was permitted to promise the daughter, not yet of age, and even as a mere child, in marriage; but the Mishnah and the Talmud have in such cases prevented an abuse of parental authority.

279

On the day the daughter becomes of age, she is at liberty to reject the intended before witnesses, and is then free to choose another husband. In case the wife becomes a widow, she enjoys, besides all the rights of majority, also the right of minors, to return to the parents and receive the prescribed support.

A very essential question is that of the dowry of the young wife. As she could not inherit in case there were brothers, the dowry included a compensation. The Talmud, which refers, wherever feasible, to the authority of the Bible, cites the example of Caleb, who gave his daughter, Achsah, in marriage to the young hero, Othniel: *And it came to pass, when she came to him, that she moved him to ask of her father a field, and she alighted from her ass, and Caleb said unto her, "What wilt thou?" And she said unto him, "Give me a blessing, for thou hast set me in the Southland; give me therefore springs of water." And Caleb gave her the upper springs and the nether springs* (Judges 1:14, 15).

In case the father is too poor to give a dowry to his daughter, the community assumes this charitable duty. Up to this day there exist Jewish societies, mostly composed of women, which provide dowries for poor brides.

The dowry of daughters is generally set aside before any inheritance is settled on sons or other relatives; similar care is taken in behalf of the wife.

According to the old formula, the *kethubah,* the document wherein the husband enumerates his obligations towards his wife, begins thus: "Be my wife according to the laws of Moses and Israel, and I will work for thee, honor thee, support thee, and provide for thee according to the custom of Jewish husbands, who work for, honor and support their wives and provide for them in verity."

Touching, indeed, are the repeated admonitions of the

280

Bible to protect the widows and orphans, and it is a proof of a grand and lofty moral conception that provisions were made, first of all, for the "stranger." "Ye shall not afflict any widow or fatherless child. If thou afflict them in any wise, and they cry at all unto me, I will surely hear their cry, and my wrath shall wax hot." (Exodus 22; Deuteronomy 24; Isaiah 10; Jeremiah 7; 6, etc.)

By the agricultural laws, certain portions of each field were reserved, among the Jews, for the stranger, the widow and the orphan. The widow was not only permitted to remain in the house of the deceased husband, but she could claim the right to be supported and to be waited on by the servants of the house. R. Judah Hanassi, the compiler of the Mishnah, was the originator of this privilege. Before he died he called his sons and admonished them to honor their stepmother, his second wife, and to let her enjoy all advantages and privileges which she had enjoyed during his lifetime. It can be surmised that the habitually industrious Jewish woman, in return, helped actively to further the family's welfare during her widowhood.

It is remarkable that the wife had the right to select the first dwelling place after the marriage. In case of a refusal by the husband, they could be divorced, without any detrimental consequences to the wife in any respect, either morally or pecuniarily. Of what consequence such a rule was, opposing a certain roaming disposition in some men, is obvious.

All these rules and precepts make it clear that the Jewish people found the expression of being the "chosen people" preeminently in the sanctification of life. And where could this sanctification find a truer expression than in family life? On the preserving of a pure and spotless family life depended the preservation of the Jewish people. Not to keep family life intact, meant to stop up the source of the godly life of the true Jew. And to whom was entrusted the immediate care, on whom rested the greatest responsibility for the sanctification of the home? On woman, on the wife, on the mother.

The greatest responsibility rested on her, but she was also invested with the greatest dignity in the home. The husband being actively engaged in his office, or at his trade, or becoming so absorbed by his studies that often his eyes rested but dreamily on his nearest surroundings, the eye of the wife had to be keener and clearer for his, for her, for the whole family's sakes.

Rigorous punishment was inflicted on the husband who knowingly brought false accusations against his wife. Seduction of a girl was likewise subject to the full severity of the law; besides being liable to penalties, one could atone for it only by marriage, which was indissoluble in contradistinction to a marriage by free consent; but the girl had the right of refusal. He who had misled a married woman was sentenced to die; his transgression could not be atoned for by marriage; he was deemed equal to a murderer, and was put to death. All these precepts and laws are an evidence of the elevated position Jewish woman held in the old Mosaic legislation.

Somewhat strange seem the Biblical regulations of divorce. According to them, only the husband can demand a divorce, and often for apparently trifling causes (Deuteronomy 24:1-5).

The Talmud, so often defamed by ignorance and malevolence, is always found interceding for the weak and helpless. It supplements the Bible text in favor of woman.

The Talmud grants also to the wife the right to demand a divorce, and if her claim is deemed valid, the husband is forced to a separation by the judges; finally, at the Synod in Metz (1020) Rabbenu Gershom passed an interdiction against seeking a divorce without the acquiescence of the wife. In case the wife claimed and obtained the divorce, she naturally remained in the possession of all her property and marriage portion. The small children were entrusted to her care, while

282

the father had to provide for their support. If the child was a boy, the father could claim him at the age of six years; the daughters stayed with the mother, who, independently, conducted their education.

Where the daughter's or the widow's rights seem curtailed, as in the laws of inheritance, etc., ample provisions were made, often securing for her even more than the full value of the property in question.

When a woman had brought punishment upon herself, then special care was taken not to violate her modesty. Scourging of women, as it is practiced in Russia even today, would have been considered atrocious among the ancient Jews.

The Mosaic laws are not only more humane and show a deeper insight into human nature than those of any other nation of that time, but the unwritten statutes are even more refined and on a higher plane.

The Jewish view of marriage is loftier than that of any other nation. The main quest is not submission and blind obedience on the part of the wife; what is required of her are morals and morality. There is no question of a gloomy, silent subjection, but of a loving alliance; of a union of purpose and aspirations. The wife is not the slave of her husband, but, as God Himself calls her, his "helpmate." Her place is at his side; love and peace she shall spread around him, like a sheltering canopy. "His house," says the Talmud, "that is, his wife." The same book tells, further, if an important proposition was made to the husband, he would say, "I will go and consult my wife." With the Greeks, however, all that the husband undertook in accordance with the counsel of his wife could be annulled and declared as not binding. It is one of the moral laws of the Talmud that man should marry, but *only* when he is able to support a family adequately. In choosing a wife, man should not be guided by outward charms and riches, but by her moral qualities. *House and riches are the inheritance of fathers, but a prudent wife is from the Lord* (Proverbs 19:14). *A woman that feareth the Lord, she shall be praised* (*ibid.* 31:30).

A covenant of God is called the marriage contract, which requires not mere outward fidelity, but the fidelity of the heart. Husband and wife, each of them performing his or her duty, each of them invested with equal authority, shall share faithfully the joys and the sorrows of life. To forsake the wife *covereth the altar of God with tears and with crying out,* says the Prophet (Malachi 2:13). The Jewish sages commanded the husband to honor the wife more than himself, to love her as himself, and in proportion to his fortune to supply her with the comforts of life. He should not excite fear in her (contradictory to the Christian precept, "But the wife shall fear the husband"), but commune with her quietly and gently, and not be gloomy nor angry with her (Maimonides).

The following characteristic maxims are found in the Talmud: "A husband's death is felt by no one as much as by his wife; a wife's death is felt by no one as much as by her husband." "It is the wife through whose efforts the blessings of the Lord come to the house; she teaches the children, encourages the husband to visit the house of God and the school, and welcomes his coming home; she fills the house with godliness and purity; on all her doings rests the blessing of the Lord." Among the innumerable anecdotes and narrations of the Talmud there is found a very characteristic one about the wife of Rabbi Akiba. She is a typical "helpmate" of the husband; she relieves him of all domestic toil and trouble, in order to enable him to apply himself undisturbed to his studies. She, the spoiled child of the rich Kalba Sabua, whom she exasperated and estranged from herself by following the poor, but beloved husband—she even sold her wonderful hair to support him in a time of distress.

It is an ever-recurring phenomenon, the taking care by

284

Jewish women of all domestic and even business affairs which are essential for the support of a family, in order that the husband might gain leisure for study—a fact hardly to be met with among any other nation.

IN THE DARK MIDDLE AGES

. . . The dispersed Jews found everywhere smaller and larger Jewish settlements, for many of their forefathers had emigrated, centuries ago, on account of persecution. . . . Already during the sway of the Romans, Jews had settled in Cologne. By inherited habits they cultivated vineyards, became farmers and craftsmen—only a few of them turned to trade. . . .

Manslaughter became canonically sanctioned by the crusades. More than seven million men were slain "to the glory of God," and just as many were reduced to beggary.

It was the women who encouraged the men fearlessly to meet death. When, during the first crusade, the Jews in Mayence were threatened by the rabble with death in case they did not submit to baptism, then the wives assembled with their children, requesting the husbands first to slay them, and then to commit suicide. . . .

It is well known how the ridiculous accusations of the killing of Christian children, and of poisoning the wells, were circulated among the populace, how they were credited, and of what endless misery they were the cause. The priestly slaughterers gradually became aware that the steadfast adherence of the Jews to their faith had to be ascribed, in most cases, to the heroism of Jewish women. As a consequence, the persecution of women increased. In the year 1501 sixty-seven Jewesses were burned. A number of women drowned themselves in despair; in other places they were driven away. We read repeatedly of women who sought death in the floods.

Their prototype is Esther, the daughter of the magistrate

of a synagogue, who, in the eleventh century, with a number of companions, all weighted down with stones, threw themselves into the Moselle. Nearly one hundred thousand women and girls sought death in this manner in order that they should not be forced to be faithless to the God of Israel, to the One and Only God.

More fortunate was a Jewess by the name of Maria Nunnes Pereyra. On her flight from Holland she was made a captive by an English ship. Her charming ways and the dignity of her deportment made such a deep impression on the owner of the vessel, who was an English duke, that he wooed her with passionate eagerness. He offered her his hand, and although she refused his offer, because in order to become his wife she would have had to renounce her faith, he still hoped to win her.

He remained near her at their arrival in London, and introduced her to Queen Elizabeth. The Queen herself soon felt so deep an interest in the beautiful and highly educated Jewess that she asked her to accept Christianity and to become the wife of the duke. The favor of the Queen could not fail to impress the fugitive, who needed protection in the foreign land; nevertheless, she remained faithful to the Eternal, and declined conversion. Finally the Queen dismissed her, not ungraciously, and she went to Holland. In Amsterdam she gathered around herself a number of faithful adherents of the Mosaic law. This was the beginning of the subsequently large and influential Jewish community.

Another interesting Jewess of superior attainments ought likewise to be mentioned here: *Donna Grazia Nasi*, who was born in Portugal in the year 1501. She was left a widow in her twenty-fifth year, and had to face most trying circumstances.

The establishment of the Inquisition, which from year to year exacted enormous sums from the Jews on the most trivial pretenses, forced Donna Grazia to flee to Holland, in order to

286

save her life and fortune. Here she had to deny her belief; but she could not endure this dissimulation, and was anxious to move to a place where she could openly acknowledge her faith. Only after enormous sacrifices and sufferings did she find a refuge in Venice. From there she went to Ferrara, and finally to Constantinople. Here, among the Turks, she obtained what Christians had refused her—the freedom to live without falsehood and hypocrisy. She openly confessed Judaism, assumed the name of Hannah, and evinced her deep religiousness by her love for her coreligionists and by works of charity.

She founded synagogues and schools, promoted learning and science in every way, and assisted the poor and persecuted.

At that time, when the Pope, Pius IV, committed horrible atrocities against peaceful Jews, Grazia-Hannah obtained the assistance of the Sultan. He gave them his protection and granted them refuge. She died deeply deplored by a host of friends in the year 1569.

❀ 7 ❀

The Elan Vital of the Jewish Woman

BY NINA H. ALDERBLUM

IN THIS ESSAY I shall seek the source out of which there may have sprung the rich and multicolored panorama of activities by Jewish women. My search is for what constitutes Jewish vitality and how it has expressed itself in the life of the Jewish woman.

There is something peculiar to the Jewish woman which distinguishes her from the rest of womankind. The Jewish woman has not only to live, but to live Jewishly; not only to carry her own life, but also that of her people. The blending of her life with that of the Jewish vision constitutes the entelechy, that is the highest form of Jewish womanhood. Her immediate flow of being carries with it the past with all its memories, and the future with all its hopes and problems. She is born with a destiny, and with a consciousness of it.

Sarah had to concern herself with the inculcation of purity and idealism in Isaac. Rebekah was faced with the conflict of Jewish and non-Jewish ideals, exemplified in Jacob and Esau; to safeguard Jacob, she was forced to worry, struggle, plan and even to use strategy against Isaac. The effect of the cruel designs of Pharaoh was, naturally, to make more firm the Jewishness of every prospective mother. Not on milk, but on Heavenly food, did mothers rear their infants during the forty years in the desert. Already in the wilderness Jewish life started: a generation raised on the manna could not but be different from the rest of the world. A history with the experience of Mount Sinai behind it and the Promised Land before it was bound to generate a life of its own, a life with a perpetual momentum. Judah Halevi reckons the exodus from Egypt, the revelation on Mount Sinai, the manna in the desert, the choice of God's dwelling, and His covenant with His people, as the fundamental elements out of which Jewish life was formed. We may even assume that he considers these historic traditions the premises, the primary stuff of experience, out of which thinking —Jewish thinking—proceeds. Judah Halevi seems to be convinced that thinking becomes possible only when we assume as our first axioms the election of Israel and the knitting of God with the fate of Israel and its land. Such convictions produced a people with the strength symbolized by Daniel, who could go into a lions' den without being devoured, and walk through a furnace without being burned. To the same beliefs we owe the Deborahs, the Hannahs, the Judiths, the Esthers, the Beruriahs, and the host of other women who consecrated their lives to the perpetuation of Jewish ideals.

288

7: Nina H. Alderblum, *The Elan Vital of the Jewish Woman*

The vision of certain ideals gives to a people self-consciousness, coherence, and its own way of thinking. By grasping the vision of a nation, we can penetrate into its history and philosophy. History written from the point of view of vision would reproduce the innermost essence of each nation and bring out its dreams, strivings, and aspirations. It seems to me the vital impetus of the Jewish woman—what one thinker calls the elan vital—is drawn from the very romance of Jewish being. The Jewish soil is fertile for nurturing the creative ideals of womanhood. It is unnecessary again to state how in each generation the woman—through the atmosphere of genuine piety that she created in the home—has been the carrier of Jewish life. The spirituality, the mystical beauty, the consciousness of spiritual strivings and creations, the nearness to God, the complete identification with the group life—all these conceptions the Jewish woman has drawn from the Jewish impetus to live a unique life of her own. Her personal life merges with the Jewish life. In our century of transition, this coalescence may not be so self-apparent, but it was a complete one even so recently as the preceding generation, when the voice of the past was not a feeble echo, when the Sabbaths and the Festivals vibrated with the strength of the ages.

I cannot yet forget the picture of my grandmother with her joys, her ecstasies, her concerns and sorrows, all bound up with the Torah. Even at the age of eighty she would get up at four in the morning to prepare breakfast for the men studying in the *yeshibah* which was in the courtyard adjoining.

The same vital force which created and maintained Jewish existence has also given character and color to Jewish womanhood. It is this impetus which has kept Judaism from being destroyed either through persecution or assimilation. This vitality which cannot be conveyed in rational terms (though it becomes rationalized in its process) can only be defined as

289

an elan vital. We may refer again to Judah Halevi, who insists that the essence of Jewish life is not rationalism, but the very romance of being. He did not use this term, but that is what he meant. The German philosophers of the nineteenth century emphasized strongly that romance was the ultimate explanation of life. One may venture to read Jewish life and history in terms of romance, which may furnish an adequate expression for much that is intangible and indefinable in Jewish life.

Romance, in its philosophical connotation, implies a lofty moral conception superior to the exigencies of life, more stern and picturesque than daily utilitarianism. It implies a belief in will-power, an endeavor to submit life to that will rather than to bend the latter to a life which is inferior. The will has to believe that underneath the surface of life—which alone is discernible—there is something totally different from the outward stubborn crust. There is a beauty above the sensuous, there is a kind of intellectual and moral beatitude, which cannot be defined. If we add to this the concept of vital impetus, we may get the rich meaning of romance which philosophers regard as the source of existence.

Like philosophical romanticism, Judaism, too, is a will to live a life different from the one which surrounds us, one which will make us partners with God—His chosen people who help Him perfect the world. God chose Israel and Israel chose God, in order that both might engage in the same task of fulfilling the moral life. The Jewish will is the will to live a life such as could even mould nature and transform it into divine symbols and permeate it with divine precepts.

There is sufficient ground for asserting that woman's natural craving for beauty and romance can find satisfaction in the essence of Jewish being. For there is beauty in a life with a vision of beyond the horizon, there is poetry in the moral striving to transform the physical into the ideal, there is loftiness in the

290

passion to draw near to the perfection of God, and there is vitality in the joy of living. The Jewish elan vital flows from this very romance which has constituted itself the Jewish being. A romance woven out of God, land, and people, fused together into an organic spiritual life, carries with it its own regenerating strength. It is romantic for the Jewish woman to be part of a history which is self-creative, and more romantic than any of our epic poems. It is a poem wrought in deeds; it is the story of human imagination welded with action, of dreams and visions knitted with life, of ideals brought to bear upon that life and not divorced from it. Life, constantly moved by the vision of the ideal, is the greatest epic poem of human creation.

The strength of the Jewish woman lies therefore in living the Jewish life in its entirety. It is incumbent upon the Jewish woman to help infuse the world with Jewish moral fervor, with the unquenchable thirst for a moral cosmos. We have not yet risen to the lofty moral principles of the Prophets and the Sages. Of course, the world-problems might have found their own respective solutions. But Jewish ethics has given them a moral timbre. Of great moment to the world is the very existence of the Jewish people—a people with a different elan vital, a moral one, a people which yearns for the moral life, and for whom the moral life is the sole purpose of existence. The nations have changed through the existence of the Jewish people— therein appears the dynamic power of Jewish thought.

The twentieth-century Jewish woman seems to be faced with the hardest task in Jewish history. It is incumbent upon her to reconstruct the Jewish home so that the values of old may interpenetrate the life of to-day and transform it into an harmonious whole. Life in the ghetto was integral and harmonious; the island within was unsplashed by the outside currents. Nowadays, however, to be born a Jew means to be born into a conflicting world, into a world which is one's own and yet not one's own. The Jewish mother can bring meaning and continuity into the life of the modern Jewish child by connecting his outer life with the living fountains of the Jewish past, and by making him realize that the Jewish past and present are inseparable links in one continuous chain—the past appearing as the retrospective present, and the present as an enlarged and richer past.

In this way the Jewish woman, who draws her strength from the impetus which gave momentum to the Jewish people, can revitalize that very source and help to make it a continuous stream.

❦ 8 ❦

Married Love in Jewish Law

BY DR. LEO JUNG

THROUGHOUT THEIR HISTORY, the Jewish people have been the classic example of domestic happiness. To us the meaning of marriage is conveyed through *Halachah,* the legal part of the Talmud and later Rabbinic literature. The Sages insisted [Kiddushin 45a] that the verse, *"Love thy neighbor as thyself"* (Leviticus 19:18), referred particularly to one's wife. The husband must entertain highest regard for his wife, and cherish her as he would himself.

WEDDING CEREMONY

The wedding ceremony illustrates this attitude dramatically. The ancient *kethubah* (marriage document) was the first in human history to guarantee to woman rights and privileges of her own, and to protect her in every contingency and situation. There are both general and specific provisions in the *kethubah.*

292

The groom pledges: "Become thou my wife according to the law of Moses and Israel, and I shall serve you, honor you, and provide for you according to the principles of a Jewish husband who should serve, honor, and provide for his wife in sincerity." But in the *kethubah*, he also makes a more specific commitment: he must put aside before the marriage, a sum of money to take care of such emergencies as his own death or a divorce, so that his wife will not be left destitute. This practice impresses the young couple with the knowledge that while there is romance in marriage, there are also concrete obligations. It is of the utmost importance that they realize in advance that marriage is more than a beautiful lark. It is a serious matter between two adults.

Why does the couple drink out of the same cup under the *huppah* or marriage canopy? Because marriage means that whatever life holds in store, man and wife "drink together." If it be a problem, it will be only half a problem because two people, deeply devoted to each other, have it together. And if, as we hope, it is *simhah*, it will be double joy because two people, devoted to each other, have it together.

Nor is marriage only a matter concerning one couple. The ideals they are to uphold add to the glory, peace, and strength of the Jewish people. Hence it is an event of communal rejoicing, and a *minyan* is required at the ceremony. The establishment of every new Jewish home offers the hope that it may produce a leader in Israel. Did not the Sages say that every Jewish school child is a potential Messiah?

In some countries, the bride walks around the groom under the *huppah*. This symbolizes her ethical sensitiveness. Refined persons do not display their love in public. By circling around her husband under the *huppah*, the bride suggests the vow that she is too modest to state aloud: "I will endeavor to surround you all my life with grace and kindness and harmony."

SACREDNESS OF MARRIAGE

Marriage in Hebrew is called *kiddushin,* "a sacred thing." This does not mean that it is under all circumstances binding unto death. Where there is absolute incompatibility between man and wife, Judaism recognizes the need to help them part. But so long as husband and wife are compatible, their marriage is a sacred union. The three R's of marriage are reverence for personality, righteousness and *rahamanuth* (unselfish love, literally mother-love). A happy marriage depends not only on sound character, intellect and healthy emotions—it draws its strongest sustenance from the principles of Jewish ethics.

Whereas figures show that between twenty-five and thirty per cent of all marriages in this country end in divorce, and an additional twenty to twenty-five per cent stay together because of parents or children, religious scruples, public opinion, or monetary considerations, the Jewish rate of divorce used to be one-half of one per cent and is now about two per cent. How explain this difference? At least in part it is due to the Jewish attitude toward marriage, brought about by the laws of Judaism as against those prevailing in the world without. Even today, in most civilized countries, if a man cohabits with a woman below the age of consent, he is considered as having committed rape, and, if convicted, is sent to jail. But if a man marries a woman, she is, even by the laws of our own fifty states, expected to be physically at his disposal whenever he so desires. Hence the notices in newspapers: "My wife having left my bed and board, I will no longer be responsible for her debts." A Jewish husband may never approach his wife without her consent. He is bound to respect marriage as *kiddushin,* a sacred institution which demands mental, moral, and physical discipline. By Jewish law, it is unlawful for a man and a woman —unless they are married to each other—to be alone in a closed apartment. To some this may seem old-fashioned and harsh, but it reflects a noble attitude that has prevented sexual laxity, and has kept the relations between man and woman on a high plane.

ATTITUDE TOWARD WOMEN

The Sages, esteeming woman's esthetic awareness and moral significance, state in the Mishnah that to her was entrusted a threefold mission: "to justify possession by charity, love by purity, and life by spirituality." No more eloquent tribute to woman can be found in all of world literature.

R. Akiba, one of the greatest Sages, said of his wife [Kethuboth 63a]: "I owe everything I am to her," and that, "if the whole Bible is holy, the *Song of Songs* (dealing with love between man and wife) is the holiest of the holy" [Yadayim 3, 5]. He once made a statement which, on the surface, is rather startling. On the last page of the Talmud tractate *Gittin* [90a] there is a discussion of what constitutes ground for divorce. One rabbi said "immorality," another "malice." But Rabbi Akiba held that if a man found another woman more beautiful than his own wife, he could divorce her. The profundity of this statement may not be immediately apparent. Unless a Jewish husband felt from the day of the wedding and beyond the diamond anniversary that his wife remained the most beautiful woman on earth, he should, grant her a divorce, for he no longer deserved her. Curiously enough, this is echoed by Robert Ingersoll: "The essence of our attitude toward woman is that, when we have married her, she must remain the most beautiful creature from now and forever."

In this ennobling of marriage among Jews and in assuring women their rights as human beings, the Talmud has been of greatest influence. In its view [Pesahim 49b], a father who marries his daughter to an *am ha'aretz* (literally "a man of the soil," but bearing the connotation of "an uncouth lout") commits a grave sin, as though he had thrown her to a lion: "Just as a lion does not ask its victim's permission to devour him, so the *am ha'aretz* debases his wife by approaching without her consent." The stricture against the exploitation of women in marriage is basic in Jewish law, and most remarkable for the fact that it was set down in the Mishnah almost two thousand years ago, at a time when other nations treated their women as though they were chattel.

ATTITUDE TOWARD SEX

Unlike the teachings of other religions, Halachah has no contempt for physical love. While the early Christian Church looked upon marriage as the work of the devil—only monks and nuns being free of his influence—the Torah teaches that we are made of body and soul, and therefore love with body and soul. Provided that love is genuine, that it implies not merely desire but also respect for the partner, it is precious and beautiful.

The wisdom of Halachah concerning sex in marriage has been lauded by many authorities, among them the late Doctor Marie Stopes, one of the world's great authorities on marriage, and the only woman member of the Royal Society of Great Britain. In her book *Married Love* (first attacked as lewd and lascivious, but now regarded as one of the soundest manuals ever written), she states: "I have studied all systems, literatures, and laws dealing with married love. I have found only one to protect the physical and spiritual welfare of young women— the Jewish twelve-day law."

This law is so sacred in Jewish tradition that Jewish women throughout the ages ignored every inconvenience and danger in order to conform with it. In essence, the Jewish "twelve-day law" was intended to guard woman's dignity, to make her feel at all times that she remained in possession of her body and soul, even in marriage. While the law states that a husband must never approach his wife without her consent it also emphasizes that when husband and wife are physically, mentally, and emotionally in good condition, there is nothing wrong in physical union. But there must be unity of heart and mind before unity of the body is lawful. The Jewish law insists that during the period of menstruation and for seven days thereafter —that is, for twelve days every month except in pregnancy— there must be no sexual union whatsoever.

There is an excellent reason for this stricture beyond the purely physiological. These twelve days serve as a period of renewal, when man and wife rediscover other facets of love: a sense of belonging, consideration, respect, companionship. Sex is important but it is neither everything nor nothing, and it must not overshadow the enduring qualities of marriage. The serenity of knowing, without any sexual act, that one loves and is loved; the opportunity to convey devotion by a word or a look; the chance to exchange one's deepest thoughts in a quiet atmosphere untroubled by powerful physical urges— these are all vital to a happy, lasting marriage. And when the twelve days are over, the normal longing for each other has returned, so that, in accord with Halachah, when the love cycle is renewed, there is a new honeymoon every month.

This practice of observing sexual abstinence for twelve days would have vanished long ago had Jewish law not given it the support of ritual and ceremony. To protect woman, and through her to protect man and the sanctity of marriage, the Torah set forth the rule that the love cycle was not to be resumed until the woman had taken a ritual bath, which in turn could not be taken until the end of the twelve days.

The term "ritual bath" or *mikvah* has an unfortunate connotation today. Some modern Jews tend to sneer at it as an outmoded custom, but they have never understood its nature or function. The *mikvah* has nothing to do with cleanliness of the body. It is part of a religious ceremony to insure the quality of married love. Marriage is a fragile bark that needs protection against the storms of life. By interrupting the love cycle on the night before the woman expects her period, and resuming it not earlier than twelve days later, after the prescribed immersion in the *mikvah,* married people learn to control their impulses and to consider the mate's feelings. Free from excess their love will never grow stale. Adherence to the twelve-day law prevents married relations from becoming drab routine and makes it possible for marriage to be considered, even many years after the *huppah,* as an institution on the highest moral level, a source of abiding happiness to the partners.

When non-Jews praise the stability of Jewish marriages and the wisdom of the "twelve-day law," it is a tribute to the solid achievement of Jewish law in raising the quality of married love and binding husband and wife in a devotion that rests on mutual respect and compassion. The law of the *mikvah* is not outmoded. Never more blissful than today, it is a symbol of the Torah's injunction: *Sanctify yourself and you will be holy* [Leviticus 11:44, 20:7].

The Jewish people have survived through all these centuries not only because Judaism is a living faith, but also, in great part, because the Jewish code of marriage has served as a constant, unfailing source of renewal. We must be wise enough to observe these laws. Only thus shall we perpetuate the spiritual and ethical level of Jewish homes, and enable them to continue as sanctuaries of harmony and peace in a chaotic world.

298

☗ 9 ☗

Mixed Pews

BY RABBI MORRIS MAX

WITHIN the three centuries in which orthodox Judaism has been a part of the American scene, and certainly during the past fifty years, environmental forces of major weight have challenged the perpetuation of its unique character and institutions. American Jewry can therefore find satisfaction in the fact that the overwhelming majority of its over 4,000 congregations remain loyal to orthodox belief and practice. This is particularly striking in view of the insidious forms which the means of assimilation are apt to assume, notable among which is that of "mixed pews."

Mixed pews—that is, the mingled seating of men and women at services—is a problem which has plagued numerous synagogues at one time or another. A departure from traditional Jewish usage which has characterized the Reform and Conservative movements since their inception, mixed seating has become the very symbol of assimilationist retreat from the Jewishly-oriented view of life. The rise of a generation tragically unschooled in Jewish teaching has widened the ranks of those who suffer the illusion that mixed pews form a touchstone to a supposed "modernization" and who fail to perceive that traditional Jewish practices are each an integral part of the great pattern whose total is Judaism. The orthodox Rabbi visiting a new community is very apt to find himself faced with the question: "Why not change the seating arrangement of the synagogue so that men and women may sit together at services and thereby make the synagogue modern and attractive to youth?"

299

The time has come when we must bring this matter out in the open. Our views must be clear and forthright, so that Jewish men and women everywhere may know where orthodoxy stands and why we take that stand. In far too many instances have congregations been cut off from their ancient moorings, via the deceptive path of mixed pews. Using ill-informed individual members as catspaws, anti-orthodox groups have exploited the issue of mixed pews in such fashion as to gain entry to circles foreign to them. The Conservative group, in its studied attack upon the strongholds of Judaism, has been particularly energetic in using the mixed pew technique as the first prong of a pincer movement—the second being the foisting upon congregations of subsidized Conservative "Rabbis"—whereby synagogues have been captured. More than one leader of an orthodox congregation, Rabbinic and lay, has been tempted to go along, to swim with the tide. But this tide is rather a treacherous current amidst the ocean of Judaism. It leads to fatal destruction.

Let us note the reasons given for mixed pews by its advocates. They can be set down briefly as follows: (1) The equality of men and women in the social, political and industrial fields of life makes it imperative that in the synagogue the same equality should prevail. (2) The women, whose Jewish education has been sorely neglected—even more than that of the boys and men—need help in following the prayers of the service. The men can extend that help to them, if they sit close by during the service. (3) The girls and women feel that they are segregated and are not considered part of the congregation. Segregation breaks up the feeling of unity that should pervade the atmosphere of the synagogue as it pervades the home. (4) The Torah does not specifically enjoin separate seating. And (5) customs must change with the times, and the trend is irresistible.

Let us analyze these arguments and see how they stand

300

up in the light of genuine Jewish tradition and in the light of the religious needs of people today.

EQUALITY

The synagogue was established for regular public worship to be conducted not once a week but three times a day—morning, afternoon and evening. According to the Halachah, women have been freed from the obligation of observing those positive commandments which must be performed only at a particular time of the day or season of the year (Kiddushin 29a). The reason for this ruling is to be found in the natural superiority that woman has over man for the upbringing and training of children. No man would be so carried away by the enticing slogan of "equality" as to insist that he be given equal "rights" in the daily routine chores of raising his children. Nature has endowed woman with traits of character that make her uniquely suitable for motherhood—qualities that man cannot equal.

Recognizing this superiority of woman as an indisputable asset to Jewish social living, our Heavenly Father decreed in the Torah that no religious law should interfere with the woman's unique aptitude and capability of raising her children properly. We can readily see the wisdom of this law. What would happen to our children if Jewish women were to be obligated, as are Jewish men, to go to the synagogue every morning, don *tallith* and *tefillin* and to participate in the services three times a day? The religiously observant woman would be forced to neglect the needs of her children.

Yet, the Jewish woman was required to participate in the synagogue service insofar as she was able to do so. We can, therefore, well understand that for the sake of preserving the regularity of public worship the custom arose to have the main synagogue set aside for the boys and men—for those who were obligated to come three times a day, while the balcony or any other part of the synagogue which was partitioned from the main auditorium was set aside for the women who, because of the reason mentioned above, can attend only at certain times.

It is, therefore, evident that when the opponents of tradition advocate mixed pews in order to establish the "equality" of men and women, they do not mean that they want the women to be obligated as the men to participate in the service three times a day. What they really desire is that Jewish men should become "equal" to Jewish women—that is, free from the obligation of observing the positive commandments of the Lord as are the Jewish women!

The time has come for all to understand that the slogan of "equality" is only a catch word exploited by non-orthodox bodies to gain entry into the orthodox communities and then to continue their destructive work of undermining our fundamental principles one after another. Let me but mention one example which has been brought to my attention, and which is typical of what is happening in different parts of the country.

The Conservative leaders decided that they must gain a foothold in a certain city which was known as a stronghold of Orthodoxy and which did not have a single Conservative temple. Aiming their "big guns" at one group which showed signs of religious weakness, they sent down (gratis of course) some of their biggest names—"Rabbis" who were nationally known because of their Zionist activities, who delivered lectures. These visits were accompanied by all the fanfare of modern publicity. After this softening-up process they sent their chief missionary to that community for the High Holy Days. In true demagogue fashion, he made the coup de grace in his *Rosh Hashanah* sermon, which he concluded dramatically by shouting to the women in the balcony: "The time has come for you women to come down from the balcony and take the place that you deserve down here among the men." Of course he carried the day. Even

302

the religious-minded men were in favor of engaging a Conservative minister.

They realized their mistake, however, only too late after they heard the new "Rabbi" tell their hitherto observant coreligionists that they could ride to the synagogue in their automobiles on the Sabbath and holidays if it were more convenient; that they could put on their electric lights at home on the Sabbath—and as a proof he flashed signals to the choir leader on the Sabbath by putting an electric light on and off; that they could sponsor fish dinners cooked and served in *trefah* dishes at any hotel or restaurant; that they could pray in English rather than in Hebrew if they found it more convenient; that they could have their children circumcised by gentile doctors as long as he, the "Rabbi," was there to put his blessing on the operation; and that he, the "Rabbi," would officiate at the wedding of any divorced man or woman even if no Jewish divorce (*get*) had been granted, as long as the parties had a civil divorce. They realized what a wicked trap had been set for them by that slogan of "equality" after they saw everything which was sacred to the religious Jew discarded—and all that with the "blessings of the Rabbi" too.

AID TO WOMEN WORSHIPPERS

Now let us analyze the second argument. It is as unsound as the first. Mixed pews' proponents seem to be concerned about helping the ladies follow the prayers of the congregational service. We can note, though, that it is customary for the Conservative "Rabbi" to lead the congregation in prayers. He announces the pages. Surely, the "Rabbi" does not consider himself less effective in directing the congregants to prayer than the man who sits next to his wife! Proper decorum would demand that the worshipers direct their attention to the one who leads them in prayer. His directives could therefore be followed by the ladies sitting in the women's section of the synagogue equally as well as when they sit next to the men.

The idea of keeping the family together in the family pew, unknown to the synagogue, was not born among the Reformists and Conservatives as an original religious motif, chosen on its Jewish merits. It is merely their imitation of the Christian idea of a church. The desire to adopt this practice could not rise from the will to foster more intensive religiousness, to conserve Jewishness, to guide the untaught along the path of Israel. Such a will must necessarily be manifested by effort to uphold practices which have enabled Israel to reach spiritual heights untouched by any other people. It must be signalized by effort to emphasize to the maximum the customs and laws distinctive to Judaism, to enlighten the people as to their character, to familiarize them with their practice. It must promote measures making for the Judaization of the environment and must seek to surmount the forces making for the nullification of Jewish life. But "mixed-pewism," to the contrary, abandoning religious values, is inspired merely by the wish to ape the gentile; it poses a church practice as a model for Jews and implicitly assumes that the standards and practices of the church milieu should be adopted by Jews.

Fervent religious purpose has never in history—and certainly not in Jewish history—been characterized by the wish to assimilate to those of a different faith, but by the very opposite. Our mixed pew assimilationists are such not by virtue of religious conviction but by lack of such conviction. Their action can lead in but one direction—downward.

SEGREGATION

Let us, therefore, really see whether there is any validity to this argument that the ladies when sitting in the balcony or

304

in the special section of the synagogue feel that they are alone and separate from the congregation.

The purpose of prayer is to bring the individual into close touch with God. This is not easily accomplished. It requires concentration; the heart as well as the mind must be wrapped up in the thought of God. Any distraction from the central purpose of synagogue worship has no place in the synagogue. Hence, there are laws in the *Shulhan Aruch* which stress the importance of absolute decorum, so that no individual will disturb the religious thoughts of his neighbor. Only such prayers as will lift the individual out of his routine occupation and thoughts and set his mind and heart upon the higher spiritual pursuits of life will serve to make a better man or woman of the worshiper and will bring down upon him or her the blessings of God.

The purpose of synagogue worship, then, is to put the individual in a prayerful mood, so that he can detach himself from mundane associations and make contact with God. The separate seating arrangement was instituted to enable every Jew to pray with all his heart and mind and soul. This arrangement was proven to be least disturbing since it produced maximum decorum, especially among the young men and women. Consequently, separate seating has always formed an essential part of the synagogues—and until 100 years ago there were only orthodox synagogues. Far from leading to family disunity, it has been a pillar of that lofty, harmonious family life which has distinguished Israel through the ages and which—as more than one sociologist has noted—yet continues to distinguish Torah-loyal families in the modern world of today.

Although we are living in an age when the intermingling of the sexes in schools and public gatherings is commonplace, there is no doubt that when absolute concentration is necessary as in prayer and when the mind is apt to wander as the individual strives to conceive and feel the ideas of Godliness, the presence of the opposite sex that may lead to socializing may become a distracting factor.

The ideal which the orthodox synagogue strives to attain is to make every worshiper feel every moment of his stay in the synagogue what our patriarch Jacob experienced when he exclaimed: "How awe-inspiring this place is; it is none other than the house of God." Only such an atmosphere is conducive to genuine prayer.

If there are men and women today who complain that they cannot experience this spiritual ecstasy from the orthodox Jewish services, they should take to heart an ancient parable.

When a king once spoke to his subjects in glowing terms about the benefits of prayer, a loyal subject of his approached him with the complaint that he could not experience the thrill in prayer that the king evidently derived from it. Realizing that this person was sincere but incapable of concentrating on the higher thoughts embodied in the prayers, the king decided to teach him a lesson. He ordered him to carry a bowl filled with hot oil on his head down the street and back to his palace, warning him that if he spilled a drop of the oil his head would be cut off. The young man sorrowfully accepted the order of the king, placed the bowl on his head, walked down the street and returned without spilling a drop of the oil.

The king then asked him why he did not answer his mother as she called him while he was walking down the street. He berated him for being discourteous and disregarding the call of his sweetheart who cried out to him as he was carrying out the king's order.

"Your majesty," answered the bewildered young man, "my thoughts were concentrated upon that bowl of oil and I was oblivious of everything else. How could I see or hear my mother or sweetheart when I had such a life-saving task to perform?"

306

"My dear son," answered the kindly king, "if you will concentrate on God when you pray as you concentrated your heart and mind on that bowl of oil, you too will finish your prayers with a feeling of ecstasy and spiritual elevation. For then you will have experienced the thrill of having elevated yourself from this earthly existence to reach the sublime spiritual heights of God, your Heavenly Father."

JEWISH LAW

Those who claim that the Torah did not decree the segregation of the sexes during services ignore the role which the Oral Law occupied in Jewish life throughout the ages. Simultaneously with the Written Law, Moses received on Mt. Sinai the Oral Torah which was transmitted and elucidated by word of mouth to every generation until it was written down in the Mishnah and the Gemara.

Rabbi Samuel Gerstenfeld, in an article in the volume *Eidenu,* first published in 1942 [reprinted in this volume as source 2 to chap. III] disproves the contention of Dr. Louis M. Epstein in his recent book, *Sex Laws and Customs in Judaism* (page 78) that "there was apparently no separation of the sexes at worship in the First Temple." R. Gerstenfeld [above, p. 164] shows that from Maimonides (Laws of the Temple, Number 5) and the *Yalkut Shim'oni* (on Deuteronomy 23:15), "the fact is that Solomon's Temple did have an *ezrath nashim,* a special section for the use of women for the purpose of prayer"; and Solomon's Temple was modeled after the Tabernacle in the wilderness. So that "it is proven that the *ezrath nashim* is an ancient institution existing in both Temples and, according to the *Yalkut,* is part of a Biblical commandment" [above, p. 167].

He traces the development, after the destruction of the Temple, of the Synagogue, which was called by the Prophet Ezekiel the *mikdash me'at*—the little sanctuary—and concludes that "the old synagogue bears witness to the continuity of the law concerning *ezrath nashim* and its acceptance by Israel. . . . A synagogue without an *ezrath nashim* is a violation of the Law, and ought altogether to be shunned. . . . It is better to pray alone and be with Him who hears all prayers and who promised 'In every place where I shall *permit my name to be mentioned* I shall come to thee and bless thee' " [pp. 168-9].

IRRESISTIBLE TREND

The claim that the sentiment in favor of mixed pews is an irresistible trend is spurious, tendentious propaganda reminiscent of that once spread by the "wave of the future" emissaries of the Nazis. Quite contrary to this propaganda, the overwhelming majority of congregations, as mentioned earlier, remain orthodox in their practice. To the extent that such sentiment exists, it falls directly counter to the historic Jewish spirit, which impels us to determine our course not on the basis of what prevails in the non-Jewish world but on what the Lord requires of us. The will to live according to our distinctive beliefs has upheld us, against every "trend," since the days of our Father Abraham; in our day the will to be Jewish has brought us *medinath Israel* —against every "irresistible trend," the will to worship and live Jewishly will, with God's help, continue to sustain us amidst the quicksands of *hefkeruth*.

In this spirit, and in this spirit alone, Judaism legitimately faces the problem of "changing with the times." We strive to shape the ever-changing circumstances with which life confronts us to the standard of a Torah which is unchangeable, yet is always fluidly applicable to the needs of the time, through the Halachic expositions authoritatively propounded by the legitimate orthodox Rabbinate. This alone—never the recalcitrant presumptions of unqualified, self-appointed individuals—forms the valid, disciplined means of determining questions of Jewish

308

law, practice and doctrine. Our long history is a tribute to the unique success of this concept.

Amongst the limited number of congregations which have yielded to mixed pews, increasingly successful efforts are being made to recover them for Judaism. In some of these congregations, orthodox Rabbis have taken upon themselves the responsibility of accepting pulpits for the specific purpose of winning them back to the orthodox path. Despite its laudable aim, this course is opposed by many, for it is felt that, despite the *kavvanah*, principle is compromised and public misinterpretation can compound the evil. The Rabbinical Council of America, composed of 400 *musmachim,* duly ordained orthodox Rabbis, holding pulpits in 40 states, some time ago adopted a policy of limiting to a period of five years the length of time in which any of its members serving mixed pews congregations might remain with them in the effort to raise them to orthodox status. At the last Rabbinical Council Convention it was decided that a survey be made to determine the progress achieved.

Although the survey has not been completed, sufficient evidence is at hand to show that a number of synagogues have restored or have newly-instituted separate seating. In more than one case, substantial expense in re-modeling has been involved, and in others the change has been incorporated in new structures, testifying to the strength of enlightened conviction. In most cases, however, the architectual problem was simple, involving slight cost—a circumstance which would probably apply to most synagogues seeking this desirable change.

The evidence of this kind is of course not conclusive. It will, in any case, not affect the view of those who maintain that consistent refusal by orthodox Rabbis to serve congregations with mixed pews is the only proper—and in its general salutary effect the only decisive—way to face the problem.

Recognizing that the source of this and related problems

lies in mis-education, much is being done to bring wider knowledge, understanding and appreciation of the orthodox service and, in particular, to help women lacking such training to follow and partake in these services to the proper extent. Adult classes and study courses, applying techniques which take account of present-day minds, are being instituted in an increasing number of communities. Attracting large numbers of young men and women, they are replacing ignorance with knowledge of Jewish beliefs, Hebrew, Jewish liturgy and other aspects of Judaism. The time-honored Siddur is becoming an open book to the young people. They are becoming aware of a genuine equality that they can possess in common with all the generations of Jews which have upheld genuine Judaism throughout the ages down to this present day.

They will soon recognize the truth of the words of an American jurist, who in speaking of the Jewish concept of justice said, "the world owes its conception of justice to the Jew. *God gave him to see through the things that are ever changing, the things that never change.* Compared with the meaning and majesty of this achievement every other triumph of every other people sinks into insignificance." With the organized efforts of the orthodox Rabbis and laymen our young people will recognize through all the changing fads the unchanging fundamental principles of genuine religion and sincere prayer.

Let our orthodox leaders, therefore, understand that by insisting on our time-honored customs in the synagogue they are not being old-fashioned; instead, they are fashioning as of old spiritual men and women, whose lives will become enriched by the God idea that they will take with them from the synagogue into their homes and daily pursuits. Let them not be confused by the false slogan of "equality" and become drunk with transient whims and fads. Instead, let them keep Jewish men and women the "God intoxicated people," who will proclaim with the Psalm-

310

ist (Psalm 27): *One thing I have asked of the Lord, that will I seek after; That I may dwell in the house of the Lord all the days of my life; To behold the graciousness of the Lord and to visit early in His Temple.*

❧ 10 ❧

Separate Pews in the Synagogue
a social and psychological approach

BY RABBI NORMAN LAMM

THE PROBLEM of "mixed pews" versus "separate pews" in the synagogue is one which has engaged the attention of the Jewish public for a number of years. It has been the focus of much controversy and agitation. More often than not, the real issues have been obscured by the strong emotions aroused. Perhaps if the reader is uninitiated in the history and dialectic of Jewish religious debate in mid-twentieth century America, he will be puzzled and amused by such serious concern and sharp polemics on what to him may seem to be a trivial issue. If the reader is thus perplexed, he is asked to consider that "trivialities" are often the symbols of issues of far greater moment. Their significance often transcends what is formally apparent, for especially in Judaism they may be clues to matters of principle that have far-reaching philosophic consequences. In our case, the *mechitzah* (the physical partition between the men's and women's pews) has become, in effect, a symbol in the struggle between two competing ideological groups. It has become a *cause celebre* in the debate on the validity of the Jewish tradition itself and its survival intact in the modern world. The *mechitzah* was meant to divide physically the men from the women in the synagogue. In our day it has served also to divide spiritually synagogue from synagogue, community from community, and often rabbi from layman. This division has become a wide struggle, in which one faction attempts to impose contemporary standards—whatever their quality or worth—upon the inherited corpus of Jewish tradition, which it does not regard as being of divine origin; conversely, the other side seeks to preserve the integrity of Jewish law and tradition from an abject capitulation to alien concepts whose only virtue is, frequently, that they are declared "modern" by their proponents. The purpose of this essay is to demonstrate the validity of the Jewish tradition in its view that separate seating for men and women ought to prevail in the synagogue.

THE LAW

The separation of the sexes at services is not a "mere custom reflecting the mores of a bygone age." It is a law, a *Halachah,* and according to our outstanding Talmudic scholars an extremely important one. Its origin is in the Talmud,[1] where we are told that at certain festive occasions which took place at the Temple in Jerusalem great crowds gathered to witness the service. The Sages were concerned lest there occur a commingling of the sexes, for the solemnity and sanctity of the services could not be maintained in such environment. Hence, although the sexes were already originally separated, and despite the reluctance to add to the structure of the Temple, it was ruled that a special balcony be built for the women in that section called the *ezrath nashim* (Women's Court) in order to reduce the possibility of frivolousness at these special occasions. The same principle which applied to the Sanctuary in Jerusalem applies to the synagogue,[2] the *mikdash me'at* (miniature Sanctuary), and mixed pews are therefore proscribed.

---

1. Sukkah 51b.
2. Megillah 29a; *Tur* and *Shulhan Aruch Orah Hayyim* 151; *Sefer Yere'im* 324.

Thus Jewish law clearly forbids what has become known as "mixed pews." We do not know, historically, of any syna-gogue before the modern era where mixed pews existed. No documents and no excavations can support the notion that this breach of Jewish law was ever accepted by Jews. Philo and Josephus both mention separate seating in the days of the Second Commonwealth.[3] The principle was upheld as law in the last generation by such eminent authorities as Rabbi Israel Meir ha-Kohen (the *Hafetz Hayyim*) in Lithuania, Chief Rabbi Kook in Palestine, and Rabbi Dr. M. Hildesheimer in Germany. In our own day, it was affirmed by every one of the Orthodox rabbinical and lay groups without exception, and by such con-temporary scholars as Chief Rabbi Herzog of Israel, Chief Rabbi Brodie of the British Empire, Rabbis Moses Feinstein and Aaron Kotler, and Dr. Samuel Belkin and Rabbi Joseph B. Soloveitchik of Yeshiva University.

Of course, one may argue that "this is only the Orthodox interpretation." We shall not now argue the point that "Ortho-doxy" is the name one must give to the three thousand years of normative Judaism no matter what our contemporary pref-erence in sectarian nomenclature. But aside from this, and aside from the fact that there is abundant supporting source material, both Halachic and historic,[4] antedating the fragmenta-

---

3. Philo, *De Vita Contemplativa* 32-34; Josephus, *Wars of the Jews,* v. 5. 2.

4. The following is only a random sample from the Halachic literature confirming the absolute necessity for separate pews: *Hatham Sofer* (Responsa), *Hoshen Mishpat* 190, *Orah Hayyim* 28; *Maharam Shick* (Responsa), *Orah Hayyim* 77; *Teshuboth Beth Hillel* 50; *Dibre Hayyim, Orah Hayyim* 18. For a more elaborate treatment of the text of the Talmud in Sukkah 51b, and for other Halachic references, see Rabbi Samuel Gerstenfeld, "The Segregation of the Sexes," *Eidenu,* New York, 1942, 67-74 [reprinted in this volume, pp. 159-169]. Additional historical references may be found in: the Jerusalem Talmud, Sukkah 5, 1; Tosefta, Sukkah 4, 6; *Terumath ha-Deshen* 353; *Mordechai* quoted in *Ture Zahab, Orah Hayyim* 351, 1; cf. Cecil Roth's introduction to G. K. Loukomski, *Jewish Art in European Synagogues*, p. 21.

tion of the Jewish community into the Orthodox-Conservative-Reform pattern, it is interesting to note the position of the Conservative group. This is the group whose leaders still feel it necessary to defend their deviations from traditional norms, and whose attitude to Jewish law has usually been ambivalent. It is a fact, of course, that the overwhelming majority of Conservative Temples have mixed pews. But, significantly, some of their leading spokesmen have not embraced this reform wholeheartedly. Rabbi Bernard Segal, Executive Director of the United Synagogue (the organization of Conservative temples) recently had this to say:

> We have introduced family pews, organ music, English readings. Our cantors have turned around to face their congregations. In some synagogues we have introduced the triennial cycle for the reading of the Torah. *All of these were never intended to be ends in themselves or principles of the Conservative Movement. . . .* Unfortunately, in the minds of too many these *expedients* have come to represent the sum and substance of the Conservative Movement.[5]

We thus learn that Conservative leadership has begun to recognize that mixed seating in the synagogue is not entirely defensible, that it was meant to be only an "expedient" and not an in-principle reform. From another Conservative leader we learn that the Law Committee of the Rabbinical Assembly (the Conservative rabbinic group) has for years only "condoned" but not "approved" the system of family pews! The very same group that encourages its members to drive the automobile to the Temple on the Sabbath—only "condones" but does not "approve" of mixed pews![6] And of course those who

---

5. *United Synagogue Review* (Winter, 1958), p. 10. Italics are mine.
6. Jacob B. Agus, *Guideposts in Modern Judaism*, p. 133f., and in *Conservative Judaism*, Vol. XI, No. 1 (1956), p. 11.

have visited the Jewish Theological Seminary in New York know that the synagogue of the Conservative Seminary itself has separate seating for men and women. We are dealing here with a *din,* with a *Halachah,* with a binding and crucial law, with the very sanctity of the synagogue, and religious Jews have no choice but to insist upon separate seating as an indispensable and irrevocable feature of the synagogue.[7]

The references made so far should not be taken as a full treatment of the Halachic and historical basis for separate seating. A considerable literature, both ancient and modern, could be cited as documentation of the thesis here presented. However, as the subtitle of this essay indicates, our major interest here is not in articulating the Halachah as much as in explaining it. Our main concern in this essay is to demonstrate that the separation of the sexes at religious services makes good sense even—or perhaps especially—in America, where woman has reached her highest degree of "emancipation." What we will attempt to show is that if there were no law requiring a *mechitzah,* we should have to propose such a law—for good, cogent reasons. These reasons are in the tradition of *ta'ame ha-mitzvoth,* the rationale ascribed to existing laws, rationales

---

7. It is true that there are Orthodox rabbis who minister to family pew congregations. Yet there is a vast difference between the Conservative who at best "condones" a mixed pews situation, without regrets, and the Orthodox rabbi who accepts such a pulpit with the unambiguous knowledge that mixed pews are a denial of the Halachah and hence an offense against his own highest principles. An Orthodox rabbi accepts such a post—*if* he should decide to do so—*only* with the prior approval of *his* rabbi or school, *only* on a temporary basis, and *only* with the intention of eliminating its objectionable features by any or all of the time-tested techniques of Jewish spiritual leadership. The difference, then, is not only philosophical but also psychological. This spiritual discomfort of the authentic Orthodox rabbi in the non-conforming pulpit constantly serves to remind him of his sacred duty to effect a change for the better in the community he serves. Any reconciliation with the anti-Halachic character of a synagogue which is permanent, does undeniable violence to the most sacred principles of Judaism, and is hence indefensible.

which may or may not be identical with the original motive of the commandment (assuming we *can* know it), but which serve to make immutable laws relevant to every new historical period.

Because of the fact that Tradition clearly advocates separate seating, it is those who would change this millennial practice who must first prove their case. Let us therefore begin by examining some of the arguments of the reformers, and then explain some of the motives of the Halachah (Jewish law) in deciding against this commingling of the sexes at services.

Those who want to reform the Tradition and introduce mixed pews at religious services present two main arguments. One is that separate seating is an insult to womanhood, a relic of the days when our ancestors held woman to be inferior to man, and hence untenable in this era when we unquestioningly accept the equality of the sexes. The second is the domestic argument: the experience of husbands and wives worshipping next to each other makes for happier homes. The slogan for this argument is the well-known "families that pray together stay together." These arguments deserve detailed analysis and investigation to see whether or not they are sufficiently valid premises upon which to base the mass reform of our synagogues.

THE EQUALITY OF THE SEXES

The source of the value of man, the sanction of his dignity, is God. The Bible expresses this by saying that man was created in His image. But woman too is in the image of God. Hence she derives her value from the same source as does the male of the species. In value, therefore, she is identical with man. She is liable to the same punishment that a man is—no more, no less—when she breaks a law, and she is as deserving of reward and commendation when she acts virtuously. A famous rabbinic dictum tells us that the spirit of prophecy, the *ruah ha-kodesh,* can rest equally upon man or woman. Our people had not only Patriarchs, but also Matriarchs. We had not only Prophets, but also Prophetesses. In the eyes of God, in the eyes of Torah, in the eyes of Jews, woman was invested with the full dignity accorded to man. Equality of value there certainly was.

Furthermore, a good case can be made out to show that our Tradition in many cases found greater inherent value in womankind than in mankind. The first man in history received his name "Adam" from the *'adamah,* the earth from which he was created. His wife, Eve, has her name *Havvah,* derived from *em kol hai,* meaning "the mother of all life." Man's very name refers to his lowly origins, while woman's name is a tribute to her life-bearing functions. Moses is commanded to give the Ten Commandments first to "the house of Jacob" and then to "the house of Israel"; and our Rabbis interpret "the house of Jacob" as referring to the Jewish women, while "the house of Israel" refers to the menfolk.[8a] Our Sages attribute to women greater insight—*binah yetherah*—than men.[8b] They maintain that the redemption from Egypt, the leitmotif of all Jewish history, was only *bizechut nashim tzidkaniyot,* because of the merit of the pious women of Israel.[8c]

Of course, such illustrations can be given in the dozens. Much more can be written—and indeed, much has been published—on the Jewish attitude towards women. This is not the place to probe the matter in detail and with documentation.

It is useless to match statement with counter-statement, to marshal the commendations against the commendations. There is a far more basic direction than isolated quotations or fine legal points by which to judge the traditional Jewish attitude to woman. And that is, the historic role of the Jewess—her exalted position in the home, her traditional standing and stature

---

8a. [*Mechilta', bahodesh* 2.] 8b. [*Niddah* 45b.] 8c. [*Sotah* 11b.]

in the family, her aristocratic dignity as wife and mother and individual. By this standard, any talk of her inferiority is a ridiculous canard, and the chivalry of those who today seek so militantly to "liberate" her by mixing pews in the synagogue is a ludicrous posture of misguided gallantry.

The Jewish woman, therefore, as a person and as a human being was and is regarded by authentic Judaism as anything but inferior. Judaism orients itself to women with a deep appreciation for their positions as the mothers of our generations and as daughters of God. Their position is one of complete honor and dignity, and talk of inequality [to impute to Orthodoxy an attitude of "male superiority"] is therefore absurd.

But while it is true that woman is man's equal in intrinsic value in the eyes of Torah, it is not true—nor should it be— that her functions in life are all identical with those of man. She has a different role in life and in society, and one for which she was uniquely equipped by her Creator. By nature there are many things in which women differ from men. And the fact that men and women differ in function and in role has nothing to do with the categories of inferiority or superiority. The fact that the Torah assigns different religious functions, different *mitzvoth,* to men and to women no more implies inequality than the fact that men and women have different tastes in tobacco or different areas of excellence in the various arts.[9]

---

9. The blessing recited as part of the morning service, " . . . who hast not made me a woman," is to be understood in the light of what we have written. This is not a value-judgment, not an assertion of woman's inferiority, any more than the accompanying blessing " . . . who hast not made me a heathen" imputes racial inferiority to the non-Jew. Both blessings refer to the comparative *roles* of Jew and non-Jew, male and female, in the religious universe of Torah, in which a greater number of religious duties are declared obligatory upon males than females, upon Jews than gentiles. The worshipper thanks God for the opportunity to perform a larger number of commandments. The woman, who in general is excused by the Halachah from positive commandments the observance of which is restricted to specific times, therefore recites a blessing referring to *value* instead of *function* or *role*: " . . . who

That modern women have suffered because they have often failed to appreciate this difference is attested to by one of the most distinguished authorities in the field, anthropologist M. F. Ashley Montagu:

> The manner in which we may most helpfully regard the present relationships between the sexes is that they are in a transitional phase of development. That in the passage from the "abolition" phase of women's movement to the phase of "emancipation" a certain number of predictable errors were committed.
>
> The logic of the situation actually led to the most grievous of the errors committed. This was the argument that insofar as political and social rights were concerned women should be judged as persons and not as members of a biological or any other kind of group. As far as it goes this argument is sound enough, but what seems to have been forgotten in the excitement, is that women, in addition to being persons, also belong to a sex, and that with the differences in sex are associated important differences in function and behavior. *Equality of rights does not imply identity of function,* yet this is what it was taken to mean by many women and men. And so women began —and in many cases continue—to compete with men as if they were themselves men, instead of realizing and establishing themselves in their own right as persons. Women have so much more to contribute to the world as women than they could ever have as spurious men.[10]

---

hast made me according to His will." The latter blessing is, if anything, more profoundly spiritual—gratitude to God for having created me a woman who, despite a more passive role, is, as a daughter of God, created in His image no less than man.

10. "The Triumph and Tragedy of the American Woman," *Saturday Review,* September 27, 1958, p. 14; and cf. Margaret Mead in *N. Y. Times Magazine,* February 10, 1957.

Furthermore, this selfsame confusion in the traditional roles. of male and female, a confusion encouraged by this mistaken identification of sameness with equality, is largely responsible for the disintegration of many marriages. Writing in a popular magazine,[11] Robert Coughlan cites authority when he attributes the failure of so many modern marriages to the failure of men and women to accept their emotional responsibilities to each other and within the family as *men* and *women,* male and female. There appears to be a developing confusion of roles as the traditional identities of the sexes are lost. The emerging American woman tends to the role of male dominance and exploitativeness, while the male becomes more passive. Consequently, neither sex can satisfy the other—they are suffering from *sexual ambiguity.* And Prof. Montagu, approving of Coughlan's diagnosis, adds:

> The feminization of the male and the masculinization of the female are proving to be more than too many marriages can endure. The masculinized woman tends to reject the roles of wife and mother. In compensation, the feminized male wants to be a mother to his children, grows dissatisfied with his wife, and she in turn with him. These are the displaced persons of the American family who make psychiatry the most under-populated profession in the country.[12]

And not only are women themselves and their marriages the sufferers as a result of this confusion of roles of the sexes, but *children* too are falling victim as they are increasingly uncertain of the roles they are expected to play in life. The more masculine the woman becomes, and the more feminine the male tends to be, the more are the children perplexed by what it means to

---

11. *Life,* December 31, 1956.
12. Ashley Montagu, "The American Woman," *Chicago Jewish Forum,* Vol. XVII, No. 1 (1958), p. 8.

be a man or a woman. It is more than a matter of a passing phase as "sissies" or "tomboys." It is a question of the whole psychological integrity of the growing child. A lot of the wreckage ends up on the psychiatrist's couch, as Prof. Montagu said. Some of the less fortunate end up in jail—only recently Judge Samuel Leibowitz attributed the upsurge in juvenile delinquency to this attenuation of the father's role in the family. So that this confusion in the traditional roles of the sexes—a confusion that has hurt modern women, endangered their marriages, and disorganized the normal psychological development of their children—is the very source of the foolish accusation hurled at the Orthodox synagogue, that its separate seating implies an acceptance of woman's inequality and hence ought to be abolished, law or no law.

FAMILIES THAT PRAY TOGETHER

The second line of reasoning presented in favor of mixed pews in the synagogue is that of family solidarity. "Families that pray together stay together," we are told day in, day out, from billboards and bulletin boards and literature mailed out both by churches and non-Orthodox synagogues. Family pews make for family cohesion, for "togetherness," and the experience of worshipping together gives the family unit added strength which it badly needs in these troubled times.

The answer to this is not to underestimate the need for family togetherness. That is, within prescribed limits, extremely important. One of the aspects of our Tradition we can be most proud of is the Jewish home—its beauty, its peace, its strength, its "togetherness." Christians often note this fact, and with great envy. So that we are all for "togetherness" for the family.

And yet it is because of our very concern for the traditional togetherness of the Jewish family that we are so skeptical of the efficacy of the mixed pew synagogue in this regard. If there is

321

any place at all where the togetherness of a family must be fashioned and practiced and lived—that place is the home, not the synagogue. If a family goes to the theater together and goes to a service together and goes on vacation together, but is never *home* together—then all this togetherness is a hollow joke. That is the tragedy of our society. During the week each member of the family leads a completely separate and independent existence, the home being merely a convenient base of operations. During the day Father is at the office or on the road, Mother is shopping, and the children are at school. At night, Father is with "the boys," Mother is with "the girls," and the children dispersed all over the city—or else they are all bickering over which television program to watch. And then they expect this separateness, this lack of cohesion in the home, to be remedied by one hour of sitting together and responding to a rabbi's readings at a Late Friday Service! The brutal fact is that the synagogue is not capable of performing such magic. One evening of family pews will not cure the basic ills of modern family life. "Mixed pews" is no solution for mixed-up homes. We are wrong, terribly wrong, if we think that the rabbi can substitute for the laity in being observant, that the cantor and the choir and organ can substitute for us in praying, and that the synagogue can become a substitute for our homes. And we are even in greater error if we try to substitute clever and/or cute Madison Avenue slogans for the cumulative wisdom expressed in Halachah and Tradition.

If it were true that "families that pray together stay together," and that, conversely, families that pray in a *shul* with a *mechitzah* do not stay together, then one would expect the Orthodox Jewish home to be the most broken home in all of society, for Orthodox Jews have maintained separate pews throughout history. And yet it is precisely in Orthodox Jewish society that the home is the most stable, most firm, most secure.

322

One writer[13] has the following to say on this matter. After describing the pattern of Jewish home life in the Middle Ages, with the "love and attachment of the child for his home and tradition," and the "place where the Jew was at his best," with the home wielding a powerful influence in refining Jewish character, so that "Jewish domestic morals in the Middle Ages were beyond reproach," he writes:

> Particularly in those households where Orthodox Judaism is practiced and observed—both in Europe and in cosmopolitan American centers—almost the entire rubric . . . of Jewish home life in the Middle Ages may be observed even today.
>
> In those homes where the liberties of the Emancipation have infiltrated there exists a wide variety of family patterns, conditioned by the range of defection from Orthodox tradition.

The reader should be informed that this tribute to the Orthodox Jewish home—whose members always worshipped in a synagogue with a *mechitzah*—was written by a prominent Reform rabbi.

So that just "doing things together," including worshipping together, is no panacea for the very real domestic problems of modern Jews. "Li'l Abner," the famous comic-strip character, recently refused to give his son a separate comb for his own use because, he said in his inimitable dialect, "th' fambly whut combs together stays together." We shall have to do more than comb together or pray together or play baseball together. We shall have to build homes, Jewish homes, where Torah and Tradition will be welcome guests, where a Jewish book will be read and intellectual achievements reverenced, where parents will be respected, where the table will be an altar and the food blessed; homes where prayer will be heard and where Torah

---

13. Stanley R. Brav, *Marriage and the Jewish Tradition*, p. 98.

will be discussed in all seriousness. Madison Avenue slogans may increase the attendance at the synagogues and Temples; they will not keep families together.

In speaking of the family, we might also add the tangential observation that it is simply untrue that "the younger generation" invariably wants mixed pews. The personal experience of the writer has convinced him that there is nothing indigenous in youth that makes it pant after mixed seating in the synagogue. It is a matter of training, conviction, and above all of learning and understanding. Young people often understand the necessity for separate pews much more readily than the older folks, to whom mixed seating is sometimes a symbol of having arrived socially, of having outgrown immigrant status. The writer happily chanced upon the following report of a visit to a Reform Sunday School in Westchester, N. Y.:

> When the teacher had elicited the right answer, he passed on to the respective positions of women in Orthodox and Reform Judaism. He had a difficult time at first because the children, unexpectedly, expressed themselves in favor of separating men and women in the synagogue—they thought the women talked too much and had best be segregated—but finally they were persuaded to accept the Reform view.[14]

There is a refreshing naivete about this youthful acceptance of separate seating before being "persuaded" of the Reform view.

ON THE POSITIVE SIDE

Thus far the arguments of those who would do violence to our Tradition and institute mixed pews. What, now, are the reasons why the Halachah is so firm on separating the sexes at

---

14. Theodore Frankel, "Suburban Jewish Sunday School," *Commentary*, June, 1958, p. 486.

every service? What, on the positive side, are the Tradition's motives for keeping the *mechitzah* and the separated seating arrangement?

The answer to this and every similar question must be studied in one frame of reference only. And that is the issue of prayer. We begin with one unalterable premise: *the only function of a religious service is prayer,* and that prayer is a religious experience and *not* a social exercise. If a synagogue is a place to meet friends, and a service the occasion for displaying the latest fashions, then we must agree that "if I can sit next to my wife in the movies, I can sit next to her in the Temple."

THE JEWISH CONCEPT OF PRAYER

To know the effect of mixed seating on the Jewish religious quality of prayer, we must first have some idea of the Jewish concept of prayer. Within the confines of this short essay we cannot hope to treat the matter exhaustively. But we can, I believe, present just a few insights, sufficient to illuminate the question at hand.

Prayer in Hebrew is called *tefillah,* which comes from the word which means "to judge one's self." When the Jew prays, he does not submit an itemized list of requests to God; he judges himself before God, he looks at himself from the point of view of God. Nothing is calculated to give man a greater feeling of awe and humility. The Halachah refers to prayer as *abodah she-be-leb,* which means: the service or sacrifice of the heart. When we pray, we open our hearts to God; nay, we *offer* Him our hearts. At the moment of prayer, we submit completely to His will, and we feel purged of any selfishness, of any pursuit of our own pleasure or satisfaction. The words of the Talmud, "Know before Whom you stand," have graced many an Ark. When we know before Whom we stand, we forget ourselves. At that moment we realize how truly insecure and lonely and abandoned we really are without Him. That is how a Jew approaches God—out of solitude and insecurity, relying completely upon Him for his very breath. This complete concentration on God, this awareness only of Him and nothing or no one else, is called *kavvanah*; and the direction of one's mind to God in utter and complete concentration upon Him, is indispensable for prayer. Without *kavvanah,* prayer becomes just a senseless repetition of words.

DISTRACTION

For *kavvanah* to be present in prayer, it is necessary to eliminate every source of distraction. When the mind is distracted, *kavvanah* is impossible, for then we cannot concentrate on and understand and mean the words our lips pronounce. And as long as men will be men and women will be women, there is nothing more distracting in prayer than mixed company.

Orthodox Jews have a high regard for the pulchritude of Jewish women. As a rule, we believe, a Jewess is beautiful. Her comeliness is so attractive, that it is distractive; *kavvanah* in her presence is extremely difficult. It is too much to expect of a man, sitting in feminine company, to concentrate fully upon the sacred words of the *siddur* and submit completely to God. We are speaking of the deepest recesses of the human heart; it is there that prayer originates. And how can one expect a man's heart to be with God when his eyes are attracted elsewhere? We are speaking of human beings, not angels, and the Halachah recognizes both the strength and weakness of a man. It is simply too much to ask of a man that he sit in the company of women, that he behold their loveliness—and at the same time undergo a great religious experience. What man can feel the nearness of God when if he but raises his eyes from the corner of the *siddur* he finds himself attracted to more earthly pursuits which do not exactly encourage his utter devotion to

326

the pursuit of Godliness? (And what woman can concentrate on the ultimate issues of life and feel the presence of God, when she is far more interested in exhibiting a new dress or new chapeau? How can she try to attract the attention of God when she may be trying much harder to attract the attention of some man?) When the sexes are separated, the chances for such distraction are greatly reduced.[15]

---

15. This argument has often been objected to on the grounds that it takes an unrealistic and exaggerated view of man's erotic responsiveness and that certainly devout Jews who come to pray should not be suspected of romantic daydreaming. That such objections can be raised seriously in our present post-Freudian culture and society is unthinkable. Evidently, our Sages, who lived in a society of much greater moral restraint, had a keener and more realistic insight into psychology than many of us moderns in our sophisticated society where the most grievous moral offense is no longer regarded as particularly shocking.

The late Dr. Kinsey's works prove that the intuitive insights of the Jewish sages are confirmed by modern statistics and sexological theory. In his first book (Kinsey, Pomeroy, and Martin, *Sexual Behavior in the Human Male* [Phila. & London: W. B. Saunders Co., 1948] p. 363), Kinsey and his associates inform us of an inverse relationship between full sexual expression and erotic responsiveness to visual stimulation. Upper-level males have much lower frequency of full sexual outlet than lower-level males; they are therefore far more responsive to external sexual stimuli, such as the very presence of women, than the lower level males. In addition, "the higher degree of eroticism in the upper level male may also be consequent on his greater capacity to visualize situations which are not immediately at hand."

Thus, greater erotic responsiveness is experienced by higher class men, both because of their greater restraint from full sexual outlet and because of their greater capacity for imagining erotic situations. It is well-known that the great majority of American Jews fall into this category of "upper-level males." And certainly the more advanced education of so many American Jews needs no documentation here. Add to this the fact that, according to Kinsey's statistics, the more pious have a lower rate of sexual activity than the less pious (*ibid.*, 469-472), and it is fairly evident that if erotic thoughts are to be prevented during worship, as indeed they must be, then the synagogue-going Jew needs the safeguard of separate seating certainly no less than anyone else.

This Jewish insight into the human mind, upon which is based the institution of separate pews, is thus neither exaggerated nor insulting; it is merely realistic. We might add that women find it more difficult to accept this thesis than men. This is a quite understandable phenomenon. Women have

327

FRIVOLITY

And it is not only that what one *sees* prevents one from experiencing *kavvanah,* but that mixed company in general, in the relaxed and non-business-like atmosphere of the synagogue, is conducive to a kind of frivolity—not disrespectful, but levity nonetheless. And if a synagogue is to retain its character as a holy place, it must possess *kedushah,* or holiness. Holiness in Judaism has a variety of meanings, but mostly it means transcendence, the ability to grow above one's limits, the ability to reach upwards. Holiness is defined by many of our Sages as *perishah me'arayoth*—separation from immorality or immoral thoughts. That is why on Yom Kippur, the holiest day of the year, the portion of the Torah read in the afternoon deals with the *'arayoth,* with the prohibitions of various sexual relations, such as incest, adultery, etc. For only by transcending one's biological self does one reach his or her spiritual stature. Only by separating one's self from sensual thoughts and wants can one achieve the state of holiness. It may be true, as modern Jews like to hear so often, that Judaism sees nothing inherently wrong or sinful about sex. But that does not mean that it is to be regarded as a harmless exercise not subject to any control or discipline.[16] And its control, even refraining from any

---

greater purity of mind than do men. According to Prof. Kinsey, they are half as responsive to visual stimulation as are men. (Kinsey, Pomeroy, Martin, & Gebhard, *Sexual Behavior in the Human Female* [Phila. & London, W. B. Saunders Co., 1953], p. 651). No wonder that Orthodox rabbis often find it harder to convince women than men of the propriety of separate pews!

16. We are indebted to Dr. Kinsey for recording the intriguing paradox of, on the one hand, the openness and frankness of Jews in talking about sex and, on the other hand, their relatively greater restraint in its full biological (and especially illicit) expression (*Sexual Behavior in the Human Male,* p. 486). *Perishah me'arayoth* is a matter of principled self-discipline, not prudishness. And this and other such Jewish attitudes color the lives even of those non-observant Jews who have had very little contact with Judaism. "The influence of several thousand years of Jewish sexual philosophy is not to be ignored in the search for any final explanation of these data."

thoughts about it, is indispensable for an atmosphere of *kedushah* or holiness. So that the very fact of mixed company, despite our very best intentions, gives rise to the kind of milieu which makes holiness impossible. "Know before Whom you stand," we were commanded, and not "know next to whom you are sitting." "It requires a great effort *to realize before Whom we stand,* for such realization is more than having a thought in one's mind. It is a knowledge in which the whole person is involved; the mind, the heart, body, and soul. To know it is to forget everything else, including the self."[16a] That is why Halachic authorities have ruled that a synagogue with mixed pews loses its status as a holy place before the Holy One.

BASHFULNESS

In addition to distraction and frivolousness, there is yet another aspect of mixed seating which makes it undesirable for an authentically Jewish synagogue: the matter of bashfulness.

Few of us are really "ourselves" at all times. We "change personalities" for different occasions. The man who at home does nothing but grumble and complain is all charm when talking to a customer. The harried housewife who shouts at her children all day speaks in a dignified whisper when the doctor comes to visit. And especially when we are in mixed company we like to "put up a front"; we take special care to talk in a certain way, smile a certain way; we become more careful of posture, of looks, of expression, of our sense of humor. These things are not necessarily done consciously—they just happen as part of our natural psychological reaction.

Now prayer, real Jewish prayer, the kind we should strive for at all times though we achieve it rarely, demands full concentration on our part. It must monopolize our attention. It

16a. *God in Search of Man,* Abraham J. Heschel (New York: Farrar, Straus and Cudahy, 1955), p. 407.

insists that we be unconcerned with our outer appearance at that time. And full and undiminished concentration on the holy words of the *siddur* can sometimes result in unusual physical expression. Sometimes it can move us to tears. Sometimes the spiritual climate of a particular passage makes us want to smile with happiness. At other times we feel inclined to concentrate strongly and shut out all interference from the outer world, so that our foreheads become wrinkled and our eyes shut and our fists clenched—the physical symptoms of intense thought. Sometimes we feel like reciting a verse aloud, of giving full vocal expression to our innermost feelings. *All my bones shall say, Lord, who is like Thee* (Psalms 35:10)?

And can this ever be done in a mixed group? When we are so concerned with our appearances, can we ever abandon ourselves so freely to prayer? When we tend to remain self-conscious, can we become fully God-conscious? Are we not much too bashful, in mixed company, to give such expression to our prayer? In congregations maintaining separate seating, it is usual to *hear* the worshippers worshipping, each addressing God at his own rate and in his own intonation and with his whole individual being. Do we ordinarily hear such *davenning* at the Temples? Is the mechanical reading-in-unison and the slightly bored responsive reading and the deadly-silent silent-meditations —is this *davenning*, the rapturous flight of the worshipper's soul to God? Have not the mixed pews and the attendant bashfulness thoroughly frustrated the expression of prayer?

The poet James Montgomery once wrote that prayer is
The motion of a hidden fire
That trembles in the breast.
Prayer is the burden of a sigh,
The falling of a tear,
The upward glancing of an eye
When none but God is near.

330

Note that the inner experience of prayer results in an outward physical expression as well. And in the mixed company of a family-pew-Temple, who is not going to be bashful? Who will tremble just a bit, and give vent to a sigh, and shed a tear, and glance upward with a pleading eye? Who is brave enough and unbashful enough to risk looking ludicrous by becoming absorbed in prayer and letting the innermost thoughts and feelings show outwardly, without any inhibition? Bashfulness presents enough of a problem as is, without the added complication of mixed seating, which takes *kavvanah* out of the level of the difficult and into the realm of the highly improbable.

THE SENSE OF INSECURITY

To understand the next point in favor of *mechitzah,* we must mention yet one other argument in favor of family pews that merits our serious attention—the desire of a wife to sit next to her husband because of the feeling of strength and protection and security that his presence gives her. (The old and oft-repeated desire for mixed pews because "he has to show me the page in the *siddur*" is no longer relevant. In most synagogues there are regular announcements of the page from the pulpit, if necessary, to serve this purpose.) That such feeling exists we cannot doubt—and it is a genuine one too.

What is the verdict of our Tradition on this issue? First, it should be clear that when we pray, we must do so for *all* Israel and for all humanity, not just each for his own little family. Only occasionally is there a special prayer for the members of one's family or one's self; usually our prayers are phrased in the plural, indicating our concern for all the community. Praying in public *only* for the family is a relic from ancient days when the family worshipped as a tribal unit. And Judaism has from the beginning rejected the pagan institution of the household idol and all its trappings.

331

Second, as Rabbi J. B. Soloveitchik has pointed out,[17] this reliance upon a husband or a wife is precisely the opposite of the Jewish concept of prayer. As was mentioned before, the approach of the Jew to God must be out of a sense of isolation, of insecurity, of defenselessness. There must be a recognition that without God none of us has any security at all, that my husband's life is dependent on God's will, his strength on God's favor, his health on God's goodness. Standing before God there is no other source of safety. It is only when we do not have that feeling of reliance on others that we can achieve faith in God. When we leave His presence—then we may feel a sense of security and safety in life.

Third, and finally, when Orthodoxy tells the modern woman not to worship at the side of her husband in whom she so trusts, it reveals an appreciation of her spiritual competence much greater than that of the Reformers and half-Reformers who offer mixed pews for this very reason. Torah tells her that she need not rely upon a strong, superior male. It tells her that she is his spiritual equal and is as worthy of approaching God by herself as he is. It reminds her that women are the daughters of God no less than men are His sons, and that our Father is no less disposed to the company of His daughters than of His sons. It tells her to address God by herself; that she both cannot and need not rely on anyone else.

MIMICRY

The final reason we offer in favor of the age-old system of separate seating at all religious services is to avoid religious mimicry, copying from other faiths. The principle of Jewish separateness is fundamental to our people and our religion. We are different and we are unique. There is no other people

---

17. *The Day-Morning Journal*, November 22, 1954, p. 5 [reprinted in this volume; see above, p. 116].

about whom no one can agree whether they are nation, race, or religion, because they are all three, and more. There is no other people that has lived in exile for two thousand years and then returned to its homeland. We are different in the way we pray, in the food we eat, in the holidays we observe, in the strange hopes we have always entertained for the future. And it is this separateness, this anti-assimilation principle, which has kept us alive and distinct throughout the ages in all lands and societies and civilizations.

The source of this principle in the Bible is the verse, *Neither shall ye walk in their ordinances* (Leviticus 18:3) and similar verses, such as, *And ye shall not walk in the customs of the nations* (*ibid.* 20:23). Our Tradition understood this prohibition against imitating others to refer especially to the borrowing from gentile cults and forms of worship. Our ritual was to be completely Jewish and in no way were we to assimilate any gentile religious practices. But this is more than a mere verse. According to Maimonides, this principle is so fundamental that it is responsible for a major part of the Torah's legislation. Many a *mitzvah* was given, he says, to prevent our mimicking pagan rituals. Most of Part III of the *Guide for the Perplexed* is an elaboration of this principle.

We can now see why from this point of view the whole idea of mixed seating in the synagogue is thoroughly objectionable. It is an unambiguous case of religious mimicry. The alien model in this case is Christianity; worse yet, the specifically *pagan* root of Christianity.

In its very earliest history, while still under the influence of classical Judaism, Christianity maintained a traditional Jewish attitude towards women's participation in religious services, and already found a strong pagan undercurrent making itself felt in opposition. It was Paul who found it necessary to admonish the Corinthian Christians to prevent their women from

333

preaching in the church.[18] The position of the early church was against allowing its women to take part audibly in public worship, and included a prohibition on praying in mixed company.[19] The Pauline position was clearly "a rule taken over from the synagogue and maintained in the primitive church."[20] The Corinthian Church proved, however, to be a channel for the introduction of pagan elements into Christianity, foreign elements which later were to become organic parts of that religion. Corinth itself was a city of pleasure, noted for its immorality which usually had religious sanction. It was full of prostitutes, thousands of courtesans attached to the temple of Aphrodite. This pagan environment, with its moral laxity, had a profound effect upon the Corinthian church.[21] The effort to introduce mixed seating and women's preaching is thus part of the pagan heritage of Christianity, just as Paul's initial efforts to resist these reforms were part of Christianity's Jewish heritage. The pagan influence ultimately dominated, and today mixed seating is a typically Christian institution.

When Jews agitate for mixed pews they are guilty, therefore, of religious mimicry. In this case, as stated, it is a borrowing from paganism[22] transmitted to the modern world by way of Christianity. In the more immediate sense, it is a borrowing from Christianity itself—for who of us stops to consider the historical antecedents of a particular ritual or institution which attracts us? Mixed seating thus represents a desire by Jews to Christianize their synagogues by imitating the prac-

18. I Corinthians 14:34, 35.
19. Charles C. Ryrie, *The Place of Women in the Church* (New York: Macmillan Co., 1958), pp. 78-80.
20. F. Godet, *First Epistle to the Corinthians* (Edinburgh: T. & T. Clark, 1887), II, pp. 324, 325.
21. *Ibid.*, pp. 7, 60, 62, 140.
22. This point was conceded by the late Prof. Louis Ginzberg, the Talmud expert of the Conservative movement, in a letter quoted in *Conservative Judaism*, Vol. XI (Fall, 1956), p. 39.

tices of contemporary Christian churches. And this kind of mimicry is, as we pointed out, a violation not only of a specific law of the Torah, but an offense against the whole spirit of Torah.

Lest the reader still remains skeptical of our thesis that mixed seating represents a pagan-Christianization of the synagogue, he ought to consider the origin of mixed pews in the synagogue itself. Reform in Europe did not know of mixed seating. It was first introduced in America by Isaac Mayer Wise, in about 1850, when he borrowed a Baptist Church for his Reform services in Albany, N. Y., and found the mixed pews of the church so to his liking that he decided to retain this feature for his temple![23]

We thus have only one conclusion as far as this is concerned—that those who have favored family pews have unwittingly advanced the cause of the paganization and Christianization of our Synagogues. Understanding that it is wrong to assimilate *Jews,* we are now witnessing the attempt to assimilate *Judaism.* And when a congregation finds itself wondering whether to submit to the pressure for mixed pews, it must consider this among other things: Are we to remain a Jewish synagogue—or a semi-pagan house of worship? Are we to incorporate the *ezrath nashim* of the Holy Temple—or the family pew of the Baptist Church? Are we to carry on in the spirit of Jerusalem—or of Corinth? Are we to follow the teachings of Hillel and R. Akiba and Maimonides—or of Isaac Mayer Wise and his ministerial colleagues?

CONCLUSION

In conclusion, we do not mean to imply that the rationale elaborated in this essay should be the primary motive for the

---

23. Samuel S. Cohen, "Reform Judaism" in *Jewish Life in America* (ed. Freedman and Gordis) p. 86.

observance by moderns of *kedushath beth ha-knesseth,* the sanctity of the synagogue, which requires the separate seating of men and women in its confines. The Halachah is essentially independent of the reasons the Jews of every succeeding age discover in and ascribe to it, and its sacred origin is enough to commend its acceptance by faithful Jews. What we did want to accomplish—and if we have failed it is the fault of the author, not of Orthodox Judaism—is to show that even without the specific and clear judgment of the Halachah, separate seating ought to be the only arrangement acceptable to serious-minded modern Jews; for it is consistent not only with the whole tradition of Jewish morality and the philosophy of Jewish prayer, but also with the enlightened self-interest of modern Jewish men *and* women—and children—from a social and psychological point of view.

VII

no room for compromise

GAINST THE VIEW that the law is immutable, however, another major objection has been raised: "Many orthodox rabbis and congregations have accepted mixed pews."

It is true that a number of rabbis who consider themselves orthodox, and are even members of orthodox rabbinical organizations, hold positions in synagogues with mixed seating. This has often been quoted as proof that mixed pews are permissible. However, it must be realized that these rabbis themselves do not so maintain; as pointed out before, they actually cannot do so if they want to be recognized as orthodox rabbis, for they would then be contradicting the law which they are supposed to apply. To quote again:

"No rabbi, however great in scholarship and moral

integrity, has the authority to endorse, legalize, or even apologetically explain, this basic deviation. Any rabbi or scholar who attempts to sanction the desecrated synagogue, *ipso facto* casts a doubt on his own moral right to function as a teacher or spiritual leader in the traditional sense of the word" (Rabbi Joseph B. Soleveitchik, chapter II, source 13).

The orthodox rabbis serving in synagogues with mixed pews readily admit that it is wrong to have mixed seating; they will strongly object to synagogues changing to mixed pews; and they will defend the right of orthodox worshipers not to be interfered with in their desire to worship in an edifice of prayer that will not do violence to their conscience with its seating arrangement. They will merely stress the fact that "a generation tragically unschooled in Jewish teaching . . . suffers the illusion that mixed pews form a touchstone to a supposed 'modernization,' and fails to perceive that traditional Jewish practices are each an integral part of the great pattern whose total is Judaism" (Rabbi Morris Max, chapter VI, source 9). These rabbis accept synagogues with mixed pews only with the hope to lead the errant congregation back to proper orthodox authority and practice.

Their argument carries some weight. *Jewish Action,* April-May 1957, lists fourteen synagogues which recently reinstalled *mechitzoth.* It cites a statement by the Rabbinical Council of America that this development shows "a reversal of that trend toward abandonment of Torah standards . . . infiltration of influence foreign to Judaism . . . adulteration of Jewish worship and of the Jewish concept of life. . . . Among the congregations which had suffered deviations in Jewish practice, a steadily increasing number are rising again to re-affirm the sovereignty of Halachah in

Jewish life, and the sanctity and indestructible unity of our sacred Jewish tradition" (1).

However, the policy of accepting positions in deviating synagogues, even for a limited period of time, has been strongly challenged by many authorities who feel that even the most idealistic considerations cannot permit countenancing a violation of the Law of the separation of the sexes in a House of Worship. "Some congregations do attempt to combine mixed seating with otherwise traditional Jewish forms of service, and the status of these congregations, having undertaken a grave religious deviation, is very much in question" (Union of Orthodox Jewish Congregations).

In any case, even if we concede any merit to the view of those rabbis who have accepted posts in deviating synagogues, and even if their number were much larger than it is, the legal position would not be altered: "We must remember that an ethical or Halachic principle decreed by God is not rendered void by the fact that the people refuse to abide by it" (R. Joseph B. Soloveitchik, chapter II, source 13). This applies to the lack of a *mechitzah* as well as any other improper practice that congregations may adopt, and clearly establishes the obligation of an orthodox Jew to reject deviation.

Jewish ACTION

Published by: THE UNION OF ORTHODOX JEWISH CONGREGATIONS OF AMERICA

APRIL-MAY, 1957   418   VOL. XI., No. 1   NISAN-IYAR, 5717

14 Synagogues Install Mechitzoth; Viewed as Marking Upward Trend

Fourteen congregations during the past year have re-erected or newly installed mechitzoth, the separation between the men's and women's seating sections required for public worship by Jewish law, a study by UOJCA headquarters has disclosed. The congregations which have effected the change to Jewish seating practice are located in various parts of the country and vary widely in size and in historic background.

A list of the synagogues, together with the names of their rabbis and presidents, is printed in an adjoining column.

The development is viewed by the country's Rabbinate and lay leaders as a significant manifestation of the mounting tempo of the Torah-ward current in American Jewish life. A statement by Rabbi Solomon J. Sharfman, president of the Rabbinical Council of America, said:

Symbol of Re-birth

"This inspiring development testifies to a reversal of that trend towards abandonment of Torah standards which in the past has posed so ominous a threat to American Jewry. Entire congregations, as well as great numbers of individuals, have been the victims of that trend.

CONGREGATION	RABBI	PRESIDENT
Cong. Anshe Emes of Williamsbridge, Bronx, N. Y.	Hyman E. Bloom	
B'nai Abraham of S. Flatbush, Brooklyn, N. Y.	Solomon Shapiro	Aaron Levine
Cong. Ahavath Sholom, Grange, N.J.	Lieb Trachs	Louis Margolies
Beth Hamedrosh Hagodol, Brooklyn, N.Y.	Jacob Zaikhes	Hughes Tannenbaum
Jewish Center of Hyde Park, Brooklyn, N. Y.		
Cong. Agudath Israel, Brooklyn, N.Y.	Joseph Fraade	Joseph Tracey
Cong. Adath Jeshurun, Bronx, N.Y.	Solomon Kornfeld	
Ozone Park Jewish Center, Ozone Park, N. Y.	Moboch Schneider	Morris P. Wecker
Beth Jacob Cong., Miami Beach, Fla.	Samuel Laska	Murray Tredwold
Baron Hirsch Cong., Memphis, Tenn.	Tibor H. Stern	David Wiseman
Homestead Hebrew Center, Homestead, Pa.	Hyman Gorelons	Philip Br's
Springfield Gardens Jewish Center, Springfield Gardens, N.Y.	Hyman Shapiro	
University City, Mo.	Josh Adler	
Beth Jacob Cong., Columbus, Ohio	Charles Hartman	Herman B. Madden
With Jacob Cong.	Solomon Pemphs	Milton Leaman

The synagogues cited above have either re-erected or newly installed mechitzoth — the separation of the men's and women's section. According to Rabbi Solomon J. Sharfman, President of the Rabbinical Council of America, the development is viewed as "a reversal of the trend towards abandonment of Torah standards."

"The removal of mechitzoth was the symptom of the infiltration of influences foreign to Judaism, and its inevitable accompaniment has been the adulteration of Jewish worship and of the Jewish concept of life. In no case has this deviation — however well-meaning may, in some instances, have been its motivation — achieved its supposed aim of increasing synagogue attendance. The very contrary has been the inevitable result.

"Today, thank the Almighty, we see the rise of a truer understanding, we see many who had been estranged turning to a re-awakened appreciation of the Jewish heritage and a determination to uphold and fulfill it. Among the congregations which had suffered deviations in Jewish practice, a steadily increasing number are rising again to re-affirm the sovereignty of Halachah in Jewish life and the sanctity and indestructible unity of our sacred Jewish tradition. The erection or restoration of mechitzoth in the synagogues is a symbol of a profound re-birth.

tablishment of a separate Publications Division. All UOJCA periodicals and literature, otherwise demonstrated, mater-

is also Editor of JEWISH LIFE, with M. Judah Metchik serving as Assistant Editor.

On Other Fronts

sion call for intensified tempo in these fields, with regional gatherings blueprinted on a coast-to-coast basis.

(Continued on Page 8)

Feuerstein Urges U.S. to Ensure Freedom of Transit in Suez Canal

UOJCA President Moses I. Feuerstein, together with the leaders of sixteen other major American Jewish organizations, called upon the Government of the United States this month to lose the full weight of its influence and authority to other ways, about an end to Israel's continued military occupation and immediately to secure to Israel United Nations control of Gaza and freedom of transit now in the Gulf of Aqaba and the Suez Canal.

"Our Government's behavior in this issue will be regarded as a yardstick by all nations of the free world whose future is bound to their faith in America and its pledges," the Jewish leaders said.

source for chapter VII

❦ 1 ❦

A News Report on New Mechitzoth

FROM "JEWISH ACTION," APRIL-MAY, 1957

14 SYNAGOGUES INSTALL MECHITZOTH; VIEWED AS MARKING UPWARD TREND

Fourteen congregations during the past year have re-erected or newly installed *mechitzoth,* the separation between the men's and women's seating sections required for public worship by Jewish law, a study by the headquarters of the Union of Orthodox Jewish Congregations of America disclosed. The congregations which have effected the change to Jewish seating practice are located in various parts of the country and vary widely in size and in historic background. . . .

The development is viewed by the country's Rabbinic and lay leaders as a significant manifestation of the mounting tempo of the Torah-ward current in American Jewish life. A statement by Rabbi Solomon J. Sharfman, president of the Rabbinical Council of America, said:

SYMBOL OF REBIRTH

"This inspiring development testifies to a reversal of that trend toward abandonment of Torah standards which in the past has posed so ominous a threat to American Jewry. Entire congregations, as well as great numbers of individuals, have been the victims of that trend.

341

"The removal of *mechitzoth* was the symptom of the infiltration of influences foreign to Judaism, and its inevitable accompaniment has been the adulteration of Jewish worship and of the Jewish concept of life. In no case has this deviation— however well-meaning may, in some instances, have been its motivation—achieved its supposed aim of increasing synagogue attendance. The very contrary has been the inevitable result.

"Today, thank the Almighty, we see the rise of a true understanding; we see many who had been estranged turning to a reawakened appreciation of the Jewish heritage and a determination to uphold and fulfill it. Among the congregations which had suffered deviations in Jewish practice, a steadily increasing number are rising again to re-affirm the sovereignty of Halachah in Jewish life and the sanctity and indestructible unity of our sacred Jewish tradition. The erection or restoration of *mechitzoth* in the synagogues is a symbol of a profound re-birth."

342

VIII

conclusion:
the case
in court

T WAS on the basis of the facts presented in this book that the Mount Clemens case was fought. The defenders of authentic Jewish tradition could not accept the introduction of mixed pews. However, it should be on record that they made every effort to avoid a conflict in the civil courts. They offered to take the entire issue before a Jewish religious court competent to rule on Jewish Law. Only when this was refused, and the trustees of the congregation proceeded with the introduction of mixed seating, was the case reluctantly taken to the civil courts with a Bill of Complaint (1), supported by a Brief (2), in our search for an injunction to stay their hand.

The basis for civil action readily emerges from the present book. This synagogue was built by its founders

343

in the strictest accordance with established Jewish law and practice, and in definite contradiction to the procedures of Reform synagogues, which were then already well established.

When these founders stated in the congregation's Constitution that its object shall be "the furtherance of Jewish religion," they very obviously meant the historically established Jewish religion. They wanted to further it in those ways which, by Jewish law, are incumbent upon a congregation: by the provision of a place of worship and a place of study such as the Synagogue has traditionally been.

Thus the leaders of the congregation were obliged to make available these services according to the rules of Jewish law. This is borne out by the fact that the synagogue did, in fact, follow orthodox practices and fulfill all obligations of Jewish law. Any change from this course of action, such as an alteration in seating arrangements, which would force an orthodox member either to leave the congregation or to do violence to his religious principles, represents a violation of the fundamental purposes for which the congregation was founded. (It should be noted that, when a form of ecclesiastical support was sought to defend the change in mixed pews, it was a Conservative clergyman who was called upon.) It furthermore deprives the conscientious orthodox members of their established property rights. Not even a majority of members, at any given time, can do that.

It is not sufficient to argue that the congregation will remain orthodox despite the changed seating arrangements. Orthodoxy does not depend on statements of allegiance but on actual compliance with the Law. Since there will be no such compliance, conscientious orthodox members

344

have no other source of relief but the courts in order to protect their established rights and the purposes for which the congregation was established, just as they did in the New Orleans case, referred to in chapter I (see source 3 there).

To our regret, the case led to unfortunate statements in print which only served to add confusion and rancor to an issue already emotionally beclouded. For the record we have included one typical statement in the sources (3), along with a courageous and heartwarming answer by a stalwart defender of our faith, of the younger generation, Rabbi David Hollander (4).

Meanwhile, the initial Bill of Complaint, with its supporting brief, failed in its purpose; it was necessary to appeal to the higher court for a reversal of the unfavorable decision. Toward this end the plaintiffs, through their attorneys, presented a fuller brief, marshalling the facts more cogently, and documenting them more thoroughly(5). Mr. Samuel L. Brennglass, vice-president of the Union of Orthodox Jewish Congregations of America, and a brilliant attorney, prepared another, most effective brief, which the Rabbinical Council of America and the Union presented as *amici curiae,* "friends of the Court."

It is only left to record, with humble gratitude, that by the grace of God, a favorable decision was rendered by the Supreme Court of the State of Michigan. It is reprinted here in full (7), together with the decree which the Court issued subsequently (8).

This decision establishes a bulwark in Michigan State law to defend orthodox Jewish faith against inroads by would-be "modernizers" and "reformers." We can but hope that it will also help our brethren in other states of the Union by setting a significant precedent.

345

But it is with no sense of victory or triumph that we receive this decision.   It is with the hope and the prayer that as Jewish religious practice continues unchanged in the synagogue, it may lead our fellow-Jews away from a modern jet-age of speed, confusion and emptiness to a glimpse of man's ability to commune with the Divine beyond the reaches and ravages of time.

346

sources for chapter VIII

❧ 1 ❧
The Bill of Complaint

IN THE MOUNT CLEMENS CASE

[No. 25233] presented in the Circuit Court for the County of Macomb, State of Michigan, in Chancery, by Walsh, Walsh, O'Sullivan, Stommel & Sharp, Attorneys for Plaintiff, September 7, 1955.

MEYER DAVIS, SAM SCHWARTZ and BARUCH LITVIN, Members of Congregation Beth Tefilas Moses, Plaintiffs, vs. J. N. SCHER, MORRIS FELDMAN (Dr.), SAM LEVINE, SAM GORDENKER, MAX SCHWARTZ, HARRY MALBIN, MAX ELKIN, BERNICE LITVIN, ALICE FARBER, REVA CHAITMAN, SAM GINSBURG and SAM LEVINE, Members of the Board of Trustees of Congregation Beth Tefilas Moses, an Orthodox Jewish Congregation, Defendants.

The plaintiffs above named respectfully aver unto this honorable court as follows:

I

That plaintiffs are members of the Congregation of Beth Tefilas Moses, an Orthodox Jewish Congregation, organized and existing under the laws of the State of Michigan and located in the City of Mt. Clemens in the County of Macomb and State of Michigan.

For technical legal reasons, every member of the Board of Trustees was listed as a defendant whether or not they agreed with the Board's view on this issue.

347

II

That the defendants are the duly elected and constituted members of the Board of Trustees of said congregation and purport to with respect to the within controversy in their representative capacity.

III

That defendant trustees, in accordance with the constitution of Congregation Beth Tefilas Moses, have the full and complete physical control and direction of the activities and property of the Congregation including the synagogue or place of worship of the Congregation; but do not have power or authority under ecclesiastical or civil law to abrogate or change the form of worship of said Congregation.

IV

That the real property of the Congregation on which is located the synagogue and its appurtenances was conveyed to the Congregation by instruments of conveyance described in schedule A attached hereto and made a part hereof.

V

That defendant trustees hold the title to the synagogue and its appurtenances by virtue of their office, as trustees for the purposes for which the Congregation was formed and dedicated, to wit: as a place of worship of an orthodox Jewish congregation.

VI

That the synagogue was built in the year 1921, and thereafter other improvements were added to the real estate presently held by the defendant trustees aforesaid; therewith the holdings have a present value of upwards of forty thousand dollars; that the synagogue and other improvements were built from the

348

funds and contributions of orthodox Jews of the Mt. Clemens community as well as from the funds and contributions of orthodox Jews who have come to Mt. Clemens from time to time to the health resorts of that community; that the funds and contributions of orthodox Jews, including the plaintiffs herein, have maintained the synagogue and its appurtenances down to the present time.

VII

That the Jews' religion is based upon the *Halachoth,* or authoritative statements of the rules of conduct as guides to the exact fulfillment of the Divine commands found in the Talmud, the chief body of Jewish tradition, which in turn is based upon the interpretation of the Hebrew Scriptures, particularly the Torah or great body of Mosaic law.

VIII

That in accordance with the *Halachoth,* it is forbidden to pray in a synagogue where men and women sit together, as such synagogue under the orthodox Jewish tradition has no *kedushah* or congregational sanctification; that the separation of the sexes has been strictly adhered to in the orthodox Jewish practice for upwards of three thousand years, and orthodox Jews, such as the plaintiffs herein and those whose funds and contributions built and maintained the synagogue of Congregation Beth Tefilas Moses, cannot conscientiously worship contrary to orthodox custom and tradition in a synagogue where the sexes are not separated.

IX

That on or about the 28th day of July, 1955, at a special meeting of the members of the Congregation of Beth Tefilas Moses, certain members constituting a reform movement, so-called, within the Congregation, voted by a majority vote to

349

introduce mixed seating within the synagogue, and the defendant trustees, as plaintiffs are informed and have reason to believe, are making arrangements to carry out the dictates of the aforesaid vote; that the plaintiffs are informed and have reason to believe that said mixed seating will be put into effect in the synagogue for the High Jewish Holidays approaching, namely, Rosh Hashanah occurring on September 16, 1955, Yom Kippur occurring on September 26, and the Feast of the Tabernacles commencing on October 5, 1955, as well as at other times.

X

That if mixed seating is established or permitted by the defendants as aforesaid, the plaintiffs and the members of the Congregation who adhere to the orthodox Jewish tradition and practice will be deprived of the beneficial use of the synagogue, particularly during the High Holidays approaching, and at all other times; that there is no other orthodox synagogue in the Mt. Clemens community, and the plaintiffs and other adhering members of the Congregation will be forced to leave the city and seek a place of worship elsewhere; and that the contemplated acts of the defendants aforesaid in instituting or permitting mixed seating will deprive the plaintiffs and the adhering members of the Congregation of their property rights in the synagogue and its appurtenances as adhering orthodox members of the Congregation, as it was organized and as it existed down to the time of the vote aforesaid and the contemplated action of the defendant trustees based upon said vote.

XI

That the action of members constituting the reform group, so called, of the Congregation is radically and fundamentally opposed to the doctrines, customs, usages and practices of Congregation Beth Tefilas Moses and orthodox Judaism recognized, accepted and practiced by the Congregation prior to the reform movement referred to herein.

XII

That the amount in controversy exceeds the sum of $100.00 and the plaintiffs have no adequate remedy at law.

Wherefore, the plaintiffs pray:

1.   That the defendants may, without oath (all answers upon oath hereby expressly waived), full, true, direct and perfect answer make to all and singular the matters hereinbefore stated and charged.

2.   That the plaintiffs may have an order directing the defendants and each of them to show cause on a day certain sufficiently in advance of the commencement of the High Jewish Holidays mentioned in Paragraph IX of this bill of complaint so as to protect the property rights of the plaintiffs therein, why a restraining order should not issue enjoining and restraining the defendants from instituting or permitting mixed seating in the synagogue, particularly during the said High Jewish Holidays and at all other times pending the hearing of this cause.

3.   That the court find that the action of the Congregation in voting mixed seating was contrary to the established practice of orthodox Judaism as recognized by the Congregation from the date of its organization to the time of said vote.

4.   That the true congregation of Congregation Beth Tefilas Moses are the plaintiffs and those who adhere to the established tradition and practice of orthodox Judaism as recognized by the Congregation prior to the vote aforesaid.

5.   That the vote of the Congregation in favor of mixed seating was not the vote of the true Congregation and constituted an illegal interference with the property rights of the plaintiffs and the other adherents of orthodox Judaism.

351

6. That the defendant trustees be enjoined and restrained from instituting or permitting mixed seating in the synagogue of Congregation Beth Tefilas Moses or otherwise carrying out the vote of those members who by their action do not constitute the true Congregation aforesaid.

7. That the plaintiffs may have such other and further relief in the premises as shall be agreeable to equity.

Meyer Davis, Sam Schwartz, Baruch Litvin

ꕤ 2 ꕤ

Brief

IN SUPPORT OF PLAINTIFFS' APPLICATION FOR A PRELIMINARY INJUNCTION

PLAINTIFFS HEREIN, by Walsh, Walsh, O'Sullivan, Stommel and Sharp, their Attorneys, respectfully submit the following brief in support of their application for a preliminary injunction in this matter.

CONTENTS

A. The facts as shown by the Bill of Complaint.

B. The issue presented.

C. The applicable law.

D. The defendants' Motion to Dismiss fails to set forth any legal or equitable basis for dismissal or for refusing the granting of the preliminary injunction.

E. The relief prayed.

THE FACTS AS SHOWN BY THE BILL OF COMPLAINT

The undisputed material facts shown by the sworn Bill of Complaint in this matter are:

352

1. The Congregation was founded as a Jewish Orthodox Congregation over 30 years ago.

2. The real property upon which the Synagogue and the other appurtenances were built was conveyed to a congregation that was Jewish Orthodox.

3. The Synagogue was built over 30 years ago and was dedicated to the Jewish Orthodox form of worship.

4. That in an Orthodox congregation, the men and women do not sit together in worship, and mixed seating is a desecration, and orthodox Jews cannot, in conscience, worship in a synagogue where mixed seating is allowed.

5. That the plaintiffs and others adhere to the orthodox practice and ritual.

6. That the defendant trustees have no power of authority under ecclesiastical or civil law to abrogate or change the form of worship of the congregation.

7. That in the congregation is a group that favors a form of worship not in accordance with orthodox Jewish practice and doctrine; that through the efforts of this group, the defendant trustees have been directed and plan to establish mixed seating during the High and solemn Holidays of Rosh Hashanah, Yom Kippur, the Feast of the Tabernacles and the other holidays now approaching.

8. That the plaintiffs and others who adhere to the orthodox Jewish practice and doctrine will suffer irreparable injury as a result thereof in that they will be deprived of the opportunity to worship during said holidays in the synagogue of the congregation and will be compelled to go elsewhere.

THE ISSUE PRESENTED

The issue here is not a question of the right of a majority of a church organization to exercise its prerogative upon a matter of church policy within its jurisdiction. Instead, it is a question of whether a majority of a church congregation can institute a practice within the church fundamentally opposed to the doctrine to which the church property is dedicated, when a minority of the congregation adhere to the established doctrine and practice.

THE APPLICABLE LAW

The right of a member of a congregation to the beneficial use of the church property as a place of worship is a property right, and the judicial determination of property rights as between two church groups claiming church property does not constitute an unlawful interference with the ecclesiastical affairs of a church. *See: United Armenian Church vs. Kazanjian, 322 Mich. 651.*

Such judicial determination is not the adjudicating of the right of any person to a religious belief or practice contrary to a state constitution or the first amendment of the constitution of the United States. *See: Reid vs. Johnson, 85 SE 2nd 114; Supreme Court of North Carolina, decided December 15, 1954.*

The weight of authority is to the effect that the majority faction of an independent or congregational society, however regular its action or procedure in other respects, may not, as against a faithful minority, divert the property of the society to another denomination *or to the support of doctrines fundamentally opposed to the characteristic doctrines of the society, although the property is subject to no express and specific trust. See: 8 ALR 113; 70 ALR 83; Bear vs. Heasley, 98 Mich. 279; Fuchs vs. Meisel, 102 Mich. 357; Borgman vs. Bultema, 213 Mich. 684; Hanna vs. Malick, 223 Mich. 100; United A. Church vs. Kazanjian, 332 Mich. 651; Cong. Conf. vs. U. Church of Stanton, 330 Mich. 561; to the same effect see: 45 American Jurisprudence Religious Societies, sec. 55; 76 Corpus Juris Secundum, Religious Societies, Sec. 71; The rule is well stated in the Reid vs. Johnson case, 85 SE 2nd 115 (citing the above authorities and others.):*

"A majority of the membership . . . may not, as against a faithful minority, divert the property of the church to another denomination, or to the support of doctrines, usages, customs and practices radically and fundamentally opposed to the characteristic doctrines, usages, customs and practices of that particular church recognized and accepted by both factions before the dissension, for in such an event the real identity of the church is no longer lodged with the majority group, but resides with the minority adhering to its fundamental faith, usages, customs and practices, before the dissension, who though small in numbers, are entitled to hold and control the entire property of the church."

The conveyances of the land to the original trustees and to the congregation in this case, by implication of law, conveyed the land in trust for the purposes for which the congregation was formed; namely, a Jewish Orthodox place of worship. *See: Reid vs. Johnson, 85 SE 2nd 115; Fuchs vs. Meisel, 102 Mich. 357.*

In *Fuchs vs. Meisel, 102 Mich. 357,* the Michigan Supreme Court said: "A conveyance or bequest to a religious association or to trustees for that association, necessarily implies a trust." With respect to such a trust, the rule is well established: "Where property has been dedicated by way of trust for the purpose of supporting or propagating definite religious doctrines or principles, it is the duty of the courts to see that the property is not diverted from the trust which has been thus attached to its use. So long as there are persons who are qualified within the original dedication, and are also willing to teach the doctrines prescribed in the act of dedication, and so long as there is anyone so interested in the execution of the trust as to have a standing in court, a diversion of the property or fund to other and different uses can be prevented. . . . It is not within the power of the congregation, by reason of a change of views on religious subjects, to carry such property to the support of a new and conflicting doctrine; in such case, the secular courts will, as a general rule, interfere to protect the members of an ecclesiastical organization who adhere to the tenets and doctrines which it was organized to promulgate, in their right to use the property, as against those members who are attempting to divert it to purposes utterly foreign to the organization, and will enjoin its diversion from the trust." *45 American Jurisprudence, Religious Societies, Sec. 61.*

THE DEFENDANTS' MOTION TO DISMISS FAILS TO SET FORTH ANY LEGAL OR EQUITABLE GROUND FOR DISMISSAL OF THE BILL OF COMPLAINT OR FOR REFUSING THE GRANTING OF THE PRELIMINARY INJUNCTION.

The first three grounds of the defendants' motion to dismiss, namely, that the bill does not state a case of action, the court is without jurisdiction because it is claimed that no property rights are involved, and finally, that the case involves the application of ecclesiastical doctrines with which the court is without right to interfere, would appear to be without merit: first, because they are not in accordance with the Applicable Law of the case; and secondly, they are in the nature of a demurrer and admit the truth of all the allegations of fact well pleaded in the bill of complaint. *Hatch vs. Wolack, 316 Mich. 258; Det. 1. 1. Ex. vs. Det. M., 337 Mich. 50; Prawdzik vs. City of G.R., 313 Mich. 376; Bishop vs. Hartman, 325 Mich. 115.*

The fourth ground of the motion, namely, that the action taken is not radically and fundamentally opposed to the doctrines of a Jewish Orthodox Congregation, is improperly pleaded in that it is the allegation of a matter in the nature of a special demurrer not within the rule of practice governing motions to dismiss, and even if it were, it is unsupported by affidavit and is properly a matter of answer and proofs.

RELIEF PRAYED

A preliminary injunction will not deprive the defendants and the majority of the congregation of any right of worship or enjoyment of the property they have not had for the past thirty years and upwards.

A preliminary injunction is necessary to preserve the status quo of the property until a hearing on the merits of the case. Granting it will not harm the defendants and the majority of the congregation, failure to grant it will cause the plaintiffs and others who adhere to the orthodox practice forbidding mixed seating irreparable injury in being deprived of the beneficial use of their place of worship during the said solemn holidays approaching.

In *Niedzialek vs. B. Union, 331 Mich. 296,* our Supreme Court quoted with approval the following:

"An injunction pendent lite should not usurp the place of a final decree, neither should it reach out any further than is absolutely necessary to protect the rights and property of the petitioner from injuries which are not only irreparable, but which must be expected before the suit can be heard on its merits. Only those issues will be determined which are necessary factors in granting or denying a temporary restraining order. It is not necessary that the complainant's rights be clearly established, or that the court find that complainant is entitled to prevail on the final hearing. It is sufficient if it appears that there is a real and substantial question between the parties, proper to be investigated in a court of equity, and in order to prevent irremediable injury to the complainant, before his claims can be investigated, it is necessary to prohibit any

357

change in the conditions and relations of the property and of the parties during the litigation."

In the same case, the court further said:

"In granting or withholding injunctive relief pendent lite . . . it is highly proper and quite essential for a court to consider whether the rights of the respective litigants will best be subserved by granting temporary injunctive relief if sought. If the personal rights or property rights involved will be best preserved by granting temporary injunctive relief in a suit presenting issues of controverted merit, such relief should be granted."

It is respectfully submitted that a preliminary injunction should be granted in this case pending a hearing on the merits thereof as prayed in the Bill of Complaint.

❦ 3 ❦

The Mount Clemens Story

The following appeared as an editorial in the Jewish Spectator, *January, 1957, written apparently by its editor, Dr. Trude Weiss-Rosmarin.*

FOR SOME TIME the Jewish community of Mt. Clemens, Mich. has been convulsed by a bitter struggle over the conversion of their Orthodox congregation into a house of worship following what goes by the name of Conservative Judaism. The preponderant majority of the Congregation has voted for following the Conservative ritual, but a small and vociferous minority insists that this change would be unconstitutional and must not come to pass. They argue that the Congregation was incorporated as an Orthodox house of worship and this, they insist, obligates the successors to the original founders to abide by the

358

Orthodox pattern. Moreover, the Orthodox minority maintains, in Jewish religious matters it is not the consent of the majority that matters but the authority of the Torah. The Torah, however, is unconditionally binding, the Orthodox group of Mt. Clemens, Mich. declares. And as the Torah, as interpreted by Orthodox Judaism, outlaws such deviations as Conservative Judaism and considers them heresy, it is clear that the opinions and preferences of those subject to the Torah should carry no weight.

All Jews, the Mt. Clemens zealots argue, must submit to the Torah as interpreted by Orthodoxy and order their lives in accordance with its laws. Determined to prevent heresy and the desecration of an Orthodox synagogue, the Mt. Clemens zealots, defeated in their own community, are now appealing to national Orthodox organizations and to Orthodox Jews everywhere to strengthen their hands so as to enable them to *force* their will upon the majority of the community who have voted for transforming the Orthodox synagogue into a Conservative house of worship. For some time now the Yiddish press and some Orthodox magazines printed in English have published appeals for funds to support "the holy war" of the Mt. Clemens Orthodox minority, so that they may be able to carry their case into the secular courts and sue for an injunction to prevent the majority of the Mt. Clemens Jewish community from committing "the heinous rape" of an Orthodox synagogue by "the camp of Conservative sinners."

As the main argument of the Mt. Clemens Orthodox minority is that the Divine authority of the Torah does not depend on the consent of those governed by it and that democratic principles are suspended in the religious sphere, it is indicated to probe whether these views, which are diametrically opposed to the democratic convictions of virtually all American Jews, are authenticated by the Torah. Our inquiry leads us first of all to the Pentateuchal passage: *Thou shalt not follow a multitude to do evil, neither shalt thou bear witness in a cause to turn aside after a multitude to pervert justice* (Exodus 23:2). By means of interpretation, the Sages derived from this passage the principle that the majority decision is binding in all cases of doubt about what the law is. By delimiting the validity of majority opinions to that which is *not* evil and does *not* pervert justice, the Pentateuch pursues the same line of common sense as modern democracy in stipulating that the prohibition of crying "fire!" in a crowded hall is not a delimitation of free speech.

Jewish law throughout the ages was developed by upholding the principle of the power of the majority decision. The differences of opinion between the various "schools" during the Talmudic period were resolved by the democratic procedure of deciding doubtful questions of the Law in accordance with the opinion of the majority. It is significant that whenever a minority opinion attempted to soar to victory on the wings of the invocation of Divine authority, the spokesmen for the majority invoked the Pentateuchal passages: *For this commandment which I command thee this day, it is not too hard for thee, neither is it far off. It is not in heaven . . .* (Deuteronomy 30:11, 12). Even when "heaven," as it were, testified on behalf of a minority interpretation of the Law, the Sages, committed to the democratic principle of the rule of the majority, refused to be swayed. The unswerving loyalty of the Makers of the Talmud to the traditional interpretation of the universal sway of freedom in the interpretation of the Torah, predicated on democratic procedure, is strikingly attested by Rabbi Eliezer's experience with some of his Rabbinic colleagues who refused to accept an interpretation of his. The Talmud (Baba Metzia 59b) relates that "once Rabbi Eliezer adduced all possible arguments to prove his opinion, but the Rabbis did not accept it. Then he said: 'If I am right, may this carob tree move a hundred yards from

360

its place.' And it did move. But the Rabbis said: 'No proof can be adduced from a tree.' Thereupon Rabbi Eliezer caused the waters of the canal to flow backward and the walls of the House of Study to bend inward, but still the Sages refused to go along with him. Finally, Rabbi Eliezer cried, 'If I am right let the heavens prove it!' And sure enough, a Heavenly Voice (*Bath Kol*) was heard proclaiming: 'Why do you oppose Rabbi Eliezer? The *Halachah* always backs him up.' " But even when the very heavens supported Rabbi Eliezer, the Sages would not be moved from their democratic convictions. "Rabbi Joshua rose and said: 'It (the Torah) is not in heaven'; this means, as Rabbi Jeremiah said: 'The Law was given us from Sinai. We pay no attention to a heavenly voice. For already from Sinai the Law said, *By a majority you are to decide.*' "

Speculating on God's reaction to this declaration of independence from Heaven, the *Aggadah* has it that, following this incident, Rabbi Nathan met Elijah the Prophet and asked him what God did in the hour when the Sages rejected His support of Rabbi Eliezer's minority opinion. Elijah answered: "He laughed and said, 'My children have conquered Me.'" (Baba Metzia 59b.)

The authoritative Jewish sources, especially the Hebrew Bible, prove conclusively that the free consent of the governed and the principle "by a majority you are to decide" are the twin pillars on which the Torah is built. It is instructive to ponder that according to the authoritative text of the Bible, and not only according to the folklore of the Aggadah, did God accede to the will and decision of the people. When the tribes of Israel demanded, *Give us a king to judge us* (I Samuel 8:6) it was not only Samuel whom "the thing displeased." God Himself was "displeased," and yet He told Samuel: *Hearken unto the voice of the people in all that they say unto you, for they have not rejected you, but they have rejected Me, that I should not be king over them. According to all the works which they have done since the day that I brought them out of Egypt even unto this day, in that they have forsaken Me, and served other gods, so do they also unto thee. Now therefore hearken unto their voice* (I Samuel 8:7ff.).

Israel rejected the "Kingship of God" and demanded a king of blood and flesh; and God not only "submitted" to this demand of the people for the duration of the life-span of that generation but "authorized" the change to a monarchical form of government on principle, to wit, the Prophets' visions of the renewal of the kingship under the House of David.

The Orthodox minority of Mt. Clemens, Mich. is not only opposing the majority of the community but the letter together with the spirit of Jewish law in arguing that "the majority does not count" in deciding what forms of religious worship should be followed. Jewish history conclusively proves that Jewish law and religion have followed an orientation which goes far beyond the equation of the Voice of the People with the Voice of God.

As we see it, the Orthodox minority of Mt. Clemens, Mich. has no case. By no stretch of the imagination can it be argued that the espousal of Conservative Judaism is tantamount "to do evil . . . and to pervert justice," which would justify the literal application of Exodus 23:2 to the situation. We hope that should the Orthodox zealots of Mt. Clemens go through with their planned *hillul hashem* and bring their case before a secular court for litigation, the earthly judge will be guided by the rulings of the Heavenly Judge, as recorded in Bible and Talmud.

362

✿ 4 ✿

In Answer to an Editorial

BY RABBI DAVID B. HOLLANDER

DEAR DR. ROSMARIN:

In the January 1957 issue of the *Jewish Spectator,* under the heading, "The Mount Clemens Story," you begin with premises in Jewish law that are unfounded and, hence, you arrive at conclusions which have no basis either in logic or Jewish law.

I shall seek in these following lines to prove the validity of the stand of the Mount Clemens "zealots" and to disprove the validity of your stand in the article referred to above. I realize fully that in presenting my views through your magazine, I must address myself primarily to your readers rather than to you, the author of the article. This is due to the fact that your presentations are a mixture of objective reporting in the opening paragraph and possibly also in the third paragraph on the one hand, and blind (I hope not wilful) prejudice on the other; and they are climaxed by a "prayer" that the *hillul hashem* (desecration of His Name) involved in bringing their case before a secular court for litigation, may be averted by that same court's rejection of the case.

In order to avoid the tempting pitfalls of answering you in kind, I shall limit myself to several factual refutations of the points you make.

You state that "Jewish law throughout the ages was developed by upholding the principle of the power of the majority decision"; therefore the main argument of the Mount Clemens minority that "in Jewish religious matters it is not the consent of the majority that matters but the authority of the Torah," is, according to you, "not only opposing the majority of the community, but the letter together with the spirit of the Jewish

363

law." Your position is made utterly untenable by the very sources you adduce to sustain your point. Of course the majority of the *Sages* were able to overrule the opinion of Rabbi Eliezer (Baba Metzia 59b), but that was a case of a dispute *among* Sages, among experts on Jewish law, among Rabbis of unquestioned scholarship and fear of God. In such a case we have clear instruction in Torah and Talmud that the majority opinion of the Sages prevails. Also, you talk of a dispute, but there is no dispute of law in the case of mixed seating. Regardless of what anyone might say or write, these facts are clear: 1) There is no orthodox rabbi in the world of *any* recognized standing in the eyes of existing orthodox rabbinical bodies, who will state that mixed seating is *not* a violation of Jewish law. 2) From the President of Yeshiva University to the heads of so-called ultra-orthodox *yeshiboth* in the United States and Israel, these leaders will not worship in any synagogue if it has mixed seating. 3) The Chief Rabbi of Israel, on his visits to the United States, has carefully refrained from entering a synagogue with mixed seating arrangement. Therefore, it does not matter how many (and I believe that there are not too many) Rabbinical Council or other orthodox rabbinic members have synagogues with mixed seating. The rabbi may be guilty of violating the law, the law remains binding on all.

But is it not utterly ridiculous to equate the Mount Clemens case with that of a dispute among Rabbis of the Talmud (or even with a dispute among rabbis of our times)? In the Mount Clemens case we have a majority of men and women who do not even claim to be either learned or pious in the observance of the Sabbath, *taharath ha-mishpahah* (family ritual purity), etc.; it is they who voted the change in a clear rejection of the oral and written pleas made to them by every orthodox Rabbinic body in the U.S.A. (I, in my capacity as president of the Rabbinical Council went there and met with a small committee of perhaps ten people, and pleaded with them not to insist on going through with the violation of the Torah.) My plea was only a faint echo of the much more authoritative request of the world orthodox Rabbinate, who in turn merely reaffirmed the elementary principles of Jewish law in this matter of mixed seating; all were rejected, not by rabbis, nor even by learned and/or pious laymen, but by men and women who, as I said before, laid no claims to adherence to the *Shulhan Aruch,* even aside from the question of mixed seating.

And while I am on this phase of the subject, may I just make a short reference to another article in your magazine written by some one from Mount Clemens and signed by the pseudonym, *Rodef Sholom* (why does not the writer reveal himself?) where I came personally under attack. I am not worried about that because God knows whether those words are sincere or not, and His knowledge is enough for me. Still, in keeping with the principle of *vihiyithem nekiyyim mehashem umiyyisra'el—ye shall be clear before the Lord and before Israel* (Numbers 32:22), I wish to state that it is not true that I was invited to address the congregation in Mount Clemens. I was permitted to meet with a small committee in someone's private home, and was told that "the die was cast." (Two days later a large meeting was held which I might have been able to crash, but I was certainly unwelcome.)

Moreover, I was told that the fact that Mr. Baruch Litvin brought me down to Mount Clemens would militate against me and my stand. True, Mr. Litvin is a "controversial figure"; (I wish to God there were more unpopular controversial figures who are sincere in seeking to uphold the truth, whether in Judaism or Americanism;) but is there "guilt by association"? Shall an *issue* suffer in the eyes of the "just and democratic majority" of Mount Clemens because of "controversial figures" like Litvin or the present writer? There were also complaints about "outsiders" coming in to interfere in the local matter. These mut-terings smacked of the complaint made in certain cities when lawyers from the North came to defend those who stood accused before a hostile and prejudiced majority.

* * *

You make much of the will of the majority being ignored by a minority. But the fact remains that religious and moral principles are superior to all majorities. The majority may, and does have more *power* than the minority, but that does not make it *right*. The whole function of religion is to get the majority to voluntarily submit to the authority of religion. The minority is not right by virtue of *being a minority*, but neither is it wrong *on that account*.

It is dangerous to speak of the "rightness" of the majority where religion, ethics, and justice are involved.

We, the Jewish people who suffered from so much persecu-tion, and are still as individuals and as a group the victims of prejudice and "double standard" justice, can hardly find refuge in the position that the majority is *right*. Unfortunately, only small minorities, nationally and internationally, were friendly to the Jews—the majority was *not*. The whole concept of the majority being right *because it is aligned against a minority* is a repudiation of both the Jewish and American conception of justice. The current court decision on rights of Negroes is probably not in keeping with the majority opinion of the people *in* the cities and states where these decisions are applicable; shall we say that *therefore* the court is wrong and the democratic majority (with a small "d") are right? It is interesting in this connection that those who denounce the court, do so behind the convenient but deceptive facade of *constitutional* govern-ment; I am afraid I see a parallel between that approach and the one which says that "a small and vociferous minority" wants to retain orthodoxy in Mount Clemens, and by so insisting,

366

they, the orthodox, are guilty of *hillul hashem* (desecrating His Name). According to this topsy-turvy logic, they who defend the law desecrate the Torah, and by implication, those who reject the law sanctify the name of God.

*　　*　　*

You speak with resentment about this issue going to a secular court. On this point I wish to answer: 1) Before going to a secular court, every effort was made, as I stated above, to persuade with *only* peaceful means, by pleading and begging, to get the rebels against the authority of Jewish law to repent, and to permit the synagogue to proceed in consonance with its orthodox beginnings. 2) The decision was by a majority of men and women themselves not qualified by learning or piety to *pass on*, let alone *change* Jewish law; do they constitute a *religious* court? Are they not infinitely less authentic than an American secular court full of the prejudice of a majority, which did not want to listen publicly to the orthodox point of view offered by a Detroit member of the Rabbinical Council of America and myself, but did listen to a spokesman of the conservative United Synagogue? 3) The term *hillul hashem* in connection with going to a secular court signifies, of course, that we would thus tell the non-Jewish community of our religious differences. I never believed that the non-Jewish American was so naive that he did not realize that we have "grown up," and from *one* Judaism we now have in addition to classical orthodoxy two denominations, Reform and Conservative. Do you believe that the Christian American is unaware that usually there are three types of Jewish houses of worship and rabbis in small and large cities? And finally, is not *hillul hashem* at its worst, the demonstration by Jews that they desecrate the Sabbath, patronize *trefe* restaurants and hotels, permit their synagogues to be empty of worshipers, and then on top of that arbitrarily and without even a *semblance* of Halachic approval alter the traditional character of the synagogue? It is *that* kind of *hillul hashem,* which we demonstrate in the streets and public places for non-Jews to see—that we, the People of the Book, reject the teachings of the Book—which ought to disturb us. But how can it, when we are so busy pinning that label of *hillul hashem* on those who sanctify His Name bearing all the ridicule and insults of a practically "one-party" Anglo-Jewish press in order to salvage some Judaism from the flood of invective and ignorance that has inundated our community.

* * *

Finally, I would turn to those to whom the issue of *introducing* mixed seating has become no less an "ideal" than to preserve traditional seating is to the truly orthodox. I turn to them in a plea in these difficult times not to flout the law of the Torah, not to take the personal and collective risk involved in raising one's hand against the Torah. Suppose you succeed in changing the seating arrangement; will that save *Judaism?* Is it not a fact that non-orthodox rabbis are complaining that their temples, even at the late Friday night service (which itself is bound up with many features of Sabbath violation) are pitifully empty unless some kind of special "gimmick" is employed which "attracts" the people, but not on the basis of the compelling sanctity of religion. Hence, when the "gimmick" is not there, the people are not there, and this despite all the concessions that the temple has made to the *imagined* yearning of the American Jew. Parking lots, mixed choirs, organs, mixed seating—all these have not brought the people to the temple. Those that do come are primarily children of those who still were attached to the orthodox synagogue. The children of parents who themselves were members of Conservative and Reform temples are conspicuous by their absence.

Also, did you ever consider the moral and American aspects—aside from the religious—of changing the traditional character of the synagogue? 1) It is morally wrong because we are interfering with the plans of those who are now dead, but who during their lifetime built the synagogue to be orthodox. These dead people cannot vote, but it is a case where "the blood of thy brother cries out to thee from the earth." Can we turn a deaf ear to their clear intention as spelled out in their lives and in the concrete structure of the synagogue? (Except for the last ten years or so, when many Conservative temples were built anew, the majority of Conservative temples have been "created" through voting power, which changed the orthodox character of the synagogue.) Are the living fair to the dead who worked and sweated to build those edifices, when we by a vote dissipate and squander that "easy" heritage?

2) It is especially un-American where, as in Mount Clemens, there is only one synagogue. Surely no advocate of mixed seating will say that it violates his religious conscience to attend an orthodox synagogue (many Conservative and Reform Jews and rabbis attend the *yahrzeit* of their Orthodox parents *only* in an *Orthodox* synagogue). At best the advocate of mixed seating can argue that it violates his sense of esthetics or convenience. But the Orthodox Jew has no choice. His religion tells him that he must pray at home without a *minyan* (religious quorum for group prayer) rather than attend a synagogue with mixed seating.

Dr. Soloveitchik, in his convention message to the Rabbinical Council convention of July 1955, states clearly that even on High Holidays one must miss *teki'ath shofar* if necessary, rather than attend such a synagogue. Therefore, in a choice between violating one's convenience or one's religious conscience, American fair play will undoubtedly require that the religious conscience must be given priority.

This above point is especially valid when you consider that numerically the orthodox produce a greater number of worshipers, pro rata at least, than the Conservative and Reform. It is interesting that of the "majority" that voted *for* mixed seating in Mount Clemens only a *small minority* attended the synagogue throughout the year, while of the minority that voted for traditional seating, the majority attended synagogue daily and on the Sabbath.

As you may know, I have recently returned from an historic tour of Russia and other countries where religion has had a stubborn struggle of a different nature than we know that struggle to be elsewhere. There is a substantial minority that has held fast. I ask all fair minded people to judge whether, if these Jews had been reared on a non-orthodox religious diet, they would have displayed the same obstinate quality of "holding on to the Torah" that they now do. I leave that answer to fair-minded people, because they must conclude that when the "chips are down," when real *mesirath nefesh* is required, only those who accept the yoke, discipline and authority of the Law will hold on to the tree of life, the Torah.

❧ 5 ❧
Brief for Plaintiffs and Appellants

presented in the Supreme Court of the State of Michigan, in appeal from the Circuit Court for the County of Macomb, in chancery; Hon. Edward T. Kane, Circuit Judge.

STATEMENT OF QUESTIONS INVOLVED

I. *May a majority of a church congregation institute a practice within the church fundamentally opposed to the doctrine to which the church property is dedicated, as against a minority of the congregation who adhere to the established doctrine and practice?*

The lower court answered the question "Yes".

Appellant contends the question should be answered "No".

II. *What is the established doctrine or practice claimed to be violated?*

The violation would appear to be undisputed inasmuch as no proofs were offered by the appellees and the trial court made no finding on the question.

III. *Is the act attempted by the defendants violative of that doctrine or practice?*

The violation would appear to be undisputed inasmuch as no proofs were offered by the appellees and the trial court made no finding on the question.

IV. *Would the action, unless restrained, deprive the plaintiffs of a valuable property right?*

The lower court answered the question "No".

Appellant contends the question should be answered "Yes".

STATEMENT OF FACTS

The plaintiffs-appellants are members of Congregation Beth Tefilas Moses, an Orthodox Jewish Synagogue located in the City of Mt. Clemens in Macomb County, Michigan. The defendants-appellees constitute the Board of Trustees of the Congregation.

The Congregation was founded in the year 1911 and was incorporated in 1912 under Act 209 of the Public Act of Michigan of 1897 as an ecclesiastical corporation. The Charter of the Corporation lapsed for failure to file reports in 1934 and the Congregation has continued as an unincorporated association down to the present time.

The original Constitution was adopted in 1918 and was printed in Yiddish, the traditional language of Orthodox Judaism. The land on which the Synagogue was built in 1921 was acquired by the Congregation between 1912 and 1919. When the Synagogue was built, it was constructed with a women's balcony, which has remained and has been used as such to the present controversy.

Under the Orthodox practice, the men and women do not sit together during prayer. Until the mixed seating practice attempted by the defendants, this was the established and practiced seating of the Congregation. The men sat in the main portion of the Synagogue; the women in the balcony. At all times, the Congregation was served by Orthodox Rabbis.

Plaintiff Litvin is a businessman and has been a member of the Congregation for over twenty years. He served at one time as financial secretary of the Synagogue and later as its president. In or about the year 1954 agitation for mixed seating arose in the Congregation. A vote was called by the proponents of the matter and thirty-three members voted against the proposal and thirty members for it. A year later the group in the Congregation advocating mixed seating procured the appointment of a committee which called a meeting on July 14, 1955 for the purpose, among others, of considering the practice of mixed seating.

Plaintiff and other members of the Congregation opposed the move, pointing out that the Orthodox practice forbade mixed seating, and references were made to the literature on the subject. However, the majority of the Congregation voted for mixed seating, which the defendants-appellees thereafter proposed to carry out. Mr. Schwartz, the President of the Congregation, and Mr. Litvin, plaintiffs herein, did not participate in the vote and Mr. Schwartz then resigned the presidency in protest.

After the pending litigation was instituted and during the pendency of the temporary injunction restraining mixed seating, some instances of mixed seating were attempted and the plaintiffs, consistent with the requirement of Orthodox Jewish practice, were forced to leave the Congregation and worship in an Orthodox Synagogue in Detroit.

The major alignments of Jewry in the United States are Orthodox, Conservative and Reform. There are theological differences between these groups, but the major one is that the Orthodox Jew believes in Divine Revelation, namely that the Torah given to the Jewish People on Mt. Sinai represents the dedicated Word of God and is not subject to change, although its application might be varied by the duly authorized Rabbinical Authorities. The Orthodox Jew firmly believes in Divine Revelation; the Conservative and Reform groups have rejected the full authority and binding character of the Jewish Law. The written law and the oral law and the later commentaries on these constitute the Torah or *Halachah*. Halachah is the binding decision of Jewish Law. In that sense, Torah and Halachah are synonymous. The law is immutable, and all Jews who describe themselves as being faithful to their religion must accept its authority.

In the Orthodox view, only a properly qualified Rabbi may apply Jewish Law. The Rabbi must be a scholar ordained by the proper authority, and he must himself be pious and accept fully and without reservation the full authority of the law.

The Rabbinical Council of America, comprising approximately seven hundred members serving Orthodox congregations throughout the United States and Canada, and of which the Rabbi serving Beth Tefilas Moses is a member, has issued various declarations on the subject of mixed seating affirming the immutable Jewish Law prohibiting prayer in a Synagogue where men and women pray together without the proper separation.

The prohibitions against mixed seating are found in the sacred scriptures (testimony of Rabbi Hollander and testimony of Dr. Weiss). The prohibition does not infer or suggest an inferiority of women in the Jewish religion. It suggests that men are not capable of keeping attention on the Almighty and the prayer directed to the Almighty in the presence of women; since prayer demands complete attention and devotion to the Almighty, the presence of women is considered distracting, and the separation is intended to achieve the desired dedication and devotion.

An Orthodox Jew cannot in conscience worship in a Synagogue where mixed seating is permitted. In such case the Synagogue with mixed seating loses the character of a Synagogue, and no Jew who believes in the authority of the Torah is permitted to pray in such a Synagogue. Contrarywise, an adherent of the Reform or Conservative Movements may worship in an Orthodox Synagogue without violating his religious principles.

Where mixed seating is practiced, no Orthodox Rabbi may serve such a Synagogue without the consent of the Rabbinical authorities. This authority is sometimes permitted after a proper analysis of the Congregation in an attempt to bring the Congregation back into the accepted practice. The purpose of permitting temporary assignments of a Rabbi to a mixed pew congregation is to regain the congregation. From the Rabbinical standpoint, the only one who worships in such a congregation with permission in such a case is the Rabbi, as he is there to effect the separation of the sexes.

The Reform and Conservative movements practice mixed seating. Upon entering a Synagogue, the immediately observable thing would be that the men and women in the Orthodox Synagogue are required to be separated and in the Conservative and Reform Synagogue they would not. Where a balcony is

374

not used and a partition is substituted in its place, the partition in Jewish Law is called a *mechitzah*. A *mechitzah* may consist of any substance as long as it achieves the purpose of the law to give the men and women the attitude of mind necessary to concentrate entirely on the sacredness of the worship. Men and women worshipping together in a congregation where no physical spacing separated them would constitute mixed seating. In the earlier Synagogues, the mechanical way of achieving the separation was to build a balcony. In more recent years new architectural designs and concepts have succeeded in separating the aisle of men from women. The law is regarded as adhered to where there is a physical separation even without a balcony.

The reference in Article 2 of the present Constitution of the Congregation to the purpose of "furthering the Jewish religion" refers to Orthodox Judaism. In the Orthodox view, the term "Judaism or Jewish religion" without the qualifying adjective (Orthodox), which is of recent vintage, must necessarily refer to Orthodox Judaism. The practice of using the term "Orthodox" has been more recently adopted to distinguish it from the Reform and Conservative movements.

The reference in the original Constitution of the Congregation stipulating that praying should follow the Rite of the Ashkenaz Jews refers to Orthodoxy. The Ashkenazic Rite refers to Eastern European countries, Poland, Russia, Germany, Hungary and other countries where a certain form of prayer was used as distinguished from that of the Jews of Spain. Mixed seating under this Rite was not allowed.

The defendants-appellees presented no proof in the case, and upon the close of the proofs, the lower Court made a finding that the Congregation was autonomous, and its Rites would be governed by a majority of its members. From a Decree dismissing the Bill of Complaint, the plaintiffs-appellants respectfully take this appeal.

ARGUMENT

I. *A majority of a church congregation may not institute a practice within the church fundamentally opposed to the doctrine to which the church property is dedicated, as against a minority of the congregation who adhere to the established doctrine and practice.*

Preliminarily, it may be stated that this case does not involve a question of the right of the governing body of a church to exercise its prerogative upon a matter of church policy within its own organization. Instead, the question is whether a majority of a church congregation can institute a practice contrary and fundamentally opposed to the doctrine recognized by both factions prior thereto as against a minority of the congregation who adhere to the established doctrine or practice.

The Bill of Complaint and the proofs in this case clearly show the appellees' attempt to institute mixed seating in this Synagogue in which the appellants are members. The proofs clearly show that such practice is contrary to the Orthodox practice and that the appellants and others who adhere to the Orthodox practice cannot worship in a Synagogue where mixed seating is permitted. It is the position of the appellants that the action of the appellees deprives the appellants and those who adhere to the established practice of a valuable property right, to-wit: the use of the Synagogue to worship in accordance with the established doctrine of the Congregation.

The action of the appellees in practical effect is a diversion of the Synagogue of this Congregation to the use of a reform group whose tenets, rites and practices are as fundamentally opposed to those of Orthodox Judaism as those of other denominations.

Does the membership of a congregation have the right to effect, by vote of a momentary majority, a change in religious practice, not conformable with the origin and historic character of the Congregation as against those who faithfully adhere to the characteristic doctrine of the Congregation?

The weight of authority is to the effect that the majority faction of an independent or congregational society, however regular its action or procedure in other respects, may not, as against a faithful minority, divert the property of the society to another denomination *or to the support of doctrines fundamentally opposed to the characteristic doctrines of the society, although the property is subject to no express and specific trust. 8 ALR 113; 70 ALR 83; Bear v. Heasley,* 98 Mich. 279; *Fuchs v. Meisel,* 102 Mich. 357; *Borgman v. Bultema,* 213 Mich. 684; *Hanna v. Malick,* 223 Mich. 100; *United A. Church v. Kazanjian,* 322 Mich. 651; *Cong. Conf. v. U. Church of Stanton,* 330 Mich. 561; *76 Corpus Juris Secundum, Religious Societies,* Par. 71, Page 853.

To the same effect see: *45 American Jurisprudence, Religious Societies,* sec. 55; *76 Corpus Juris Secundum, Religious Societies,* sec. 71. The rule is well stated in *Reid v. Johnson,* 85 SE 2d 115 (citing the above authorities and others):

"A majority of the membership . . . may not, as against a faithful minority, divert the property of the church to another denomination, *or to the support of doctrines, usages, customs and practices radically and fundamentally opposed to the characteristic doctrines, usages, customs and practices of that particular church recognized and accepted by both factions before the dissention, for in such an event the real identity of the church is no longer lodged with the majority group, but resides with the minority adhering to its fundamental faith, usages, customs and practices, before the dissension, who though small in numbers, are entitled to hold and control the entire property of the church.*"

The lower Court's finding that a Jewish Congregation is

autonomous does not militate against the rule of law that the property interest of a member of a Jewish Congregation upon the continued maintenance of a house of worship adhering to the fundamental principles of the founders is paramount.

II. *The prohibition against mixed seating in the Orthodox Jewish practice was clearly established.*

The appellees' attempt to obtain a dismissal of the appellants' cause of action in the lower Court upon the Bill of Complaint and the evasive answer and amended answer of the appellees together with their failure to offer proofs in the case rather clearly emphasizes the inability of the appellees to defend the practice of mixed seating.

Congregation Beth Tefilas Moses was founded as an Orthodox Jewish Congregation. Its Synagogue was constructed and maintained from the time of its founding by Orthodox Jews whose contributions improved the property as a place of worship for all those who adhered to the Orthodox practice.

The distinguishing feature of the Orthodox ritual as compared to that of the Reform and Conservative movements is separate seating for the men and women. The most concrete evidence of the Orthodox practice in Congregation Beth Tefilas Moses is its women's balcony which has been consistently used from the time of the founding of the Congregation down to the present controversy.

The Orthodox Jew believes in a continuous Judaic tradition based upon a divinely revealed Bible. The Orthodox Jew regards the observance of the rituals and ceremonies as basic to the values of Judaism. The prohibition against mixed seating found in the scriptures has been carefully observed in the ritual of Orthodox Judaism for over three thousand years. Diametrically opposed to the Orthodox practice is that of the Conservative and Reform groups which practice mixed seating and other ceremonies which these groups do not regard as Divinely required because they do not believe in the principle of Divine Revelation as accepted by Orthodoxy.

In *Fisher v. Congregation B'Nai Yitzhok* (Penn.) 110 A 2d 881, the Orthodox practice of not permitting mixed seating is well indicated. In that case the plaintiff was an ordained Rabbi of the Orthodox Hebrew faith and was engaged as a cantor for High Holiday services for an agreed compensation. Shortly before the Holidays the congregation moved into a new Synagogue in which, instead of separating the men from the women, they set aside four rows for the men, the next four rows for the women and the remaining rows for mixed seating. The plaintiff took the position that he could not serve as a cantor for the defendants as long as the men and the women were not sitting separately as this would be a violation of his beliefs. He did not officiate and subsequently sued the congregation for his contract price. The opinion states:

" . . . up to the time of the execution of the contract, the defendant congregation conducted its religious services in accordance with the practices of the Orthodox Hebrew faith. On behalf of the plaintiff there is evidence that under the law of the Torah and other binding authority of the Jewish law, men and women may not sit together at services in the Synagogue. In the Orthodox Synagogue, where the practice is observed, the women sit apart from the men in a gallery, or they are separated from the men by means of a partition between the groups."

"Judge Smith accepted the testimony of three Rabbis learned in Hebrew law, who appeared for plaintiff, to the effect: 'That Orthodox Judaism required a definite and physical separation of the sexes in the Synagogue.' And he also considered it established by the testimony that an Orthodox Rabbi cantor, 'could not conscientiously officiate in the *trefeh* Synagogue, that is, one that violates Jewish law.' And it was specifically found that the old building which the congregation left 'had separation in accordance with Jewish Orthodoxy.' "

III. *The acts attempted by the appellees were clearly violative of the established Orthodox Jewish law and practice.*

The prohibition against mixed seating being such a characteristic practice of Orthodox Judaism and having its origin in the scriptures which the Reform and Conservative groups do not regard as binding, clearly points up a basic difference between the groups.

While a Reform or Conservative Jew might worship in an Orthodox Synagogue with his conscience unaffected by the seating arrangement, on the other hand, an Orthodox Jew cannot, in conscience, worship in a Synagogue where mixed seating is permitted. Indeed, he is prohibited by Rabbinical directive from so doing. Consequently, the action of those in charge of the temporal affairs of a congregation in instituting a practice so fundamentally and radically opposed to the characteristic doctrine, usage, custom and practice of an Orthodox Congregation, certainly violates that characteristic doctrine, usage, custom and practice.

The testimony of the learned Rabbi Hollander and Dr. Weiss established without question the basis in scripture of the prohibition against mixed seating, the binding effect of Rabbinical directives upon Orthodox Judaism and the effect of a violation of the prohibition, namely, that a Synagogue in which mixed seating is permitted, cannot be used for prayer by an Orthodox Jew.

IV. *The violation of the established Orthodox Jewish law and practice resulted in a deprivation of the property rights of the appellants who adhered to the established doctrine and practice.*

380

The direct result of the action of the appellees is that the Orthodox Jew must leave his Synagogue and worship in a Synagogue that has the *kedushah* or congregational sanctity required under the Orthodox practice. Thus, he is as effectively deprived of the use of the property of his Congregation as though he were evicted therefrom.

The right of a member of a congregation to the beneficial use of the church property as a place of worship is a property right and the judicial determination of property rights as between two church groups claiming church property does not constitute an unlawful interference with the ecclesiastical affairs of a church.

"In the case at bar property rights are involved, namely, which group has the exclusive use and control of the church property." *Holt v. Trone,* 341 Mich. 169 at Page 174.

"Judicial interference in the purely ecclesiastical affairs of a religious organization is improper. Property rights, however, are the concern of the courts." *United Armenian Church v. Kazanjian,* 320 Mich. 214 at Page 217.

"Such judicial determination is not the adjudicating of the right of any person to a religious belief or practice contrary to a state constitution or the First Amendment to the Constitution of the United States." *Reid v. Johnson,* 85 SE 2d 114 (North Carolina).

The conveyances of the land to the original trustees and to the congregation in this case, by implication of law, conveyed the land in trust for the purposes for which the congregation was formed; namely, a Jewish Orthodox place of worship.

"A conveyance or bequest to a religious association or to trustees for that association, necessarily implies a trust." *Fuchs v. Meisel,* 102 Mich. 357 at Page 369.

"Property held for an unincorporated religious association

must be held by trustees." *Trustees First Society, ME Church of Newark v. Clark,* 41 Mich. 730.

With respect to an express trust, the rule is well established.

"Where property has been dedicated by way of trust for the purpose of supporting or propagating definite religious doctrines or principles, it is the duty of the courts to see that the property is not diverted from the trust which has been thus attached to its use. So long as there are persons who are qualified within the original dedication, and are also willing to teach the doctrines prescribed in the act of dedication, and so long as there is anyone so interested in the execution of the trust as to have a standing in Court, a diversion of the property or fund to other and different uses can be prevented . . . *it is not within the power of the congregation, by reason of a change of views on religious subjects, to carry such property to the support of a new and conflicting doctrine; in such case, the secular courts will, as a general rule, interfere to protect the members of an ecclesiastical organization who adhere to the tenets and doctrines which it was organized to promulgate in their right to use the property, as against those members who are attempting to divert it to purposes utterly foreign to the organization, and will enjoin its diversion from the trust.*" 45 *American Jurisprudence, Religious Societies,* Sec. 61, Pages 771, 772.

"No one disputes, where property is dedicated to the use of a religious denomination it cannot thereafter be diverted to the use of those who depart from that faith, but must remain for the use and benefit of those who still adhere to the faith." *Borgman v. Bultema,* 213 Mich. 684 at Page 689.

In *Protestant Reformed Church v. DeWolf,* 344 Mich. 624, this Court said:

"It is obvious that the real dispute in this case between the Hoeksema church group and the DeWolf church group has for its objective the ownership of the church property and the *right of its possession and control. While Courts do not interfere in matters of church doctrine, church discipline, or the regularity of the proceedings of church tribunals, and refuse to interfere with the right of religious groups to worship freely as they choose, the question of property rights of the members is a matter within the jurisdiction of the Court and may be determined by the Court."*

The Court further quoting from *Calvary Baptist Church of Port Huron v. Shay,* 292 Mich. 517, said:

"The judicial determination of property rights as between two church groups claiming church property does not constitute an unlawful interference with ecclesiastical affairs of a church."

"A church organization cannot change its fundamental faith or religion for the promotion of which it was organized and devote its property to a different faith without the consent of all its members. The property which it owns is charged with a trust, though not expressed in the instrument by which it is acquired. It is to be devoted to the fundamental faith or doctrine of the church, and cannot be changed as against the protest of a single member." *Blauert v. Schupmann,* (Minn.) 63 NW 2d 578.

The purchase of land and the erection of a Synagogue by a Jewish Orthodox Congregation followed by years of use of that property by succeeding generations practicing the Orthodox Rite shows beyond any doubt a dedication of that property to that Rite. The founders and succeeding membership of the Congregation who adhered and continue to adhere faithfully to Orthodox Judaism and whose funds built and maintained the Synagogue over these many years have a property right in that property which a Court of equity will protect as against the irreparable injury the act of the appellees will cause.

RELIEF SOUGHT

The Decree of Dismissal entered by the lower Court should be reversed and a Decree granting the injunctive relief prayed in the Bill of Complaint be ordered.

Respectfully submitted,

WALSH, O'SULLIVAN, STOMMEL & SHARP,
Attorneys for Appellants,
307 Michigan National Bank Bldg.,
Port Huron, Michigan.

July 30, 1958.

Brief Amici Curiae

OF THE RABBINICAL COUNCIL OF AMERICA AND THE UNION OF ORTHODOX JEWISH CONGREGATIONS OF AMERICA

presented in the Supreme Court of the State of Michigan, in appeal from the Circuit Court for the County of Macomb, in chancery; Hon. Edward T. Kane, Circuit Judge.

STATEMENT OF QUESTIONS INVOLVED

I. *Was Congregation Beth Tefilas Moses of Mt. Clemens founded as an Orthodox Jewish Congregation and its property dedicated to the doctrines of Orthodox Judaism?*

The lower court by its decision answered the question "No".

The Amici Curiae contend the question should be answered "Yes".

II. *Do the doctrines of Orthodox Judaism proscribe mixed seating and may an adherent of such faith in conscience worship in a synagogue where such practice is permitted?*

384

The lower court by its decision answered "No" to the first question and "Yes" to the second question.

The Amici Curiae contend the first question should be answered "Yes" and the second question "No".

III. *Can the majority of a congregation, as against a faithful minority, institute a practice radically and fundamentally opposed to the characteristic doctrines to which the congregational property is dedicated?*

The lower court by its decision answered the question "Yes".

The Amici Curiae contend the question should be answered "No".

IV. *Do civil courts have jurisdiction to determine the issues presented?*

The lower court by its decision answered the question "No".

The Amici Curiae contend the question should be answered "Yes".

STATEMENT OF FACTS

The Statement of Facts set forth in the Brief of Plaintiffs and Appellants is hereby adopted.

ARGUMENT

Preliminary Statement
(All italics ours unless otherwise noted.)

By permission of this Honorable Court dated November 12, 1958, the Rabbinical Council of America and the Union of Orthodox Jewish Congregations of America were granted leave to file a brief *amici curiae*. The Rabbinical Council of America has a membership of over 700 Orthodox Rabbis serving congregations throughout the United States and Canada and nearly all of its members have received their secular education and religious training in the United States. The Union of Orthodox Jewish Congregations of America, organized in 1898, is the national body for the Orthodox Jewish Synagogues throughout the United States and Canada. It was founded by Congregation Shearith Israel of New York City, the oldest Congregation in America, which was established in 1654.

The interest of these two organizations in the disposition of this case is identical with that of the plaintiffs-appellants. At the trial of this suit the two principal witnesses in behalf of the plaintiffs were the immediate past president of the Rabbinical Council and the executive vice-president of the Union of Orthodox Jewish Congregations. The crucial questions involved herein are of vital concern not only to the immediate parties to the litigation but also to the large Orthodox Jewish community in the State of Michigan and to the millions of adherents of the Orthodox Jewish faith throughout the United States.

We have carefully read the excellent brief submitted by counsel for the plaintiffs-appellants and support the Statement of Questions Involved, the Statement of Facts and the arguments made therein. We shall endeavor to confine our discussion in the main to additional factors and supplementary material to be considered against the background presented by the plaintiffs-appellants.

The bill of complaint, filed August 26, 1955, alleges that the plaintiffs are members of Congregation Beth Tefilas Moses, an Orthodox Jewish Congregation located in Mt. Clemens, Michigan, and that the defendants are members of its Board of Trustees; that the defendants have physical control and direction of the activities and property of the Congregation including the Synagogue or house of worship, but do not have authority to change the form of worship; that the Synagogue was built and has been maintained from funds and contributions of Orthodox Jews.

386

It is further set forth that the Jewish religion is based upon the Halachah or authoritative rules of ecclesiastical law; that in accordance with the Halachah, "it is forbidden to pray in a synagogue where men and women sit together, as such synagogue under the Orthodox Jewish tradition has no *kedushah* or Congregational sanctity;" that the separation of the sexes in Synagogue practice has been strictly adhered to for over 3,000 years, and that Orthodox Jews "cannot conscientiously worship contrary to Orthodox custom and tradition in a synagogue where the sexes are not separated."

It is further alleged that on July 28, 1955, at a special membership meeting, certain members constituting a "reform movement" voted by a majority to introduce mixed seating; that defendants-trustees intend to effect such change which is "radically and fundamentally opposed to the doctrines, customs, usages and practices" of the Congregation and Orthodox Judaism; that if mixed seating is permitted, the plaintiffs and other members of similar Orthodox conviction will be deprived of the beneficial use of the Synagogue; and that the contemplated deviation to mixed seating "will deprive plaintiffs and the adhering members of the Congregation of their property rights in the synagogue and its appurtenances."

In their prayer for relief the plaintiffs sought a declaration that the action in voting mixed seating was contrary to the doctrine and practice of Orthodox Judaism and "constituted an illegal interference with the property rights of the plaintiffs;" "that the true Congregation of Congregation Beth Tefilas Moses are the plaintiffs" and other members of similar Orthodox conviction; and that in order to protect the plaintiffs' property rights, the defendants be enjoined from permitting mixed seating.

The amended answer of the defendants (20a-23a) denies that the Congregation is " 'orthodox' in the true sense and meaning of the word" and that it "was formed and dedicated

as a place of worship of an 'orthodox' Jewish Congregation."
The defendants "admit that the 'Halachah,' the 'Talmud' and
the 'Torah' represent the authoritative bodies of law within the
Jewish religion, . . . and accordingly leave plaintiffs to their
proofs thereof."

It is most significant that the defendants at the trial refused
to cross-examine the witnesses appearing in behalf of the plaintiffs or to produce proofs in support of their answer. In such
state of the record the plaintiffs' allegations must be deemed
conclusively established. Accordingly, the defendants' sole permissible reliance is upon their motion to dismiss, renewed at the
conclusion of the trial, which is based upon the erroneous
grounds that the Court is without jurisdiction and that the introduction of mixed seating constitutes no radical and fundamental
change in the doctrine and dogma of the Congregation Beth
Tefilas Moses. The Court below based its decision solely upon
the former ground.

In essence, this case presents the issue whether a Jewish
Congregation, founded upon the Halachic principles of Orthodox Judaism, may, through the action of a transient majority,
alter its dogma and deviate from such principles, through the
introduction of a radical change, in this instance, mixed seating.
We respectfully submit that the decisions of this Court, with
which the overwhelming weight of authority in other jurisdictions is in accord, mandate a negative answer with a resultant
reversal of the decree appealed from.

I. *Congregation Beth Tefilas Moses of Mt. Clemens was
founded as an Orthodox Jewish congregation and its property
dedicated to the doctrines of Orthodox Judaism.*

Both the defendants and the Court below advert to the
fact that the word "Orthodox" does not expressly appear in
the Articles of Association or the Constitutions of the Syna-

gogue. The defendants would make the presence of this precise word the sovereign talisman as regards the original tenets of the Congregation and the intent of its founders. Its absence, they urge, is fatal to a conclusion that Beth Tefilas Moses was founded as an Orthodox Jewish house of worship. The law happily rejects such narrow formalism and instead looks to any competent evidence proving the original tenets of the congregation and the intended use of its property, such as the constitution and by-laws, declarations of faith and practice, customs and usages in existence when the congregation was organized and the usages accepted by all prior to the controversy (see *Zollman, American Church Law,* §§247-8; *United Armenian Church v. Kazanjian,* 322 Mich. 651, 661; and authorities cited *infra* under subdivision B).

A.

Manifestly, members of the judiciary, like other intelligent laymen, are frequently unfamiliar with the doctrines and dogmas of religious faiths other than their own. Indeed, mere generality of ideas concerning other faiths sometimes involves misconceptions; as, for example, that the prohibition against eating pork is presently adhered to by all branches of Judaism. This is not so as to reform elements who have rejected all adherence to dietary laws. Nonetheless, in the settlement of the legion of intrachurch disputes over which the civil courts have accepted jurisdiction, the courts examine religious creed and dogma and resolve them in the same manner as other disputed questions of fact (see, *e.g., Bear v. Heasley,* 98 Mich. 279, involving a comparison of original and amended Confessions of Faith of the Church of the United Brethren; *cf. Schlichter v. Keiter,* 156 Pa. St. 119, 27 Atl. 45; *Kuns v. Robertson,* 154 Ill. 394, 40 N.E. 343, considering the same Confessions but reaching as questions of fact a contrary result).

389

The record makes clear that the term "Orthodox" as applied to a particular group within the Jewish faith is of comparatively recent origin. Originally, the word "Judaism" represented that which is now known as "Orthodox Judaism" based upon literal Divine Revelation. It was only when departures from normative Judaism arose in the last century, that is, "Reform" and later "Conservative" Judaism, that the term "Orthodox" was applied to that which had been originally called "Judaism." "Orthodox" by definition means holding right, true or correct opinion (Webster's New International Dictionary [2d ed.]; Murray, New English Dictionary), and is meant to imply that this is the original historic Judaism. Obviously, therefore, the use of the word "Orthodox" is neither definitive nor essential as it is meant to distinguish it from the deviational Reform and Conservative movements.

"Well, I would say that whenever the term Judaism or Jewish Religion is used without a qualifying adjective of recent vintage, it must refer to Orthodox Judaism, as a matter of fact, we only use the term 'Orthodox' because we have been forced in order to make it authentic to use it, otherwise we would simply say Judaism or Jewish Religion."

We may note in passing that notwithstanding the defendants' discursive comments on "what is Jewish and who is a Jew," the fact remains that there are three major alignments in Judaism in the United States, namely, Orthodox, Conservative and Reform; that the difference between Orthodox on the one hand and the other two groups is *a profound theological one, a qualitative one,"* while the difference between Conservative and Reform is only "quantitative," and that each group has a separate congregational association—for the Orthodox, the present *amicus curiae,* the Union of Orthodox Jewish Congregations of America; for the Conservative, the United Synagogue of

390

America, and for the Reform, the Union of American Hebrew Congregations.

B.

Where there might be some doubt as to what were the original tenets of the Congregation and the intent of the founders, the courts will receive any competent evidence shedding light thereon (*Zollman, American Church Law,* §§247-8). Thus, examination is made of the constitution and by-laws (*Fuchs v. Meisel,* 102 Mich. 357, 369; *Baker v. Ducker,* 79 Cal. 365, 373, 21 Pac. 764, 765); of declarations of faith and practice when the funds were obtained (*Park v. Chaplin,* 96 Iowa 55, 65, 64 N.W. 674, 677); of contemporaneous usage (*Bakos v. Takach,* 14 Ohio App. 370, 383, 32 O.C.A. 569, 578; *Presbyterian Congregation v. Johnston,* 1 Watts & S. 9, 37 [Pa.]; and the usages accepted by all prior to the controversy (*Baer v. Heasley, supra,* 98 Mich. 279, 316; *Greek Catholic Church v. Orthodox Greek Church,* 195 Pa. St. 425, 434, 46 Atl. 72, 75). As stated by Lord Eldon in the frequently quoted and approved case of *Attorney General v. Pearson,* 3 Merivale 353, 400, 36 Eng. Rep. 135, 150:

"[W]here an institution exists for the purpose of religious worship, and it cannot be discovered from the deed declaring the trust what form or species of religious worship was intended, the Court can find no other means of deciding the question, than through the medium of an inquiry into what has been the usage of the congregation in respect to it; . . . I take it to be the duty of the Court to administer the trust in such a manner as best to establish the usage, considering it as a matter of implied contract between the members of that congregation."

C.

In the light of the criteria set forth in the preceding authorities, there cannot exist even a scintilla of a doubt that

391

Congregation Beth Tefilas Moses was founded as an Orthodox Jewish Congregation and its property dedicated to the doctrines of Orthodox Judaism. The fact that the precise term "Orthodox" does not expressly appear in the Articles of Association or the Constitutions of the Synagogue is, under the compelling circumstances described immediately below, immaterial.

Examination of the 1918 Constitution demonstrates conclusively the Orthodox character of the Congregation. The entire document is instinct with Orthodoxy, as witness the following:

(a) The Constitution was written in Yiddish, "the vernacular of the immigrants who came from Poland, Russia, [and] Hungary." This language factor is significant because the founders "wanted to point out while in another new home and new country they cling to the traditions of their forefathers of which, of course, are Orthodox." A Yiddish constitution for a non-Orthodox congregation would be a curiosity, an anomaly.

(b) "Praying shall follow the form according to the *rite of the Ashkenaz Jews,* for this form was also adhered to by our fathers." This refers unmistakably and exclusively to Orthodox Judaism, since such nomenclature is foreign to the Conservative and Reform movements. In Orthodox Judaism, there are two forms of prayers or rites, namely, the Ashkenazic and the Sephardic,[1] neither of which of course permits mixed seating. The dichotomy between the Ashkenazic and the Sephardic rites may be loosely compared to that between the Western or Latin rites churches and the Byzantine or Eastern rites churches which differ in no essential dogma and acknowledge the supremacy of the Pope (see *Bakos v. Takach, supra,* 14 Ohio App. 370, 32 O.C.A. 569; *Greek Catholic Church v. Orthodox Greek Church, supra,* 195 Pa. St. 425, 46 Atl. 72).

---

1. Adherents of both rites are found in the membership of the *amici curiae.*

(c)   The reference in the Constitution to such practices and functionaries as a *mikveh* (ritualarium for religious ablutions), a "burial society," and to the reservation of definite space in the cemetery for suicides, again bears the indelible imprint of Orthodox Judaism. These are matters foreign to the non-Orthodox movements in Judaism and would be considered by the followers thereof in the same light as the dogma of the Assumption of the Virgin Mary proclaimed by the late Pope Pius XII may be considered by non-Roman Catholics.

While the present Constitution, adopted in 1953 or 1954 without the vote of plaintiff Litvin, is written in English and expresses the purpose of "furthering the Jewish religion," "[i]t does not, by any stretch of the imagination, postulate another kind of Jewish Religion than the one originally adhered to." The new Constitution was designed to eliminate the numerous outdated *minutiae* in the old (*e.g.,* failure to attend services with an attendant 25 cent fine) and was written in English as the language of the present congregants. There is nothing in the present Constitution which indicates an intention to depart from the fundamental principles of Orthodox Judaism expressed and inherent in the original Constitution—assuming, contrary to the legal principles set forth under Point III, *infra,* that a new constitution could validly effect radical departures from the original tenets.

The record shows that since the founding of the Congregation almost fifty years ago, the men and women did not sit together at religious services; the men sat in the main portion of the Synagogue, the women in the balcony. The Congregation has always been served by Orthodox Rabbis.

Accordingly, the constitutions, the contemporaneous usage and the usage accepted by all prior to the controversy conclusively demonstrate the Orthodox character of the Congregation Beth Tefilas Moses.

393

II.   *The doctrines of Orthodox Judaism proscribe mixed seating, and an adherent of such faith cannot in conscience worship in a Synagogue where such practice is permitted.*

To those unfamiliar with the dogmas and doctrines of faiths other than their own, the materiality and significance of particular rituals and practices of such other religions may not be readily apparent. Thus, the introduction of instrumental music during religious services or of a changed attire of the clergy or worshippers at such services may signify a radical departure from cardinal principles of a faith.[2] Pertinent is the observation of the Court in *Landis' Appeal,* 102 Pa. St. 467, 473, involving a schism among Mennonites:

"The second Master in his report has said that the primary cause of the differences between these people had its origin in the cut of the Rev. Mr. Overholtzer's coat. Undoubtedly such was the fact, for this new-fangled coat, when it first made its appearance in the conference, symbolized rebellion, a change of principles, and it is not the first time that the cut or turning of a coat has signified something of much more importance than was apparent either in its style or texture."

While the defendants would treat the separation of the sexes at Divine worship as without doctrinal significance and the introduction of mixed seating as "at most a matter of church practice," the proof is overwhelming (if not conclusive in view of the defendants' failure to defend) that the separation of the sexes during Divine worship has been a cardinal principle and fundamental tenet of Orthodox Judaism for over 3,000 years; that an adherent of this faith cannot in conscience worship in a Synagogue where mixed seating is permitted since such Temple

---

2. Among the radical departures from the basic tenets of Orthodox Judaism are: (1) playing of instrumental music during Sabbath and holy day services; (2) praying by males in the Synagogue with uncovered heads; (3) embalming a corpse and burial in metal coffins.

394

lacks the necessary *kedushah* or sanctity; that a follower of the Conservative or Reform movements may worship in an Orthodox Synagogue without violating his religious principles, and that the first visible distinguishing feature of the Orthodox ritual vis-a-vis that of the Reform and Conservative movements is separate seating for men and women. The bases of this age-old proscription against mixed seating are set forth in the record, and mention should be made that such prohibition does not in the slightest infer or suggest an inferiority of women in the Jewish religion—on the contrary, "[t]he fact is that it bespeaks to the properly trained religious mind the glory and respect of Jewish women, womanhood."

That the separation of the sexes during Divine worship is a cardinal principle and basic requirement of Orthodox Judaism was recognized by the Superior Court of Pennsylvania, the statewide intermediate appellate court, in the recent case of *Fisher v. Congregation B'nai Yitzhok*, 177 Pa. Super. 359, 110 A. 2d 881. *Fisher* and the incontrovertible proof herein demonstrate that the introduction of mixed seating constitutes a radical and fundamental change in the Congregation's theology, and not merely "shades of opinion on the same doctrine or dogma" (*Mertz v. Schaeffer*, 271 S.W. 2d 238, 242 [Mo. App.]; *Mt. Zion Baptist Church v. Whitmore*, 83 Iowa 138, 148, 49 N.W. 81, 84). Unlike the situation in *Mertz*, which involved a comparison of the "Common Confession" of the Missouri Synod of the Lutheran Church with corresponding portions of the Orthodox Lutheran Doctrine promulgated by the Orthodox Lutheran Conference, the plaintiffs herein, as the testimony discloses, cannot in conscience worship in the Synagogue if mixed seating is effected "without departure from the faith upon which the church was founded" (*Mertz*, at 242 of 271 S.W. 2d).

The defendants' plaint that "[c]ertainly none will claim that the same worship and the same ritual previously used by a congregation become, by the mere fact of mixed seating, un-Jewish or that the worshippers are no longer Jewish or are guilty of a diversion of church property," assumes the premise that there are no differences of dogma and doctrine between Orthodox Judaism on the one hand and the Conservative and Reform movements on the other, and that the separation of the sexes at Divine worship is without fundamental doctrinal significance. Since the proof demonstrates that the defendants' assumption is unfounded, the inference drawn by them is clearly erroneous.

Accordingly, it has been established that mixed seating constitutes a radical departure from the tenets of Orthodox Judaism to which the Congregation was dedicated.

III. *The majority of a congregation cannot, as against a faithful minority, institute a practice radically and fundamentally opposed to the characteristic doctrines to which the congregational property is dedicated.*

Religious societies are generally divided into three categories as to their form of government, namely, monarchical or prelatical, with authority being centralized in the spiritual leader; associated, with authority vested in a governing body such as an assembly, and independent or congregational (*Protestant Reformed Church v. Blankespoor,* 350 Mich. 347, 350; *Thomas v. Lewis,* 224 Ky. 307, 312, 6 S.W. 2d 255, 257; 3 Stokes, Church and State in the United States 376). Jewish congregations, like the one involved herein, fall within the third category.

By the overwhelming weight of authority, the courts will exercise their powers to protect a minority in a congregationally governed church, however regular the action or procedure of the majority may be in other respects, against a diversion of the society's property to another denomination *or to a group*

396

supporting doctrines fundamentally opposed to the characteristic doctrines of the society or disavowing the tenets and practices hitherto followed, even though the property is subject to no express and specific trust (45 Am. Jur., Religious Societies, §55, p. 765; 76 C.J.S., Religious Societies, §71, p. 853; Annotations, 8 A.L.R. 105, 113; 70 A.L.R. 75, 83). This Court has consistently adhered to the principle that those who adhere to the original fundamental tenets and doctrines, though a minority, are the true congregation; and that the church property may never be diverted from its intended use—use by the congregation for the benefit of those who still adhere to the faith and the customs and usages that existed prior to the dissension (*Bear v. Heasley, supra,* 98 Mich. 279; *Fuchs v. Meisel,* 102 Mich. 357; *Borgman v. Bultema,* 213 Mich. 684; *Michigan Congregational Conference v. United Church of Stanton,* 330 Mich. 561). For representative recent cases elsewhere, (see *Reid v. Johnston,* 241 N.C. 201, 85 S.E. 2d 114; *Whipple v. Fehsenfeld,* 173 Kan. 427, 249 P. 2d 638, *certiorari denied,* 346 U.S. 813, 918; *Parker v. Harper,* 295 Ky. 686, 175 S.W. 2d 361; *Blauert v. Schupmann,* 241 Minn. 428, 63 N.W. 2d 578). In the application of the governing principle, the protest of a *single* member is sufficient to prevent a diversion (*Rock Dell Norwegian E.L. Church v. Mommsen,* 174 Minn. 207, 212, 219 N.W. 88, 90; *Kemp v. Lentz,* 46 Ohio L. Abs. 28, 31, 68 N.E. 2d 339, 341).

As against this overwhelming array of authority, the defendants rely principally upon *Katz v. Goldman,* 33 Ohio App. 150, 168 N.E. 763, a 1929 decision by one of the nine district courts of appeal in Ohio. Because of the great reliance placed by the defendants upon *Katz,* careful analysis thereof is essential.

At the outset it should be observed that procedurally the issues therein were disposed of on the basis of a motion for judgment on the pleadings, namely, the amended petition and the answer. *No proof was presented by either side; no evidence such as was adduced at the trial of this suit was availed of by the court.* Moreover, a coordinate branch of the same court had previously overruled a demurrer to the amended petition, thus indicating a difference of opinion (at 151 of 33 Ohio App., 168 N.E. at 764). Furthermore, *Katz* has never been cited in any reported Ohio decision.

In support of its position that absent an express trust, independent congregations are solely controlled by a numerical majority, the action of which is not subject to judicial scrutiny, the court cited *Kenesaw Free Baptist Church v. Latimer,* 103 Neb. 755, 174 N.W. 296; *Watson v. Jones,* 13 Wall. [80 U.S.] 679, and two lower Federal court decisions following *Watson.* *Kenesaw* is a leading exponent of the minority view that there is no limitation on the control of the numerical majority in a religious society with an independent form of government (see Notes, 22 U. of Cin. L.Rev. 273, 275; 23 Tulane L.Rev. 572, 573). The dictum in *Watson* expressing a "hands off" policy as regards the action of a majority of an independent church has been frequently criticized (Annotations, 8 A.L.R. 105, 112; 24 L.R.A. [n.s.] 692, 698-9, 703), and has not been followed in the great majority of later decisions by state courts. "This decision [*Watson v. Jones*], however, departed from the uniform current of prior American authority, as well as the British cases involving non-established Churches; and, while seldom expressly repudiated [*Bear v. Heasley supra,* 98 Mich. 279, is one of four cases cited to such effect in the footnote], it is rarely followed outside of the federal courts, and is usually distinguished" (Note, 46 Yale L.J. 519, 522).

Further light upon the aberrant character of *Katz v. Goldman* is shed by *Bakos v. Takach, supra,* 14 Ohio App. 370, 32 O.C.A. 569, decided by the same district court of appeal a few years earlier. In the opinion for reargument, the court stated (at 385 of 14 Ohio App., 32 O.C.A. at 579-580):

"A rule, which is established by the weight of authority, *at least outside of Ohio,* is, that the majority faction of an independent or congregational society, whether incorporated or not, however regular its action or procedure may be, cannot, as against a faithful minority, divert the property of the society to another denomination, *or to the support of doctrines radically and fundamentally opposed to the characteristic doctrines of the society, even though the property is subject to no express or specific trust.* . . . In view of the early decisions in Ohio, in *Keyser v. Stansifer,* 6 Ohio, 363; *Heckman v. Mees,* 16 Ohio, 583, and *Bartholomew v. Lutheran Congregation,* 35 Ohio St. 567, it is not our purpose to hold that this rule is operative to the full extent as stated above . . ."

One naturally wonders how the same tribunal even forgot to mention this rule in the *Katz* opinion!

Furthermore, the rationale of *Katz* is opposed to the later case of *Kemp v. Lentz, supra,* 46 Ohio L. Abs. 28, 68 N.E. 2d 339, where the Court said (at 341 of 68 N.E. 2d, 46 Ohio L. Abs. at 31-2):

"We think the law has very definitely determined that a church organization, even though congregationally controlled, may not affiliate itself with another denomination and transfer its property so long as a single member of such a church objects to its transfer of property. *This principle is also given application where a local church, while not changing its name or identity, yet departs from the church doctrines so that it can no longer be said that it is following the creed of the organized church.*"

The basic infirmity of *Katz v. Goldman* is highlighted by the statement that "certainly this court could not define Jewish orthodoxy and traditional Judaism *except from the testimony of experts,* and it is an inevitable fact that such an inquiry would result in multiplying dissension, instead of eliminating it" (at 163 of 33 Ohio App., 168 N.E. at 767). The incontrovertible fact is that the use of expert testimony in this class of dispute is standard procedure. Such evidence has frequently been considered by this tribunal and the numerous other courts adhering to the principle that even in a congregational society, the majority cannot depart from the original tenets. (It appears that the Ohio court in *Kemp, supra,* did take evidence and on appeal additional exhibits were introduced for the first time.) As to the solicitude expressed in the latter part of the quoted sentence from *Katz, supra,* we may observe that an attitude of judicial non-intervention in this situation concretizes the might of the numerical majority as the legal right.

Katz may also be distinguished on its facts since such elements as consolidation of two congregations, acquiescence over a period of years in the innovations, etc., were present. But enough has been shown to demonstrate the inherent weakness of that decision as a matter of rationale and of precedent. So slender a reed has become the defendants' chief support— a support opposed to the great weight of authority in Michigan and other jurisdictions.

IV. *The civil courts have jurisdiction to determine the issues presented.*

The principle is firmly established that while courts are reluctant to take cognizance of the purely ecclesiastical affairs of religious societies, independent or otherwise, in suits between contending factions they will assume jurisdiction to determine such issues as which group is entitled to the use and control of the church property (*Holt v. Trone,* 341 Mich. 169, 174; *United Armenian Church v. Kazanjian, supra,* 320 Mich. 214, 217). As stated in 76 C.J.S., Religious Societies, pp. 873-4:

"While the civil courts have no jurisdiction over, and no

concern with, purely ecclesiastical questions and controversies, they do have jurisdiction as to civil, contract, and property rights even though such rights are involved in, or arise from, a church controversy."

The bill of complaint which was occasioned by the defendants' announced intention to introduce mixed seating beginning with the High Holy Day services in the fall of 1955, alleged that the contemplated action of the defendants would force the plaintiffs to leave the Synagogue and worship in one (necessarily outside of Mt. Clemens) which possessed the essential *kedushah* or congregational sanctity. The evidence fully supports such allegations. In other words, the action of the defendants would bar the plaintiffs from the use of the Synagogue just as effectively as a forced eviction or a changed lock would.

Under the circumstances, it is obvious that the real dispute in this case involves the ultimate issue, which group has the right to the use, enjoyment and control of the congregational property. The resolution of this issue necessarily involves civil and property rights as does the plaintiffs' request in their prayer for relief that "the true Congregation of Congregation Beth Tefilas Moses are the plaintiffs and those who adhere to the established tradition and practice of Orthodox Judaism as recognized by the Congregation prior to the vote aforesaid."

Moreover, as this Court observed in the leading case of *Fuchs v. Meisel, supra,* 102 Mich. 357, which was cited recently in *First Protestant Reformed Church v. DeWolf,* 344 Mich. 624, 633, the issue may be one of control and use rather than ownership. In *Fuchs* it was said (p. 371):

"In the present case the bill recognizes the defendant trustees as the lawful trustees, in charge and in possession of the church property. No attempt is made to deprive them of its control or possession when used in a legitimate manner. The only purpose is to compel them to permit the use of the church and parsonage according to the discipline, rules, usages, and polity of the church. It is immaterial in whom the legal title stands. One party may hold the title, and another be entitled to the use and possession of the property; or, as in this case, both may be entitled to its joint use and possession. It may be admitted for the purposes of this hearing that the title is in the local society or its board of trustees. The question is not, as in many of the cases cited in the briefs of counsel, in whom is the title to the property? but, in whom is the right to its use for religious worship both as pastor and layman? . . . The question presented relates exclusively to property rights, over which the proper courts have almost universally exercised jurisdiction. If the defendants' position be the true one, it follows that they are in no manner bound to the faith and tenets of this church, and that they may withdraw, and take the property to any other denomination of Christians."

Apart from the considerations discussed above, another basis exists to satisfy any jurisdictional requirement, to wit, the plaintiffs' membership in Congregation Beth Tefilas Moses. Whether characterized as a traditional property right or a personal, civil right, the modern trend is to recognize such membership as a right which the courts will protect (*Randolph v. First Baptist Church*, 120 N.E. 2d 485 [Ohio]; Annotation, 20 A.L.R. 2d 421, 458).

CONCLUSIONS

The proof is incontrovertible that Congregation Beth Tefilas Moses was founded as an Orthodox Jewish Synagogue and its property dedicated to, and for almost fifty years used to further, the doctrines of Orthodox Judaism. The separation of the sexes at Divine worship is a fundamental doctrine of this faith maintained in this Congregation since its founding, and an adherent thereof cannot in conscience worship in a Synagogue where

402

mixed seating is permitted. Under established principles of law the rights of the plaintiffs to the continuance of the Synagogue as an Orthodox house of worship will be protected by the courts.

RELIEF SOUGHT

The Decree of Dismissal entered by the lower court should be reversed and a Decree granting the relief prayed for in the Bill of Complaint should be ordered.

Respectfully submitted,

SAMUEL LAWRENCE BRENNGLASS,
Attorney for Amici Curiae,
103 Park Avenue,
New York, New York.

Dated: December 19, 1958.

The Decision of the Michigan Supreme Court

DAVIS *v.* SCHER

1. RELIGIOUS SOCIETIES—COURTS—JURISDICTION—ECCLESIASTICAL QUESTIONS —PROPERTY RIGHTS.
   A civil court has no jurisdiction over ecclesiastical questions unless property rights are involved.

2. SAME—COURTS—PRACTICE OF RELIGION.
   Civil courts do not have the right to interfere with the practice of religion in any way whatsoever.

3. SAME—COURTS—FREEDOM OF RELIGION.
   It is the duty of courts to preserve freedom of religion and its practice and to protect the rights of minority groups.

REFERENCES FOR POINTS IN HEADNOTES
[1, 2, 3] 45 Am Jur, Religious Societies §§ 40, 41.
[4, 5, 6, 8] 45 Am Jur, Religious Societies § 55.
[7] 45 Am Jur, Religious Societies § 59.
[9, 10] 45 Am Jur, Religious Societies § 48.

4. SAME—CHANGE IN PRACTICE OF RELIGION—PROTECTION OF MINORITY.

> The membership of a congregation, which is one of several congregations belonging to a particular religious faith to which the local church property and practice is dedicated, does not have the right to effect, by vote of a momentary majority, a change in religious practice, not conformable with the origin and historic character of the faith of the church of which the local congregation is one member, as against those who faithfully adhere to the characteristic doctrine of the church, and thereby deprive the minority of the use of the church property.

5. SAME—DIVERSION OF PROPERTY BY MAJORITY.

> The majority faction of a local congregation or religious society, being one part of a large church unit, however regular its action or procedure in other respects, may not, as against a faithful minority, divert the property of the society to another denomination or to the support of doctrines fundamentally opposed to the characteristic doctrines of the society, although the property is subject to no express or specific trust.

6. SAME—ORTHODOX JEWISH CONGREGATION—MIXED SEATING—USE OF PROPERTY.

> An Orthodox Jewish congregation, which is prohibited from participation in services where there is mixed seating of the sexes, may not be deprived of the right to such use of their property by a majority group contrary to law.

7. SAME—COURTS—ECCLESIASTICAL MATTERS—PROPERTY RIGHTS.

> Civil courts do not interfere in matters of church polity purely ecclesiastical, but when property rights are involved they are to be tested in the civil courts by the civil laws.

8. SAME—PROPERTY—DEDICATION—DIVERSION.

> Property of a religious society that is dedicated to the use of a religious denomination cannot thereafter be diverted to the use of those who depart from that faith, but must remain for the use and benefit of those who still adhere to the faith.

9. SAME—PROPERTY—TRUSTS.

> A conveyance of land to the original trustees of a religious society conveys the land in trust for the purposes for which the congregation was formed.

10. SAME—PROPERTY—TRUSTS.

> A conveyance or bequest to a religious association or to trustees for such association, necessarily implies a trust.

11. SAME—ORTHODOX JEWISH CONGREGATION—PROPERTY—SEPARATE SEATING OF SEXES.

> Undisputed testimony that Orthodox Judaism requires that sexes be separately seated in the synagogue during religious services provided for a use of the property dedicated to the use of an Orthodox Jewish

404

congregation which was subject to protection by the civil courts, notwithstanding a majority of the congregation had voted to have mixed seating.

Appeal from Macomb; Kane, (Edward T.), J., presiding. Submitted January 7, 1959. (Docket No. 20, Calendar No. 47,666.) Decided June 5, 1959.

Bill by Meyer Davis, Sam Schwartz and Baruch Litvin against J. N. Scher, Morris Feldman and other members of the Board of Trustees of Congregation Beth Tefilas Moses, an Orthodox Jewish congregation, to enjoin use of synagogue property in certain manners not in accord with Orthodox practice. Bill dismissed. Plaintiffs appeal. Reversed and remanded.

Walsh, O'Sullivan, Stommel & Sharp, for plaintiffs.

Charles Rubiner and *Arthur James Rubiner,* for defendants.

Amici Curiae:

Rabbinical Council of America and Union of Orthodox Jewish Congregations of America, by *Samuel Lawrence Brennglass.*

BEFORE THE ENTIRE BENCH,
KAVANAGH, J.

Plaintiffs-appellants are members of Congregation Beth Tefilas Moses, a Jewish synagogue located in the city of Mt. Clemens in Macomb county, Michigan. The defendants-appellees constitute the board of trustees of the congregation.

The congregation was founded in the year 1911 and was incorporated under PA 1897, No. 209, as an ecclesiastical corporation. The charter of the corporation lapsed for failure to file reports in 1934 and the congregation has continued as an unincorporated association down to the present time. The original constitution was adopted in 1918 and was printed in Yiddish. The present constitution was adopted in 1953 or 1954. The land on which the synagogue was built in 1921 was acquired by the congregation between 1912 and 1919. When the synagogue was built, it was constructed with a women's balcony which has remained and been used as such down to the present controversy.

Plaintiff Litvin is a businessman and has been a member of the congregation for about 20 years. He served at one time as financial secretary of the synagogue and later as its president. In or about the year 1954 agitation for mixed seating arose in the congregation. On a vote the issue was voted down. A year later a committee was appointed for the purpose of considering the practice of mixed seating. Plaintiff Litvin and other members of the congregation opposed the move, pointing out that the Orthodox practice forbade mixed seating. However, the majority of the congregation voted for mixed seating and the defendants-appellees thereafter proposed to carry it out.

Following the vote to permit mixed seating, plaintiffs-appellants filed their bill in chancery, and a temporary injunction restraining mixed seating was entered. During the pendency of the temporary injunction some instances of mixed seating were attempted and the plaintiffs, consistent with their contention as to the requirement of Orthodox Jewish practice, left the synagogue and worshipped in an Orthodox synagogue in Detroit.

Defendants filed a motion to dismiss alleging, among other things, that the court was without jurisdiction to adjudicate the dispute between the parties hereto, for the reason that such dispute is with respect to doctrinal and ecclesiastical matters only and not in relation to property rights; and it would be inconsistent with complete religious liberty for the court to assume such jurisdiction.

Defendants subsequently filed an answer to the bill.

The chancellor denied the motion to dismiss without prejudice to the rights of defendants to renew the same at the close of plaintiffs' proofs, and restrained any different seating arrangement for the holidays in September and October of 1955 than had prevailed for the corresponding holidays in 1954.

On the trial of the issue, before plaintiffs introduced their proofs, the court was informed by counsel for the defendants that they did not wish to cross-examine witnesses or present any proofs in the case and they would rely upon their motion to dismiss at the end of plaintiffs' proofs.

Plaintiff Litvin testified that he had been a member of the congregation for approximately 20 to 21 years. He further testified he had been an officer for a portion of this time and was familiar with the original constitution written in Yiddish. Mr. Litvin stated in response to a question as to whether the congregation had ever been served by other than Orthodox rabbis:

"*A.* Not to my recollection, ever since 1929 that I have been around Mt. Clemens they have been all Orthodox rabbis and those rabbis prior, which I know, they were also Orthodox rabbis."

A plan of the synagogue was identified and introduced in evidence which indicated that the plan called for a balcony for the seating of women. Plaintiff Litvin testified that segregated seating had been the rule, with the exception of rare instances where women were permitted because they were sick or invalids to use the benches in the extreme southwest part of the synagogue. He testified that this was the Orthodox practice that men and women do not sit together during prayer and that this congregation was served by Orthodox rabbis. Mr. Litvin further testified that after the institution of this suit he and others left the synagogue when mixed seating was attempted.

Rabbi David B. Hollander was then sworn and testified that he was at that time the honorary president of the Rabbinical Council of America and, also, Rabbi of the Mount Eden Jewish

Center in the borough of Bronx. He testified that the Rabbinical Council is an organization of Orthodox rabbis. He further testified that the law prohibiting mixed seating of the sexes is a fundamental law of the Jewish religion. He stated that in the past few years in America there have grown two new movements in the Jewish religion, one referred to as the Conservative, the other the Reform movement, and that both practiced mixed seating. Rabbi Hollander stated in response to a question:

"*Q.* Now, if you walked into a synagogue, Rabbi Hollander, would there be any immediate observable difference, any differentiation, let's say, between an Orthodox, Conservative or a Reform synagogue?"

"*A.* That's correct, the immediate observable thing would be that the men and women in the Orthodox synagogue would be required to be separated and the Conservative and Reform they would not."

Rabbi Hollander further stated that the mixed seating arrangement with reference to the Mt. Clemens synagogue had been called to the attention of his council and they had condemned it. In reply to a question by the chancellor, Rabbi Hollander testified that an Orthodox Jew could not worship in a synagogue where there is mixed seating.

Similar testimony was offered by Rabbi Dr. Samson R. Weiss. Rabbi Weiss also testified that the original constitution adopted in 1918 was a constitution of a synagogue which wishes to be an Orthodox traditional synagogue.

At the close of plaintiffs' proofs defendants were asked if they cared to present any proofs. They again informed the court that they did not wish to do so but would rely on their motion to dismiss. The court granted the motion on the theory this controversy was strictly a religious question and the matter of a property right was not involved.

408

Plaintiffs appeal to this Court.

It is admitted that a civil court has no jurisdiction over ecclesiastical questions unless property rights are involved. It is not the responsibility or duty of our civil courts, nor have they the right, to interfere with the practice of religion in any way whatsoever. Hundreds of thousands of people came to the shores of the United States of America seeking the right to practice their religion in accordance with the dictates of their own conscience, driven in most instances by either majority in numbers or by power of enforcement to refrain from practicing their own particular religion and join in a State religion. The drafters of our Constitution had this in mind and have provided that the State cannot in any way interfere with the practice of religion. Under the Constitution and Bill of Rights, however, it is made equally clear that it is the courts' duty to preserve freedom of religion and its practice and to preserve the rights of minority groups. It is upon this theory of religious liberty that this country has enjoyed more religious freedom than any country in history.

The Michigan Supreme Court has held on numerous occasions that the membership of a congregation, which is one of several congregations belonging to a particular religious faith to which the local church property and practice is dedicated, does not have the right to effect, by vote of a momentary majority, a change in religious practice, not conformable with the origin and historic character of the faith of the church of which the local congregation is one member, as against those who faithfully adhere to the characteristic doctrine of the church, and thereby deprive the minority of the use of the church property.

The weight of authority in Michigan is to the effect that the majority faction of a local congregation or society, being one part of a large church unit, however regular its action or procedure in other respects, may not, as against a faithful minority, divert the property of the society to another denomination or to the support of doctrines fundamentally opposed to the characteristic doctrines of the society, although the property is subject to no expressed trust.

The defendants herein had an opportunity to present testimony to dispute plaintiffs' testimony. This they refused to do. Therefore, we are faced under the proofs with these unchallenged facts: (1) that this congregation was an Orthodox Jewish congregation; (2) that under the Orthodox Jewish law Orthodox Jews cannot participate in services where there is mixed seating; (3) that if mixed seating was enjoyed in this congregation Orthodox Jews would be prohibited from participating in services there. Clearly plaintiffs would be deprived of their right to the use of their synagogue—in other words deprived of the right of the use of their property and the use of the property by the majority group contrary to law. In the very early case of *Fuchs* v. *Meisel,* 102 Mich 357, 373, 374 (32 LRA 92), Justice GRANT, writing for the Court, said:

"In the freedom of conscience and the right to worship allowed in this country, the defendants and the members of this church undoubtedly possessed the right to withdraw from it, with or without reason. But they could not take with them, for their own purposes, or transfer to any other religious body, the property dedicated to and conveyed for the worship of God under the discipline of this religious association; nor could they prevent its use by those who chose to remain in the church, and who represent the regular church organization."

The same rule of law was followed in *Holwerda* v. *Hoeksema,* 232 Mich 648. It was also followed in *Borgman* v. *Bultema,* 213 Mich 684, in an appeal from Muskegon County.

Justice STEERE, writing in the case of *Hanna* v. *Malick,* 223 Mich 100 (syllabus), held:

410

"Where the articles of incorporation and the by-laws of a local Orthodox Greek church, as drafted and adopted by the original incorporators, who were natives of Syria, clearly express the intention to bring the church under the supreme authority and jurisdiction of the Patriarch of Antioch, those who adhere to that declaration of faith and recognized jurisdiction are entitled to the possession, control, and use of its property for its declared purpose as against those seceding from the original organization and seeking to divert its use and control to the jurisdiction of a Holy Russian Synod or patriarch."

Justice BUSHNELL in *Calvary Baptist Church of Port Huron* v. *Shay,* 292 Mich 517, 520, 521, quoted from *Komarynski* v. *Popovich,* 232 Mich 88, 89, as follows:

" 'In matters of church polity purely ecclesiastical, civil courts do not interfere, but when property rights are involved they are to be tested in the civil courts by the civil laws.' "

Justice SHARPE, writing in *Holt* v. *Trone,* 341 Mich 169, 174, said as follows:

"In the case at bar property rights are involved, namely, which group has the exclusive use and control of the church property. We have no concern with ecclesiastical disputes, and whether the 'New Testament' authorizes and empowers a life tenure for elders with divine right to rule is not a proper subject for our determination."

Justice BOYLES, in the case of *First Protestant Reformed Church* v. *DeWolf,* 344 Mich 624, 633, said:

"While courts do not interfere in matters of church doctrine, church discipline, or the regularity of the proceedings of church tribunals, and refuse to interfere with the right of religious groups to worship freely as they choose, the question of the property rights of the members is a matter within the jurisdiction of the courts and may be determined by the court."

Justice DETHMERS, writing in the case of *Michigan Congre-*

gational Conference v. *United Church of Stanton,* 330 Mich 561, 575, 576, said:

"It is the well-established law of this State, declared in *Fuchs* v. *Meisel,* 102 Mich 357 (32 LRA 92); *Borgman* v. *Bultema,* 213 Mich 684; *Hanna* v. *Malick,* 223 Mich 100; and *United Armenian Brethren Evangelical Church* v. *Kazanjian,* 322 Mich 651, that while members of a church undoubtedly possess the legal right to withdraw from it, with or without reason, they may not, in so doing, take with them, for their own purposes, or transfer to any other religious body, property previously conveyed to, or dedicated to the use of, the religious denomination from which they are withdrawing or one of its member churches, but such property must remain for the use and benefit of adherents to that denomination or those who represent it. Not inconsistent is the earlier case of *Wilson* v. *Livingstone,* 99 Mich 594, when viewed as having been predicated. on the theory that the property involved in that case had not been dedicated to the use of any religious denomination.

"The property involved in the instant case belonged, originally, to the First Congregational Church of Stanton and was, as such, dedicated to the use of the religious denomination commonly called Congregational, of which the Stanton church was a part. When, in the year 1937, members of the First Congregational Church of Stanton dissolved its corporate existence and undertook to take its property with them into the newly-incorporated United Church of Stanton (defendant), the legality of that attempt depended upon whether the new organization was a part of the religious denomination commonly called Congregational. If it was not, they could not, in leaving the Congregational denomination, take the property with them into the new church organization and convey it to the latter."

Justice BOYLES in *United Armenian* . . . 322 Mich 651, 660, quotes from *Borgman* v. *Bultema,* 213 Mich 684, 689:

412

" 'No one disputes, where property is dedicated to the use of a religious denomination it cannot thereafter be diverted to the use of those who depart from their faith, but must remain for the use and benefit of those who still adhere to the faith.' "

The conveyance of the land to the original trustees and to the congregation conveyed the land in trust for the purposes for which the congregation was formed.

"A conveyance or bequest to a religious association, or to trustees for such association, necessarily implies a trust." *Fuchs* v. *Meisel, supra.* (Syllabus.)

As to an express trust, the rule is well established and set forth in 45 Am Jur, Religious Societies, §61, pp 771, 772, as follows:

"Where property has been dedicated by way of trust for the purpose of supporting or propagating definite religious doctrines or principles, it is the duty of the courts to see that the property so dedicated is not diverted from the trust which has been thus attached to its use. So long as there are persons who are qualified within the meaning of the original dedication and are also willing to teach the doctrines or principles prescribed in the act of dedication, and so long as there is anyone so interested in the execution of the trust as to have a standing in court, a diversion of the property or fund to other and different uses can be prevented. *** It is not within the power of the congregation, by reason of a change of views on religious subjects, to carry such property to the support of a new and conflicting doctrine; in such case, the secular courts will, as a general rule, interfere to protect the members of an ecclesiastical organization who adhere to the tenets and doctrines which it was organized to promulgate in their right to use the property, as against those members who are attempting to divert it to purposes utterly foreign to the organization, and will enjoin its diversion from the trust."

In the case of *Fisher* v. *Congregation B'nai Yitzhok,* 177 Pa Super 359 (110 A2d 881) the superior court of Pennsylvania dealing with a similar proposition of law dealt with it in accordance with the Michigan rule. Plaintiff was an ordained rabbi of the Orthodox Hebrew faith. He was a professional rabbi-cantor. Defendant was an incorporated Hebrew congregation with a synagogue in Philadelphia. Plaintiff, in response to defendant's advertisement in a Yiddish newspaper, appeared in Philadelphia for an audition before a committee representing the congregation. As a result, a written contract was entered into on June 26, 1950, under the terms of which plaintiff agreed to officiate as cantor at the synagogue of the defendant congregation "for the High Holiday Season of 1950," at 6 specified services during the month of September, 1950. Compensation for the above services was to be $1,200. The congregation up to that time had been conducted without mixed seating of the sexes. At a general meeting of the congregation on July 12, 1950, on the eve of moving into a new synagogue, the practice of separate seating by the defendant formerly observed was modified. When plaintiff was informed of the action of the defendant congregation, he, through his attorney notified the defendant that he . . . would be unable to officiate as cantor. When defendant failed to rescind its action, plaintiff refused to officiate. He was able to obtain employment as cantor for one service which paid him $100. He sued for the balance of the contract price.

Testimony of 3 rabbis learned in Hebrew law appeared for the plaintiff and testified to the effect "that Orthodox Judaism required a definite and physical separation of the sexes in the synagogue." Testimony was also established that an Orthodox rabbi-cantor could not conscientiously officiate in a synagogue that violates such Jewish law. Judgment for the plaintiff in the sum of $1,100 was entered plus interest. The court on appeal said:

414

"In determining the right of recovery in this case the question is to be determined under the rules of our civil law, and the ancient provision of the Hebrew law relating to separate seating is read into the contract only because implicit in the writing as to the basis—according to the evidence—upon which the parties dealt."

The court affirmed the judgment of the lower court.

The rule above set forth for Michigan has been followed in other States.

In their contention that ecclesiastical matters above are involved, defendants rely heavily upon *Katz* v. *Goldman,* 33 Ohio App 150 (168 NE 763). Here the court adopted (p 163) a theory that if they were to try to define just Orthodox and Traditional Judaism there would be such a divergence of opinions that it would result in multiplying dissension instead of eliminating it.

Here, because of defendants' calculated risk of not offering proofs, no dispute exists as to the teaching of Orthodox Judaism as to mixed seating.

The case is reversed and remanded for entry of a decree in accordance with this opinion. Costs in favor of plaintiffs-appellants.

Dethmers, C.J., and Carr, Kelly, Smith, Black, Edwards, and Voelker, J.J., concurred.

The Final Decree

State of Michigan
in the Circuit Court for the County of Macomb
in chancery (No. 252-33)

DECREE

AT A SESSION of said Court held continued in the Court House in the City of Mount Clemens, said County and State, on the 21st day of September, 1959.

Present: Honorable Edward T. Kane, Circuit Judge.

An Opinion in this matter having been rendered by the Michigan Supreme Court on June 5, 1959, and the matter having been remanded to this Court for entry of a Decree in accordance with said Opinion;

NOW THEREFORE, THIS COURT DOES FIND, ORDER AND ADJUDGE AS FOLLOWS:

1. That the Plaintiffs are members of Congregation Beth Tefilas Moses, an Orthodox Jewish Congregation located in the City of Mount Clemens, in Macomb County, Michigan.

2. That the Defendants are the duly elected and constituted members of the Board of Trustees of said Congregation.

3. That the doctrines of Orthodox Judaism proscribe mixed seating, that is the seating of men and women together in the Synagogue without a definite and physical separation of the sexes.

4. That an adherent of Orthodox Judaism cannot in conscience worship in a Synagogue where mixed seating is permitted.

416

5. That the acts attempted by the Trustees as representatives of the Congregation, to-wit: the institution of mixed seating in the Synagogue of Beth Tefilas Moses were clearly violative of the established Orthodox Jewish law and practice.

6. That the acts of the Defendants in instituting mixed seating in the Synagogue of Beth Tefilas Moses deprived the plaintiffs and all who adhered to the established Orthodox Jewish practice of the right of use of their property contrary to law.

7. That the Defendants and their successors in office be and they are hereby enjoined and restrained from instituting or permitting mixed seating in the Synagogue of Congregation Beth Tefilas Moses.

8. It appearing that, before the controversy involved herein, it was the practice in the Synagogue of Congregation Beth Tefilas Moses to assign one bench in the Southwesterly corner of the main floor to elderly women who were crippled or otherwise by reason of disease unable to ascend the stairs to the balcony, nothing in this Decree contained shall be construed to prevent the continuance of that practice. It is further ordered that the Defendants and their successors in that capacity provide such usher facilities and/or signs as shall be reasonably calculated to carry out this paragraph of the Decree.

9. It further appearing that the actions of the Defendants in this matter as Trustees of the Congregation were carried out in their representative capacities, Plaintiffs may tax their costs and have execution therefore against the membership of the Congregation as an unincorporated association in the manner and form by law provided.

s/ EDWARD T. KANE
Circuit Judge

December 19, 1958

IX

aftermath of the Michigan Supreme Court decision

Sivan 5 5719
June 11, 1959

Mr. Baruch Litvin
57 Lodewyck
Mount Clemens, Mich.

Dear Mr. Litvin:

We have just heard the good news of your great victory and we
hasten to express our great pleasure and congratulations to you
who have been the real bearer of the brunt of this battle.

It is a great victory and we pray that its effect will be felt
in all parts of our land.

Cordially,

Rabbi Emanuel Rackman
President

Rabbi Israel Klavan
Executive Vice President

420

מכתובת:
הרבנות הראשית לישראל, ירושלם
ת. ד. 179

Address:
THE CHIEF RABBINATE OF ISRAEL, JERUSALEM
P. O. B. 179

Telegrams:
"CHIEF RABBINATE JERUSALEM ISRAEL"

Reply to the a/m address only

Jerusalem 18 Sivan 5719
Tel. 3219 June 24, 1959

Mr. Baruch Litvin
57 Lodwyck Street
Mt. Clemens, Michigan

Dear Mr. Litvin,

I have great pleasure to acknowledge in behalf of their Eminences, the Chief Rabbis, the receipt of your letter dated the 8th of Sivan. It will no doubt be of interest to you to learn that the Israeli press gave prominent space to the report.

We share your hope that the legal victory you scored singlehanded at the Michigan Supreme Court will be a source of encouragement to other communities and their leadership. The protection of sanctity and reverence in the Houses of Prayer and Study—which must ultimately be relocated in Eretz Israel (Talmud) — is a matter of grave concern at this moment.

As for Congregation Beth Tefilas Moses, we trust that with the aid of other guardians of our Faith in the large metropolitan center of Detroit, you will be in a position to maintain the synagogue in conformity with Torah law and the historical tradition, for which you fought so valiantly.

Our very best wishes to you.

Sincerely yours,

Rabbi M. J. E. Wohlgelernter
General Secretary

421

The Jewish Center

RABBI'S STUDY
131-135 West 86th Street
New York 24, N. Y.

Phone SChuyler 4-2700

Cable Address "Rosester" New York

June 10, 1959

Dear Mr. Litvin:

Thank you very much for your letter of June 8th.
My warmest congratulations on your great victory!

I give my permission with pleasure to reprint
the article by Dr. Alderblum....

With every good wish,

Sincerely yours,

Rabbi Leo Jung

LJ:MW

CONGREGATION SHAARAY TEFILA
THE JEWISH CENTER OF FAR ROCKAWAY

June 10th, 1959.

Dear Mr. Litvin,

Congratulations! I was very happy to learn
from the Yiddish Press and from your letter
of the great success that was yours and ours.
May the Lord bless you for all that you did.

Warmest personal regards and best wishes.

Yours as ever,

Rabbi Emanuel Rackman

422

JEWS' COLLEGE, LONDON
11 Montagu Place
London, W. 1.

10th June, 1959.

Dear Mr. Litvin,

Mazel Tov and heartiest congratulations on your success. I shall be informing the Chief Rabbi who, I am sure, will be equally pleased to hear the outcome of your action.

With kindest regards and best wishes,

Yours sincerely,

RABBI DR. I. EPSTEIN
Principal

DEB012 SYA064
SY NNB244 CGN NL PD=BROOKLYN NY   JUN 6=
BARUCH LITZIN=
    57 LOEDWICK MTCLEMENS MICH=

HEARTFELT MAZELTOV ON SUPREME COURT VICTORY. YOU HAVE
EARNED EVERLASTING GRATITUDE OF TORAH JEWRY FOR YOUR
SINGLEHANDED FIGHTING AGAINST ALL ODDS TO HELP SAVE THE
SANCTITY OF THE SYNAGOGUE OF AMERICA   YOUR DETERMINED
STRUGGLES HAS WRITTEN JEWISH HISTORY TECHEZAKNA YEDEICHEM=
    AGUDAH ISRAEL OF AMERICA RABBI MOSHE SHERER EXECUTIVE
    VICE PRESIDENT=.

B Y   W E S T E R N   U N I O N

victory for
synagogue sanctity

AN EDITORIAL FROM
"JEWISH LIFE" OF JUNE, 1959

H ISTORIC is most certainly the right word for the decision of the Supreme Court of Michigan, announced June 5th, in the celebrated Mount Clemens "mixed seating" case. Reversing the earlier decision of a lower court, the Michigan Supreme Court unanimously upheld the case of the minority group opposing the abandonment of separate seating of men and women at religious services at Congregation Beth Tefilas Moses of Mount Clemens, Mich. As in the similar case of Congregation Chevra Thilim of New Orleans, La. last year, the court found that the projected seating change constituted a violation of synagogue sanctity and hence of members' religious and property rights. But going beyond the decision of the Louisiana court, the Michigan Supreme Court held that whether or not the property is subject to an "express trust," breach of religious freedom and of property rights are alike entailed when "a majority faction of a local congregation" diverts the congregational property "to another denomination or to the support of doctrines fundamentally opposed to the characteristic doctrines of the society."

In the light of the fundamental religious issues and legal questions underlying the "mixed seating" issue, the decision of the Michigan Supreme Court bears wide ramifications. It protects congregations of historically orthodox character whether or not their charters or constitutions expressly bear the word "orthodox." It upholds the premise that traditional synagogue practices based on fundamental Jewish doctrine are not subject to change by "vote of a momentary majority" of lay members of a congregation. Upheld too, on the basis of the unchallenged evidence, was the contention that adoption of mixed seating, a hallmark of the Reform and Conservative movements, violates Jewish law and removes the sanctity of the synagogue, and the observant Jew may no longer properly worship there.

The successful outcome of this case underscores the position held by orthodox Jewry that issues deriving from questions of Jewish law are rightfully adjudicable only within the terms of such law and by tribunals of recognized Halachic authorities. In rejecting Halachic adjudication, the proponents of mixed seating at services have given further demonstration that they are motivated by disregard for sacred Jewish law and tradition. Thus there has been forced upon the defenders of synagogue sanctity the alternatives of either yielding religious principle or defending their right in the civil courts.

The Mount Clemens decision spells the end of an era of anarchy in congregational life. As the decision put it:

"It is not the responsibility or duty of our civil courts, nor have they the right, to interfere with the practice of religion in any way whatsoever. . . . Under the Constitution and Bill of Rights, however, it is made equally clear that it is the court's duty to preserve freedom of religion and its practice and to preserve the rights of minority groups. . . ."

Thus the decision serves notice to all that those opposed to sacred Jewish norms have every right, under American freedom, to withdraw from the orthodox syna-

425

gogue and set up such institutions as they may choose. But they have no right and henceforth may no longer arrogate the power to usurp the religious freedom of their religiously-loyal brethren by imposing heterodox doctrines and practices on orthodox synagogues. Agitation-inspired ballot may no longer be used with impunity in deciding the fate of orthodox congregations.

The Jewish community is lastingly indebted to Mr. Baruch Litvin, who, standing alone in Mount Clemens, carried on an unceasing struggle against the proposed change for more than five years. Carrying his cause far and wide throughout the country, Mr. Litvin has aroused many to the realization that the "mixed seating" issue is a focal point in the battle for the sanctity of the synagogue and of Torah law, for the integrity and endurance of true Judaism. In giving aid and guidance in this as in similar cases, the Union of Orthodox Jewish Congregations of America, with the cooperation of the Rabbinical Council of America, has made a major contribution. Particular tribute must be paid to Samuel Lawrence Brennglass, UOJCA vice-president and noted attorney who prepared the brief of the Union and the Rabbinical Council, as *amici curiae* in support of the plaintiffs, upon which the Michigan Supreme Court's decision was based.

The historical significance of the Mount Clemens case must be appraised in the context of pregnant developments. Many signs indicate an awakening to the sanctity and glory of the Jewish heritage among Jews everywhere. From coast to coast there can be seen the rise of new orthodox synagogues, the expansion of many others, continual increases in the number and enrollments of Day Schools, the waxing of institutions of Torah learning, the fruitful spread of traditional religious endeavor in a variety of forms,

426

above all the upsurge of a positive Jewish spirit, of respect for Jewish law, and of personal and home observance. Scores of synagogues which had fallen into the "mixed pews" deviation have, during the past few years alone, recognized their error and have restored or newly instituted the *mechitzah,* the separation of the men's and women's seating sections required by Jewish law.

This does not gainsay the fact that a contrary spirit of flight from Jewish values and principles, a spirit of assimilation to the non-Jewish world, remains a potent factor on the Jewish scene. There can be no neutrality for these two opposing trends. A battle on wide fronts emerges.

For the Torah forces, the campaign must be waged primarily with education, with programs for the spreading of Jewish knowledge and enlightenment. Greater unity, more cohesive organization must be and is being brought to bear. But, under all circumstances, unshakable determination to meet the realities of the situation must govern all efforts. There must be the realization that not one synagogue or community, or for that matter not one home and not one Jew, is expendable.

Epitomizing as it does the struggle for defense of Jewish foundations, the "mixed seating" issue cannot be treated as a peripheral problem; upon it hinges the question whether synagogues will remain Jewish sanctuaries or will, Heaven forfend, be made over into the likeness of the church. The Mount Clemens decision denotes that the will to confront the problem even under the most adverse conditions has come to the fore and that this will must triumph. The spirit symbolized in the Mount Clemens case will, with the blessing of the Almighty, spur on to new heights the forces of creative Jewish endeavor and yield manifold blessings to our people.

implications of the

THE MICHIGAN SUPREME COURT *unanimously decided, on Friday, June 5, 1959, for the Plaintiffs and Appellants in the "Mount Clemens Case."*

Mr. Samuel Lawrence Brennglass, UOJCA Vice President and Chairman of its Communal Relations Commission, had entered a "Brief Amici Curiae" on behalf of the UOJCA and the Rabbinical Council of America. The decision of the Michigan Supreme Court is based, in its salient points, on this brief, which has been classified by leading experts as a masterpiece, and to which Mr. Brennglass devoted many weeks of research.

Mr. Brennglass, an eminent attorney, was Chairman of the Ad Hoc Committee which had also dealt with the New Orleans, Louisiana case involving Congregation Chevra Thilim. He was in constant contact with the attorneys for the plaintiffs throughout the involved legal proceedings in both the New Orleans, La. and Mount Clemens, Michigan cases and developed the legal strategy which led to their successful conclusions.

What follows is an analysis of the implications of the Michigan Supreme Court decision, prepared by Mr. Brennglass. The protective provisions which Mr. Brennglass recommends to our congregations for the protection of their orthodox character, were developed by Mr. Brennglass upon his analysis of the Louisiana Court decision. Their validity has now been further underscored by the opinion of the Michigan Supreme Court.

DR. SAMSON R. WEISS
Executive Vice-President,
Union of Orthodox Jewish
Congregations of America

428

Michigan Supreme Court decision

BY SAMUEL L. BRENNGLASS

T HE UNANIMOUS DECISION of the Supreme Court of the State of Michigan concerning the abolition of the separation of the sexes during worship by majority decision of the members of Congregation Beth Tefilas Moses in Mount Clemens, Michigan, directs the Board of Trustees of the congregation to reinstitute separate seating. This decision has far-reaching implications for congregational Jewish life throughout the United States. Some of these implications are as follows:

(1) Practices of a synagogue based on fundamental and doctrinal teachings of Judaism, cannot be changed by majority vote. Such practices are recognized by this decision (as they were by the decision of the New Orleans, Louisiana Court in the prior case of Congregation Chevra Thilim) as not subject to change "by vote of a momentary majority" against a "faithful minority." Consequently, there is now high decisional authority that a congregation may not change its fundamental religious practices as long as even a single member objects.

(2) The decision of the Michigan Supreme Court, goes beyond the New Orleans, La. ruling in at least two important ways.

The latter is based on an express trust established and accepted by the congregation for the purpose of main-

429

taining an orthodox synagogue. The orthodox character
of this synagogue was further clearly stipulated in its charter and constitution. The intended change to mixed pews
was, therefore, considered by the Louisiana Court as a
violation of property rights protected by such trust, charter
and constitution.

The Michigan Supreme Court upheld the contention,
set forth in the legal brief submitted by this writer, that
a conveyance, bequest or donation to a synagogue necessarily implies a trust for the purposes for which the congregation was formed. An implied trust is as much entitled
to judicial protection as an express trust. In neither case
may a temporary majority disavow the fundamental tenets
and practices hitherto followed.

(3) The Michigan Supreme Court further upheld
the contention of this writer that the fact that the word
"orthodox" does not expressly appear in the charter and
constitution of a synagogue, is not material. The court
will look to any competent evidence proving the original
tenets of the congregation and the intended use of its
property, such as the practices and usages in existence
when the congregation was organized. Indeed, the very
absence of a descriptive and qualifying phrase denoting
the congregation as "conservative" or "reform," makes a
congregation organized for Jewish worship *ipso facto* an
orthodox congregation when in keeping with the intentions
of its original founders and in keeping with the practices
they introduced. Regardless, therefore, of any specific
protective provisions in the charter and the constitution
of a congregation, the Michigan Supreme Court ruled that
the intentions of the founders as expressed in the initial
practices of a synagogue determine its fundamental character for its entire future.

430

(4) The Michigan Supreme Court, upon the testimony of our experts submitted upon the trial in the lower court, held that mixed seating is a fundamental and doctrinal deviation from orthodox Judaism and that its introduction, therefore, would deprive orthodox Jews of "their right to the use of their synagogue—in other words of the right of the use of their property and [constitute] the use of the property by the majority group contrary to law."

This means that the Michigan Supreme Court has recognized the validity of the contention expressed by our experts, Dr. Samson R. Weiss, UOJCA Vice President, and Rabbi David B. Hollander, Past President of the Rabbinical Council of America, that the introduction of mixed seating is not merely a violation of one of the sacred tenets and traditions of Judaism but an attempt to change the character of the synagogue in a fundamental manner, robbing it of its previous *kedushah*. In this aspect, the present decision concurs with the earlier judgment of the Louisiana Court.

(5) The Michigan Supreme Court reiterates the principle that separation of Church and State does not imply that the civil courts can have no jurisdiction whatsoever in any issue arising out of a religious conflict. On the contrary, the Court declared that "under the constitution and bill of rights, however, it is made equally clear that it is the courts' duty to preserve freedom of religion and its practice and to preserve the rights of minority groups."

Whenever, therefore, an internal religious dispute or disagreement involves civil, contract or property rights of a religious entity, the courts *do* have jurisdiction and must investigate whether or not minority rights are violated by the decision of the majority. If such violation is established, it is the task of the courts to correct by its decree such violative action.

While the majority of the courts in the various states will protect implied trusts as well as express trusts, the latter receive universal protection. Accordingly, the UOJCA earnestly recommends to our congregations to study their charters and constitutions and, if found lacking therein, to amend them to include protective provisions clearly defining the orthodox character and practices of the congregation and safeguarding them from deviational involvements.

Upon request, the Union will mail you its memorandum on such protective provisions.

The Lesson of Mount Clemens

BY RABBI MOSHE SHERER

In the month of Sivan, 5719 (1959), Orthodox Jewry in America celebrated the "Victory of Mount Clemens." Now, however, after the initial feelings of triumph and satisfaction, the time is surely right for an incisive analysis of the meaning of the Mount Clemens *mechitzah* battle, whose climax was the Michigan Supreme Court's decision. The victory in Mount Clemens will not be a victory if Orthodox Jewry, its rabbis and lay leaders, celebrate it without understanding its long-term ramifications and useful lessons.

The victory at Mount Clemens is not that a civil court delivered a verdict in favor of the Orthodox position, which steadfastly opposed the removal of holiness from a Jewish holy place; it is not that a Gentile judge expressed a stern warning about those ultra-modern Jews, a "passing minority," who seek to "change religious practice and blatantly ignore the historical character of its religious tenets and belief."

What is important is not so much the ruling in the Mount Clemens case—which we will soon show has great historical meaning—as the battle itself. This battle, which was fought during a period of about five years, made the subject of *mechitzot* a live issue, a topic of discussion and debate. And the present Supreme Court decision and its natural prominence has provided great encouragement to those who waged this battle.

The removal of the *mechitzot* in tens of synagogues all over the land had, for many years, been an issue muffled in complete silence. In many Orthodox circles, this trend was considered an inevitable evil. The feeling was that there was no effective chance of combating it, and it was no longer deemed useful to even discuss the issue. And the moment the

433

issue ceased to be discussed, the "germ" began to spread uncontrollably.

Mount Clemens, a small town, hardly noticeable on a map, will be remembered as the place where a Jew appeared who, with traditional Jewish stubborness, put a stop to the conspiracy of silence on the issue of *mechitzah*. Because this outstanding Jew, Reb Baruch Litvin, clamored incessantly in a clangor so loud it was heard from one end of the land to the other, the problem of *mechitzot* has become a live issue. This in itself (the end of the period of silence during which *mechitzah* opposition blossomed) was the major historical step forward in the campaign to uphold the sanctity of synagogues in this country.

The battle in Mount Clemens has another much deeper meaning. Reb Baruch Litvin, with his initiative not to permit the removal of holiness from his synagogue in Mount Clemens, introduced in America the battle cry for authentic Torah Judaism and set an example for others.

For a considerable period of time, proceedings had been taking place to remove *mechitzot* in congregations. These "Reform operations" were carried out undeterred and without disagreement. At the whim of one upscale Jew in town who aspired to assimilate or acculturate within the social coteries of non-Jewish neighbors and business associates, a "motion" would be placed on the agenda to modernize the synagogue. Inevitably, the response, in a surprising display of choral unity, would be a secularly resounding "Amen." No one had the courage to stand up in opposition. Certainly, there were Jews here and there who were disturbed by all this. But they quickly came to terms with the situation, concluding, "These are new times," "We must follow," or even, "We must run blindly with the new winds and not challenge the 'holy right' of the majority."

So it happened in many towns all over the land. Until the

434

advent of Reb Baruch Litvin; a Jew, not a rabbi and not a *gaon*. A Jew, a simple businessman, or as he describes himself—a carpenter. This Reb Baruch mustered the courage to shout a resounding "No!" And suddenly, an echo was heard from other Jews all over the country as camps of courageous opposition began to develop.

Reb Baruch Litvin, with his battle in Mt. Clemens, became a national symbol of Jewish resistance spirit, and it was this spirit that rescued more than one holy place from the Reform deluge which tried to subvert it. Reb Baruch Litvin, with his campaign, helped salvage the sanctity of synagogues in a manner that few could ever imagine.

Take, for example, a small episode which is personally familiar to the writer of these lines. In a small town in Pennsylvania, a group of *baalai batim* joined together at a board of trustees meeting and proposed the removal of the *mechitzah*. Had this motion been presented before the Mount Clemens battle, it would have been pushed through with the ease and haste that such motions were passed in tens of other communities. But a different group of *baalai batim* had apparently heard something about the campaign of Baruch Litvin. One member of this second group arose to speak, and in a neat play on words ended the discussion. He declared, "It would be advisable to remove the motion rather than the *mechitzah*. Otherwise, we'll bring out that Jew with the long beard from Mt. Clemens. So all this is not worthwhile."

Many people wonder why the conscious Orthodox leadership places so much importance on the *mechitzah* issue when there are so many other "evils" in Jewish life in America. Both the battle and the Supreme Court decision about the Mount Clemens case best express the deeper significance of this problem.

Aside from the actual severe halachic problem connected with the removal of a *mechitzah*—one of the cornerstones of

435

synagogal sanctity—the subject reaches a major question of principle, which touches upon the very foundations of our religion, i.e., who establishes religious standards—the eternal, yet flexible *halachah* or G-d forbid, a majority of hands.

During the "Americanization" process, many Jews, completely devoid of *Torah* became so imbued with the concept of democracy and the principle of "majority rule," that they indiscriminately applied it in every sphere of life. This attitude became part of the Jews' ingrained behavior pattern, in all areas of personal life, and even in the untouchable Holy of Holies of our belief.

It is the unbounded extrapolation of the concepts of democracy from politics to religion which has led, and still leads, from one catastrophe to the next in Jewish religious life. The divinely commanded, profound, and eternally-binding *halachah* has been pushed aside by a new idol, which sanctifies the hands of "the voters" in matters of cardinal importance in our belief.

The *mechitzot* have become the battlefield upon which these two diametrically opposed concepts have confronted each other and every single effort to maintain the *mechitzah* becomes ipso facto a battle to uphold authority of *halachah* as the single dominating factor in Jewish life. Every victory in the battle to keep *mechitzot* in synagogues is, therefore, also a victory on a greater scale, to uphold and to strengthen the sovereignty of *Torah*.

For those misdirected individuals who think that worshipping the idol of "majority rule," is a holy American principle, the Michigan Supreme Court decision is a bitter disappointment. They certainly could not expect that such an authoritative American court would tear down the "holiness of majority rule" and declare that there are even "higher" laws, next to which every man-made law becomes null and void.

436

In this sense, the Michigan Supreme Court decision can be presented as a victory for Orthodoxy. Maybe our misdirected and confused Jews who, with all their reforms, simply want to imitate the Gentile, will now come to their senses. The court decision informed them that their "way" is not even the Gentile one.

What has been denominated in Orthodox circles as the "Victory of Mount Clemens," should rather, it seems, better be entitled as the "Challenge of Mount Clemens," the greatest victory resulting from the court decision will occur when Orthodoxy understands how to address this challenge, which has been placed before it as a result of the battle of Mount Clemens.

A reading of the transcript of the first court case leads to the conclusion that at the defense table sat not only the confused Jews of the Board of Trustees of the Mount Clemens synagogue of Reb Baruch who decided to remove the *mechitzah*, but with them sat American Orthodox Jewry, which with its neglect of the issue, actually brought about the problem.

Reading further, one cannot avoid being disturbed by the questions the judge posed to Rabbis David Hollander and Samson Raphael Weiss, who acted as the Orthodox experts: Are there Orthodox synagogues that do not have *mechitzot*? Are there Orthodox rabbis who take positions in such synagogues? And what about the rabbi in the Mt. Clemens synagogue? Is he a member of any Orthodox rabbinical organization? The Orthodox experts had no choice but to answer a sorrowful yes. Though they intelligently presented the specific circumstances of such situations, they must remain, for us, unanswered questions. Even more so, do they show clearly the ease with which the Jewish masses handled the *mechitzah* issue, its roots and causes, and the inconsistency with which a certain segment of Orthodox leadership has for so many years approached this problem.

437

This problem is clearly brought to the forefront in a letter which a rabbi publicized in the "Rabbinical Council Record," (Teveth, 1959), a publication of the Rabbinical Council of America, in which the conscientious Rabbi speaks from the heart:

> We have up until now knocked ourselves out trying to stand face to face with the problem (of *mechitzot*). We have a substantial group in our membership, especially in the West, who think all is lost. . . . But before we decide what to do, we must first clarify that mixed pews are a violation of *Halachah*. We, in the Rabbinical Council of America, have grappled with this problem. Earlier we had a five year law, but we never carried it out and it cannot be taken seriously any more. We gave the responsibility over to the "placement bureau" and they, with the precision of an automatic machine, supported anyone who took a position in a *shul* with mixed pews to acquire membership in the Rabbinical Council of America.
>
> Let us cease fooling ourselves. Let us stand up and wage a battle. But before we educate our congregations, we must convince them and ourselves of our true consciousness. It makes no sense to preach against mixed pews when our organizations and Yeshivot secretly "protect" them. After speaking once in my *shul* about *mechitzot*, a "*Baal Habas*" came up to me and said, "Rabbi, tell all this to the President of your Yeshiva and to the Rabbinical Council of America. You cannot tell me not to pray in a synagogue without a *mechitzah* when your Yeshiva and organization look the other way . . ."

And herein lies the tragedy of the problem. Orthodox rabbis procure positions in synagogues without *mechitzot* and still remain "Orthodox" rabbis and full-privileged members in an Orthodox rabbinical organization; Yeshivot send their graduates to take up positions in *shuls* without *mechitzot*; a rabbi in

Mount Clemens positions himself on the side of the *baalai batim* who want to remove the *mechitzah* and, worse, who claim during the court case that they are absolutely not Orthodox—and this same rabbi remains a member of good standing in an Orthodox rabbinical body.

What can be expected from unknowledgeable *baalai batim* in such a situation, who are flooded from all sides by so many inconsistencies in the Orthodox camp itself?

The battle of Mount Clemens, therefore, must serve as a demand to the Orthodox for consistency. If the Orthodox camp wants the victory to be everlasting, there is but one way, and that is consistency in position and clarity in approach. Once and for all, clear standards and defined boundaries must be established as to what is an Orthodox *shul* and as to who is an Orthodox rabbi.

However, this is still not a complete solution for this painful problem. What is needed is not merely firmness, clarity, and steadfastness in rabbinic and lay leadership circles, but also an information campaign covering the length and breadth of the land against the crazed psyche of "mixed pews."

It seems to me that we have much better chances of victory in this battle for synagogue sanctity than in other areas. It is probably difficult to influence a Jew to become Sabbath-observant. It is, however, much easier to speak to the common sense of a Jew about respecting the holiness of a *shul*. It is, perhaps, hard for the Jew to rid himself of old sins. But it should be easier to prevent him from committing new ones.

There are Jews all over the country who do not even know that a *shul* with mixed pews cannot be a holy place. They must be educated. The American Jew, including the irreligious, has respect and reverence for the synagogue, for a holy place. He must be taught that mixed pews degrade the sanctity of a synagogue and convert the holy place into a fashion hall, into a modern salon. People with a fine feeling for religion will understand. The Jewish woman must be made aware of her elevated position in Jewish law and that the *mechitzah* separation means absolutely no degradation of her prominent place in Jewish family and communal life.

It is interesting how our opponents, the apostles of mixed pews, are terrified of such an education campaign. Proof of this phenomenon can best be offered by the case of Mount Clemens. When the board of trustees in the Mt. Clemens synagogue decided to remove the *mechitzah,* Rabbi Hollander, then the president of the Rabbinical Council of America, visited the town. The board members discussed the issue and when Rabbi Hollander saw that they refused to budge from their decision, he made a small request: "Allow me to speak to the members of the congregation." The board members in no way would permit that. The reason: they were afraid. They knew that though they have the members' support, the members would not consent to the removal of the *mechitzah* if they would only be enlightened a bit about the true essence of a holy place.

Therefore, Reb Baruch Litvin's initiative to publish an all-encompassing book which is a collection of the explanations and sources regarding the sanctity of the synagogue in all its aspects, should be acclaimed. He took upon himself the publication of this monumental work because throughout the years of his campaign, when he travelled the length and breadth of this land many times, he felt the great damage caused by the lack of proper material about the entire problem. The present book will be a major collection of material dealing with themes like the revelation at Mt. Sinai, when, according to the *Midrash Pirkei De-Rabbi Eliezer,* there was a separation of men and women. It will also include the latest responsa of our *Torah* Sages of the present generation. All this is in addition to convincing clarifications which can be used to combat the psychotic race to "gentilize" our synagogues.

Meanwhile, until Orthodoxy can develop such effective propaganda, the decision of the Michigan Supreme Court has given the *Torah* community a vital weapon. It will serve as a legal means of temporarily preventing synagogues, that are about to take the tragic step of liquidating their *mechitzot* from doing so. In the interim, the precious time thus won can be used to open the eyes and minds of confused Jews.

If there ever was an opportune time for a new offensive to salvage the sanctity of our synagogues, it is now. The battle of Mount Clemens with its Supreme Court victory has created a favorable climate to mobilize Orthodox strength both inwardly and outwardly in preparation for a holy battle for the sovereignty of G-d's *Torah* on all fronts in the House of G-d.

Let us rise up to the call of the day.

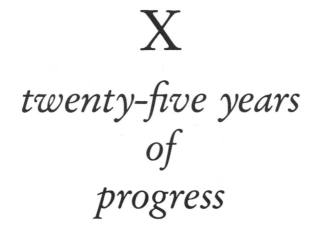

X

twenty-five years of progress

In the years following the momentous Michigan Supreme Court decision and the publication of *The Sanctity of the Synagogue,* great progress was made in the area of *mechitzah.* Synagogues that had been hesitating whether or not to install a *mechitzah* took courage from the news of Baruch Litvin's success and took the leap required to install one. Other synagogues that had been contemplating removing their *mechitzah* with the hope of increasing their membership rolls, decided to keep their *mechitzah* rather than face the possibility of a court battle with members who desired to keep the *mechitzah.* These synagogues were to benefit greatly from a new wave of young professionals seeking affiliation with an authentic orthodox synagogue. This search was apparently a by-product of the phenomenon of searching for one's roots that was prevalent in the decade of the 70s. Already, in the

442

mid-60s, there was a noticeable movement of raising the *mechitzah* in synagogues that had for many years maintained one of only minimal height.

One powerful demonstration of the impact of the court decision and subsequent publication of *The Sanctity of the Synagogue* is demonstrated by the following article written by Abraham Dere, a layman from Richmond, Virginia. As you will read, Mr. Dere specifically cites his reading of *The Sanctity of the Synagogue* as the prime motivator in giving him the courage to break away from his non-*mechitzah* synagogue, of which he had been a member of long standing, and create a vibrant new *mechitzah* synagogue.

Congregation Kol Emes Richmond, Virginia

BY ABRAHAM DERE

Congregation Kol Emes in Richmond, Virginia, was founded in 1964. At the time, there was only one other orthodox Jewish synagogue in Richmond. Though carrying the label orthodox, that synagogue had for the last fifty years, not maintained separate sections for seating men and women.

Kol Emes was founded by two individuals (the writer of these words being one of the two) who were no longer content with that situation. The founders of Kol Emes read *The Sanctity of the Synagogue* several times and then passed the book to friends. The book inspired the founders and others to establish Congregation Kol Emes in accord with truly orthodox form and standards. That this was accomplished was due in no small measure to the example set by Baruch Litvin. He showed that with proper commitment for a true *Torah* cause, even one person can do the seemingly impossible.

By the time Kol Emes's new building was ready to open its doors, the two founding members had been joined by many more people. The congregation had a *minyan*! The *minyan* has continued uninterrupted for the three daily services each day for the past twenty years.

Kol Emes has also had a profound and lasting effect on the Jewish community in Richmond. A day school, which was first housed on Kol Emes's premises, is now large enough to occupy its own building. The local Jewish Federation was persuaded to adhere to a policy that at all community functions only Kosher food shall be served. Also, a *mikveh* built on the Kol Emes premises is used by large numbers of Richmond's Jews.

Most notable, however, was the installation of a *mechitzah* in the old and established orthodox congregation. For so long, it had called itself orthodox though it did not require men and women to sit in separate sections. Now it is truly orthodox in name and in practice.

One cannot minimize the time, money, and effort sacrificed by a dedicated membership for more than twenty years now. The accomplishments of Kol Emes, for itself and for Richmond, were a direct result of all that. But one cannot write about our synagogue's history and its accomplishments without paying special tribute to Baruch Litvin and his book *The Sanctity of the Synagogue*. Both were important factors in inspiring those devoted to Kol Emes in their work to build and sustain it.

To this writer, Baruch Litvin was truly a "Profile in Courage." He labored during a period when orthodox Judaism in America was at a low ebb. Reform Judaism, with a membership greater in number and greater in wealth, was the powerhouse in American Judaism. The Conservative movement, at the time, was striving to imitate the Reform movement. Orthodoxy was still, basically, comprised of immi-

444

grants seeking and searching to adjust and establish themselves as a discernible Jewish element in the United States.

Oblivious to these realities, Baruch Litvin refused to concede to prevailing trends and was determined not to abdicate his beliefs. Those who thought they could destroy the sanctity of Baruch Litvin's synagogue by resorting to democratic principles of majority rule were confronted by Baruch Litvin's own adaptation of classic American principles, to wit, that certain rights, and rituals, are inalienable. The strength of Baruch Litvin's commitment and the force of his personality gave orthodox Jews throughout the United States the courage to persevere and the fortitude to hold their heads high in an era when America's Jews were inclined to be more American than Jewish.

Baruch Litvin taught us all that a democracy is based on principles which cannot be emaciated at the whim of a majority, that adherence to those principles breeds respect and honor. As a layman, he paved the way for orthodox Jews in America to feel safe, secure, and proud in their undiluted brand of Judaism. He liberated them from their apprehension, awakened them from their apathy and gave them the courage to become the guiding force of American Jewry.

Today, this holds true for orthodox Judaism in America and for Congregation Kol Emes in Richmond.

Letters to Baruch Litvin

The following letters, found among Baruch Litvin's correspondence files, further demonstrate the shift in mood in orthodox synagogues across the United States during the 1960s and 1970s.

KNESSETH ISRAEL CONGREGATION

בית ישראל

3225 Montevallo Road • Mountain Brook, Alabama • Telephone 879-1664

ב״ה

NAHUM M. BENATHEN
RABBI
RESIDENCE 879-1142

April 7, 1964

Mr. Baruch Litvin
57   Lodewych Street
Mount Clemens, Michigan

Dear Mr. Litvin:

As an old friend of your grandson Joseph and a newly
ordained rabbi, I greet you and express my thanks and
appreciation for your book.

Strange as it may seem, we too, at this moment are
engaged in attempting to install the beginning of separate
seating with a partial mechitsa in our synagogue. Your
volume comes at a very opportune time.

Again many thanks.

Very sincerely yours,

Nahum M. Benathen, Rabbi

NMB:lp

KNESETH ISRAEL CONGREGATION

1415 EUCLID AVENUE
MIAMI BEACH 39, FLORIDA
PHONES: JE 8-2741 - 2

RABBI DAVID LEHRFIELD   CANTOR ABRAHAM SEIF

March 24, 1964

Mr. Baruch Litvin
57 Lodewyck
Mount Clemens, Michigan

Dear Mr. Litvin:

I hasten to answer the letters you sent me. With regard to the locking of the fence around my house. You are perfectly correct. We will rectify this in the near future, and I thank you for your kind and generous interest in our behalf.

With regard to the "mechitzah", you have heard a false rumor. Our synagogue is not going to make a "mechitzah" of 40". It is going to be much higher. The problem we have in our synagogue is a simple one. We want the ladies to be able to see the pulpit and the rabbi and the cantor as they daven and preach. We are not yet in the category of Beth Israel to construct a 7 ft. "mechitzah". We called Rabbi Dr. J.B. Soloveitchik long distance, and we asked him what was his opinion for the minimum height of the "mechitzah". He told us 48" or four feet. Our "mechitzah" is going to be 52". It is not going to be the highest in the land, nor is it going to be the lowest in the land, and seeing as we have Rabbi Soloveitchik's approval for a 48" "mechitzah", we are building it 4" higher. We feel that he is a great enough man upon whom we can rely. We also checked upon the heights of "mechitzahs" throughout the country, and we have found that ours will exceed the average height of the standard "mechitzah".

I do hope that this note finds you and your wife enjoying the best of health. Please accept my wishes

To Mr. Baruch Litvin   -2-   March 24, 1964

for a most hearty, happy, and Kosher Passover, and
again I am indebted to you and to your sefer for
the inspiration you have given to me and the countless other rabbis throughout the country. May G-d
reward you with many years of fruitful endeavors in
the vineyard of Judaism.

Sincerely yours,

Rabbi David Lehrfield

DL:ps

YESHIVA COLLEGE

500 West 185th Street / New York, N.Y. 10033 / (212) 568-8400

ב"ה

Tzom Gedaliah
4 October 1970

Dear Mr. Litvin,

I received your letter of the 23rd and do want to thank you for your good wishes for the New Year. Permit me to reciprocate and to wish you a year of good health and much happiness with peace for all Israel.

As a matter of fact, Mr. Litvin, you were very much in my mind because of the following incident--a maaseh shehoyoh, as they say--that occurred on the first day of Rosh Hashonah, a mere three days ago. For the past twenty years I have been a Ba'al Tefilah during the Yomim Noraim in various shuls. This year I was in Beth Jacob Congregation of Astoria (Queens), N. Y. When I was interviewed for the position I inquired, as I always do, whether the shul is a kosher shul with a mechizah. I was assured that it was and was given the name of the Orthodox rabbi in the shul, Solomon Rybak, who would vouch for it. On the first day of Rosh Hashonah four women insisted on sitting on seats outside the mechizah. Rabbi Rybak, who had been assured that the mechizah would not be violated, arose before the reading of the Torah and stated that if he would be forced to leave the shul, and I would have left with him, if the women did not retreat behind the mechizah. It took several minutes before the women left. I thought of your wonderful work in Mount Clemens and of your excellent volume on the <u>Sanctity of the Synagogue</u> in which you report at some length on a case in Pennsylvania where a chazan was paid his fee because the congregation failed to live up to its implicit agreement, thus making it impossible for him to daven there.

I am, of course, flattered, Mr. Litvin, that you still remember what I said in Miami Beach four a half years ago about the two hundred thousand Jews of Alexandria. You may be interested in reading my article, "The Orthodoxy of the Jews in Hellenistic Egypt," which appeared in <u>Jewish Social Studies,</u> volume 22 (October, 1960), pp. 215-237.

All good wishes to you, Mr. Litvin.

Sincerely,

Louis H. Feldman

בעזהשי"ת

CONGREGATION BETH JACOB

DR. EMANUEL FELDMAN, Rabbi

1855   LA VISTA   ROAD
Atlanta, Georgia 30329   (404) 633-0551

HERBERT J. COHEN   Ed. Dir. & Asst. Rabbi
BENJAMIN STIEFEL   Chazzan
FRED GLUSMAN   Exec. Dir.

July 14, 1972

Mr. Baruch Litvin
57 Lodewyck
Mt. Clemens, Michigan

Dear Mr. Litvin,

Thank you for your letter of June 26th. I
was away for two weeks in Russia and found your
letter upon my return.

It was good of you to write me about my
article, "The Inscrutable Israeli." I deeply
appreciate your comments, since they come from
a person as learned and as knowledgeable as
you.

As a man who has fought the lonely battle for
mechitzah in your community and throughout the
country, you will be gratified, I know, to learn
that we in our congregation have raised the mechitzah by some eight inches this year. I know that
were it not for the lonely and courageous battle
fought by you against all odds a decade and more
ago, there would be no modern synagogues in this
country today with a vestige of this hallowed
aspect of a Shul. Your work was certainly not in
vain.

I am enclosing for your perusal two recent
articles of mine which you might find of interest.

Sincerely yours,

Rabbi Emanuel Feldman

EF:sh

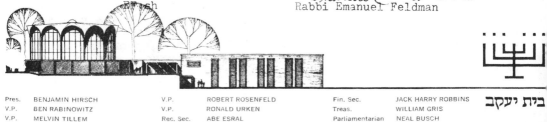

Pres.	BENJAMIN HIRSCH	V.P.	ROBERT ROSENFELD	Fin. Sec.	JACK HARRY ROBBINS	בית יעקב
V.P.	BEN RABINOWITZ	V.P.	RONALD URKEN	Treas.	WILLIAM GRIS	
V.P.	MELVIN TILLEM	Rec. Sec.	ABE ESRAL	Parliamentarian	NEAL BUSCH	
			MRS. TILLIE SHAPIRO, Honorary Treasurer			

Don

397-3457

The Unsuccessful Stories

Most of the stories related to the editor and collected for the third edition of this volume had a successful outcome. Yet there still remained certain elements which continued to resist the developing groundswell toward acceptance of the basic standard that a truly orthodox synagogue must have a *mechitzah*. Unfortunately, as the next three stories illustrate, not all *mechitzah* struggles since the historic court decision have ended successfully.

1. Most disappointing of the unsuccessful stories is, sadly, that of Mount Clemens, itself. The Jewish community there never made its peace with Baruch Litvin. For forcing them to continue to have a *mechitzah* in their synagogue, he was consciously ignored by all synagogue members. Except for his family, no member socialized with him after the court battle. As long as he was physically able, Mr. Litvin attended services daily, sitting in the corner of the last pew. Invariably, he sat alone, unless a son or grandson joined him.

Within a few months of his death, the synagogue was sold to the city of Mount Clemens. It was then torn down to make way for a senior citizen's housing development. The congregation was given another piece of property nearby on which to build a new synagogue. There were those who tried their best to convince the board of trustees to build the new synagogue with a *mechitzah*—but to no avail.

Baruch Litvin did not succeed in maintaining the sanctity of *his* synagogue after his passing. However, as most of the stories in this third edition attest, he did succeed in awakening communities across the nation to restoring the sanctity of their synagogues.

2. In the 1950s, three synagogues in Houston, Texas, with orthodox affiliations merged. There was no *mechitzah* in

the new synagogue they built. The thought at that time was that the synagogue could better compete for members if there were no *mechitzah*.

In the late 1960s, a new principal, Rabbi Nachum Zvi Josephy, was engaged by the local Hebrew day school. He made it a condition of his accepting the position that a *minyan* with a *mechitzah* be established in the synagogue separately from the main sanctuary *minyan*, which still did not have a *mechitzah*. The *mechitzah minyan* was to begin services at 7:30 A.M. and thus not be competitive with the *minyan* in the main sanctuary.

Over the next few years, this early *minyan* attracted some new members who were more committed to orthodoxy. On *Yom Kippur* in 1975, Rabbi Kenneth Hain, then the synagogue's rabbi, spoke about the *mechitzah* issue from the pulpit, stating that it was about time to make one *minyan* and discontinue the two separate services. He lobbied intensively for about six months to obtain the two-thirds vote required for such a structural change. In the final vote, the *mechitzah* advocates were six votes short of the two-thirds needed.

The status quo continued until 1980, when the issue of a *mechitzah* for the main sanctuary was brought up again by the more-committed laymen of what came to be known as the "side *minyan*." The rabbi did not feel that the time was yet right to wage a fight on this particular issue. However, the lay members felt they had been patient long enough. Saul Quinn, a new member of the congregation, called a friend in New York to ask where he could obtain materials to help him convince the other members of the board of the importance of a *mechitzah*. The friend recalled the book *The Sanctity of the Synagogue*. Since the book was out of print he was reluctant to part with his copy. He photocopied articles by several rabbis from the book, including those of Rav Moshe Fein-

452

stein, Rav Aaron Kotler and (*Y'L*) Rav J. B. Soloveitchik, and forwarded them to Houston.

The articles were first passed among the members of the side *minyan*, helping to strengthen the resolve of these congregants. Then the articles were circulated among the members who regularly attended services in the main sanctuary. It created quite a lively debate among the members and culminated in a proposal by one of the members of the board of directors, Dr. Max Mintz, to adopt an amendment to the constitution of the synagogue allowing for the installation of a *mechitzah* when requested by a family celebrating a Bar Mitzvah in the main sanctuary.

There was much heated discussion at the meeting but the vote was postponed on a technicality. The *mechitzah* advocates utilized this additional time to persuade more board members toward their point of view so that when the vote was taken about a month later, the amendment passed by one vote! The first request for a *mechitzah* for a Bar Mitzvah came a few months following the successful vote. The request was honored despite vocal complaints from several members.

In 1986, the synagogue still has its *minyan*, its side *minyan* and the occasional requests for a *mechitzah* in the main sanctuary for Bar Mitzvah celebrants.

3. There was another unsuccessful *mechitzah* struggle that must be related. [Names have been omitted per request.] Although the results weren't positive for the specific synagogue involved, they were positive for the future of orthodoxy.

In the mid-1960s, a midwestern non-*mechitzah* synagogue with orthodox affiliations, decided to build a new sanctuary. The rabbi hoped that this might be the opportune time to install a *mechitzah*. He made arrangements with the architect, who was also orthodox, to build the new synagogue

453

with a *mechitzah* without obtaining prior approval from the Board of Directors of the synagogue. Of course, there was quite a furor when this was discovered. The non-permanent part of the *mechitzah* was removed as soon as it was set up. However, the rabbi and the orthodox architect had built a permanent separation into the design for the structure, but most of the congregants continued to sit together during services. The synagogue, however, maintained its identification as an orthodox synagogue.

A traditional day school with more than five hundred students was housed in this synagogue. The principal at the time was an orthodox rabbi who declined to attend services in the synagogue because it was lacking a *mechitzah*. As principal, he used his influence to encourage the older students to participate in Yeshiva University outreach seminars which were held periodically in the area. As a direct result of these seminars, about one hundred youngsters organized a *minyan* in another section of the synagogue building. This *minyan* had a *mechitzah* from the first day of its creation.

From 1969 to 1971, this *minyan* continued without the board members being aware of the *mechitzah*. When they did find out, the principal was called in and asked to explain why he had set up the *minyan* without their approval. The principal explained that the teenagers themselves organized and maintained the *minyan*. Whereupon a board meeting was called to discuss the issue. Before the meeting, the teenagers formed a telephone squad and called all of the members of the board of directors, hoping to ensure a positive vote for continuation of their *mechitzah minyan*.

Discussions were heated at the meeting. At one point, the teenagers informed the board that if it wouldn't allow their *minyan* to continue with a *mechitzah*, they would go to the media with the story. The board backed down and agreed to allow the *minyan* to continue. It did continue—but not for long.

The rabbi and the principal both accepted positions in other orthodox institutions where *mechitzah* was not a debatable issue. Shortly after their departure, the *mechitzah* was dismantled, and not long after that, the *minyan* itself disbanded. Most of the teenagers left the congregation and began to attend services at a local Young Israel *minyan*. While the courage and strength of these youngsters was not enough to restore the sanctity of this synagogue, their perseverance and fortitude bode well for the future of orthodox Judaism.

Rethinking the Mechitzah
BY RABBI PINCHAS STOLPER

For most orthodox Jews, the days when we battled over the *mechitzah* in the synagogue are a dim memory. Our synagogues, with few exceptions, have long resolved this issue. We are now at the point where the overwhelming majority of people who regularly attend synagogues insist there be a *mechitzah* or they just won't walk in.

This is more and more true of young people. Wherever they attend synagogues, they are generally to be found in orthodox, *mechitzah* congregations.

Furthermore, it is extremely difficult to find a serious graduate of any orthodox rabbinical seminary who, upon graduation, is prepared to accept the pulpit of a non-*mechitzah* congregation. And in those instances where a rabbi is prevailed upon to accept such a position, it is usually on the promise that the membership is leaning towards, or is amenable to, a *mechitzah*. If the rabbi does not succeed after a year or two, chances are that he will seek and find a *mechitzah* congregation elsewhere.

But what about the congregation that then remains without a *mechitzah*? Many could be preserved for orthodoxy and countless families would thereby remain within the *Torah* community—were more of an effort made to show concern for their spiritual welfare, the key to which, possibly unbeknown to these congregations, is very much dependent on the status of the *mechitzah*. I have undertaken to review some of the rationales for *mechitzah* observance so that those of us who have the opportunity to influence the holdout congregations may be better informed.

1. A HOLY NATION

The goal of Jewish life is to transform the Jewish people into a "kingdom of priests and a holy nation" (Exodus 19:6). The synagogue is built with a separation between the men's and women's sections because the synagogue is that one place where we make our strongest attempt to live up to the ideal of "a holy people you shall be to Me" (Exodus 22:30). After all, the synagogue is G-d's house, a place for serious thought and prayer, a place where we most intensely concentrate on our relationship with G-d and on the serious business of prayer. The synagogue is not a place for socializing, conversation, or any form of interaction between the sexes.

2. GUESTS IN G-D'S HOUSE

If the synagogue is G-d's house, whether or not each and every one of us observes all of His laws carefully and meticulously in each and every instance, there should be general agreement that at least in His house, His rules and laws are to be supreme. But if we banish Him from His house, if we decide that *we* will decide on the proper arrangement of the

456

furniture, then it is no longer G-d's house—it becomes a house in which the mind and will of man reign supreme.

Let's put it a bit differently. If I were a guest in your home, you would treat me with respect and deference. You would set the table with your best cloth, your best silver, your best china. But what if—while I was sitting in your living room, waiting for you to invite me to the meal you had meticulously and carefully prepared—I decided that I did not fancy the arrangement of your furniture and proceeded to unilaterally and arbitrarily rearrange it, putting the sofa over there, the chair somewhere else. I think you would forget about the meal and swiftly escort me to the nearest door. Once I began rearranging the furniture in your house, I ceased to be the guest and became the master.

3. WORKING AT PRAYER

Prayer is neither responsive reading, the lyric entertainment of the cantor, nor the mumbling of words without meaning. Our rabbis call prayer *avodah she-balev,* the worship of G-d with the heart. But the word *avodah* literally means work and that's what prayer is really all about.

It's no secret that the *yaitzer hara* can, for some, be strongest in the synagogue, the one place where we would hope these thoughts would not intrude. The goal of prayer is *kavanah,* concentration, but the mind may wander—especially if we create conditions which promote such wanderings. Under such circumstances, the synagogue is no longer the house of G-d but a social hall.

Our rabbis tell us that the pious of their day, the *Chassidim Harishonim,* would pause in their daily pursuits for one full hour prior to praying in order to place themselves in the proper frame of mind. So much more must we—whose lives are not saturated with *Torah* and the fear of Heaven—do

457

everything possible to create an environment where *kavanah* is attainable.

The worst deception is self-deception. Anyone who deceives himself into thinking that true prayer can exist in an environment where men and women enjoy each other's company is practicing such self-deception. Such a person is either dishonest, or probably has no idea what serious prayer truly involves.

No one is so naive as to think that during the past decades, *mechitzot* were removed from American synagogues because of religious, theological, or philosophical reasons. We are all aware of the fact that the causes were social, sociological, generational—having to do with the fact that in the minds of first generation American Jews, the synagogue with a *mechitzah* was not quite American, and did not quite fit into their great desire to become Americanized as quickly as possible. Still, things that were done in the synagogue for sociological reasons do have religious implications. But now that the initial sociological motivation no longer pertains, the time has come to give weight to the religious consequences of the removal of the *mechitzah*.

A View from the Midwest
BY RABBI OSCAR Z. FASMAN

Mr. Baruch Litvin of Mount Clemens, Michigan, was one of the most remarkable men I ever met. His battle on behalf of the sanctity of the synagogue, particularly his insistence upon a *mechitzah* to separate women from men during synagogue services, should be viewed in light of the conditions of the Jewish communities not located along the eastern seaboard of the United States. That section of the country had a strong and populous element of dedicated orthodox Jews who would not countenance any departure from age-old traditions. In most of the other parts of America, however, the Reform Jewish movement was taking control of Jewish society, and many among the concerned orthodox minority sought to stem the tide by making a few concessions to what was regarded as the modern, or the American, way of life.

Specifically, it was hoped that by conceding on the issue of family seating in the synagogue, traditionalists would be able to resist encroachment on numerous other important items, such as organ music, gentile choirs, and emasculated prayer books. In addition, the orthodox leaders, while concededly compromising on a major *halachic* issue, found spiritual refuge in the fact that additional matters of great significance would not be forsaken, for example, *kashruth,* remarriage without a proper Jewish divorce, vehicular travel, smoking, and writing on the Sabbath, trespasses that Reform Judaism tolerated.

Thus, it happened that in large parts of this country, congregations founded by dietary loyalists, Sabbath observers, and daily wearers of *tephilin* were persuaded to remove the *mechitzah*. While the motivation of the sincere people was, at that time, understandable, it is certainly debatable whether any successes vis-à-vis Reform resulted. Furthermore, it is doubtful whether such successes, if any, outweighed the harm done by the initial breach of tradition and whether it did not instead lead to further retreat from the standards and traditions.

To Baruch Litvin, there was no time for endless debate. To him, the situation did not warrant compromise. Consequently, he made personal sacrifices, far beyond the ordinary, to prevent a synagogue with a *mechitzah* from removing it. He launched an amazing one-man campaign to educate those who were active in synagogues without a *mechitzah* to establish

459

one. His philosophy was simple: individual Jews may break away from one or more commandments because individuals have their weaknesses, but the public religious practice must function at the highest level.

Indeed for a number of years, before the festival of *Shavuoth,* he would write me to request that I send him the interpretation of my sainted teacher Rabbi Saul Silber on the two forms of cantillation utilized in reading the Ten Commandments; the standard chant based on notes appearing below the printed Hebrew letters and the special chant based on the notes appearing above the printed Hebrew letters. Rabbi Silber explained that the chant based on the lower notes which is reserved for personal or private reading, indicates breaks for paragraphs and sentences, but for public readings, the chant is the one based on the upper notes which connects all the paragraphs and sentences of the Ten Commandments into a single unit. Similarly, in their own private lives, people may think of themselves as unequal to the fulfillment of all the commandments and unfortunately neglect some. But the community carries the sacred responsibility of preserving in its entirety the total uninterrupted glory of all the essences of our faith. Baruch Litvin cherished this sermon all his days and devotedly preached its message.

In the year 1986, Baruch Litvin would have rejoiced to witness the creation of *mechitzah* congregations in suburbs, in new urban districts, and in small towns that had not seen a *mechitzah* in three generations. Perhaps, the most amazing aspect of this development is the cast of characters responsible for these innovations: scientists, college faculty members, and M.B.A.s from distinguished centers of academia. Moreover, many congregations that have functioned for years with family seating have yielded to the demands of younger members to allow them to worship in a separate section of the synagogue building where a *mechitzah* has been erected.

460

Indeed, in one of the largest non-*mechitzah* congregations in the Midwest, the "college crowd" organized a *mechitzah* service more than six years ago, attended by only about a dozen men. Eventually, attendance at this supposedly auxiliary service grew larger than the attendance at the main sanctuary service. The founding rabbi predicted to his membership that a *mechitzah* in the main sanctuary is inevitable.

On high, Baruch Litvin must be smiling!

A Canadian Success Story
Montreal, Canada

Congregation Chevra Kadisha–B'nai Jacob was formed by the merger of two very traditional synagogues with histories of almost 100 years each. In April, 1957, it was resolved, unanimously, to install a *mechitzah*. For reasons which are still unclear, it never was installed.

The congregation, which is now the largest orthodox synagogue in Montreal was finally moved to install the *mechitzah* under its present leadership, Rabbi Benjamin Hauer and the president, Meyer Samuels. Rabbi Hauer, who has been rabbi at Chevra Kadisha–B'nai Jacob since 1972, drew on the support of Jewish organizations in Montreal, in Canada, and in the United States.

Men and women have always sat separately at Chevra Kadisha–B'nai Jacob, but there has never been an actual physical *mechitzah*. *Halachah* requires a *mechitzah* in addition to separate seating to preclude physical contact between men and women during services.

Rabbi Hauer prodded the congregation to take this final step in 1983. In April of that year, the seven officers voted unanimously to build the *mechitzah*. The executive board then approved the same by a vote of 11–5 (there were 2 abstentions and 6 members were absent). Significant opposition arose among the membership and a petition signed by more than 200 members demanded a general meeting and a vote on the issue.

A meeting was scheduled for June 27, 1983. Prior to the meeting, seminars and discussion groups were organized to allow for a full discussion of the issues involved. Six days before the scheduled general membership meeting, events took an unexpected but conclusive turn. In a letter dated June

462

21, 1983, Mr. Samuels cancelled the scheduled general membership meeting.

In the letter, Mr. Samuels explained that based on consultations with legal counsel and with Rabbi Pinchas Hirschprung, it was determined "that to hold a vote questioning religious principles would be illegal." The letter pointed out that the bylaws prohibit the membership from "do(ing) . . . or suffer(ing) an act which is contrary to the practice or principles of Orthodox Judaism."

Consequently, since Orthodox ritual makes a *mechitzah* imperative, it would be improper to vote on a matter which the congregation's Incorporating Act mandates—and the act does mandate adherence to principles of Orthodox Judaism.

Thus, all that was left to decide was the esthetic nature of the *mechitzah,* within the legal requirements of a height of about four feet. A committee was appointed to determine the type of *mechitzah* to be installed.

Congratulatory telegrams were received from leading rabbis in Canada and the United States. The Rabbinical Council of Canada placed an ad in the *Montreal Gazette* congratulating the membership and Rabbi Hauer for their courageous and historic act.

REMINDER

To:

MEMBERS OF THE CONGREGATION

CHEVRA KADISHA - B'NAI JACOB

●

SPECIAL GENERAL MEETING

RE: MECHIZA

JUNE 27, 1983 — 8:00 P.M.

IN THE COMMUNITY HALL

●

PLEASE COME AND EXERCISE

YOUR RIGHT TO

VOTE NO

DIANE L. TESSLER
AND CONCERNED CONGREGANTS

YOU ARE CORDIALLY INVITED!!!

to an

A D U L T   E D U C A T I O N   E V E N T

in

CONGREGATION CHEVRA KADISHA-B'NAI JACOB

WEDNESDAY, JUNE 22, 1983 at 2:00 P.M.

in the Community Hall

when

MRS. NORMA JOSEPH

Lecturer at Concordia University

will discuss

A FEMINIST VIEW OF THE MECHITZA

Followed by light refreshments

RABBI BENJAMIN HAUER

Three East Coast Success Stories

Congregation Bikur Cholim–
Shevet Achim
New Haven, Connecticut
BY RABBI DAVID AVIGDOR

In 1884, a small number of New Haven Jews, 22 in all, seceded from a local established synagogue because of religious doctrinal differences. These 22 people then founded Congregation Bikur Cholim Bnai Avraham, which erected its first building in 1889.

The synagogue was built in the European architectural tradition which required women to walk up two flights of stairs to a horseshoe-shaped balcony that extended over the main sanctuary below. Bikur Cholim's membership consisted largely of *Misnagdim*.

Also during this period, early in the 1890s, many Chassidic followers of the Lubavitcher *Rebbi* had settled in New Haven and conducted their own services in a private home. In 1898, they established their own congregation and named it Congregation Sheveth Achim Anshei Lubavitch. Their synagogue also had the traditional balcony to serve as the women's section.

Both the Bikur Cholim and the Sheveth Achim synagogues flourished from the turn of the century on through the late 1940s. In the autumn of 1949, the two groups agreed to merge into one synagogue, which they named Congregation Bikur Cholim–Shevet Achim. The new congregation purchased a Christian Science Church and converted it into the beautiful synagogue still in use at the present time.

The seating arrangements in the new sanctuary remained unchanged from what it had been as a church. Twenty long benches filled the center of the synagogue flanked on both sides by two wide aisles. Two additional twenty row sections of shorter benches bordered the periphery of the large sanctuary.

Structurally, the synagogue was incapable of supporting a balcony and so a different method of separating men and women had to be designed. The membership opted for what seemed simple and natural, to seat the men in the center pews and women in the side benches of the sanctuary. Ever since, men and women have sat separately but without an actual physical partition between them. The separation thus consisted of nothing more than an aisle four feet wide, and the membership deemed that sufficient.

The synagogue prospered in the 50s and 60s. In the early 70s, the neighborhood changed, and membership and attendance began to decline. Other orthodox congregations located in different parts of the city began attracting a large number of new members while the membership of Bikur Cholim dwindled. Most of the new young orthodox families moving into the New Haven area chose to attend services elsewhere—not at Bikur Cholim–Shevet Achim. They hesitated to join Bikur Cholim–Shevet Achim because it lacked the actual physical partition of a traditional *mechitzah*. This was a defect that truly traditional couples were unwilling to overlook.

In June of 1980, as a young orthodox rabbi, I assumed the position of spiritual leader of this congregation. The membership expected their young and vibrant rabbi to draw young people to the synagogue. Aware of the deficiency of the *mechitzah*—its absence—I accepted the position only after much discussion with my father, Rabbi Isaac C. Avigdor of West Hartford, Connecticut, my rabbis, and my teachers.

During my first three years as rabbi, many meetings were held to discuss the *mechitzah* issue. Many members of the congregation were violently opposed to the erection of a traditional *mechitzah*. Those who were in favor of the change were, however, unwilling to fight for it for fear of losing those precious few members of the congregation who were keeping the synagogue alive. The synagogue thus found itself in a "Catch-22" situation. Fortunately, however, a solution was found.

In August, 1983, with the synagogue's centennial approaching, Dr. David Fischer, a prominent physician in the city of New Haven, was elected to serve as president of the congregation for 1984. Dr. Fischer was respected by all as an individual who brought prestige and honor to the synagogue. He realized that the planned centennial celebration provided what was possibly the last opportunity for increasing attendance and interest in the congregation. Dr. Fischer was also aware that for three years, I had met and communicated with many families in the community in an effort to stem the decline in the synagogue's membership. Support for construction of a *mechitzah* was now growing. There were even pledges of financial and moral support from some members if the synagogue decided to make the change.

In October of 1983, I invited a group of people to my home to meet with Dr. Fischer. Seventeen young married men attended and expressed their frank opinions about Bikur Cholim's seating arrangement. Dr. Fischer, in turn, questioned them about their backgrounds, sincerity, and standing in the community. It became clear that if the synagogue would install a traditional *mechitzah*, it would gain new members and daily parishioners.

After weeks of planning and consultation, Dr. Fischer

468

called a preliminary meeting of the board of directors for November 13, 1983. During this meeting, the recent meeting in my home was reviewed and the issues were vigorously debated. I also advised the board of the *halachic* standards. It was decided to send a letter to the entire membership, soliciting their feelings and comments on the subject. The responses were encouraging but inconclusive.

Dr. Fischer then called for a meeting of the full board of directors to decide if a permanent *mechitzah* should be installed in the synagogue. This special meeting was held in the main sanctuary on December 11, 1983. It was well attended by board members, as well as by the general membership. The meeting lasted nearly two hours and included a passionate plea made by Dr. Fischer that some action be taken so that he not be the last president of the congregation.

For the record, it is worth noting some of the major points raised at the meeting in opposition to installing a permanent *mechitzah:*

1. That the synagogue has very few "truly orthodox" members and that it would be best to make the congregation totally Conservative.
2. That those individuals who promised support for the synagogue were only doing so for the *mitzvah* of the matter but would not really attend.
3. That the *mechitzah* would cost $5,000.00 to install and that this was more than the synagogue could afford.
4. That the proposed *mechitzah* would not be sufficient because only a balcony is a true separation.
5. That once the *mechitzah* would be built and new religious families began attending the services, other demands and restrictions would be placed on the founding members of the congregation who were not as religious.

469

6. That this issue should not be raised during the centennial celebration of the congregation.
7. That the *mechitzah* issue was a devisive one and would hurt the membership if those opposed left the synagogue.
8. That the proposed change would have the effect of taking members away from other synagogues.

The 26 qualified Board members present then voted 19 in favor and 7 opposed. However, it was agreed that because the issue was so important, it should be presented to the general membership for their vote. The general membership met on December 18, 1983, and voted 34 in favor and 9 opposed. The recommendation of the board of directors to erect a partition was thus confirmed.

Reaction in the community was quick and decisive. The decision was hailed as a reaffirmation and return to traditional orthodox Judaism. Letters of congratulations were received from the Union of Orthodox Jewish Congregations of America, the Rabbinical Council of America, the Lubavitch movement as well as from many members of local and state rabbinates. The story appeared as a news item in the *Jewish Press,* the *Algemeiner Journal* and the *Forward* newspapers.

The actual partition was completed in February, 1984, and there was overwhelming agreement that it added to the beauty of the synagogue. On March 3, 1984, on the occasion of the *Shabbat* of *Parshat Hachodesh* the new *mechitzah* was dedicated at a special service attended by people from throughout the community.

The congregation's leadership is to be commended. They handled this difficult issue well. With their diplomacy, fairness and with the help of G-d, there was no loss of members. This historic event is further evidence that young orthodox Jewish families in the United States and abroad, seek and want

470

Judaism as practiced by their grandparents and great-grand-parents. They are looking for a return to tradition!

Congregation Havurat Israel
Forest Hills, New York

BY RABBI DAVID L. ALGAZE

It was surely more than a modicum of arrogance and spiritual alienation that led me to accept a position as assistant rabbi at a prominent Conservative congregation in New York. My family background is traditional. I studied under the tutelage of orthodox rabbis, and received my rabbinic ordination from a distinguished Sephardic *talmid chacham*. It did not take long for me to realize that I did not belong. I had placed myself in a predicament from which I was not to extricate myself without difficulty.

Without warning or planning, events confirmed my belated realization. The "young married" group of the synagogue dissolved. Apathy and boredom had taken their toll and people stopped participating. The leaders of the group, two couples, met with me at my home. They talked about their feeling of emptiness regarding synagogue activities. They had had enough bowling, picnics, and garage sales. They sought something more lasting and more meaningful. They wanted to learn about Judaism . . . about their heritage.

I listened to their stories and was overcome with joy. The prospect of having willing and dedicated students gave me great happiness. I responded eagerly, declaring that I would be delighted to teach and lead such an interested and concerned group.

We organized a group of families to study together on a weekly basis. A *havurah* was started. The first meetings of the *havurah* were dedicated to discussions of *Shabbat*. Each person undertook to examine a different aspect of the meaning of *Shabbat* and, on each consecutive week, made his or her presentation.

At the end of this first series of meetings, several families undertook full observance of *Shabbat*. Apparently, they had been touched by the power of *halachah* as a guide to life. They had learned the rituals and experienced *Shabbat* meals together. A strong bond had developed among the families.

The excitement and warm feelings generated by these meetings became known to other young couples. Soon others were interested in forming similar groups. In the course of a few months, this *havurah* soon spawned several more *Havurot*.

During the summer and early fall of 1980, the issues that were troubling the Conservative movement as a whole, such as participation of women in services and ordination of women rabbis, came to the fore in our synagogue. The matters were discussed at the *havurot* meetings, and everyone preferred the traditional stance. I had long ago made it clear that I disapproved of these changes. But in January, 1981, at a difficult and unfriendly board meeting, the directors of the synagogue voted to allow women, on certain occasions, to have *aliyot* to the *Torah*. *Havurah* members were vociferous and passionate in their opposition.

For members of the *Havurot,* and for myself, it was impossible to continue in that synagogue. After a few weeks of consultation and dialogue, a group of friends helped me organize an exodus.

In mid-February of 1981, we organized a separate *minyan* in the social hall of the Sephardic synagogue across the street from our synagogue. For Purim, we used the social hall of a

472

synagogue in a neighboring community, and with some extensive publicity, over 400 people attended our Purim celebration and *Megillah* reading. It was an unforgettable evening. Our *minyan* became the talk of the community. The enthusiasm grew by the day.

Soon enough, reality dawned. At a crucial meeting, we decided that our synagogue should follow halachic guidelines; precisely the kind of control and discipline that had not existed in the congregation we had left. Initially, we avoided the word "orthodox" and settled on the more neutral label of "traditional."

However, upon realizing that *halachah* required the presence of a physical structure to separate men from women during services, there was great surprise, much doubt, and even anger. This was discussed at length, and it was agreed that the matter should be accorded further study and reflection. Everyone conceded that the matter would have to evolve gradually and gently.

And so it happened. Separate seating gradually was introduced. From the outset, there was a small section reserved for men, a small section for women, and a larger section reserved for mixed seating. The expectation was that with more time and further study, the separate seating areas would grow until ultimately there would be no mixed seating at all.

Our first High Holy Days services were a great success. We rented one of the big movie complexes in Forest Hills. Over 600 people attended. With a giant screen in the background and the aroma of popcorn in the air, we welcomed the year 5742 with deep emotion and gratitude to the Almighty.

With the successful High Holiday season behind us, the struggle of a newly formed synagogue resumed. I counseled consideration of all the issues in dispute including the matter of the *mechitzah* and separate seating. Toward this end, we scheduled a series of lectures titled "The Sanctity of the

Synagogue." The lectures, which I conducted, were held in the beginning of December, 1981.

I had much help in preparing for the lectures. The words I used were right from Baruch Litvin's book, whose title I had used to name my lecture series. The statements, articles, and pronouncements in his book made me feel as if all of those great rabbis who contributed to *The Sanctity of the Synagogue* were sitting in my living room at night holding my hand, strengthening me, supporting me, and not allowing me to falter. I had felt so alone, but Litvin's book showed me that the great Jewish leaders of the day were with me.

In the opening lecture, after describing the historical background of the *mechitzah,* the philosophy behind it, and the laws concerning the sanctity of the synagogue, I quoted a long passage from Rabbi Kook. In this passage, Rabbi Kook, best known for the gentleness of his soul and the profound affection he had for all Jews, declared that it was forbidden to enter a synagogue that had no *mechitzah,* (*supra,* page 99). "*Forbidden!*" The severity of the statement, its inflexible nature, brought tears to my eyes, and I could not continue my speech. It was a highly tense and emotional moment. It was then that I knew that a *mechitzah* would have to be installed in the synagogue within a short time.

After the lecture and at numerous subsequent meetings, many questions were asked but few minds were changed. At the time, there was no one in the congregation who held orthodox views and who could not have tolerated the continuance of the status quo somewhat longer. Furthermore, there was a vocal minority that held steadfastly to a desire to remain with the Conservative philosophy, if not the movement, and who, for personal reasons, had a great distaste for orthodoxy. The erection of a *mechitzah,* they knew, would constitute the irrevocable step in the transformation of our synagogue to one

474

that is orthodox. This, they vehemently opposed. They utilized every possible tactic to sway me or to defeat me.

Fortunately, there was a third group within the congregation and this group proved to be the majority. This group felt that I was their teacher. If they had left a Conservative congregation, it was to learn Judaism from me in the manner and method which I considered most genuine. Many of them were impressed by the contents of the lectures. But, essentially, they supported my decision out of their trust in my sincerity as a teacher of Judaism.

Between the lectures, I held several private meetings with people, particularly women, who had trouble understanding the concept of separate seating. I learned a great deal from these meetings. The basic objection to the *mechitzah* was, however, not only a feminist protest, but also an unwillingness to accept the binding force of religious law. To live in a world where *halachah* is sovereign and where our destinies and actions are shaped by a legal system that is authoritative—these are alien concepts to the contemporary mind, especially one educated in the liberal branches of Judaism.

After the last lecture, the president, who until this matter arose had been one of my closest friends, asked me to hold a board meeting. The meeting of officers took place in my home. I informed the officers that commencing on the following *Shabbat* we would have to have separate seating and a *mechitzah* in place. That turned out to be *Shabbat Hanukah* (December 26, 1981).

It was quite fitting that we were removing vestiges of assimilation in the modern synagogue concomitantly with the celebration of the heroic acts of the Hasmoneans against the Greek assimilation of their times. As in the days of the Maccabees, we too, were rededicating our synagogue with full reverence for the traditions of our ancestors.

475

It was a cold and gray morning and many people had opted not to come on this first *Shabbat* with a *mechitzah* in place. We were all equally unhappy. No one had wanted to create dissension. We all wanted to love one another. But there were many who realized that love for *Torah* and Jewish law must remain supreme. These people attended that morning and continued to build the synagogue. There were a few who never again attended. The president of the congregation, and his family as well, also did not show up that morning. I grieved for them. In my heart I wished them well, though pained by the thought that I would not be their teacher any longer. They, too, were never to come back.

But the synagogue has prospered. Today, we are housed in our own building, purchased in February of 1982. The synagogue counts over 2,000 families as members. Many more attend our programs and courses. Our adult education courses, our outreach programs, and our youth activities have become well known throughout the city. The synagogue's activities have been featured in a Sunday edition of the *New York Times*.

The synagogue is now an active member of the Union of Orthodox Jewish Congregations of America (U.O.J.C.A.) and its members are active in all aspects of orthodox Jewish life in the community as well as in national projects of the U.O.J.C.A. and its youth division, National Conference of Synagogue Youth (N.C.S.Y.). We rejoice at what has been the happy result of our spiritual adventure.

476

Lincoln Square Synagogue
BY RABBI SHLOMO RISKIN

The story begins in 1963, the year in which I received *semicha* from Yeshiva University. I had just married and had already accepted a position to teach at the James Striar School of Yeshiva University, commencing in September. I had given little thought to entering the pulpit rabbinate. Rather, I was much more interested in pursuing a career in Academia. However, I had told Yeshiva's administration that in appreciation for what the institution had done for me over the years, I would be willing to do public lecturing for Yeshiva. As soon as the school year began, I was asked by the Community Services Division of Yeshiva University to address a group of people who were just beginning a synagogue in the newly developed West Side of Manhattan.

The area had previously been known as "Hell's Kitchen," and served as the backdrop for "West Side Story," the fabled play and movie. The new Lincoln Center for the Performing Arts was now the rage of the West Side. A very clever builder, Harry Zeckendorf, erected luxury apartment houses and presto—the neighborhood was experiencing a revival. It was drawing people who were upper middle class, fairly affluent, rather intellectual, and not especially oriented to religious observance.

Nevertheless, a group of 10–15 families did band together to establish a synagogue for the High Holidays utilizing facilities rented in the Esplanade Hotel on West End Avenue and 74th Street. A charter was drawn up and the synagogue was named the Lincoln Square Conservative Synagogue.

For the High Holidays of 1963, Lincoln Square enlisted the help of the Jewish Theological Seminary of America. The Seminary referred a Rabbi Geffen who served as Rabbi for

Rosh Hoshana and *Yom Kippur*. After very successful services attended by approximately 100 worshippers, Geffen
informed the membership that he would be willing to again
serve as rabbi for next year's High Holiday services but his
fee would have to be increased by one thousand dollars. To
this, the people of Lincoln Square were reluctant to agree. In
addition, they were somewhat miffed that Geffen wouldn't be
able to attend and conduct *Shabbat* services on a regular basis
throughout the year.

One of the members suggested that perhaps Yeshiva
University would send a Rabbi. Lincoln Square would still
remain a conservative synagogue and continue to have mixed
seating, but a Yeshiva University Rabbi would likely cost less
money. There was, however, much opposition to this proposal. Most of the membership didn't want a Rabbi who was
orthodox. To them, the word orthodoxy was anathema. Many
of them were actually inclined toward Reform Judaism and
did not follow *halachah* on matters such as *Shabbat* or other
rituals observed by orthodox Jews. Nevertheless, an approach was made to Yeshiva University and I was sent to
pave the way—to show them that orthodoxy is not medieval.

It was understood by Yeshiva University that I wasn't
interested in being the Rabbi of this burgeoning group, that I
certainly wouldn't go into a synagogue which didn't have a
mechitzah and that I wasn't interested in the pulpit rabbinate.
However, I certainly hoped I could be a fitting salesman for
Yeshiva University as an institution of *Torah* learning as well
as for orthodox Judaism.

The lecture was held at the home of Sidney Trompeter,
the vice-president. The president, Danny Mars, was unaltera-
bly opposed to an address by an orthodox Rabbi. The session
lasted nearly three hours. When it ended, I was asked to be
the Rabbi for *Rosh Hoshana* and *Yom Kippur*. I explained to
them that I was merely speaking on behalf of Yeshiva Univer-

sity and that I had little interest in becoming a pulpit rabbi. Furthermore, I certainly would not serve in a synagogue in which there was no separate seating. However, the more I said no, the more they insisted that I agree to serve.

When I returned to Yeshiva, I spoke to Dr. Belkin, the President. Dr. Belkin spoke to Rav Soloveitchik. Thereafter, they both urged me to accept the position for the High Holidays and, if at all possible, to establish regular *Shabbat* services. Dr. Belkin, himself, lived in the area. He told me that he saw enormous potential for this neighborhood now developing around Lincoln Center and that if I could succeed, it would be a *kiddush Hashem*. Rav Soloveitchik concurred.

Reluctantly, I agreed to serve as Rabbi for the High Holidays. However, I set the following conditions based on further discussions with Rav Soloveitchik:

1. I would not accept compensation. I could not accept money from a synagogue without a *mechitzah*. (However, Yeshiva University did compensate me for the loss I incurred. As a result of assuming the Lincoln Square post, I was compelled to relinquish a hebrew school position in New Jersey.)

2. The name of the synagogue had to be immediately changed from Lincoln Square Conservative Synagogue to Lincoln Square Synagogue.

3. As long as there was mixed seating, I would not live in the area even when *Shabbat* services would begin on a regular basis.

4. It would be made very clear that though I was present for services, I would not actually be *davening* along with the congregation. I would *daven* privately and be present at services merely to conduct and explain the prayers.

The conditions were accepted and I conducted the High Holiday services at the Esplanade Hotel. With more than two hundred worshippers attending, the appeal for increased membership was very successful as well as the appeal for a building fund which netted some five thousand dollars. With those funds, the President, Danny Mars, the Vice-President, Sidney Trompeter and I, rented apartment 1B in the Lincoln Towers apartment complex. Apartment 1B was to serve as our weekly *Shabbat* synagogue and as an adult education center. *Shabbat* services commenced during Chanukah, 1964. It was understood that I would remain as Rabbi only for a limited period of time and only under the conditions that I had originally set. Seating at the services was mixed but this discomfort only affected the *Shabbat* morning services—women did not attend services on Friday night and *Shabbat* afternoon. As a result, orthodox men from the neighborhood would often join us for those services.

At the time, I lived in Washington Heights near Yeshiva University. For *Shabbat,* my wife and I stayed on the West Side at the Westover Hotel. Soon a regular weekly class in Torah and then one in philosophy were begun. Slowly, I was becoming a part of the community of Lincoln Square.

In January 1964, our oldest daughter was born. We could no longer stay at the Westover Hotel because it was too cold and drafty to accommodate an infant. We were now compelled to spend *Shabbat* at the home of my wife's parents on Central Park South. They lived on the 29th floor and walking those floors up and down several times each *Shabbat* was very difficult. I did it for a few weeks but, for the long term a different arrangement would have to be made. I realized that the time had come to deal head-on with one of the conditions I had originally set. Either there would be separate seating, at least for *Shabbat,* or I would have to sever my connection to the congregation. I could no longer remain with my in-laws on *Shabbat.* The moment of truth had arrived.

I met with the board and told them I wouldn't remain past

Purim unless there would be separate seating for the *Shabbat* morning service. On Friday night we could still have our *Oneg Shabbat* type of service and for that I would allow mixed seating to continue. And, for the time being, I would even allow mixed seating to remain for *Rosh Hoshana* and *Yom Kippur.* As long as separate seating was required for *Shabbat* morning services, I would remain as rabbi and move into the Lincoln Square area. (Apartment 2B in the Lincoln Towers directly above the *shul* was then available.) I further advised them that this was not an issue for their consideration—a board may not vote on a *halachic* issue. They could seek to vote on me—whether I was to continue as rabbi of the synagogue—with the understanding that if they voted for me. I would immediately require separate seating.

During this period, I was under a great deal of pressure. On one hand I seemed to be making progress. The *shul* was growing. We were drawing 40–50 people for our *Shabbat* morning service. On the seating issue, there was also progress. At my behest, the usher, a young man named Barry, diplomatically, sat men and women separately as they entered. With the exception of a few couples, seating was already almost entirely separate for *Shabbat* morning.

On the other hand, there was criticism and even ridicule. A very nasty article written by Trude Weiss-Rosmarin appeared in *The Jewish Spectator.* After visiting our congregation she had written an article entitled, "Orthodoxy à la Lincoln Square." She said, in effect, that apparently, while Yeshiva University insists that *mechitzah* is a necessary feature of an orthodox synagogue, there's a different standard for an affluent neighborhood. For Yeshiva University has sent one of its promising young rabbis into the Lincoln Square area where he's establishing a successful, thriving and burgeoning synagogue but apparently because it is located in the Lincoln Center area, the absence of a *mechitzah* is overlooked. Yeshiva University sends people out to the boondocks to fight the battle of *mechitzah* but just a mere four miles from the institution itself, there seems to be no discomfort over the fact that there's mixed seating.

The article was reprinted in an orthodox publication with the postscript: "Orthodoxy à la Lincoln Square makes Trude Weiss-Rosmarin laugh, it makes us cry." I felt totally maligned and misunderstood. Here I was fighting a battle and everyone was against me. I was being criticized by all sides and factions. And, all this, just when I was confronting the board on this very same issue and success seemed close at hand.

Two individuals came to my aid. One was Baruch Litvin. He asked to meet me and we met at Yeshiva. I did not yet know anything about him, but apparently he knew plenty about me. He had read the recent articles and had heard me speak. He told me that he realized there had to be more to the story than the articles indicated and he wanted to hear the truth. I told him all that had happened and that I felt I was making much progress. Litvin offered to give me his full support in my battle for a *mechitzah*. From then on, we not only became allies in a mutual cause but close personal friends as well.

I also received a call from Dr. Belkin asking to see me. When I arrived in his office, he handed me a sheaf of papers; letters from people who had written to Yeshiva in response to the articles. A number of letter writers declared their intent to withhold support from Yeshiva University if it would continue to allow this apparent double standard. Dr. Belkin stared down at me and said, "Well, Rabbi Riskin, what do you think my response should be?" I became very upset. I was tempted to remind him that, "Dr. Belkin, you sent me into this lion's den!" But I understood he was in a difficult position. I told him that I realized that Yeshiva as an institution must come first and whatever he would decide, I would understand. To my surprise and joy, Dr. Belkin said, "I'll tell you what my decision is. How much is membership in your synagogue?" He wrote out a personal check and handed it to me stating: "If anyone criticizes you, just tell them Dr. Belkin is a member of your congregation. I believe in you—you will succeed." All his living days, Dr. Belkin remained a member of Lincoln Square Synagogue.

When the board met, it voted for me to continue as rabbi, knowing full well that it would mean separate seating on *Shabbat* morning. I was, of course, thrilled with the result. The very next day, Daniel Greer, a very good friend, accompanied me and we went to buy planters to use as a makeshift *mechitzah*. In accordance with prior statements by Rav Soloveitchik that the minimum height for a *mechitzah* was 40 inches, we bought 40 inch high planters. We placed them in the middle of the room in Apartment 1B where we held *Shabbat* morning services. The Congregation was outraged! They felt they had been duped. They insisted that I had only spoken about separate seating but now I'd put in place an actual *mechitzah*. In actuality, they were correct. I had always spoken about separate seating and apparently I was truly naive about the issue. I didn't realize that for some people there was a difference between separate seating and *mechitzah*.

There was an emergency board meeting. I appeared and explained: "I'm very sorry that I hadn't understood there to be a difference between *mechitzah* and separate seating. However, as long as I'm the Rabbi, standards cannot be lowered. They can only be raised. The *mechitzah* has come in. It has to stay." I said, once again, that the board could vote on my status but not on the *halachic* question of *mechitzah*. The *mechitzah* remained.

Only one person left the *shul* as a result of the *mechitzah* being installed for *Shabbat* morning services. The loss was minimal because our largest service was still the late Friday night *Oneg* service which still had mixed seating. There was a great deal of opposition to separate seating. One hundred people would attend Friday night but only thirty to forty were there for *Shabbat* morning services. Most of the people liked me personally and they felt that as long as there would be mixed seating on Friday evenings and on the High Holidays, they could tolerate the *mechitzah* on *Shabbat* mornings. Everyone agreed, and they were sure I would eventually realize, that it was impossible for a synagogue to get off the ground in the affluent, generally non-orthodox, upper West Side unless mixed seating was maintained for High Holiday services. And to me, it was indeed clear that in order to attract more than just the thirty to forty people who regularly attended our *Shabbat* morning services, it would still be necessary to allow mixed seating at High Holiday services to attract a broad base of people.

However, I did want to have an orthodox service with a *mechitzah* in our Lincoln Towers facility, apartment (1B), for the High Holidays. I went to the board and asked if they would agree to a *mechitzah* at the Lincoln Towers if the services at the Esplanade Hotel continued with mixed seating. They agreed to allow a service with a *mechitzah* if I would organize it without incurring any expense.

Providentially, on the following *Shabbat,* our services were graced by an unexpected guest, one Lou Eisenstadt who led us in the service with a beautiful *davening*. After *Shabbat,* he explained that he was visiting the area for family reasons and that this was his first visit to our *shul*. He realized what I was trying to do and asked how he could help. I asked him to grace us with his beautiful *davening* for the High Holidays. He consented and also agreed to blow the *shofar* and read the *Torah*. This made possible our first orthodox service in the

484

Lincoln Towers for the High Holidays. A year of struggle thus culminated with progress on the *mechitzah* issue both for our *Shabbat* services and even for the High Holidays.

The following year matters were generally calm. But on the High Holidays an unexpected and shocking event prompted me to seek an immediate resolution of the *mechitzah* issue. The two days of *Rosh Hoshana* were Thursday and Friday and, of course, *Shabbat* followed. We utilized the Esplanade for the *Rosh* Hoshana services on Thursday and Friday. For *Shabbat,* we returned to the Lincoln Towers. I had instructed the management and maintenance staff at the Esplanade not to dismantle the conference room we used as a *shul* there for *Rosh Hoshana* and *Yom Kippur* until after *Shabbat* was officially over. This *Shabbat,* was the special *Shabbat* that occurs between *Rosh Hoshana* and *Yom Kippur.* Customarily, Rabbis deliver a special address on this *Shabbat* dedicated to the theme of the *Shabbat—Teshuvah.*

In the midst of my address to a gathering of some fifty people in the Lincoln Towers apartment, we were interrupted by an individual who ran in panting and out of breath to tell us that in the Esplanade, contrary to my instructions, the *shul* was being dismantled, though it was still *Shabbat* and, most shocking, the sacred *Torah* scrolls were resting on the floor. I immediately took off for the Esplanade and sure enough the scrolls were on the floor. Obviously, the maintenance staff was unaware of the special care required for these sacred items. When I saw this, I began, involuntarily, to cry. I ran back to the apartment and reported what I'd seen. I was still quite shook up but very sure when I explained, "This is the last year there will be a mixed seating service at the Esplanade!" I believed this was the hand of G-d. From then on there was a *mechitzah* for all services except the late Friday night Oneg service.

Our next hurdle was to include a *mechitzah* in the plan for the new building. I gave many lectures on the subject. I frequently criticized the well known maxim that a family that prays together stays together. I emphasized that making a spiritual home life together will keep the family so—more than praying together. I spoke about commitment to *halachah* and that the *mechitzah* represents such a commitment. A *shul* is not a social center and the *mechitzah* expresses this truism. A *shul* is not a family affair: the home rituals are a family affair. The *shul* is the place where one stands before G-d as an individual on his/her own merits.

We planned the *mechitzah* for the new building in the least obtrusive manner possible. Rabbi Soloveitchik approved the design. Nevertheless, our first *Shabbat* in the new building, in 1970, proved distressing. The *mechitzah* was 40 inches high but because the floor in the women's section was raised above the floor in the men's section, it did not provide an adequate cover and separation between the two sections. I was heart-broken. I contacted the architect. He suggested that we make small *mechitzot* for each row at a cost estimated at more than $20,000.00. I contacted Rabbi Soloveitchik. He advised that the additional *mechitzot* weren't *halachically* necessary. The *mechitzah* does not serve to block one's vision but rather to prevent a mingling of the sexes. I was still very upset. I approached the board but they refused to allocate the funds for the additional *mechitzot*.

I was reluctant to pressure the board to allocate the additional funds. After all, they had approved the original plans presented to them. However, I couldn't live with a *mechitzah* where the visibility into the women's section was so great. Therefore, the next Thursday, my wife stayed up all night making cardboard *mechitzot* for every row. People came from all over the West Side to *daven* with us that morning. The building was not yet finished but word had spread about our beautiful, million and a quarter dollar, synagogue and they wanted to see it. Inevitably, and invariably, during the services people would lean on the cardboards and the cardboards would fall down. I would then direct all the women from that section to move over to a different section. It was an esthetically displeasing scene and caused terrible disruption in the services. After the services, the president and vice-president came over to me and said, "Rabbi, you win, we'll give you the appropriation you need."

Lincoln Square Synagogue grew by leaps and bounds. We now had 3,000 members. On *Shabbat* mornings, we now had five separate services. The synagogue offered a full range of services and a wide variety of classes. The synagogue was now home to *Torah* scholars as well as to *Ba'alei Teshuvah*. It had become *the* Jewish institution on the West Side. There remained, for me, one last task before I was to move to Israel. I was very anxious to have a *mechitzah* that would be acceptable to, and in accord with, the rulings of Rabbi Moshe Feinstein—60 inches in height. That took time. Eventually, however, a design that I liked and that I thought a majority of the people would accept, was developed. This design included a *mechitzah* that was 60 inches high with the upper half made of glass to enable the women to see through it into the men's section. This *mechitzah* was installed about a year before I settled in Israel.

One City's Progress, Los Angeles, California

Beth Jacob Congregation
BY RABBI SIMON DOLGIN

Beth Jacob Congregation of West Adams, Los Angeles, was organized in 1925, and its building was dedicated in 1928. It was organized as a Conservative synagogue with the matter of mixed seating specifically designated. Over the years, the West Adams Jewish community grew, as did the synagogue. Services and Torah studies for adults were held daily. The congregation took on an increasingly traditional image.

Despite the elements of tradition that prevailed at Beth Jacob, the issue of mixed seating did not arise. Bearded Jews (in those days a beard was considered a token of religiosity) sat alongside their wives and others' wives. Mixed seating was the norm. Neighboring Agudath Achim Congregation had had separate seating when located on Central Avenue, but upon moving to West Adams, also began to mix the pews. Both synagogues of Chief Rabbi Werner—on Custer Street and on Olive Street—had become mixed in seating. The new Beverly-Fairfax synagogues were mixed. These were all nominally Orthodox synagogues.

In 1939, Beth Jacob invited me, then newly ordained at the Hebrew Theological College of Chicago, to serve as rabbi for the High Holy Days. Afterward, a committee approached me with the call to remain permanently as rabbi. I submitted several conditions for my employment, one of which was that I could be free to use prudent judgment for the purpose of seating separately male and female worshippers during services. I did not intend to use extreme techniques, nor to split the congregation. I did, however, reserve the right to work in the direction of separation. I also set the condition that the congregation cease being identified as Conservative and join the Union of Orthodox Jewish Congregations of America. These conditions were accepted by the committee.

Initially, I began to speak to pious, elderly women, requesting that they move to the upstairs gallery to pray. Few responded, none really wanted to do so. All had become accustomed to mixed pews. However, in time, my requests succeeded and more ladies moved to the gallery. In 1943, I married. My wife sat in the ladies' section, as did a few other young ladies. Now the elderly women felt compelled to move to the gallery. After about five years, the issue of mixed seating on the Sabbath was "solved."

The next phase would be seating at *Yizkor* services of the major holidays of Passover, Shavuoth, and Succoth. The number of women attending on those occasions could not be contained in the balcony. A separate section on the main floor was reserved for ladies. The separation was not always effective, but gradually the situation improved. Still, through all the years in West Adams, pews were mixed on the High Holy Days.

In 1954, Beth Jacob moved to Beverly Hills, an "exclusive" area. Officers of the congregation turned to me requesting that the congregation forgo the matter of separate seating. They felt that only mixed seating could possibly "succeed" in the new neighborhood. The issue was temporarily resolved by my suggestion that nothing be done or said about it for two years. "Let us see what course it takes." I did indicate that at the end of two years, I would resign if matters were not resolved to my satisfaction.

With the move completed, seating at the weekly Sabbath services again became an issue. At times, seating was separate and on occasion, especially at *Bar Mitzvot,* the seating could not be separated. Gradually, much to the credit of the *gabbai,* Joseph Schnitzer, women were directed to their sepa-

rate section, "since that is what the rabbi wanted." Within a
year, separation was effected, as if by itself, on the Sabbath
and Holidays, except for the High Holy Days. In the mean-
time, service attendance increased, adult classes flourished,
and the growth of *Yiddishkeit* was in evidence in Beverly
Hills!

Apparently, however, the issue of seating was not resolved. At a meeting of the board of directors in 1957, when I
was out of the city, some members raised the issue of consistency. If separate seating was not required on the High Holy
Days, why was it required on the Sabbath and other holidays?
However, if it was required, then on the High Holy Days it
should also be separated. The Board appointed a committee
to draw up a questionnaire to be sent to the membership
requesting its opinion on the issue. When I returned and heard
of the action taken, I notified the officers that if such a
questionnaire were composed I would see my position as
usurped and would have to leave the congregation.

My position was that the people could decide whether or
not they wanted me as rabbi. However, once they accepted
me, only I could decide issues of *halachah* for the congregation. People may choose their doctor, but only he can write
the prescription.

At the next board meeting, the committee reported that
out of respect for the rabbi's position, it did not compose a
questionnaire. A full-scale debate was held on the seating
issue. After the debate, the board voted that separate seating
also be instituted on the High Holy Days out of respect for the
rabbi's position. I rose to say that if this vote, which seemed
favorable to my position, was implemented, I would be compelled to resign. The issue simply was not for decision by
vote. It was to be decided by the rabbi, who had decided that
"inconsistency" was warranted. I would now have to declare
that no change be made on the High Holy Days for two years.

490

For those who wished separate seating, this would be provided in the auxiliary service, which would be attended by the rabbi's wife and children.

In June, 1959, I met with the officers of the congregation and told them that I felt the people to be traditionally "mature" enough to accept separation on the High Holy Days. The officers under the leadership of President Sidney Eisenshtat, indicated that problems would arise, but they would stand by the rabbi.*

On July 1, 1959, notices for the New Year's dues were sent out with the announcement that pews would be separated. Shortly, letters of resignation began to arrive. I began to visit five to eight families each weekday to discuss, and sometimes to debate, the issue. My final appeal was to try separation once, if acceptable, good; if not, one would be free to leave. Most families agreed to try.

When it became obvious that I could not visit all who sent letters of resignation from the congregation, I called for a "face to face" public meeting. Several hundred members came, including a group of past presidents, who called for recall of the separation. The majority voted to express confidence in the rabbi and accept his decision.

The results of the "struggle" were that 55 families left Beth Jacob in 1959—many to return later; 62 new families joined in 1959, some because they wanted to honor the *halachah*. Interestingly, almost all of the families who left were European-born, who may still have had problems of acclimation to America. Most of those who joined were

---

*Editor's Note:

According to Sidney Eisenshtat, the president of the congregation at this time, one of the problems raised by the women was that they wouldn't be able to follow the services if they didn't sit next to their husbands. In response, Mr. Eisenshtat, an architect by profession, devised a special sign board that conformed with *halachah,* which continuously displayed the appropriate page numbers.

younger, American-born and professional people. Their problem, where there was a problem, was that they had never seen separate seating—but they were willing to try.

Since then, Beth Jacob has become a flourishing fountainhead of traditional Judaism and has set the pattern for other synagogues to return to tradition.

Pacific Jewish Center–Bay Area Synagogue
BASED ON AN ARTICLE BY PAUL COWAN

The boardwalk of Venice, California, (in Los Angeles) is one of the last places in America where you'd expect to find a revival of traditional Judaism.

Twenty years ago, elderly Jews dominated the neighborhood. Back then, many of them—Yiddish-speaking tailors, garment workers, shopkeepers—would stay outdoors until two or three in the morning, gossiping and playing bingo.

For years, they seemed to be anachronisms among the beatniks and hippies, remnants of a culture that would never be restored. But these days, on *Shabbat,* it is clear that they are vessels of a vital tradition. For the Jewish renaissance is centered at the last of their boardwalk synagogues—at the Bay Area Synagogue, located near a drug rehabilitation center, the Figtree Vegetarian Restaurant, and a store that sells some of the best skates in California.

It all grew out of a *mitzvah.* In 1976, Michael Medved, then 29, co-author of the popular book, *Whatever Happened to the Class of '65?* was sitting on the boardwalk in Venice, *shmoozing* with his father, David, 52, a physics professor at U.C.L.A. A blind old man, *Reb* Shia Winer, 87, formerly a grocery-store owner in Lithuania and a tailor in Detroit, heard their voices, figured they were Jewish, and asked them to complete the *minyan* at the Bay Area Synagogue. Medved didn't think twice about complying with *Reb* Shia's request and neither did his dad. That was the last Medved saw of *Reb* Shia for more than a year.

Medved settled in Venice, not far from the Bay Area Synagogue, but became involved with a local synagogue that had weekly services. Then, through a mutual friend, Lee Samson, Pacific Coast Executive Director of the Union of Orthodox Jewish Congregations at the time, Michael met South African-born Rabbi Daniel Lapin, then 31, the proud descendant of an esteemed rabbinical family. Rabbi Lapin defies all stereotypes. As a young man, he traveled the length of Africa on motorcycle. He is also an avid sailor. And, for all his strict orthodox preaching, he is quite open and flexible about practice. He never asks the details of anyone's personal observance. "It's not my business," he says. "Jews are commanded only to look after other people's bodies. The Almighty looks after their souls."

An instant friendship was formed between Michael Medved and Rabbi Lapin—though the South African was clearly the visionary. He believed it was possible to create a sizable, serious religious community in Venice. But he insisted that the community have a synagogue with a *mechitzah*. Medved had never before prayed in a synagogue with a *mechitzah* but was open to the idea because, as Rabbi Lapin argued, it was likely to attract a stable group of religiously committed people.

One day, Medved remembered the *mitzvah* he'd performed a year earlier and sought out *Reb* Shia. Medved offered to clean and repair the Bay Area Synagogue—and provide a weekly *minyan*. There was, however, one important condition: the newcomers would have to be allowed to put up a *mechitzah*. That was all right with *Reb* Shia, who had always considered himself to be orthodox.

The new congregants fixed the roof, cleaned up the rubble, and put up a cardboard *mechitzah*. The older people didn't like the *mechitzah*.

"I went over to the synagogue and yelled and screamed at that crew of Young Turks," recalls Maury Rosen, 50, the director of the Israel Levin Center, who'd helped *Reb* Shia keep the synagogue alive by devising programs like a "*minyan* club" where they gave out bagels and coffee to anyone who prayed. "I told them, 'This place belongs to the old people. You have no right to change their way of worship.' Then I ripped the *mechitzah* out of the synagogue. But I was sure it was hopeless. I was sure that Medved and his friends would drive the old people into the ocean."

But they revered *Reb* Shia. In the midst of a last-ditch, vitriolic meeting between the pro- and anti-*mechitzah* forces, the blind old man, who'd been silent amid the screaming said quietly: "We have to take our chances with the young people—or the synagogue will die."

"Those young people began to develop a wonderful relationship with the elderly," Rosen says.

Today, the Pacific Jewish Center is a thriving place. Its bedrock is not simply the warmth of the Bay Area Synagogue; the community draws its greatest strength from the durable institutions that Rabbi Lapin, Michael Medved and their friends have managed to create. The institutions, in turn, are cemented by a shared desire to lead a Jewish life—and by a great deal of flexibility about what, in practical terms, a Jewish life can be.

494

Ahavath Israel Congregation
BY RABBI MELVIN TEITELBAUM

It was at the first meeting after the High Holiday season in 1979, that I officially raised the issue of *mechitzah*. The intent was to allow a year for the members to get used to the physical presence of a *mechitzah* in the synagogue before the next High Holidays.

The idea was raised simultaneously with the suggestion for removing the microphone. That suggestion was quickly adopted with a proviso that a committee be appointed to review and report before *Pesach* on the effect the removal of the microphone would have, especially on those with hearing problems. The microphone was dismantled before the next *Shabbat* and, ultimately, the committee never reported. Very simply, no complaint was ever voiced by anyone.

The *mechitzah* issue was quite another matter. There was immediate concern as to how a *mechitzah* would affect the High Holiday attendees. Of greater concern, however, was the fact that, apparently, the only feasible way to install a *mechitzah* would require several women to change their seats—seats in which they had prayed for 20 to 30 years. Being seated next to a spouse was a minor concern. There were numerous widowers or widows among the membership and many others simply had not been sitting next to their spouses.

The psychological effect of such a sudden change was something I appreciated and never sought to negate. As a compromise, it was agreed that a *mechitzah* be installed and those women that were so moved would sit on the women's side of the *mechitzah*—but no woman would be compelled to change her seat.

For regular *Shabbat* services, this meant that only two or

three women who attended regularly on *Shabbat* would still be sitting on the men's side of the *mechitzah*.

The *mechitzah* was actually installed in time for *Shabbat Chanukah,* and in my sermon I could not resist comparing our installation of the *mechitzah* to the rededication of the Temple in the era of the Maccabees.

As the weeks and months passed, it became clear that the women were not going to change their seats. Also pressing was the need to decide how to utilize the *mechitzah* for the High Holidays. It was clear that a solution had to be devised that would deal fairly and decisively with both these stumbling blocks to having a synagogue with a proper *mechitzah* and properly separated seating.

During this period, there was, as one would expect, a great deal of discussion on this matter. The president, Mr. Jack Azoff, was fully in support of the *mechitzah*. The overwhelming majority of those who attended services regularly, mornings and evenings, daily and *Shabbat,* also fully supported the installation of the *mechitzah*. Opposition came from a minority—albeit a very strong and influential one, one which included a majority of the officers. Several of those who were opposed had devoted their lives to the congregation. Thus their point of view and their personal feelings had to be given careful consideration. The point they kept repeating was that for three years, I had served as rabbi without a *mechitzah,* ergo, why did it suddenly become so urgent to install one?

To this, two individuals provided very appropriate responses in support of its installation. One, Abraham Frisher (of blessed memory) explained that the rabbi had been patient. "For three years, he had been teaching us, preaching to us, providing us with proper insights and understanding, and now, as is shown by the support of those who attend regularly, we should be ready to act on all those teachings."

496

Rabbi Melvin Teitelbaum, *Ahavath Israel Congregation*

The president, Mr. Azoff, had a different, but very disarming position. He pointed to the fact that on occasion we had had visitors to the synagogue who could not pray in the sanctuary because of the microphone and because there was no *mechitzah*. Our synagogue, he continued, should be one in which every Jew should be able to pray. He also pointed out that those who require a *mechitzah* cannot pray in its absence. On the other hand, those who oppose a *mechitzah* do so not because of any *halachic* mandate but merely a strong preference. Consequently, it was appropriate to install a *mechitzah* so that no visitor to our synagogue should be compelled to pray outside the sanctuary on *halachic* grounds.

By now *Purim* had already passed and views had hardened, especially when the discussion turned to the High Holidays. I became convinced that my initial compromise suggestion had been a mistake and that the *mechitzah* would have to be installed fully and completely with all women on one side and all men on the other side.

I stated as much in my sermon next *Shabbat* and advised the congregation that I would not continue as rabbi as long as men and women sat together.

Of the three women who refused to change their seat, only one regularly attended. The other two had already declared that they were willing to change their seat if that woman would change first. This she would not do and no one felt it would be proper to force such a change. At this point, the president, Mr. Azoff, asked those men who were sitting in the section where those three women were sitting to move to a section where only men were sitting. This compromise was accepted and abided until the meeting to decide the issue with finality was called.

Prior to the meeting, I pointed out to the president, that the members could not vote on the issue of *mechitzah* any more than they could vote on whether, for example, to eliminate or shorten any prayer. They could, however, vote on whether to continue to have me as their rabbi, knowing that the only way I would continue would be if a *mechitzah* was installed.

I also explained that I would not campaign in any way. A rabbi's position is not a political job. It was up to those who supported the rabbi and wanted a *mechitzah* to see to it that the members vote to retain the rabbi.

I learned later that the president himself took charge of this campaign together with another gentleman, Avrom Aaron Goldenberg, the year-round cantor of our synagogue. The president also called a meeting of the officers, during which he explained to them that the charter of the synagogue required it to be Orthodox in accordance with the *Shulchan Aruch* and therefore a *mechitzah* was required. He further advised them that although there had not been a *mechitzah* for years, the rabbi, in researching the minutes of all the past meetings, discovered that when the congregation was first established as an orthodox synagogue in 1954, there had been a *mechitzah* and men and women were separately seated. With the numerous changes of rabbi, enforcement of the separate seating was neglected and the *mechitzah* itself disappeared from the synagogue long before the current rabbi was engaged.

The president then referred to the book *The Sanctity of the Synagogue* and to the decision of the Michigan Supreme Court, the focus of the book. He explained that each officer had potential civil liability for allowing the charter to be violated.

Also prior to the meeting, Rabbi Yisroel Kelemer of Beth Jacob Congregation of Beverly Hills spent a *Shabbat* with us to explain the importance of the *mechitzah* to the congregation. The Rabbinical Council of California passed a resolution urging the members to act in accordance with *halachah* and its then president, Rabbi Marvin Sugarman, sent the congregation a letter to that effect. By the time the meeting was set to convene, I was advised that the vote would be very clear and strong.

At the meeting, the first issue of contention was whether I should address the meeting on the issue and explain my position. On this vote, it became clear how the ultimate issue would be decided. By a margin of more than 75%, it was agreed to have the rabbi address the meeting. With the results seemingly so clear, all the opposition walked out of the meeting. The remaining members then voted unanimously to retain the rabbi.

Thus, the *mechitzah* issue was resolved, but the hardest work was yet to come. Working with the president, we designed a new *mechitzah* which would permit all women to retain their lifelong seats. It also allowed for up to twelve couples to sit side by side—but actually on either side of the *mechitzah*. The president and I personally constructed the *mechitzah*.

The more difficult task was to bring back those few members who left the congregation in reaction to the installation of the *mechitzah*. We were mainly concerned with those several people who had been members for many years. With the exception of one or two who no longer lived in the neighborhood, all eventually returned.

The *mechitzah* brought new life to the synagogue. Neighborhood people, old and new, who sought an orthodox synagogue were now able to attend. The most positive result was the strengthening of our daily services, especially in the evenings. As Mr. Azoff explained it, people had gone through an extended period of debate which ultimately led them to realize that they should be more dedicated to the synagogue. The results were very positive.

Congregation Etz Jacob

BY RABBI RUBIN HUTTLER

Founded in 1927, Congregation Etz Jacob was the first synagogue established in the Beverly-Fairfax neighborhood of Los Angeles. It was an orthodox synagogue with separate seating.

The question of separate or mixed seating often arose as an issue of contention in the more than 59 years of Etz Jacob's existence. Around 1934, a group of newer members sought to introduce mixed seating. To appease this group, a compromise was reached whereby the front rows would be exclusively reserved for male worshipers. In the back rows, mixed seating would be allowed. Gradually, however, those in favor of mixed seating prevailed and by the late 1930s, the synagogue had a mixed seating arrangement.

The synagogue, however, still considered itself orthodox and, through the years, all of its rabbis, with perhaps one exception, were orthodox.

Mixed seating was, in fact, the prevailing situation in Los Angeles for just about all orthodox synagogues during this period. The old Jewish neighborhood in the Boyle Heights section of the city was disintegrating as Jews began moving to what was at the time the West Side. The Chassidic synagogue of Grand Rabbi Eliezer Adler, *shlita,* which was the only one at the time with a *mechitzah,* was itself sandwiched between two nominally orthodox synagogues without *mechitzot.*

Gradually, the West Side of Los Angeles expanded and Jews migrated further westward to Beverly-Fairfax and Beverly Hills. Modernization was ever more the desired end, and that meant mixed seating. This move westward and the concomitant desire for modernization continued through the 1930s, 1940s and 1950s.

In 1959, the well-known Rabbi Simon Dolgin, whose

article appears elsewhere in this book, (supra, p. 488) erected a *mechitzah* in the beautiful modern structure of Beth Jacob Congregation, which had just moved westward to Beverly Hills. Within a few years, another rabbi, Rabbi Shohem, succeeded in installing a *mechitzah* in the Shaarei Zedek Congregation located in the part of Los Angeles known as the "Valley." In 1968, Rabbi William Spigelman commenced his ultimately successful struggle to install a *mechitzah* at Shaarei Tefilah, a congregation located in the Beverly-Fairfax neighborhood. These three houses of worship were all large modern orthodox synagogues.

In 1970, after having returned from a year in Israel, I began serving as the rabbi of Etz Jacob. Prior to my concluding an agreement to serve as rabbi, the president of Etz Jacob, Mr. Bernard Abend, agreed to meet with my father-in-law, Grand Rabbi Eliezer Adler, *shlita,* and with me at Rabbi Adler's home. Known as the Zviller Rebbe, Rabbi Adler had been in Los Angeles many years and was considered the rabbi's rabbi in the city. He made it clear to the president that the objective of restoring the *mechitzah* would be an integral part of my agreement to serve as rabbi. Mr. Abend agreed to work with us to help achieve this objective.

At that time, the membership of Etz Jacob comprised three distinct groups: older Jews who had come to this country early in the century at a young and tender age; older Jews who, though American born, were raised in orthodox or traditional homes; and a sizable contingent of Jews from Europe who were holocaust survivors.

Most of the members were not observant Jews and were content to have a congregation that was basically traditional though not purely orthodox. At the first board meeting I attended, I was asked whether I intended to install a *mechitzah*. I replied that I would do so only with the congregation's approval.

During this period, people began expressing concern about published demographic studies predicting that Beverly-Fairfax would soon suffer the fate of, and succumb to, the inevitable change of neighborhood, i.e., that Jews would move on and out to a better and more modern part of town and be replaced by an influx of non-Jews, resulting in the demise of one congregation after another.

Fortunately for Beverly-Fairfax, there was a better fate in store. Before any Jews began moving elsewhere, the neighborhood experienced an unexpected influx: not an influx of non-Jews, but one of Jews from various parts of the globe.

Many Russian Jews were settled in the area with the financial assistance of the Jewish Federation Council. Israelis found Los Angeles attractive because its climate was very similar to Israel's climate. Iranian Jews also arrived in large numbers. Even American-born Jews contributed to the influx. Large numbers of orthodox Jews arrived from the east coast, apparently having concluded that to live the life of an orthodox Jew in Los Angeles was now feasible. Most of them settled in the Beverly-Fairfax area of the city.

Also notable was the founding of a *kollel* in the heart of Beverly-Fairfax. It helped attract orthodox people to the neighborhood and acted as a magnet for *ba'alai teshuvah* to make their homes in Beverly-Fairfax. The neighborhood was indeed changing!

For Etz Jacob, the good fortune of the neighborhood created a serious problem—declining membership. The newly arrived orthodox couples did not join our congregation because they would not attend services in a synagogue without a *mechitzah*. The less traditional population had moved out and the elderly, sad but true, were susceptible to attrition. The board asked me for suggestions on how to attract new members. I pointed to the large number of young orthodox people in the neighborhood who could be attracted if a *mechitzah*

502

were erected. This suggestion met with a generally unfeigned contempt, though a few members were intrigued by the idea.

Having broached the idea, I set about utilizing whatever opportunities became available to expose the congregation to the *mechitzah*. An obvious, and frequent, opportunity was provided by the *Shabbatonim* organized by and for our youth group, a National Conference of Synagogue Youth (N.C.S.Y.) affiliate. With the help of Mr. Abend, who was still president, we saw to it that there were frequent *Shabbatonim* and that for each one, a *mechitzah* would be installed. Also, whenever requested, a *mechitzah* would be installed to accommodate a Bar Mitzvah or wedding celebrants and their guests.

This was all part of a calculated effort to desensitize the opponents of *mechitzah,* and thus, ultimately, make the synagogue truly orthodox. As rabbi, I initiated several changes toward that end, e.g., I ceased wearing the clerical robe and succeeded in having the microphone removed. Each change was achieved only after considerable struggle. But on the question of *mechitzah,* bitter opposition persisted.

However, Mr. Abend, now in his 14th year as president, had developed excellent diplomatic skills in dealing with such opposition. He maneuvered the congregation into accepting the *mechitzah* for a trial period. As rabbi, I was advised that the members expected to see benefits from the experiment. Consequently, I launched a major drive to enroll new members.

The trial period was to begin after the High Holidays of 1979. Such a delayed start for the proposed period would not cause any major discomfort, since during *Shabbat* services throughout the year, men and women generally sat in separate sections even though there was no *mechitzah*. Those opposed to *mechitzah* apparently concluded that they could survive this relatively brief trial period while the rabbi's "*meshigaas*" ran its course.

During the next six months, 60 people were added to the membership rolls—on paper. Of that number, only 14 were families who became active members and regularly attended services. Some were then elected to the board. One was made *gabbai*. All were given recognition in some manner to help retain them as members.

Before Passover of 1980, the end of the six-month trial period for the *mechitzah*, a general meeting was held to evaluate the *mechitzah* and its effect on the congregation and to decide whether or not to make it permanent. Almost all the "paper" members attended. So did several prominent rabbis. When the meeting ended, the *mechitzah* had been accepted.

However, what occurred at the meeting left me very troubled. In a sad way, it reflects the continuing struggle of those in favor of *mechitzah*—including my own constant struggle with the membership on this issue.

In my mind, I always believed that religiously and ideologically it was right and necessary to install the *mechitzah*. That belief most certainly sustained me throughout. However, it was still very disturbing to witness, at that momentous meeting, people who had belonged to the congregation for so many years being bullied by young, brash individuals who were no more than "paper" members and who ultimately did not remain active in the congregation.

I had entertained the hope that these young new members would stay with us and use their talent and their intellect in a manner that would eventually enlighten our older members who had so strongly opposed the *mechitzah*. This, sadly, did not occur.

In fact, retaining the *mechitzah* has been a constant struggle. Opponents utilize every opportunity to point out that, in their view, it has adversely affected Etz Jacob. When one sees empty seats on the High Holidays, it is difficult to

504

refute the argument. Every election brings with it anxiety, on my part, as to whether the pro-*mechitzah* officers, especially our president, Mr. Abend, will be retained. Opponents seek every means to elect officers who will remove the *mechitzah* and bring back the many loyal and, yes, wealthy members who were provoked to leave Etz Jacob by the installation of the *mechitzah*. One cannot be completely oblivious to the personal wounds created, though one is secure in the righteousness of the act.

Looking back one can't help but notice that nothing has changed since that 1980 meeting. Of all the new members, after two years, only one remained. Those who left had many excuses. Some were uncomfortable with the format and style of our *Shabbat* morning services, which included a cantorial performance and a sermon. Others sought to impose additional strictures which were too rigid for our older members. Still others felt ill at ease in associating with those of our members who were clearly non-observant.

In turn, this made the older members view the newer ones as young upstarts who could only make demands but were unwilling or unable to carry their share of the congregational burden. To them, it seemed that the younger members were in a constant search to find aspects of our service that they could demand to be corrected.

Fortunately, however, there is promise. Our own young people did not leave us. They had grown up in our N.C.S.Y. affiliate, which won national awards for its activities, and had become "*frum*" in their own right. This was indeed a unique display of loyalty on their part. For though they also had points of dissatisfaction, they remained with us rather than go elsewhere. They started their own *minyan* on *Shabbat* on the congregation's premises. Amidst all the misgivings, they have provided cause to be hopeful.

Progress in the 1980s

Movement on the issue of *mechitzah* in recent years continued apace albeit more quietly than it did in the 1960s and 1970s. The continuing progress is evident from the following articles and advertisements that have appeared in the Jewish press heralding each advance.

The Jewish Week & The American Examiner, Inc.   **May 25, 1984**

Park Slope Jewish Center Wins Court Battle

The Park Slope Jewish Center in Brooklyn began as an Orthodox synagogue and was led by prominent Orthodox rabbis. As late as 1960, the by-laws of the congregation stated that it shall be affiliated with the Union of Orthodox Jewish Congregations of America. In the 1960's and 70's, the congregation began to deviate from Orthodox Judaism and Conservative elements were introduced, such as mixed seating. In 1983, the congregation voted to grant women full participation in all religious services and engaged a female "rabbi."

The Orthodox faction of the congregation organized a **mechitza** *minyan* in the basement of the Center, and thus began the legal battle in which the Conservative temple attempted to oust the Orthodox shul from its midst. Led by Attorney Joel Z. Robinson, a native of New Zealand with a thriving international law practice, the Orthodox *minyan* has been declared legal members of the Park Slope Jewish Center by the courts, and looks forward to the day when its rights as an Orthodox congregation will be respected.

Mr. Robinson was appreciative of the help of the Orthodox Union in providing the services of Rabbi Moshe Faskowitz, a *musmach* of the Lakewood Yeshiva, who provided the initial rabbinic leadership necessary for the growth of the synagogue. Mr. Robinson does not view his congregation as a new Orthodox synagogue. "We are the older community. Orthodoxy was there first." The Park Slope area of Brooklyn is a community that is currently undergoing gentrification," in which many people are beginning to move into. "Therefore," says Mr. Robinson, "It is worth fighting for a shul with great potential."

Commission Reviews Union Standards

Membership Criteria

The Synagogue Standards Committee is also reviewing the Orthodox Union's standards and criteria of membership for its affiliated synagogues. "The number of synagogues fulfilling membership obligations to the Union through payment of dues has increased over 400 percent during the last five years," Rabbi Karasick explained, "and scores of other congregations are about to make their decision to join the Orthodox Union. We are reviewing applications very closely to make sure that these synagogues meet our membership criteria, especially in regard to the *mechitza* status of an applicant synagogue."

The Union's computer data bank is analyzing the status of all synagogues which call themselves Orthodox and which wish to become affiliated only with an Orthodox synagogue body. Initial analysis indicates that 94 percent of all these synagogues maintain separate seating.

WINTER 1984

Less heralded were the actions of numerous well-known synagogues, several in New York City, that restored the traditional manner of seating to preserve the balcony section exclusively for women or who raised the height of the existing *mechitzah*. Below follow excerpts from a sermon delivered by Rabbi Milton H. Polin when he brought the issue of raising the height of the *mechitzah* before his congregants.

508

Kingsway Jewish Center

BY RABBI MILTON H. POLIN

The physical separation of the sexes at worship, whether by a balcony or a *mechitzah* expresses the *Torah*'s view of the role of the sexes in Jewish life. The idea was very succinctly stated, albeit in another context, by Ruth R. Wisse in a recent issue of Commentary: "Jewish law undeniably expects different things of men and women, and though its expectations are endlessly reinterpreted, they cannot be wholly eliminated without calling into question . . . the binding nature of the law itself.

"The restricted religious role orthodox women occupy in Judaism may not satisfy modern notions of equality; even among orthodox women they have recently been subject to vigorous re-examination. But within the internal logic of Judaism, they were part of the noble and potentially sublime purpose of perfecting the Jews and human kind . . . A group that cares as much for its collective survival as for the individual self-realization of its members . . . still finds in the *halachic* system a decipherable and defensible system of social priorities . . .

". . . When the distinctions between women and men have no known consequence or meaning, it then becomes increasingly difficult to maintain Judaism's unyielding differentiations between wool and linen, between milk and meat, between *Sabbath* and week, between Israel and the nations."

On the "hidden agenda" of Kingsway Jewish Center for at least the last five years that I have served as rabbi, has been the question of the height of our *mechitzah*. I believe the time has come to put this issue on the "open agenda" of Kingsway.

Now, there is a "Catch-22" in this question: If the present *mechitzah* is acceptable, then why is there any doubt about it now? If the present *mechitzah* is not acceptable, then how was it permitted until now? There is an answer to these questions. First, my esteemed predecessor, Rabbi Samuel J. Chill, of blessed memory, must be commended for installing a *mechitzah* in what had previously been a Conservative congregation. The fact is however, that in his later years, he considered the *mechitzah* inadequate and so informed me and several other members of our congregation. Both in his letters to me and in his conversations during his visits here, Rabbi Chill expressed the hope that one day we would make the necessary improvements in our *mechitzah*. . . .

For the past five years, I have listened to the opinions of those who said that the *mechitzah* should be raised in order to attract new people to the synagogue and those who said it should be left alone in order not to drive away people from the synagogue. Considering the complexion of our community, there is merit in both opinions. I have also studied the matter, and when the Rav, Rabbi Joseph B. Soloveitchik, came to Kingsway for a wedding a little over a year ago, I asked him about our *mechitzah*. We discussed the entire matter in the presence of the Rav's students and several leading members of our congregation who happened to be present at the time. The Rav's opinion is a matter of record. So after watching and listening and studying the matter for five years, I have concluded that the time to act has now come at last.

There is good *halachic* reason to improve our *mechitzah* and making these changes in no way reflects upon the acceptability of the present *mechitzah*. What I am proposing is in no way different from what actually happened in the Temple of old. In the Temple, there certainly were no deviations from the *halachah*. Thus, when the women were within and the men without, that was *halachically* acceptable. Unfortunately, it led to levity. When the change was made so that the men were within and women were without, that was also *halachically* acceptable. Unfortunately, that too, led to levity. And so, finally, the rabbis devised a balcony as the ideal solution to the problem. The present *mechitzah* is *halachically* acceptable. Unfortunately, it leads to levity, and therefore we need to make the change.

. . . To be sure, the *mechitzah* alone will not solve all the problems of Kingsway Jewish Center . . . (but) we have brought the *mechitzah* question into the open. It is no longer on the "hidden agenda" of our congregation. There have been no decisions on the design of our new *mechitzah* nor on the date when it will be installed. There is only a realization that we need as much discussion and as little dissension as possible. When Rabbi Soloveitchik was at Kingsway, his parting words were "You must change the *mechitzah*, and you must do it peacefully." I know that we will deal with this issue with the reverence toward *Torah* and with the respect for one another that have always characterized our congregation.*

---

*The Kingsway Jewish Center was originally a Conservative congregation. When Rabbi Samuel Chill was appointed rabbi in 1947, it was with the understanding that the synagogue would become Orthodox. The new sanctuary erected in 1952, was arranged in the *Sefardic* manner with the *mechitzah* an 11-inch velvet curtain attached to the back of the last row of men's seats. Rabbi Chill considered this *mechitzah* the best that could be obtained at that time and cherished the hope that improvements would be made later.

By the time Rabbi Polin came to Kingsway, the character of the congregation had changed to the extent that the height of the *mechitzah* was an issue at his initial interview. Rabbi Polin waited five years after assuming the pulpit before attacking the problem and it took another three years until a change was implemented.

The present *mechitzah* is also attached to the back of the last row of men's seats and rises to a height of 55″ from the floor, "shoulder height on the average woman when she stands," as Rabbi Soloveitchik had told a group from the congregation when he officiated at a wedding at Kingsway Jewish Center. The *mechitzah* was constructed of materials approved by Rabbi Moshe Feinstein (*ZT'L*).

Rabbi Polin did succeed in raising the *mechitzah* in his synagogue to the desired height. But as is illustrated in this volume, *mechitzah*-related struggles can be very protracted and inconclusive.

The most egregious example that the editor has come across occurred in the state of Pennsylvania. There, in a synagogue whose members are still embroiled in just such a protracted struggle, an addition to the existing waist-high separation is often installed for special occasions such as a Bar Mitzvah or N.C.S.Y. *Shabbaton,* upon request. Incredible as it may seem, on one such occasion, this special *mechitzah,* installed for a specific event, though beautifully decorated with greenery throughout, was deemed too high by certain influential individuals. Unfortunately, they failed to realize this until they attended services Friday night. To the shock and surprise of a goodly number of the membership who arrived for services *Shabbat* morning, a different and lower *mechitzah* had somehow been substituted overnight for the higher one that had been there at the start of *Shabbat.*

Obviously, the situation in this synagogue is extremely tense. In such instances, it is most useful for nationally renowned organizations to provide encouragement and support so that tension can be eased and progress realized in a calm and tranquil atmosphere.

The central role played by orthodox organizations has been, and will continue to be, vital for continued success in this area. The commitment to increase the synagogues which have a *mechitzah* and to raise to the proper height those *mechitzot* that are below the standard accepted by Orthodox authority has not waivered on the part of such organizations. If anything, the commitment is stronger than ever, as is illustrated by the following letter to the editor:

512

Union of
Orthodox Jewish
Congregations
of America   45 WEST 36TH STREET
NEW YORK, NEW YORK 10018 (212) 563-4000

ב"ה

איחוד הקהילות החרדיות באמריקה

April 14, 1986

Ms. Jeanne Litvin
449 N. Laurel Avenue
Los Angeles, CA 90048

Dear Jeanne:

I am writing in response to your inquiry as to the
current status of non-mechitza member congregations in
the Orthodox Union.

In 1985 Sidney Kwestel, President of the Orthodox
Union, appointed Saul Quinn to chair a Special
Committee on Synagogue Membership to determine what the
Union should do with the small number of member
congregations which have not yet installed a mechitza.
On May 29, 1985 the Officers of the Union accepted the
report of this Special Committee which has since been
put into effect by the Union.

The Special Committee determined that among the 800 odd
member congregations affiliated with the Orthodox Union
there exist approximately 20 which do not have a
mechitza. The position adopted by the Union calls for
the inauguration of an intensive educational effort in
each non-mechitza congregation. The goal of this
program is to prevail upon the leadership of each
non-mechitza congregation to install a mechitza.

The Committee report states that "we stress that the
Committee recognizes the importance of giving chizuk to
these synagogues. Indeed, the Committee feels that the
Union must continue to reach out and be "m'karev" them
by using its best efforts to help them reach the goal
of compliance with Halachic requirements." "The
approach to each non-mechitza synagogue will be a
personal one." "The Union will undertake the creation
of an educational program consisting of publications,
lectures, retreats, etc., whose purpose will be to
maintain the necessary momentum, create personal
relationships and bring maximum influence to bear so
that each synagogue will give full adequate
consideration to the proposal."

The Committee will set a time limit for each
non-mechitza congregation based upon local conditions
and circumstances. Congregations which do not make
progress towards installing a mechitza will have to
sever their membership relationship with the Union. We
are convinced that in provoking a re-evaluation of the
mechitza question within each non-mechitza congregation
we will have created circumstances which have the
potential to reverse the slide of that congregation
from orthodoxy. Even in those circumstances where a
congregation's membership in the Union will lapse, it
is our feeling that the congregation will continue to
re-consider the mechitza question, and hopefully
eventually reinstate their Orthodox Union membership.
Indeed, as regards non-member congregations the report
states that "every effort will be made to maintain
contact with non-mechitza congregations who are not
members of the Orthodox Union but wish to identify as
Orthodox. The Orthodox Union will attempt to influence
both individuals and the community as a whole to
strengthen their ties to orthodoxy including
encouraging participation in Orthodox Union programs
such as NCSY and Torah retreats."

As of this writing, conversations have taken place with
the leadership of most of the non-mechitza
congregations and delegations have visited a good
number of them. Active programs are presently under
way in some, and the prospects for positive results
look very favorable.

With warm personal regards, I am

Sincerely yours,

Rabbi Pinchas Stolper

PS:LB

Conclusion

LAWRENCE H. SCHIFFMAN
Professor of Hebrew and Judaic Studies
New York University

The material assembled in this chapter is eloquent testimony to the trend observable in present-day Orthodoxy in regard to the *mechitzah*. Recent years have seen a definite reversal of the patterns of the 1950s and 1960s. In 1952, the well-known Rabbi Jekuthiel J. Greenwald, of Columbus, Ohio, wrote that in the preceding two years not a single synagogue erected in America had been built with a proper separation of the sexes. He describes eloquently his own struggle to reverse this pattern in his own synagogue, which was being rebuilt. The reversal of this trend constitutes a major achievement for American Orthodoxy. This accomplishment was aided greatly by the earlier editions of this book and by the struggle of its editor, Baruch Litvin.

The development we have observed already in the Introduction, and which is demonstrated by the material gathered here, is part of a larger picture in contemporary Orthodoxy which calls for some comment. American Orthodoxy is experiencing unparalleled growth. This growth is apparent both in quantity and in quality. Recent years have seen a definite move toward greater stringency and greater commitment. This is manifested in many areas. Among them is the desire to achieve the strictest level of observance and to be as exacting as possible in matters of *halachah*. These developments are to a great extent the result of the coming of the postwar immigrants with their uncompromising positions. At the same time, they are abetted by an American society hospitable to ethnicity and cultural and religious pluralism. The modern Orthodox community has experienced organic growth and development which has allowed it to contemplate these higher

515

standards and indeed to reach for the fulfillment of the dream that one could be a fully observant Orthodox Jew while remaining involved in the secular world. It is primarily in this community that the battle of our editor had to be waged. It is most important to note that it is among this group as well that the *mechitzah* is considered completely normative today.

These developments pose a great challenge to the Orthodox leadership, both lay and rabbinic. Finally, after years of struggle on these shores, the Orthodox community constitutes a strong and well-organized group of people who in their different ways represent the possibility that halachic Judaism can and must be lived and experienced on this continent if Judaism is to survive. This community has repeatedly demonstrated its durability in the face of the pressures of adaptation, assimilation, and the general breakdown of traditional values in America. All this at a time when the Jewish community as a whole finds itself in the throes of increasing intermarriage, loss of commitment, and confusion as to how to preserve Judaism for the future.

The Orthodoxy of today can offer itself to the wider Jewish community as the vibrant, committed way of life that it is. It can invite all Jews to join its ranks, confident in the thought that it has shown without doubt that it can resist the pressures toward compromise of essential halachic requirements, and certain that it can be attractive to the vast numbers of Jews seeking direction as to how to actualize their commitment in their daily lives. This, indeed, is the blessing of the re-establishment of the sanctity of the synagogue. Having preserved the tradition and having established itself properly, the Orthodox synagogue and its members can extend the spirit of sanctity to the entire Jewish community. This would be the true fulfillment of the dream of Baruch Litvin, for all Israel is one congregation.

IN MEMORIAM
Zichronom Livrachah
(in remembering them we are blessed)

"I went to the Rosh Yeshiva, Reb Yaakov (Kamenetsky) to ask him what type and size of *Mechitzah* should be installed in the new synagogue we were building (in McKeesport, Pennsylvania). He told me to go to Reb Moshe (Feinstein) and to abide by his ruling. 'You need not be more *frum* than Reb Moshe,' he said."

From the eulogy for Reb Yaakov delivered in Los Angeles, California on April 8, 1986, by Reb Yitzchak Chinn of McKeesport, Pennsylvania.

As this third edition was going to print, Reb Yaakov and then Reb Moshe were *niftar*. This page is specially dedicated to their memory by the editors.

Torah Tzivah Lanu Moshe Morasha Kehilas Yaakov. (Deut. 33:4)

Moshe commanded us in the laws of the *Torah*,
As an inalienable inheritance for the Congregation of Yaakov.

Appendix
Responsa of Rabbi Moshe Feinstein (ZT'L)
on *mechitzah*

28 Cheshvan 5712 (1952).
To his honor, my friend, the Rav and Gaon R. Shmuel Tuvia
Stern, Rav of Kansas City, *shlita*:

Your honor, in your *teshuvah*, concludes that where the
women's section is on the same floor as the men's section, it is
sufficient to have a *mechitzah* of token size, such as four
tefachim by ten. I cannot agree with this at all. Rather—to
conduct services in such circumstances—remains an absolute
prohibition of an edict that is scriptural in basis, for this is
considered mixed seating. In general, I do not understand
your honor's intention in prescribing a width of four *tefachim*
and a length of ten. But no matter how your intention is
interpreted—whether the ten *tefachim* constitute the vertical

or the horizontal dimension—this is forbidden. Rather, it is necessary to make a *mechitzah* along the whole length of the women's section, with a height of 18 *tefachim*. But if the women sit at this height (18 *tefachim*) above the men, then from the aspect of separation, no *mechitzah* is needed, and all that is required is a railing so that the women shall not fall.

Your honor points out that the *Berysa* in the Babylonian Talmud (Tractate *Sukkah*) states that the reason for the separation of men and women is to prevent *kalus rosh*, while in the Jerusalem Talmud the reason given is that they should not intermingle; and you conclude that this constitutes a disagreement between the Babylonian Talmud and Jerusalem Talmud. But I do not agree with you on this point either. For it is stated in *Tosefta* that (before separation was introduced) there often was *kalus rosh*, and *Tosefta* draws the conclusion that they should not be intermingled. This is obviously the same *berysa* that is cited by the Babylonian Talmud. Thus, it is clear that there is but one reason, not two. Moreover, the *Mishnah* in *Midos* states that the reason is that they should not be intermingled—and the Jerusalem Talmud would surely not take issue with this *Mishnah*. Rather, one must conclude, it is all one reason; that through the very fact that it could rise to a situation of *kalus rosh,* it is considered as if they were intermingled, as I have explained.

Your honor also writes, in accordance with your supposition that these are two different reasons, that there are practical halachic consequences: namely, that regarding the reason of *kalus rosh,* the problem is one of visibility, and the requirement is for a *mechitzah* of such height that the women cannot be seen at all; whereas regarding the reason of not intermingling, a token *mechitzah* is sufficient. This conclusion has no basis whatsoever. For the matter of visibility is not relevant here, as I have explained. Even from the women's balcony of the *Bais HaMikdash,* the women were visible. Rather, *kalus rosh* means that it is easy for the men and women to speak with each other and touch each other, as I have explained. Thus, even regarding the reason of not intermingling, the *mechitzah* needs to be 18 *tefachim* high, and this is sufficient to prevent *kalus rosh*.

Your honor reasons that in the *Bais HaMikdash,* the women's balconies were equipped with opaque visual obstructions, such as opaque glass. With this, I also do not agree at all. Rather, as I explained, the balconies required no *mechitzah*. The balcony was solid down to the ground; and in order for all the women to be able to see below, it was terraced. Its halachic effectiveness was due entirely to the fact that it was above the men, as I have explained. And since there was no obligation to make a *mechitzah* on this balcony, it may be that they made none, for none is mentioned. If they did make one, it was only for the purpose of safety and not for separation. As for the variant reading of the words in the scriptural verse, "They sat" versus "They saw," this makes no difference, for by all opinions they could see even when they were sitting, and they sat or stood as they wished. Even if we are to grant that there is some difference between the variants, it is only regarding whether or not they had a *mechitzah* for safety; for if the women were sitting, there was no danger of falling and no *mechitzah* was needed to prevent falling. However, it is more reasonable to say that there is no difference between the two variant readings.

Your honor proposes the original thesis that during the time of prayer, there is less need for a *mechitzah,* for when praying there is no danger at all of *kalus rosh,* and likewise the prohibited intermingling is absent. Hence, no *mechitzah* is needed at all during the time of prayer. And you go even further, stating that for this reason, it would be possible to sit actually intermingled—as long as they separated for prayer. G-d forbid that any such suggestion be made, and may G-d forgive your honor for this error. For the truth is that it is forbidden to enter the *Bais HaMikdash* except with an attitude of awe. Hence, people entered the Temple only for the purpose of performing some *mitzvah* or to see the *kohanim* performing the sacred service. Such observation of the *kohanim* is also a *mitzvah,* as we see from Tractate *Yoma* 70. And yet, intermingling of men and women, and *kalus rosh,* were forbidden. Thus, we see that regarding separation, the fact that people are engaged in a *mitzvah* does not result in any leniency. This is all the more true in the synagogue, where even during the time of prayer, there is not such an obligation of awe as there was in the *Bais HaMikdash;* for the obligation of awe in the *Bais HaMikdash* is explicitly commanded in a *Torah* verse. Thus, the need to prevent *kalus rosh* in the synagogue is greater than it was in the *Bais HaMikdash.*

In fact, there would be some basis for assuming that the prohibition against intermingling in the *Bais HaMikdash* stems from the obligation of awe there; for if people are there in such a way that they can come to *kalus rosh,* then awe is lacking. If so, then the prohibition in the synagogue against intermingling would be only of rabbinic status (*Talmudic* in origin), in that the Sages forbade *kalus rosh* there as well. In that case, it would still be of no effect to build the synagogue on condition that intermingling would be allowed. But even if we follow this line of reasoning, it might be that during the time of prayer the prohibition against *kalus rosh* would be of Scriptural status (Biblical in origin) even in the synagogue, since the name of *Hashem* is referred to, and words of *Torah* and holiness are uttered—and hence there would be a Scriptural requirement of awe, as in the *Bais HaMikdash.*

This line of reasoning is contradicted, however, by the *Talmudic* source of the requirement for a *mechitzah*—i.e., the *Talmud's* citation of the reference to a mourning which will be observed at the dawn of the Messianic era (see *Sukkah* 52a);

there it is implied that the prohibition applies wherever people assemble because of a halachic requirement to gather together. But, in the absence of such an obligation to assemble, intermingling would be permitted even in the *Bais HaMikdash,* as we see from the fact that Chanah (the mother of the prophet, Samuel) prayed in the *Bais HaMikdash* in the presence of Eli, the High Priest; and also from the case of the woman who "forced her way in" (see *Kidushin* 52); and *Tosafos* there states that women were permitted to enter the Temple courtyard.

I am surprised at your honor's assertion that women used to attend the sacrificial ceremony of the paschal lamb—implying that in your honor's opinion all who eat of the sacrifice are obligated to go into the Temple courtyard. In fact, it is obvious that women did not enter the courtyard the day before *Pesach,* even according to the opinion of *Tosafos* that they were permitted, in general, to enter the courtyard. Rather, one man, representing all those who were to eat of that particular sacrificial animal, would slaughter it in the courtyard, for this completely satisfies the requirements of the *Pesach* sacrifice (Paschal lamb). For this reason, *Tosafos* does not cite the *Pesach* sacrifice as evidence that women could enter the courtyard, but confines himself to proofs from the *sotah* and the *nazir.* Hence, it would seem that on the day before *Pesach* women were forbidden to enter the Temple courtyard because it was not possible then to make a *mechitzah,* and on that day there was an obligation of gathering, for the *Pesach* sacrifice is offered in groups. And, according to the opinion that women made groups of their own for the *Pesach* sacrifice, it may be that they appointed a male emissary to slaughter their sacrificial animal in the courtyard for them. Furthermore, the prohibition against intermingling does not apply to an individual woman, for the law of separation requiring that there should be no intermingling is just the opposite of the prohibition against *yichud*—for *yichud* is a prohibition which applies only to individuals not to larger groups—whereas the whole essence of the prohibition against intermingling is only when people are gathered together.

As regards gatherings where there is no *halachic* obligation to gather, and even in the case of weddings, I doubt whether the prohibition against intermingling exists—unless there is a danger of prohibited *yichud*. Rather, I lean toward the opinion that there is no prohibition against intermingling in such cases; for we find regarding the eating of the *Pesach* sacrifice that men and women would eat together in one room and a number of families would be gathered there, for there was no *Pesach* sacrifice which was not offered by a group of more than ten, as we find in Tractate *Pesachim* 64. And, it is stated in *Midrash Rabbah* that as many as 40 or 50 people would join together over one animal; and according to *Bar Kapara,* as much as 100. Moreover, according to *Rabbi Shimon,* those who have joined together to eat a particular *Pesach* sacrifice may not divide into two groups; and if they would make a *mechitzah* between the men and women, this would be considered as if it were two groups as we find in *Pesachim* 86. So from the opinion of *Rabbi Shimon,* we may infer that according to the opinion of *Rabbi Yehudah,* too, even if the original group divided into two groups, there was no obligation that the women form a separate group.

Moreover, in *Pesachim* 91a, the *Mishnah* states that "A group formed for dining over the Paschal lamb cannot be formed of women, slaves, and minors." And, even according to the interpretation of *Rava,* that women and slaves are not to form a group because of the danger of impropriety, it may be inferred that a group may be formed of Jewish women together with Jewish men. Furthermore, we find in this same passage, the opinion of *Rav Ukva bar Chinnena* that women may not form a group by themselves, but only together with

524

men. And, since *Rav Ukva bar Chinnena* follows the opinion of *Rabbi Yehudah,* this shows that according to *Rabbi Yehudah,* too, men and women can eat the *Pesach* sacrifice in one group with no *mechitzah.*

Again, in the passage in which it is stated that a bride turns her face away from the other diners, *Rashi* explains that this is because she is embarrassed to eat in the view of the men, because they may look at her. And this certainly would not be a problem if she were eating only with her father and brothers; hence it must be that other men are present. If so, this passage is explicit proof that there was no *mechitzah* between the bride and the male diners.

But in the synagogue, and at the time of prayer, there is a clear Scriptural prohibition which demands that there must be a *mechitzah* of 18 *tefachim* between the men and women, or that the women must be above and the men below, as I explained . . .

> [The last paragraph of this teshuvah is omitted, since it does not relate directly to the question of the *mechitzah.*— Ed.]

Your friend,

Moshe Feinstein

25 Tammuz 5715 (1955).
To his honor, my friend R. Mordechai Kahn, *shlita:*

Regarding the matter of the *mechitzah* between the women and the men, certainly it is desirable and good, when possible, to make its height such that the women cannot be seen at all, and especially in this country, where many women leave their hair uncovered, and also their arms bare even when they go to the synagogue, and, *ba-avonosainu harabim*, we have no power to prevent this. But where it is impossible (to make the *mechitzah* of the ideal height), I have already explained, in a *teshuvah* which has been in print for many years, that the *mechitzah* must reach at least above the shoulders and that for the average woman this is approximately 18 *tefachim*. And this is the minimum measure according to the law of *mechitzah*. In this way, even if a woman's arms are bare, they will not be seen.

As regards the hair, since we find ourselves in a *shaas hadechak*, it is possible to rely on the lenient opinions of *Rif* and *Rambam*, who rule that the hair is not considered *ervah* with regard to the recitation of the *Shema* and words of *Torah*.

Moreover, in our times, when, *ba-avonosainu harabim*, the majority of women go with their hair uncovered even though this violates a Scriptural prohibition, the author of *Aruch HaShulchan* has written (sec. 75) that even, according to those authorities who generally forbid (the recitation of the *Shema* or the speaking of words of *Torah* in the presence of uncovered hair) it is also possible to be lenient, since nowadays it is not the custom of most women to cover their hair. *Aruch HaShulchan* argues that with regard to uttering the *Shema* or words of *Torah* (which is forbidden in the presence of women who have uncovered parts of the body which should normally be covered) the mere fact that it is forbidden to uncover the hair does not classify this part of the body as one "that is normally covered." Rather, the classification depends upon what most women actually do.

In my humble opinion, a strong proof for this opinion of *Aruch HaShulchan* can be adduced from Tractate *Berachos* 24. There, *Rav Sheshes*, in order to prove that women's hair is classified as *ervah*, finds it necessary to cite the verse "*Your hair is like a flock of goats*" (*Song of Songs* 4:1, 6:5). Now, this is a verse from *divrei kabbalah*, and furthermore (the fact that hair is *ervah* is not stated directly but) is only an inference from the fact that the verse praises the women for this feature (as *Rashi* explains). It would seem that *Rav Sheshes* could have brought much better proof, namely the verse "*And he shall uncover the hair of the woman*" (*Numbers* 5:18), from which it is derived that it is forbidden for a married woman to be seen in public with her hair uncovered. *Rav Sheshes* might have argued that since this *Torah* prohibition exists, it puts the hair in the category of "parts of the body which are normally covered," and hence gives it the law of *ervah* when uncovered. But the fact that *Rav Sheshes* does not adopt this line of proof undoubtedly shows that the mere fact of its prohibition does not put the hair into the category of *ervah*, and therefore *Rav Sheshes* had to cite the verse which praises the woman for her hair, implying that this is an object of attraction (as *Rashi* explains).

It is clear, however, that the verse of praise in *Song of Songs* does not by itself give hair the status of *ervah*; for even though this verse exists, there is no prohibition against reciting the *Shema* or speaking words of *Torah* in the presence of the uncovered hair of single women, but only married women. The reason, as explained by *Shulchan Aruch*, is that single women customarily go with their hair uncovered. Thus, we see that the attractiveness of hair, as proved by *Song of Songs*, does not classify hair as *ervah* in situations where it is customary for women to go with their hair uncovered. Hence, in our time, when even married women have become accustomed to leave their hair uncovered, even though this violates a prohibition, it does not make the hair *ervah* with regard to the recitation of the *Shema* or words of *Torah*. And thus, in a *shaas hadechak*, one may rely on this permission.

But G-d-fearing men should be strict and turn their faces away (from uncovered hair) when they recite the *Shema* and throughout the entire prayer service. And where this is impossible, they should close their eyes; for since they are able to be strict with themselves, this does not constitute a *shaas hadechak* for them.

As for the question of making part of the *mechitzah* out of lace, if bare arms can be seen through the lace, it has no effect as a *mechitzah*. But if it is a type of lace through which the women appear in such a way that the uncovered parts of the body are not recognizable, then this is considered adequate concealment, since no uncovered flesh is seen, but only a plain silhouette.

When the women are in a balcony, this satisfies the law of the *mechitzah,* even when the curtain of the balcony is low, since the women themselves are above the men. But since the women leave their arms bare, it is necessary to add to the height of the curtain so that their arms cannot be seen; and if possible, it is good to add enough that their hair also cannot be seen. But those synagogues that have balconies do not trouble to adopt any further measures; and I do not know why. No doubt it is because they are unable to do anything, because their congregants will not agree. And in such synagogues, G-d-fearing men should turn their face away from the balcony when they pray.

> [The last two paragraphs of this *teshuvah* are omitted as they do not relate to the question of the *mechitzah.*—Ed.]

> Your friend,

> Moshe Feinstein

Erev Rosh Hoshana 5716 (1956).
To his honor, my friend R. Ephraim Asher HaLevi Rottenberg, *shlita,* Rav in Los Angeles:

Regarding the *mechitzah* of which approximately the upper third is made of glass: your honor has correctly written that in terms of the law of the *mechitzah*, the glass is not a defect. However, there is a different problem, for it may be that the women will be immodestly dressed, so that their flesh will be visible. Many women are accustomed to dress in this manner in this country, *ba-avonosainu harabim*. If this is the case, it will be forbidden for the congregants to pray or say words of *Torah* when they face the women's section—unless a rule is made that the women should be modestly dressed when they come to the synagogue, and unless it is known that this rule will be obeyed.

It is only with regard to uncovered hair—a prohibition which, *ba-avonoseinu harabim*, most women violate—that we do not forbid the recitation of the *Shema* in their presence. The reason is that *Rif* and *Rambam* do not classify hair as *ervah* with regard to the utterance of the *Shema* or words of *Torah*. And even according to *Shulchan Aruch* 75:4, and those of like opinion who forbid the utterance of the *Shema* or words of *Torah* in the presence of uncovered hair (of married women), the author of *Aruch HaShulchan* has written that nowadays, when many women violate this prohibition, it does not come under the category of *ervah* with regard to the recitation of the *Shema* or the speaking of words of *Torah*.

And, in my humble opinion, a strong proof for this contention of *Aruch HaShulchan* can be adduced from Tractate *Berachos* 24, where *Rav Sheshes*, in attempting to prove that women's hair is classified as *ervah*, finds it necessary to cite the verse "Your hair is like a flock of goats" (*Song of Songs* 4:1, 6:5), a verse which does not relate directly to this issue, but simply gives rise to a logical inference that (since the verse praises a woman for this feature) it has the potential of causing improper thoughts. But why did *Rav Sheshes* not cite the verse "And he shall uncover the hair of the woman"

(*Numbers* 5:18)? From that verse the law that (married women) are Scripturally forbidden to go with their hair uncovered is derived, as stated by *Tanna De-bai Rabbi Yishmael* in *Kesubos* 72a. But from the fact that *Rav Sheshes* was not able to use this latter verse as his proof, we see that the classification of hair as *ervah* does not depend solely upon the fact that (married) women must cover their hair. Hence *Rav Sheshes* required the inference that, since the verse in *Song of Songs* praises a woman for her hair, this feature of the body may lead to improper thoughts. But it is clear that this, too, does not by itself cause hair to be classified as *ervah*. For we see that the hair of an unmarried woman is not classified as *ervah* (the reason being that it is not customary for unmarried women to cover their hair).

Thus, both factors are necessary to give hair the status of *ervah*; that it be the custom to cover it, and that it be the kind of thing which can lead to improper thoughts. Therefore, if it is the custom of most (married) women to go with their hair uncovered, even though this is forbidden, it does not mean that their hair is classified as *ervah* with regard to the recitation of the *Shema* and the speaking of words of *Torah* for this classification depends only upon the reality of whether or not the married women actually cover their hair. (If they customarily do not cover it, it is not considered *ervah*.) Hence, even though it is desirable to be strict in this matter, it is not necessary to protest if men recite the *Shema* where the uncovered hair of married women is visible.

However, if women's bare skin is visible from those places on the body that should be covered, then even if they customarily leave these places uncovered, we must forbid the recitation of the *Shema* or the uttering of words of *Torah* in their presence.

Thus, if the congregation insists that the *mechitzah* be of glass, your honor should make sure that the women come to

530

the synagogue in modest dress. And if it should occasionally happen that some individual may come improperly attired, and it should be impossible to correct the situation through protest, the congregants will have to be careful not to recite the *Shema* or say words of *Torah* when facing in that direction. Turning away in this manner, however, may be relied on only for occasional incidents. But to rely on this as a regular solution to the problem is not possible.

I have heard that there is glass through which it is possible to see from only one side. It would be good to use such glass (for the *mechitzah*) so that the women can see through it, but not the men.

I remain, your friend,

Moshe Feinstein

19 Sivan 5714 (1954).
To his honor, my friend R. Ben-Zion Lapidot, *shlita,* Rav in Dayton, Ohio:

Your honor spoke with me by telephone about a certain synagogue where the men and women pray without a *mechitzah* between them but are not intermingled; rather, the men occupy one side and the women the other side. Now, certain people have come with their "rabbi" and maintained that since, in any case, it is forbidden to sit without a *mechitzah,* they want to sit actually intermingled, one next to the other. And your honor has asked the *Torah* authorities of this country whether there is any substance to their argument.

It is obvious that there is no substance to their argument, since sitting actually intermingled is a much more severe violation than sitting in two separate sections with no *mechit-*

zah as a separation. And, when people are committing a less severe offense, it is forbidden to provoke them to commit one of greater severity. On the contrary, in a place where the congregation sits actually intermingled, one should try to influence them, if possible, that, at least, they should sit separately so that their transgression should take a less severe form. A proof of this is the *Gemara* in *Sotah* 48, where *Rav Yosef* says, "If men sing and women sing responsively, this is immodest; if women sing and men sing responsively, this is like a flame in tinder. Of what halachic consequence (is this distinction)? In the matter of annulling (the custom), this (the more severe) has priority over that (the less severe)." And *Rashi* explains: "If they will not agree to annul both (customs), one should annul the (custom) which is 'like a flame in tinder.' " (And see the passage in detail.) Here, we have explicit evidence that the *Torah* court, or any individual, even if they are not able to annul the violation completely, are at least obligated to annul as much as they can—that the people should not commit the violation which is "like a flame in tinder," which is more severe, but rather only the one which is simply immodest, since that is less severe—even though it, too, is forbidden.

Hence, undoubtedly, if someone should provoke those who are committing the transgression in a less severe form to commit it in a more severe form, such a person is both sinning and causing others to sin. This is precisely the principle that applies to the matter at hand: If we see a place where the people are sitting intermingled and we cannot cause them to sit separately and to also make a *mechitzah* between them as the law requires, we are obligated to do whatever is in our power, if they will listen to us, and, at least, cause the women to sit separately on one side; and even though they will still be violating a prohibition, they will not be doing it in the more severe manner.

Appendix

Thus, in this case, where the congregation is sitting separately but without a *mechitzah*, certainly those people with their "rabbi" who wish to bring it about that they should actually be intermingled, are leading the public to sin.

Your friend,

Moshe Feinstein

4 Shevat 5719 (1959).
To his honor, my honored friend, a truly G-d-fearing man, R. Baruch Litvin, *shlita*:

Regarding your honor's question about the synagogue in which, until now, the women have sat above (in a balcony section) and they now wish to change this and sit below, with a *mechitzah* of the proper height between them and the men: You ask whether this is permissible or whether there is any halachic objection to it.

The correct ruling, in my humble opinion, is as follows: It is true that it is permissible to build a synagogue in which the women's seating is below, on the same level as the men's, separated by a *mechitzah* of 18 *tefachim*. However, it is certainly preferable if the women sit above, for it is explicitly stated in the *Talmud* in *Sukkah* 51 that in this manner it is impossible for *kalus rosh* to result, whereas the arrangement in which the women sit on the same level as the men, separated by a *mechitzah*, is only justified by *sevara*; and it may indeed be true that there is a significant difference and that it is not completely comparable to the situation in which the women sit above; it may be that a *mechitzah* is somewhat less effective (than a balcony). Thus, while on the one hand, we certainly cannot prohibit (the suggested change), as stated above, nevertheless, since the synagogue already has a section above the men's section with adequate room for all the

533

women who wish to be in the synagogue, and this has been the practice until now, they should not change and sit below in the future, even if separated by a *mechitzah*.

This is especially so since it is clear in this instance that the women wish to belittle the importance of being separated by a *mechitzah*; and they are beginning with a small modification, but in the end, they will remove the *mechitzah*, too, until finally they will sit actually intermingled with the men. This is the way of the *yetzer harah*, which on one day says, "Do such-and-such," and on the morrow it pushes on saying, "Do such-and-such," as we find in Tractate *Shabbos* 105.

Therefore, G-d-fearing people should protest the proposed change. As for the claim of the women that it is hard for them to climb the stairs, and it is for this reason that they wish to sit below, this is a weak claim and is not true, for we see that until now it never occurred to them that it was difficult to go up the stairs, and moreover, we see that for physical pleasure they will climb even more stairs. If so, then for the honor of heaven, it should be all the more easy to go up stairs. Rather, it is clear that the purpose of this change is to belittle the importance of the *mechitzah*, with an intent to depart from the holy customs of Israel. Hence, it is necessary to protest, so that this change will not be made. And through the merit of the sanctity of their synagogue, they will be blessed from heaven.

As regards the Rav, however, if he has done all that is in his power and has not been able to have any effect, and if his continued occupancy of his position is at stake and this is his means of livelihood, then he is not obligated (to give up his position over this issue), since in any case there will be a valid *mechitzah*.

Your fond friend,

Moshe Feinstein

21 Shevat 5731 (1971).

To his honor, my friend and relative, scion of great scholars, R. Pesach Zechariah HaLevi Levovitz, *shlita*:

In the matter of the obligation to have a *mechitzah* between the men and women in the synagogue, I have explained in my *teshuvah Orach Chaim*, Chapter 39, that this obligation is *de-orysa*. And, I explained that (the *mechitzah* is necessary) because (otherwise) the result could be *kalus rosh*, i.e. unnecessary chatting with women and touching their hands and bodies. For this reason, it is necessary to make a *mechitzah* which would actually prevent this. Such a partition must be at least shoulder-high. According to *Rashi* and *Tosafos*, shoulder-high is 18 *tefachim*, and according to *Rashbam*, it is approximately 17 *tefachim* (see the aforementioned *teshuvah*).

Since, however, it has been observed that in our time, the shoulder height of most women is less (than 18 *tefachim*), there is no need to protest if a lenient measure of 60 inches, i.e., five feet, is adopted—approximately the measure (of shoulder height) arrived at by *Rashbam*. Indeed, it is not unreasonable to assume that the average height of women has decreased somewhat from what it was in *Talmudic* times. But if (the height of the *mechitzah* is) less than five feet, protest should be made.

Quite aside from this aspect of the *mechitzah,* which is an obligation that applies even to the most modest of women, there is another purpose for *mechitzah*: as a safeguard to the prohibition of actually looking at parts of the body which should be covered, and which are classified as *ervah* even in our age, when *ba-avonosainu harabim,* many women dress immodestly.

It is true that it would be possible to be lenient (as to the prohibition of gazing) with regard to those (married women) who attend synagogue with their hair uncovered. In fact, the author of *Aruch HaShulchan* rules that even according to those authorities who are strict (in classifying hair as *ervah*), it is possible to be lenient in our time, when, *ba-avonosainu harabim,* the prohibition of going with hair uncovered is commonly violated. And I adduced support for this ruling (of *Aruch HaShulchan*) in my *teshuvos* (Orach Chaim, sec. 42). Thus, one may rely (on this ruling of *Aruch HaShulchan*) in a *shaas hadechak*—and especially since *Rif* and *Rambam* rule that hair is not classified as *ervah* with regard to reciting the *Shema,* praying, or learning *Torah,* as I wrote in that *teshuvah.*

But (even though it is possible to be lenient regarding the visibility of a woman's hair during synagogue services) the fact is that, *ba-avonosainu harabim,* many women appear with uncovered arms and the like; and this undoubtedly is within the category of *ervah,* and it is forbidden to pray when these are visible. And for this purpose (of preventing the visibility of bare arms, etc.), the *mechitzah* is also effective if it reaches to shoulder height.

In this regard, mention should be made of the glass *mechitzah.* Such a *mechitzah* is effective in fulfilling the basic law of *mechitzah* (to prevent *kalus rosh*). But it is not effective with regard to the prohibition of reciting the *Shema* and praying where *ervah* is visible, for *ervah* is prohibited even when seen through glass, in accordance with the statement of *Rava* in *Berachos* 25, which is cited as *halacha* in *Shulchan Aruch* 75:5. But this problem is avoided in synagogues where women with bare arms and the like are not permitted to enter. Then, by law, it is permissible to make the *mechitzah* even of glass, as I wrote in Sec. 43 (see there).

It has come about through great pressure exerted by the congregants on the rabbis that there are synagogues where the floor of the women's section has been raised a foot or more and (the congregation) does not allow the *mechitzah* to be rasied. In my humble opinion, this is not good even where the women dress modestly. For (such an arrangement) makes it easy to come to *kalus rosh* through excessive conversation and also through touching. This situation is similar to that of tall women and men who are slightly shorter than them. A solution would be to add half a foot to the *mechitzah,* so that on the men's side it would have a height of 66 inches, i.e., 5½ feet, and on the women's side, it would reach to a height of 54 inches, i.e., 4½ feet; for this would make it difficult to come to *kalus rosh.* All the same, I do not state that this (arrangement of raising the floor of the women's section) is absolutely forbidden, even where they do not raise the *mechitzah* above 60 inches (5 feet)—but such an arrangement does not seem satisfactory to me.

Therefore, in a case where the congregants have agreed to make an improvement—but only to the extent absolutely required by law—and where there is a rule that the women must be dressed modestly when they come to the synagogue, it is permissible to make the upper part of the *mechitzah* of glass in order to reach (the required minimum of) 60 inches. And, if it is possible to lower the floor of the women's section so that this *mechitzah* will have a height of 60 inches on their side as well, or to add to the *mechitzah* so that it reaches a height of 66 inches, this would be good. And (if one of these last two suggestions is not carried out) I do not absolutely prohibit, but I do not find it satisfactory.

Or course, all that I have written here concerns only the essential halachic obligation, when there is pressure from the congregants. But it is desirable to be more strict and to make the *mechitzah* high enough so that the women's heads are not visible, and to make it of an opaque material, as I wrote in that *teshuvah.*

I remain your fond friend.

Moshe Feinstein

537

To his honor, my friend, the Rav and Gaon R. Ch. Shaul Bolotnikov, *shlita,* Rav of Sioux City: (Undated)

I refer your honor to my book *Igros Moshe, Orach Chaim,* Sec. 39, where I have explained the source of the law (of the *mechitzah*) and the gravity of the prohibition (of holding services without a valid *mechitzah*). I explained, however, that it is sufficient if the *mechitzah* reaches above the shoulders, a height which, according to *Tosafos,* measures 18 *tefachim,* and according to *Rashbam,* about 17 *tefachim,* or more than 60 inches. All the same, as I said over the telephone, it is possible to be lenient and to adopt the height of 60 inches, since it is observable that in our generations a height of five feet, or 60 inches, reaches higher than the average woman's shoulder height. And it may be, as some individual authorities have ruled, that the measure is approximately 58 inches; but one should not be any more lenient than this.

I have heard, however, that due to pressure from congregants, some have adopted the leniency of making the *mechitzah* in such a way that, although on the men's side it is the proper height, or even complies with the strictness of the full 18 *tefachim,* nevertheless, on the women's side, it has a height of only four feet (i.e., the floor of the women's side is raised). But this does not satisfy the spirit of the law as laid down by our sages. For even though this fulfills the basic requirement of a *mechitzah,* nonetheless, the fact is that most of the women dress immodestly, with bare arms and even more, *ba-avonosainu harabim.* As a result, with a *mechitzah* of this sort (such that the women are visible to the men) it is forbidden to utter sacred things or to pray, for this means that the men are in the presence of actual *ervah,* and to pray, recite blessings, discuss *Torah,* and so forth, under these circumstances is, by all opinions, forbidden. While it is true that *Rif* and *Rambam* rule leniently regarding the permissibility of

538

reciting the *Shema,* the prayers, or words of *Torah* in the presence of uncovered hair, and while it is true that *Aruch HaShulchan* states that even according to the opinion of those who forbade holy utterances in the presence of uncovered hair, one may rule leniently on the matter in our age because, *ba-avonoseinu harabim,* many women do not cover their hair, even though they are thereby violating a *Torah* commandment,* and in my book (*Igros Moshe, Orach Chaim,* Sec. 42) I adduced a strong proof in support of *Aruch HaShulchan*'s conclusion. (All this, however, applies only to uncovered hair.) But regarding bare arms, even if the majority of women ignore this prohibition, it is *ervah,* and if this is visible, it is forbidden to pray, recite the *Shema,* or speak any words of *Torah.*

Therefore, it is necessary to make every effort to insure that the *mechitzah* shall be higher than the shoulder height (of the average woman) on both the women's side and the men's side, according to the measure explained above.

Your friend,

Moshe Feinstein

13 Teves 5726 (1966)
To my very honored friend R. Yerachmiel Friedman, *shlita:*

Regarding the matter of the *mechitzah* which is only 50 inches high and above which rises a second section stretching another 13 inches in height, comprised of a series of open spaces, each being 13 inches wide, it certainly is not proper to pray in this place unless the entire upper section comprised of the open spaces is covered by a curtain. Another solution would be to fill in the upper 13 inches with vertical rods

---

* All references to the prohibition against uncovered hair apply, of course, only to married women.—*Transl.*

spaced no more than 3 inches apart, since there are some authorities who are lenient and do permit this. If this solution is adopted, it cannot be gainsaid, since there are authoritative opinions both for and against it. However, it is not in accordance with the *ruach chachamim*. Therefore, in this synagogue, where many G-d-fearing and yeshivah-educated men pray, there is no reason to be lenient. Therefore, they should stretch a curtain over the height and width of the entire open-spaced area.

Your friend,

Moshe Feinstein

Erev Shabbos Kodesh, the second day of Rosh Chodesh Kislev 5729 (1968).

To his honor, my honored friend the Rav and Gaon R. Ephraim Greenblatt, *shlita*:

In the matter of the *mechitzah,* I have already explained in a *teshuvah* that it needs to be above shoulder-level, which in the opinion of *Tosafos* is 18 *tefachim* and in the opinion of *Rashbam*, approximately 17 *tefachim*, but it seems that in our generation (the average shoulder-height) is somewhat less than this.

Therefore, it would have been best for (the congregation) to do as had been done in the previous synagogue; for in these matters, there is certainly an advantage in making as great a separation as possible (between the men's and the women's sections). But by law, in a *shaas hadechak,* the greatest leniency possible is (to make the height of the *mechitzah*) no less than 60 inches from the floor in the women's section.

As for the separation that (the congregation) made in the absence of (a valid) *mechitzah*—viz., that the women's section was set off at a distance of 2½ *amos* from the wall of the

540

(insufficiently high) *mechitzah* and that the men's section was likewise set off at a distance of 2½ *amos* from it—this is of no effect in this matter.

Thus, to the *mechitzah,* which was made with a height of 54 inches, an extension addition of at least 6 inches must be made.

And it is my hope that all the congregation want to act in accordance with the law of the *Torah* and that peace will prevail among you.

I close with a blessing to your honor, and likewise to the congregation and in particular to my friend the rav of the synagogue.

Your respectful friend,

Moshe Feinstein

3 Kislev 5729 (1968)
To my honored friend the Rav and Gaon R. Aryeh Abba Levine, *shlita,* Rav of the Anshei Sefarad synagogue in Memphis:

I received your letter yesterday, immediately after Shabbos. As regards the answer to your query, your honor should see what I wrote to my friend the Rav and Gaon Rav Ephraim Greenblatt, *shlita.* However, I shall also reply to your honor, in particular because of the honor due to you, and also to answer the objection you raised as to how I arrived at the figure of 18 *tefachim* (as the minimum height for a *mechitzah*).

I mentioned in the responsum to Rav Greenblatt that this height—18 *tefachim*—is cited explicitly by *Tosafos, Shabbos* 92a, s.v. *Ishtakach,* and *Rashi* states likewise (see *ibid.,* s.v. *Ishtakach*: the required height for a *mechitzah* is that of a man's shoulders. Both *Tosafos* and *Rashi* state that this height is three cubits—hence 18 *tefachim*).

541

However, according to *Rashbam,* the height of 18 *tefachim* includes the head as well as the shoulders (see *Bava Basra* 100b, s.v. *Vehakuchin).* Accordingly, taking into consideration the statement of the *Gemara* there that the Ark, when carried on the shoulders, was above 10 *tefachim,* we must conclude that shoulder height is no less than 16²/₃ *tefachim*—even if the height of the *Levites* was only three cubits, like our height today. This theory of *Rashbam* is a lone opinion, and one with which *Tosafos* differs.

Hence, it would be proper to require 18 *tefachim* as the minimum height of a *mechitzah.* However, under *shaas hadechak* e.g., when the congregants will not agree to this, it is possible to be lenient and adopt the measure given by *Rashbam,* for in a *shaas hadechak,* one may rely on a lone opinion; we also find that *Ramban,* in his *Chidushim* on *Bava Basra* agrees with the *Rashbam.* Furthermore, it may also be true that women of our day and age are slightly shorter than the women of the Talmudic era.

The height of three *amos* (18 *tefachim*), when calculated for the purpose of *mikvah* construction, is 72 inches. (An *amah* is 24 inches and a *tefach* is 4 inches.) According to the lenient view of *Rashbam* (16²/₃ *tefachim*) it is more than 66 inches. However, there is a measure of the *amah* smaller than that used for *mikvah* construction: only 22 inches. Accordingly, 18 *tefachim* would be 66 inches. Using this smaller measure of an *amah,* and combining it with the lenient opinion of *Rashbam,* I wrote that in a *shaas hadechak* one may be lenient and require only 60 inches. Apparently, your honor did not see what I wrote to R. Greenblatt.

And as to what your honor wrote that he saw a *Mechitzah* in a certain synagogue that is 70 inches high only on the men's side but on the women's side it is only 30 inches, (i.e. the floor on the women's side was raised). Your honor knows that the raising of the floor on the women's side was not done based on any counsel from me. Many things are said in my name that I never did say. Indeed it is required that the *Mechitzah* on the women's side rise to a height of 60 inches.

I have heard that there are synagogues in which the floor in the women's section is raised—this is not appropriate. However, they do not hold Rabbis of those synagogues to account because it is possible that they concluded that they could not do otherwise and, thus, they acted on their own in a lenient manner. Quite likely the important factor of earning a livelihood (compelled them to so act). Perhaps, they nevertheless intended (their act) to serve a heavenly purpose for the Rabbis of those synagogues were concerned that if they would leave, the synagogue would turn Conservative, G-d forbid. I am reluctant to judge on a matter on which I was not asked.

However, in your synagogue it appears that (the congregants) do want to act properly. In addition, the livelihood factor is not present and neither is there the alternative concern (described above) which would compel one to act (leniently) for a heavenly purpose.

And as to what your honor wrote that the men and women nevertheless do not sit close to each other that, in any case is a good (safety measure) to add on—but that is no reason to decrease the height (of the *Mechitzah*) below 60 inches.

And so I remain, your dear friend who hopes, that you will do things properly—no less than 60 inches as the law requires, that peace will always reign and conclude with a blessing.

Moshe Feinstein

22 Tammuz 5736 (1976)
To his honor, my very honored friend R. Yaakov Reiner, *shlita*, Rav of Congregation Ohev Tzedek:

Our noteworthy friend R. Shlomo Meir Klein, *shlita,* has sent me two samples of a beautifully decorated fine wood. As part of the decoration, open spaces have been carved out of the wood, and he asks, apparently on your behalf, if they are fit for use in separating the women's section of the synagogue from the men's section. He requests that I send the answer to you.

Hence, I am replying in this letter that, in my humble opinion, they are fit for making a *mechitzah,* since it is impossible for *kalus rosh* to result from these spaces (or openings) carved in the wood. Also the height of the *mechitzah* from the floor in the women's section should be no less than 60 inches.

(The Rav) should also endeavor to exert his influence to make it a rule that the married women should not come to the synagogue with their hair uncovered. For even if they cannot be influenced to adopt this practice (of covering the hair) in their homes, they will certainly agree to have their hair covered in the synagogue.

And as your friend, I bless you that you will be able to influence your congregation in such a way as to bring them ever closer to faith and to the awe of *Hashem*—for that is the main aim of the rabbis in every time and place, and especially in our place and our time.

Moshe Feinstein

glossary

Abbaye	Renowned Talmudic personality from the *Gemorah*.
Abodah Zarah	The name for one of the major treatises of the *Talmud*. Discussion therein generally relates to laws prohibiting all forms of idol worship and polytheism.
Aboth	The name for one of the minor tractates of the *Talmud*. Discussion therein is devoted to ethical standards and the appropriate traits of good character.
Aggadah	Story; anecdote; homiletic commentary or interpretation.
Ahduth (Achdus) ha-Shem	Monotheism; unity of the divine.
Akshanuth	Obstinacy.
Aliyot	Plural for *Aliyah* (step up, move up). During the service, on the Sabbath, Mondays, Thursdays, and holidays, portions of the *Torah* are read. Anywhere from 3 to 7 or more people are given the honor to be "called up" to the *Torah* for an *aliyah*.
Amah	A linear measure from Talmudic times: Various contemporary authorities have determined that its modern equivalence is within a range of 18 to 24 inches.
Amecha	Laity; ordinary people.
Amos	Plural of *Amah*.
Anav	A humble individual.
Arebuth	The concept that each Jew is responsible for the act of every other Jew and is obligated to help

	every other Jew observe all of the 613 commandments.
Ark	A specially built cabinet placed at the front of the synagogue. The *Ark*'s purpose is to house the handwritten parchment scrolls of the *Torah*. It is symbolic of the *Ark* in the *Bais ha-Mikdash* which housed the tablets on which were inscribed the Ten Commandments.
Aruch Hashulchan	Anthology of rulings in Jewish Law contained in the *Shulchan Aruch* and other works. The *Aruch Hashulchan* was authored before the turn of the century by Rabbi Yechiel Michel Epstein.
Avodah	Work, labor, service. Ritually, it is confined to Temple service. In the absence of the Temple, prayer is deemed a substitute.
Avodah she-ba-Lev	Service of the heart.
Azaroth	Sections; courtyards.
Baal ha-Bas	see *Baal ha-Bayis.*
Baal ha-Bayis	Owner of the house. Colloquially used to identify the laity of a synagogue or congregation; assertive individual.
Baal'e Bos	Yiddish transformation of the term Baal ha-Bayis.
Baalai Batim	Plural of *Baal ha-Bayis* or *Baal'e Bos*.
Baal Teshuvah	Returnee. Individual who, after years of not observing, has returned to a way of life committed to observing Jewish law and ritual.

546

Glossary

Baalai Teshuvah	Plural of *Baal Teshuvah*.
Ba-Avonoseinu ha-Rabim	Because of our many sins. In the development of Jewish law through the ages up to and including the contemporary period, it has always been a given that observance of the law deteriorates with each successive generation. Hence, our generation is considered to be quite sinful.
Bais ha-Mikdash	House that is sanctified. Holy Temple. The name for the singular house of worship first built by King Solomon, rebuilt by Herod and destroyed by the Romans. The Western Wall in Jerusalem is today the only remnant of the *Bais ha-Mikdash*. Animal sacrifices and high priest services are by *Torah* law confined solely to the *Bais ha-Mikdash*. Jews await the coming of the Messiah to begin the Messianic era which will see the *Bais ha-Mikdash* rebuilt—never again to be destroyed.
Bais ha-Midrash	House of study; synagogue.
Bar Kapara	Talmudic personality from the *Gemorah*.
Bar Mitzvot	Plural for Bar Mitzvah.
Baruch ha-Shem	Bless the name; Thank G-d.
Bava Basra	The name for one of the major treatises of the *Talmud*. Discussion therein generally relates to laws regarding rights in property.
Behira (Bechira)	Choice.
Ben Torah	An educated and pious person.
Berachos	The name for the opening treatise of the *Talmud*. Discussion therein

547

	generally relates to laws regarding foods, blessings, and order of prayers.
Berysa	Extramural *Talmudic* source, in rank of *Talmudic* authority nearly equivalent to *Mishnah*.
Beth Din	Court of Jewish Law.
Beth ha-Knesseth	Synagogue.
Beth Midrash	House of study.
Bimah	A podium. Frequently located at the center of the synagogue. When reading from the *Torah* scroll, the scroll is placed on the *bimah*.
Bocherim	Young lads; *Yeshiva* students.
Chasid	As used herein—Disciple of a Rabbi who adheres to the teachings of the 18th Century founder of a movement based on mysticism, prayer, joy and religious zeal.
Chasidic	Of the *Chasid* movement.
Chasidim	Plural of *Chasid*.
Chasidim ha-Rishonim	Conscientious individuals of olden days.
Cheder	Grade school.
Cheshvan	Second month in the current Jewish yearly calendar.
Chidushim	Innovations; new insights. The writings of certain commentators are divided in sections or volumes and frequently one such section is labeled as *Chidushim*.
Daven	Yiddish word meaning to pray.
Davening	Anglo-Yiddish word for praying.
De-Orysa	Aramaic word meaning "from the *Torah*." A rule of law based on

548

	Torah (biblical) authority, thus requiring greater care in adherence to such law and its every detail.
Din	Law.
Divrei Kabalah	Words of tradition. Words from scriptural writings other than the writings of the Five Books of Moses. Scriptural writings such as the Books of the Prophets, Psalms, Ruth, and Esther are considered as historical accounts and not as authoritative for purposes of framing standards of *halachah* as are the writings of the Five Books of Moses.
Eben ha-Ezer	One of the four sections of the *Shulchan* Aruch. It sets our laws regarding marital relations.
Emunath Yisrael	Faith of Israel.
Erev (Rosh ha-Shanah)	Eve of the holiday inaugurating the New Year.
Ervah	Nakedness. Arousing the senses by exposing portions of the body that should remain covered.
Ethrog	Citron. Used in special rituals during *Succoth* holiday in combination with the *Lulab*.
Frum	Yiddish word for an individual who is pious in that he/she is dedicated to observance of Jewish law and ritual.
Ezras Nashim	Women's section in the *Bais ha-Mikdash* (Temple) court.
Gabbai	Sexton.
Gaon	Title of address accorded to heads of academies in the immediate post-*Talmudic* period. Subse-

quently, it has obtained a more general use to describe individuals possessed of immense knowledge and great piety.

Gemara	The greater portion of the *Talmud*, which expounds upon the more concise (and earlier) portion, denominated *Mishnah*.
Gemorah	Same as *Gemara*.
Get	Bill of divorce.
Hak'hail	Gathering. Specifically, the annual gathering in the *Bais ha-Mikdash* for completing the cycle of weekly *Torah* readings.
Halachah	The way to go; Jewish law.
Hashem	The name. A substituted reference for the ineffable names of G-d.
Havurah	Group; study group.
Hefkeruth	Anarchy.
Hillul (Chilul) ha-Shem	Causing G-d's name to be held in disrepute.
Hurban (Churban)	Destruction (usually referring to the *Bais ha-Mikdash*).
Igros Moshe	Letters of Moshe. Multi-volume compendium of rulings on contemporary issues of Jewish law by Rabbi Moses Feinstein (*ZT'L*). Most of the rulings were made by correspondence in response to questions submitted to Rabbi Feinstein by letter.
Ishtakach	Found; apparent. As used here, it is merely a reference guide for the first word of a section of commentary for the citation given.
Kaddish	Prayer sanctifying G-d; It is most

550

Glossary

	widely known in the format in which it is recited by mourners.
Kalus Rosh	Frivolity.
Kashruth	The status of being *kosher*.
Kavanah	Concentration. An individual's intense effort to make his or her prayer meaningful.
Kedushah	Holiness; sanctification.
Kedushas Bais ha-Knesses	Sanctity of the synagogue.
Kelmer Maggid	See *Maggid*. A *maggid* from the city of Kelm.
Kesubos	Marriage contracts. The name for one of the major treatises of the *Talmud*. Discussion therein generally relates to the laws regarding marriage contracts.
Kiddush ha-Shem	To act in a way which glorifies G-d's name.
Kiddushin	Betrothal. The name for one of the major treatises of the *Talmud*. Discussion therein generally relates to laws regarding betrothal.
Kislev	Third month of the current Jewish yearly calendar.
Kodesh	Holy.
Kohanim	Every Jew belongs to one of three groups—*Kohanim, Leviim,* or *Yisraelim.* The *Kohanim* are direct descendants of Aaron, the brother of Moses. Their function is to devote their lives to service in the *Bais ha-Mikdash.* Today, in the absence of the *Bais ha-Mikdash, Kohanim* are still accorded special treatment due to their status. There are also special laws which they are still obligated

551

	to observe despite the absence of the *Bais ha-Mikdash*.
Kollel	A postgraduate academy supported by local communities whose citizens provide funds to make available stipends for families so that young and newly married husbands can continue their *Torah* studies, full time.
Korban	Ritual animal sacrifice.
Kosher	Fit or proper according to *halachah*.
Lehabdil (Lehavdil)	To separate; to distinguish.
Leviim	See *Kohanim*. *Leviim* served as aides to the *Kohanim* in carrying out *Bais ha-Mikdash* services. Like *Kohanim*, they are accorded a degree of special treatment and are expected to observe certain special laws even in the absence of the *Bais ha-Mikdash*.
Levites	Same as *Leviim*.
Lulab	Palm frond. Used in special rituals on the holiday of *Succoth*.
Maggid	A wandering spiritual and scriptural raconteur.
Makkoth	The name for one of the major treatises of the *Talmud*. Discussion therein generally relates to the laws regarding the court ordered biblical punishment of flogging.
Mashgiach	Supervisor. Usually refers to an individual who supervises the provision of foods and/or food

	services to ensure their *Kashruth*.
Mattan Torah	Giving of the Ten Commandments by G-d to the Jewish people.
Mechilta	Anthology of *Halakhic* and *Midrashic* items.
Mechitzah	Wall; separation. The term is used to describe the item that serves as the physical separator between the men's and women's sections in the synagogue.
Mechitzot	Plural of *mechitzah*.
Mechitzoth	See *mechitzot*.
Medinath Israel	Land of Israel.
Megillah	Scroll, usually referring to the biblical Book of Esther. The name for one of the major treatises of the *Talmud*. Discussion therein generally relates to laws regarding reading of the *megillah* on the holiday of *Purim*.
Meshigaas	A Yiddish form of a word of Hebrew origin. In its Yiddish form as used here, it is best defined as an idiosyncracy.
Mesiras Nefesh	Altruism; unbounded devotion to a person or a cause.
Midos	Measurements, character traits. The name for one of the minor treatises of the *Talmud*. Discussion therein generally relates to the measurements of the *Bais ha-Mikdash*.
Midrash Pirkei De-Rabbi Eliezer	Homiletic work attributed to Rabbi Eliezer Ben Hyrcanos, a

	noted personality of the *Mishnah*.
Midrash Rabah	Great Midrash. Ancient and classic homiletic compendium interpreting and commenting upon the *Torah* and the books of Esther, Ruth, Song of Songs, Lamentations, Ecclesiastes.
Mikvah	Gathering (of water); ritual bath. Immersion therein is usually one of the requirements for purifying people or objects that have become unclean or defiled.
Milchamah	War.
Minyan	Number. The quorum (10 males) required for recitation of certain official congregational prayers and for performance of certain rituals.
Mishnah	The primary portion of the *Talmud*. Compiled and edited by Rabbi Yehudah ha-Nasi (The Prince). Therein are compiled the views of leading authorities, including conflicting views. The *Gemara* contains discussions based on the rulings contained in the *Mishnah*. Together, *Mishnah* and *Gemara* comprise what is generally identified as the *Talmud*.
Misnagdim	Opponents; generally used to identify opponents of the *Chasidic* movement.
Mitzvah	Commandment. Jewish law is

Glossary

	based on 613 commandments.
Mitzvot Ma'asioth	Commandments, the performance of which requires a physical act.
Mohel	A man trained and educated in the art of performing ritual circumcisions.
Mosheh	Moses.
Musmach	A person with *Semichah*.
Musmachim	Plural of *musmach*.
Nagar	Carpenter.
Nazir	A person who abstains. The name for a person who undertakes, by means of a vow, to abstain from grapes and any product derived from grapes; the name for one of the major treatises of the Talmud dealing with all the aforementioned.
Niftar	Passed away; departed.
Orach Chaim	One of the four sections of the Shulchan Aruch. It sets out the *halachah* for daily, Sabbath and holiday rituals.
Orysa	Aramaic word meaning the *Torah*.
Parshat ha-Chodesh	One of the four Sabbaths prior to the Passover holiday dedicated to a special theme. *Parshat ha-Chodesh* is dedicated to the theme of celebrating the significance of the Jewish month of *Nissan*.
Pesach	Passover. The name for the Paschal lamb—the animal offering

555

eaten at the Seder (Passover dinner) when there is a *Bais ha-Mikdash*.

Pesachim Plural of *Pesach*. The name for one of the major treatises of the *Talmud*. Discussion therein generally relates to the laws regarding the Passover holiday.

Pesochim Same as *Pesachim*.

Pirkei De-Rabbi Eliezer See *Midrash Pirkei De-Rabbi Eliezer*.

Posekim Decisors of *halachah*.

Posuk A verse in the *Torah*.

Purim Lots. Festival celebrating the Jews' deliverance from an evil decree, based on lots drawn by Haman, as related in the scriptural Book of Esther.

R. Abbreviation of a rabbinic title.

Raba *Talmud* personality from the *Gemorah*.

Rabbanim Mubhakim Rabbis with the requisite expertise.

Rabbi Shimon Talmud personality from the *Mishnah*.

Rabbi Yehuda Talmud personality from the *Mishnah*.

Rambam As written in Hebrew, the letters are the acronym for *Rabainu Moshe ben Maimon* (our Rabbi Moshe, the son of Maimon). Twelfth-century scholar and authority on Jewish law. Compiled the first widely distributed comprehensive anthology of Jewish law. Many of his contemporaries were opposed to that anthology because of their concern that Jews would cease studying the *Torah* and the *Talmud* and simply resort to the anthology for resolving legal questions as they arose.

Ramban

As written in Hebrew, the letters are the acronym of *Rav Moshe ben Nachman. Ramban* is a leading *Torah* and *Talmudic* authority. During his life (1194–1270), he wrote books of commentary on the *Torah* and *Talmud*.

Rashbam

As written in Hebrew, the letters are the acronym of *Rav Shmuel ben Meir.* Born in 1080, he was a noted commentator on the *Torah* and *Talmud.* A grandson of *Rashi, Rashbam*'s commentary is used to fill the lacunae in *Rashi*'s commentary on the *Talmud* for portions of the treatises of *Pesachim* and *Bava Basra.*

Rashi

As written in Hebrew, the letters are the acronym of *Rav Shlomo (ben) Yitzchak. Rashi*'s commentary to the *Torah* and *Talmud* is the primary reference for all who study *Torah* and *Talmud* in the original text. *Rashi* lived from 1040–1105.

Rav

A rabbinic title.

Rav Sheshes

Talmud personality from the *Gemorah.*

Rav Ukva Bar Chinnena

Talmud personality from the *Gemorah.*

Rav Yosef	Talmud personality from the *Gemorah*.
Rava	Talmud personality from the *Gemorah*.
Reb	A rabbinic title often used as a respectful form of address even for non-rabbis.
Rebbi	A rabbinic title, especially for a Chasidic rabbi.
Rif	As written in Hebrew, the letters are the acronym for *Rabbi Yitzchak (Al) Fasi*. The code of Jewish law *Rif* compiled was the most significant one until that of *Rambam*. *Rambam* said of *Rif*'s code that its decisions were all but "unassailable." *Rif* lived at the close of the *Gaonic* period (1013–1103) and was himself often addressed by the title *Gaon*.
Rosh Chodesh	The beginning of a new month.
Rosh Yeshivah	Dean of *Talmudic* academy.
Roshe Yeshibah	Deans of *Talmudic* academies.
Ruach Chachomim	Spirit of scholars. Said of one who comports himself in accord with the law and spirit of the scholars of the *Talmud*.
Sanhedrin	As used herein, the name for one of the major treatises of the *Talmud*. Discussion therein generally relates to laws regarding judges, judicial bodies, and their decisions.
Sefardic	Identifies Jews from Spain and Portugal (and their descendants) who developed a somewhat different set of rituals, customs and liturgy.

558

Glossary

Sefer	Book.
Sefer ha-Chayim	Book of life.
Seforim	Books; plural of *sefer*.
Semichah	Rabbinic ordination.
Sevara	Reasoning; logical deduction.
Shaas ha-Dechak	A time of urgent need; emergency.
Shabas	Rest; day of rest.
Shabbat	See Shabas.
Shabbaton	In contemporary usage, the word denotes a gathering for a special event or purpose for the entire *Shabbat*, e.g., religious retreat.
Shabbatonim	Plural of *Shabbaton*.
Shabbos	See *Shabas*; as used herein also refers to one of the major treatises of the *Talmud*. Discussion therein generally relates to the laws of *Shabas*.
Shavuoth	Holiday celebrating the receipt of the Ten Commandments by the Jewish people.
Shema	Hear. The first word (and also the title) for one of the most prominent portions of Jewish prayer—"Hear O Israel . . ."
Shemirath (Kashruth) (Shabbat)	Observance, adherence to the laws of (Kosher Food) (Sabbath).
Shemitah	Sabbatical year. In Israel every seventh year is a *shemitah* for agricultural activity.
Shevat	The fifth month in the current Jewish yearly calendar.
Shlita	As written in Hebrew, the letters are the acronym of a blessing for a good and long life.

Shmoozing	Conversing; (colloquially: rapping) (Anglo-Yiddish)
Shochet	Ritual slaughterer.
Shofar	Ram's horn sounded on *Rosh ha-Shana* and at the conclusion of *Yom Kippur*.
Shul	Synagogue.
Shulchan Aruch	A set table. A massive four-part work compiling the most authoritative source for contemporary *halachah*.
Siddur	Order. The prayer book containing the general order of prayer.
Sifra	Midrash on the biblical book of Leviticus.
Sifre	Midrash on the biblical books of Numbers and Deuteronomy by scholars of the *Mishnah*.
Sifri	See *Sifre*.
Simchat Bet ha-Shoeva	A most joyous celebration at the water drawing ritual in the *Bais ha-Mikdash* commencing the second night of the holiday of *Succoth*.
Sivan	The ninth month in the current Jewish yearly calendar.
Sofer	Scribe; writer of Scriptural texts in a special style, with special ink and on special parchment.
Sotah	The name for one of the major treatises of the *Talmud*. Discussion therein generally relates to laws regarding marital infidelity.
Succoth	Holiday celebrating a specific aspect of the life of the Jewish people in the desert upon their exodus from Egypt.

560

Sukah	Hut; temporary dwelling. The name for one of the major treatises of the *Talmud*. Discussion therein generally relates to the laws of the festival known by the same name. Those laws include the requirement that eating and drinking during the festival be confined to a *Sukah* built especially for the festival.
Sukkot	See *Succoth*.
Taanith	Fasting. The name for one of the major treatises of the *Talmud*. Discussion generally relates to laws regarding days for which fasting is decreed or undertaken.
Taharath ha-Mishpacha	Family purity.
Tallith	Four-cornered cloth (wool) draped over the head and body during prayer. *Tzitzith* are draped from each of the four corners.
Talmid Chacham	Scholar; sage.
Talmud	Study. Written record of the discussions on Jewish law and customs by the sages during the years 200 to 500. The *Talmud* is comprised of the *Mishnah* and *Gemorah*. There is a Babylonian *Talmud* and a Jerusalem *Talmud*. The Babylonian *Talmud* is a much more massive work and is the source for contemporary *halachah*. Jewish law and custom is based on the written *Torah*—the Pentateuch and the oral *Torah*—the *Talmud*. As an emer-

	gency measure, the *Talmud* was reduced to writing in its current format early in the sixth century.
Talmud Torah	School. In the United States it usually refers to a religious school which conducts classes in Hebrew and religion as a supplement to the public schools.
Tammuz	The tenth month in the current Jewish yearly calendar.
Tanna De-bai Rabbi Yishmael	From the works taught at the academy of Rabbi Yishmael.
Tefach	Handbreadth. A linear measure from *Talmudic* times: See *Amah*. Six *tefochim* equal one *amah*. Various contemporary authorities have determined its modern equivalent to be within a range of 3 to 4 inches.
Tefachim	Plural of *Tefach*.
Tefochim	See *Tefachim*.
Tekiath Shofar	Sounding of the ram's horn.
Tephilin	Special ritual item donned at daily services by men and worn throughout the morning service on days other than Saturdays and Festivals.
Teshuboth	Responsa.
Teshu'ah	Salvation.
Teshuvah	Repentance. (See *Baalai Teshuvah*); responsum.
Teves	The fourth month in the current Jewish yearly calendar.
Teveth	See *Teves*.
Torah	The Five Books of Moses.

562

Glossary

Torah Min ha-Shamayim	The *Torah* has its source from heaven; it is of divine origin.
Toras Chayim	The *Torah* (Bible) is life sustaining.
Tosafos	See *Tosefos*.
Tosefos	The name for one of the two major commentaries on the *Talmud* (*Rashi* being the other). *Tosefos* is a compilation of comments of numerous great scholars, mostly from France, who lived in the thirteenth and fourteenth centuries.
Tosefta	The name for a special collection of *Mishnah* compiled and edited by the *Talmudic* scholars *Rav Chiya* and *Rav Oyshya*.
Traif	Not *kosher*.
Trefah	See *Traif*.
Trefe	See *Traif*.
Tzedakah	Charity.
Tzitzith	Fringes draped from the four corners of a *tallith*.
Tzofim	Visionaries; lookout points, e.g., Har ha-Tzofim (Mount Scopus).
Vehakuchin	Cave, cavity. As used here, it is merely a reference guide to a section of commentary for the citation given.
Yaitzer Hara	A driving evil force. Jewish belief is premised on the concept of a constant struggle between good and evil. Within each individual that struggle is forever ongoing between the *yaitzer*

hara, the driving evil force and the *yaitzer tov,* the driving beneficent force. Each individual must forever strive for his or her *yaitzer tov* to overcome his or her *yaitzer hara.*

Yahrzeit	The anniversary date of a death.
Yeshibah	House of study; school.
Yeshiboth	Schools.
Yeshivah	House of study; school.
Yeshivos	Schools.
Yichud	Privacy, especially between a male and a female.
Yiddishkeit	Judaism in Yiddish.
Yizkor	Special memorial service conducted four times a year on specified holidays.
Y'L	(Acronym for *Yibodel L'Chaim*—shall be separated for purposes of life.) In Jewish custom when the name of a living person is mentioned together with names of persons who have died *Y'L* is inserted to mark a separation and, in effect, wish continued life for the living individual.
Yoma	The name for one of the major treatises of the *Talmud.* Discussion therein generally relates to the laws regarding the holiday of *Yom Kippur* including the services performed on that day by the *Kohanim* and *Leviim* in the *Bais ha-Mikdash.*
Yom Kippur	Day of Atonement.
Yom Tov	Holiday; festival.

Glossary

Yoreh De'ah	One of the four sections of the *Shulchan Aruch*. Most notably it sets out laws of *Kashruth*. Mastering key sections of Yoreh De'ah is generally one of the pre-requisites for obtaining *Semichah*.
Zebahim	The name for one of the major treatises of the *Talmud*. Discussion therein generally relates to laws regarding sacrifices in the *Bais ha-Mikdash*.
Zeda	Grandfather in Yiddish.
Zevachim	See *Zebahim*.
ZT'L	(Acronym for *Zaicher Tzadik L'Vracha*—the memory of a righteous person shall be a blessing). This acronym is generally appended to the mention of the name of a great *Rav* or *Gaon* after his passing.

index

Index

Index

Index